THE SOCIETY FOR
POST-MEDIEVAL ARCHAEOLOGY
MONOGRAPH 4

ESTATE LANDSCAPES:
Design, Improvement and Power in the
Post-Medieval Landscape

ESTATE LANDSCAPES:
Design, Improvement and Power in the Post-Medieval Landscape

Edited by
JONATHAN FINCH *and* KATE GILES

Papers given at the Estate Landscapes Conference, April 2003, hosted by
The Society for Post-Medieval Archaeology

Boydell & Brewer Ltd
2007

© Contributors and The Society for Post-Medieval Archaeology 2007

All Rights Reserved. Except as permitted under current legislation
no part of this work may be photocopied, stored in a retrieval system,
published, performed in public, adapted, broadcast,
transmitted, recorded or reproduced in any form or by any means,
without the prior permission of the copyright owner

First published 2007
The Boydell Press, Woodbridge

Disclaimer. Statements in the volume reflect the views of the authors
and not necessarily those of the Society, editors or publisher

ISBN 978-1-84383-370-3

The Boydell Press is an imprint of Boydell & Brewer Ltd
PO Box 9, Woodbridge, Suffolk IP12 3DF, UK
and of Boydell & Brewer Inc.
668 Mt Hope Avenue, Rochester, NY 14620, USA
website: www.boydellandbrewer.com

A CiP catalogue record for this book is available
from the British Library

This publication is printed on acid-free paper

Printed in Great Britain by
CPI Antony Rowe Ltd, Chippenham, Wiltshire

CONTENTS

	PAGE
Preface	
By JONATHAN FINCH & KATE GILES	VII
Introduction: Archaeological Perspectives on Estate Landscapes	
By TOM WILLIAMSON	1

LANDSCAPES & IMPROVEMENT

Pallas, Flora and Ceres: Landscape Priorities and Improvement on the Castle Howard Estate, 1699-1880	
By JONATHAN FINCH	19
Vaynor: a Landscape and its Buildings in the Severn Valley	
By ROBERT SILVESTER & JUDITH ALFREY	39
Fields, Property and Agricultural Innovation in Late Medieval and Early Modern South-West England	
By SAM TURNER	57

LANDSCAPES & MATERIAL CULTURE

Estate Landscapes and the Cult of the Ruin: A Lesson of Spatial Transformation in Rural Ireland	
By CHARLES E. ORSER	77
'Animated Prospect' – An 18th Century Kiln at 'The Pottery House in the Old Park', Dunster, Somerset	
By DAVID DAWSON & OLIVER KENT	95
Reflecting a Stance: Establishing a Position; Moving Beyond Description and Function in Designed Estate Landscapes?	
By PAUL EVERSON	113
Thomas Jefferson's Landscape of Retirement	
By BARBARA J. HEATH	129
Monuments and Memory in the Estate Landscape: Castle Howard and Sledmere	
By HAROLD MYTUM	149

COLONIAL LANDSCAPES

English Colonial Landscapes in the South-West of Ireland
By COLIN BREEN — 177

'In What Manner Did They Devide The Land'? The Early Colonial Estate Landscape of Nevis and St. Kitts
By ROGER H. LEECH — 191

'Material Improvements': the Archaeology of Estate Landscapes in the British Leeward Islands, 1713-1838
By DAN HICKS — 205

INDEX — 229

Preface

By JONATHAN FINCH & KATE GILES

The papers in this volume were originally given at the Society for Post-Medieval Archaeology's annual conference, at the University of York in April 2003. The aim of the conference was to explore the increasing interest amongst archaeologists in the study of post-medieval landscapes in general, and the form of the 'estate landscape', in particular. This volume is the product, not only of the lively debates which resulted during the conference, but also of authors' continued research on the themes and issues raised by the types of estate landscape with which they are concerned. It also includes papers that were commissioned after the conference to reflect the global aspect of the topic and include research undertaken by North American colleagues. It is organised into three sections that reflect the main themes and forms of evidence within the research – improvement, material culture and the colonial context.

In the Introduction, Tom Williamson argues that the form of the post-medieval estate – with a central core of house, gardens and park, set within the wider penumbra of the estate landscape beyond – is a distinctively modern phenomenon, which contrasts markedly with its medieval and early modern precursors. Many of the papers which follow attempt to understand how such estates came into being, exploring their relationship to the antecedent landscapes of the late medieval and early modern periods in Yorkshire (Jonathan Finch) and in the south-west of England (Sam Tuner). In some cases, as Robert Silvester and Judith Alfrey demonstrate at Vaynor in the Severn Valley, estates appear to have been created in a rather piecemeal, haphazard manner. In others, such as those in the south-west of Ireland studied by Colin Breen, and Thomas Jefferson's Poplar Forest estate in Bedford County, Virginia, discussed by Barbara Heath, the Anglicised idea of the estate appears to have been used as a template in a number of landscape contexts. This process can also be identified in St. Kitts, Nevis and the Leeward Islands, although as Roger Leech and Dan Hicks demonstrate, these areas also share forms distinctive to the colonial context.

The impact of improvement upon the framework and features of the landscape is central to many of the papers. The transformation of boundaries, roads and field systems during phases of enclosure is shown to relate to the manipulation and incorporation of antecedent features such as woodland, fishponds and warrens. Together they create a new aesthetic expressed through carefully framed views and vistas, as well as in the estate architecture and industrial features, that formed visual foci or 'eye-catchers'?

Williamson argues that the creation of the estate landscape both structured and reflected new attitudes to property and aesthetics, and needs to be understood in the context of wider historical processes such as capitalism, enclosure and the cultural imperative for improvement. The papers explore the complex interplay of different motivations behind the development of estate landscapes. At one level changes might seem purely functional: the improvement of the landscape through enclosure, the regularisation of routeways and field boundaries (Sam Turner); the improvement of farming methods through the use of watermeadows and new drainage methods to facilitate experimentation with livestock (Jonathan Finch); and the exploitation of industries such as fishing (Colin Breen), sugar cane (Roger Leech and Dan Hicks) and the pottery industry (David Dawson and Oliver Kent). Yet all these authors emphasise the complex and often contradictory motivations behind such changes. Estates, it seems, were not always in the vanguard of change. Personal aspirations and preferences, political and ideological concerns, all had a profound effect on the timing and development of new productive processes within estate landscapes.

The complex meanings of estate landscapes, for their designers and contemporary viewers is another important area addressed by a number of the authors. Some reflect 18th and 19th century aesthetics, such as the idea of the 'animated prospect' created at Dunster (David Dawson and Oliver Kent), the 'cult of the ruin' at Tanzyfort House, County Sligo (Charles Orser Jnr) and the relationships established between ornamental elements within the agricultural landscape (Jonathan Finch). In other cases, the style and design of the central house itself made an important statement, as Barbara Heath explores in relation to Thomas Jefferson's 'Anglo-Saxon' house, and Paul Everson argues in relation to the choice of Artisan Mannerism at Wyford, Hants and Chesterton, Warwicks. Elsewhere, the manipulation of vernacular buildings such as workers' houses and slave quarters, could be equally significant, encouraging the inhabitants of estate landscapes to 'improve' their own living conditions by segregating living and working/agricultural space. Within the estate landscape, it appears that what appear superficially to be functional agricultural features, such as warrens and fishponds or industrial pottery-kilns and sugar factories, were loaded with symbolism and significance.

The interplay between estate owners and indigenous communities features prominently in the final section of the volume. The tensions and controversies between plantation owners and indigenous communities in the Caribbean are considered by Roger Leech and Dan Hicks. In Ireland, both Colin Breen and Charles Orser also look closely at the relationships between settlers and the previous landowners. All stress the crucial role played by the material culture of the estate landscape in structuring distinctive forms of estate identity, within and between aristocratic and mercantile elites, and between such elites, estate workers and slaves. In Ireland, North America and the Caribbean, this was the expression of colonial identities and mercantile 'cosmopolitanism'; in Yorkshire, monuments for both the families and estate workers were used to create a sense of communal identity and collective memory (Charles Orser Jnr, Harold Mytum).

What emerges from this collection is the need for greater sensitivity to integration within the modern landscape. Divisions and characterisations that have structured research within the discipline of post-medieval or historical archaeology are now outdated and inhibit further development. All the papers demonstrate how understanding the landscape demands that researchers break through their own conceptual boundaries and address issues raised in agricultural economics, literature, philosophy and politics. We have unparalleled sources for the period concerned here and in order to capture the complexity of the landscape in the past, even the recent past, requires an ambition amongst researchers to harness new methodologies, new technologies and an engagement with research agendas. The historic landscape is one of the most complex archaeological challenges that we face. The apparent familiarity of its material form can be disarming, yet the lives and motivations that shaped it, and the narratives embedded within it, can be as foreign and as partially preserved as those from more distant periods.

Archaeological Perspectives on Landed Estates: Research Agendas

By TOM WILLIAMSON

This chapter examines some of the ways in which a specifically archaeological perspective can throw new light on the history and character of estate landscapes in England. It concentrates on the ways in which archaeology can help to produce a typology of estates, their spatial organisation and distribution. It emphasises how landed estates were a specifically modern phenomenon, associated with the emergence of a global economy. It argues that, of all disciplines, archaeology is best placed to consider the estate as a unity: the landscapes of the estate 'core', and the periphery of tenanted land, can only be fully understood in relation to each other. Lastly, it suggests a broad typological model for the development of English estate landscapes in the period between the 16th and the 19th century.

INTRODUCTION

Landed estates have been studied for many decades by British historical geographers and economic and social historians.[1] It is only comparatively recently, however, that archaeologists have become involved. True, archaeological research into the 'core' areas of estates – mansions, gardens and parkland – is well established, in terms of excavation, field survey, and theoretical interpretation.[2] But the study of the estate as an entity, in its entirety, including the wider penumbra of tenanted farmland, is only just beginning. What particular matters ought we to place on the research agenda – what should be the principal aims and objectives of an 'archaeology of the landed estate'? Or, to put it another way, what can a specifically archaeological perspective contribute to our understanding of estates and their landscapes?

DEFINING ESTATES

Before we address this question we need first to define what we mean by 'landed estate', for the term is used in a variety of ways. In a British context an estate may be defined as an extensive and continuous or near-continuous area of land, owned as absolute private property by an individual, although not necessarily (following the elaboration of the institution of the strict settlement in the later 17th century) his or hers to alienate at will. Such units had (as already intimated) a recurrent spatial structure. They featured a central core of mansion and garden, often accompanied by a park and 'home farm', which were kept 'in hand'. Beyond this lay an outer penumbra of farms and farmland which were leased, for defined periods of time, to tenants; together with a scatter of smaller areas which were again kept in hand by the owner, especially plantations and game covers. Even a definition as basic as this, it must be emphasised, would exclude some of the 'estates' which appear in the archaeological literature, especially in a colonial context. On the east coast of America in the eighteenth and nineteenth centuries, as in the West Indies, much of the above description simply would not apply for beyond any designed 'core', large properties were usually kept in hand and managed directly, while in place of tenant farmers and farm labourers there were often populations of slaves or bonded labourers.

Other difficulties of definition arise from questions of scale. There were, in a British context, important differences between the really large properties – those belonging to the group that Clemenson has defined as 'great landowners' – which extended over 10,000 acres or more; and those of the local gentry, embracing a parish or two and ranging from around 1,000 to 10,000 acres.[3] These differences, between the properties of the nationally rich and the locally wealthy, had cultural and political correlations, in that while individuals in the former group often had a role on the national stage, made much of their money from the proceeds of office, and had both the political need and the financial means to keep abreast of national if not international fashions in architecture and landscape design, members of the latter tended to be more provincial in their outlook, to have cultural horizons which were often limited by the county boundary, and to make rather different demands on their lands.[4] Such correlations are, it is true, complicated to some extent by the poor correspondence between the inherited status (and associated political position) of individual owners, and the value of their landed property. But in general significant landed wealth brought – if not immediately, then over a relatively short period of time – political importance and extended cultural contacts.

A more serious difficulty is that wealth expressed in acres never had any very close relationship with wealth measured in terms of rental income. A thousand acres in the Highlands of Scotland in the late 18th century, as today, compared poorly in financial terms with ten acres in central London; and many spatially challenged estates grew wealthy on the income from coalfields or other minerals. In all these and other ways, the term 'estate' remains problematic, and one useful task for archaeology would be to do something no other discipline has yet really managed: produce a typology of estates, which would recognise their diversity (in Britain and beyond) and allow us to make meaningful comparisons, and identify significant differences, across time and space.

ESTATES IN CONTEXT

Large landed properties unquestionably played an increasingly important role in many aspects of social and economic life in post-medieval England, and to a significant extent in other parts of Britain, as small owners declined steadily in numbers and importance.[5] But we must be careful not to exaggerate their impact. In some areas, especially wood-pasture districts like the Weald of Kent and Sussex or the East Anglian claylands, relatively few really large estates ever existed.[6] While much of the land in such areas had, by the start of the 19th century, fallen into the hands of major landowners it was normally in the form of discrete, fragmented blocks. In general the greatest estates, by the end of the 18th century, were to be found in areas of relatively poor-quality land, and especially in areas of light, leached soils like the Lincolnshire Wolds or the East Anglian Breckland, better suited to sheep and arable than to dairying or cattle-rearing. As Thirsk and others have shown, in areas of poor arable land small owner-occupiers found it hard to make a living as a national market economy in grain developed in the course of the post-medieval period, and the large landowners who had long been prominent in these districts acquired their land steadily.[7] The crucial point is that it was in such relatively agriculturally marginal environments of heath and down, and to a lesser extent in moorland districts, that owners had the greatest opportunities to transform the landscape. These areas usually possessed, by post-medieval times, little woodland, and featured extensive commons and (in many cases) large tracts of open-field arable: they were blank canvases. Landowners did indeed effect phenomenal changes in such locations. Arthur Young typically described the achievements of the great estates of north west Norfolk:

> All the country from Holkham to Houghton was a wild sheep walk before the spirit of improvement seized the inhabitants ... Instead of boundless wilds and uncultivated wastes inhabited by scare anything but sheep, the country is all cut up into enclosures, cultivated in a most husbandlike manner, well peopled, and yielding an hundred times the produce that it did in its former state.[8]

But we must be careful not to confuse (as contemporaries often did) dramatic and visible change in the landscape with any real achievement in increasing productivity or raising wealth. The light lands of the heaths and wolds were the heartlands of the classic late 18th-century agricultural revolution, but while the adoption of the new crops and rotations, enclosure, and marling did indeed serve to raise agricultural output they generally did so from a low level. The most important areas of arable production remained the heavier clays and loams, more fertile and therefore more expensive lands in which large estates were always poorly represented.[9]

In marginal areas especially, the cores of large estates were often associated with shrunken settlements, the earthwork remains of which might be preserved in the parkland turf. This association is often interpreted in straightforward causal terms. Villages were cleared or truncated to make way for parkland, or their size was deliberately limited or reduced by landowners for other reasons.[10] In particular, both modern historians, and contemporaries, have used the terms 'close' and 'open' to characterise two broad types of parish in 18th and 19th-century England.[11] In the former, a single owner (or two large owners) limited the population in order to keep down the Poor Rates, and generally restricted development. Open parishes, in contrast, which had larger numbers of landowners, tended in contrast to grow in size and to acquire more facilities. Some historians have rightly criticised this simple model[12] - but an archaeological approach offers a novel perspective on the whole issue of the relationship between settlement size, contraction and ownership. While, as Neave and others have shown, some of these settlements were indeed depopulated by large owners in the course of the 18th century,[13] others had evidently declined before the development of the estate core.[14] The kinds of marginal environment which encouraged the growth of large properties had also, from late medieval times, experienced much voluntary out-migration, as farmers sought holdings in less demanding locations. The central cores of large estates, in other words, may often have developed where wider economic and demographic circumstances provided opportunities for them to do so. In short, in a variety of ways archaeologists can supply a tighter spatial and chronological context for the study of estate landscape, but also a longer perspective than that often adopted by historians: one which should allow a clearer understanding of causation and connections, and thus a more measured and nuanced assessment of the impact of large estates on the rural environment.

ESTATES AND MODERNITY

Throughout its history the landed estate in England has vaunted its rural and traditional character. A landed estate is a country estate, and a great house a 'country house', even if its owners lack another, specifically urban residence. Moreover, even in the seventeenth and eighteenth centuries, but even more in the nineteenth, large landowners consciously manipulated the symbols of the past. They ostentatiously employed heraldry and archaic forms of architecture, and created parks which aped, in many ways, the deer parks of earlier centuries.[15] So successful has this strategy been that modern critics of established landed wealth often describe large estates as 'relics of a feudal age'. In reality, the landed estate was something which only developed in the post-medieval world: it was a specifically modern form. Its distinguishing feature was untrammelled, or only very partially limited, power over the exploitation and physical appearance of an extensive tract of countryside. In the middle ages, large estates had seldom been held as unitary blocks and, more importantly, rights over land were usually multiple, complex and diffuse. The landed estate could only emerge in a world in which absolute rights of property in land were recognised. Far from being the archaic and traditional features they often pretended to be, landed estates were a manifestation of modernity.

Estates were, moreover, fully involved in capitalist production. Their role in the so-called 'agricultural revolution' of the late eighteenth and early nineteenth centuries has long been appreciated (arguably, as we have seen, exaggerated) by historians.[16] The estate system encouraged expansion of production because private possession of extensive acres allowed entrenched, customary systems of land use to be overridden and transformed, through engrossment, enclosure, and the replacement of customary tenures by leases, leading to an expansion in the cultivated acreage and the emergence of larger and (it is alleged) more efficient and productive farms, free of communal controls.[17] Some landowners, like Thomas William Coke, were particularly active and noted advocates of new farming methods and used prescriptive leases to enforce the adoption of new crops and rotations. In addition, the landlord/tenant farm system allowed a pooling of resources between owners and producers, the former supplying and maintaining the fixed capital of farms and fields, the latter supplying the working capital, of stock and equipment. Above all, the political power of British landowners ensured that well into the 19th century the home markets of an industrialising nation were protected from foreign competition, through the mechanism of the Corn Laws.

The role of great estates in industrial development have not perhaps been equally emphasised, but as well as exploiting the mineral wealth beneath their soil many landed families, like the Cavendishes of Chatsworth in Derbyshire, played a major part in the expansion of towns and industry, in this case turning the small settlement at Barrow in the Lake District into the great industrial town of Barrow-in-Furness in the course of the 19th century through the development of a harbour and dockyard and, in particular, iron ore mines.[18] There are numerous other examples. And large landowners were fully involved in the development of the Atlantic economy, through investments in shipping or in colonial plantations. Some probably derived as much wealth from such sources as they did from their English acres. Parks and pleasure grounds in the 18th and the 19th century proudly displayed the far-flung contacts of trade and empire, boasting a wide range of exotic plants, brought back in some cases by plant-collectors directly funded by great families; while colonial mansions often displayed the same, broadly Palladian styles of many English country houses. Archaeology should develop the work already undertaken by historians, in seeing estates as fully implicated in the emerging global economic system of the 18th century. Many have argued that the true purpose of historical archaeology is to understand the origins of capitalism and modernity[19] and it is certainly hard to argue with the more neutral suggestion that the discipline should be 'globally focussed'.[20] The landed estate can only be understood in terms of modernity and the global economy; but our knowledge of these things, conversely, can be greatly improved through an enhanced appreciation of the role of the landed estate.

ARCHAEOLOGICAL AGENDAS: WHAT HAPPENED IN HISTORY?

The simplistic notion that archaeology can 'get the facts right', or 'tell the true story', and generally present more objective and accurate accounts of the past than those based on documentary sources – with their omissions and biases - is rightly unfashionable. But we should not underestimate the extent to which physical evidence, combined with that from documents, can indeed tell us things which subvert, modify or amplify purely documentary narratives. In the study of the designed landscapes associated with landed estates, for example, an archaeological approach eschews a concentration on 'famous designers' and 'key sites', studying instead a wide range of examples using a wide range of sources - documentary, archaeological and cartographic. Such an approach can transform our understanding of even the basic chronology of garden design, showing for example how different levels of the landed gentry, and different regions of England, accepted new styles in the 18th century at very different speeds, and with very different degrees of enthusiasm.[21] Beyond the park pale, archaeological approaches can likewise provide new information about some fairly basic matters. As Paul Barnwell and Susanna Wade Martins in particular have shown, the many thousands of 18th- and 19th-century farm buildings which survive in Britain, the majority of which were erected by large estates, can tell us much about how and when new agricultural techniques were adopted, and about the investment policies of large estates: about, for example, the extent to which investment occurred when times were good and much surplus cash was available or, conversely, in times of recession, when there was competition to attract agricultural tenants of the right calibre.[22]

More importantly, archaeological approaches can serve to widen historical imaginations, and reveal the complexity of motives underlying estate management. Economic historians often write as if all estate owners were motivated primarily by a desire to maximise production. Yet while it is true that great estates were firmly a part of the modern world, their owners evidently had attitudes to land which were at once more complex, and more subtle, than those of a contemporary agribusiness farmer. Ownership of land was an end in itself as much as means to an end: possession of broad acres brought status like nothing else, and hence the universal desire of successful businessmen and entrepreneurs to purchase an extensive property. Land was to be enjoyed, and it is instructive that the most popular pastimes of the post-medieval rich, such as game shooting and foxhunting, both demanded, and demonstrated, control over extensive tracts of territory. In addition, land and the uses to which it was put were important in the game of politics, both in a direct way – economic dominance of districts ensured local obligation and dependence, and thus political support for a family's chosen candidates – but also indirectly, in terms of demonstrating acceptable values and thus legitimating the claims of the established elite to be the natural rulers of the country. Land and its exploitation were bound up in complex agendas.

In particularly marginal areas like the East Anglian Breckland the extensive improvement schemes of the 18th and 19th century were thus only partly motivated by a desire to make money. Indeed, most estates probably had little idea of how much money they were making.[23] Even when they were aware that some reclamation and improvement projects were losing money some regarded this with equanimity. When in 1774 Thomas de Grey bemoaned the costs of enclosing the heaths at Tottington in Norfolk he observed that the 'great expense ... would but ill answer, unless there was a real satisfaction in employing the labourers and bringing forth a ragged dirty parish to a neatness of cultivation'.[24] Paternalism and a desire to appear the owner of an 'improving' estate, rather than backwoods lord of a rural slum, were powerful motivations. In a similar way, the widespread tidying up of field boundaries in areas of 'ancient countryside', as described in this volume by Sam Turner, was clearly only in part motivated by practical, agrarian considerations.[25] It also represented an attempt to transform the countryside along fashionable, rational, 'improving' lines. More traditional forms of field archaeology can also contribute a great deal to our understanding of the process of enclosure and reclamation of marginal land, not least because some attempts at 'improvement' were so short-lived that they have left little clear trace in the documentary record, but abundant archaeological remains, in the form of 'narrow rig' and the earthworks of ruler-straight field boundaries.[26]

The earthworks of irrigated water meadows are a particularly good example both of the complex motives of improvers, and of the way that traditional field archaeology can throw new light on these. Meadow irrigation was practiced in southern and western England since at least the 16th century (see again Turner in this volume). By artificially inundating grassland during the winter with continually flowing water the ground temperature was raised above 5 degrees Centigrade, enough to stimulate early grass growth, thus reducing the need for winter fodder. In May the meadows were irrigated again, and substantial crops of hay taken.[27] In spite of these widely acknowledged benefits the spread of the technique into eastern districts was slow. On the Wolds of Lincolnshire and Yorkshire, in the Chilterns, on the North and South Downs, and in the sheep-corn districts of East Anglia, floating had made little headway even at the end of the 18th century. But, following the strong advocacy of the technique by agricultural writers like William Smith, the Napoleonic War years saw a flurry of new schemes in these regions, almost invariably the work of prominent improvers – estate owners or large tenant farmers.[28] Few of the systems then created (often at considerable expense) remained in use by the middle decades of the century. In reality, irrigation was never very effective in the east, where the gentle gradient of most valleys made construction expensive and the often peaty soils were unsuitable for watering, and where a dry climate made summer irrigation problematic and sharp, late frosts hindered the early forcing of grass growth.[29] Irrigated meadows in eastern England were in large part an improvers' fad, and archaeological survey reveals that some examples were actually located within landscape parks, as at Woburn in Bedfordshire or East Lexham in Norfolk. They were objects of fashionable display as much as aspects of practical agriculture, clear statements that the landowners in question were at the forefront of developments in scientific agriculture.[30] In the course of the 19th century meadow irrigation continued to be adopted in new places in which it was never really economically viable, especially in upland areas. Again, few of these systems seem to have been successful, or to have remained in operation for any length of time. Most are perhaps best interpreted as attempts on the part of large landowners to appear in the forefront of scientific agriculture, at a time when radical opinion was questioning their right to own and control vast areas of the nation. Apparently 'practical' innovations might thus be adopted for reasons which were largely social or ideological in character.

In all these and other ways an archaeological perspective can illuminate the complex and ambiguous motivations underpinning the economies of large estates. Their owners and administrators were fully a part of the modern world. Yet at the same time they were clearly influenced by considerations which went beyond the purely economic. How far their more complex views on the correct management of land represent a survival from an earlier period, how far they were associated with the landed estate as a specific economic and social form, remains an open question.

ARCHAEOLOGICAL AGENDAS: THE LANGUAGE OF LANDSCAPE

Some historical geographers have described the organisation of large estates in terms of 'distance decay'. Land close to the mansion was regarded in more aesthetic terms than that at a distance.[31] Highly ornamental estate villages thus lay close to the park gates; settlements at a distance, in contrast, might be neglected. Such an approach has considerable value but, as the case of the water meadows demonstrates, it underestimates the extent to which the 'practical' penumbra penetrated the aesthetic core, and vice versa. To put it another way, little in the landscape of the estate was either purely functional or purely ornamental, wherever it lay. The park itself was intensively used for grazing and timber production and its form modified accordingly: in the words of John Lawrence in 1801, it should serve as a 'theatre ... for the display of all the notable varieties of experimental husbandry'.[32] Conversely, woods planted at a considerable distance from the mansion were often highly decorative as well as functional and economic in character. Moreover, although 18th- and 19th-century parks were generally sealed off from the surrounding landscape by perimeter planting, 'rides' or 'ridings' - ornamented drives – often extended out into the wider countryside. As Thomas Whateley neatly put it in 1770, gardening 'Is no longer confined to the spots from which it borrows its name, but regulates also the disposition and embellishments of a park, a farm, or a riding' (helpfully adding, rather later, that the latter was an ornamented drive intended 'to lead from one beauty to another, and be a scene of pleasure all the way').[33] Recreational activities moulded the landscape far from the estate core, as Jon Finch has shown in the case of 18th-century fox-hunting in the Midlands.[34] This is where archaeologists can again make their own particular contribution. Garden historians and architectural historians look at the designed estate 'core', economic and social historians examine the life of the outer estate: archaeologists, accustomed to read the complex and layered meanings in buildings, artefacts and landscapes, are in a better position than most to understand the estate landscape as a whole, in the same way as its owners and managers appear to have done.

Yet there are other ways in which considering the designed core, and the wider countryside, as a unity can pay real dividends. The changing styles in landscape design in the 17th and 18th century doubtless owed much to developments in philosophy, foreign travel, and fashions in other forms of art. But they were also grounded in a range of indigenous contexts, associated with the working countryside: in a shared grammar of landscape which, in many respects, had been developing for centuries. As landowners laid out their grounds, they expressed their essential social values in this language, as much as in anything more esoteric or intellectual. The symbolism of designed landscapes thus involved the re-working and re-presentation of familiar, domestic, vernacular themes – themes, as it were, drawn from the outer penumbra of the estate.

The parks of 18th and 19th-century England, with their grass, trees and woodland clumps, had an immense pedigree, loaded with social significance, extending back to the deer parks of medieval times. But their essential building-blocks also had, in themselves, specific connotations. Wide areas of uninterrupted turf meant something in a world in which much land was under arable cultivation, and in which pastures were usually small and bounded by hedges. Indeed, to some extent the association of mansion, and grassland, was quite independent of the park tradition. Early maps show that the manor houses of the minor gentry in the sixteenth and seventeenth centuries had usually been surrounded by grass paddocks. Grass provided opportunities for riding, and extensive areas of uninterrupted turf for riding fast – a pastime largely reserved to the rich. Pasture, moreover, was associated with particular forms of effortless, leisured production which, in the mind of the post-medieval elite, were superior to the drudgery of arable husbandry, with its complex and laborious series of tasks (ploughing, harrowing, weeding, harvesting etc.).[35] Trees and woodlands likewise had a range of meanings in post-medieval England, as Stephen Daniels demonstrated long ago. Tree planting, being a long-term investment, demonstrated confidence in the stability of government, and in a family's continued residence upon an estate. It also displayed patriotism, because it provided the timber necessary to build the ships required by the navy.[36] At a more basic level, timber trees and woodland had always been associated with the landowning elite. Since medieval times the vast majority of managed woods had been private manorial property: and while a small landowner might plant a trees in his hedges only the larger landlord could afford to put tens or hundreds of acres down to trees, locking up land from which more immediate returns could be derived.

The meaning of the post-medieval park was thus in part constructed from a wider grammar of landscape, largely independent of the kind of literary, artistic, or philosophical influences which most interest garden historians. Much the same was true of the immediate setting of the mansion. In the sixteenth and seventeenth centuries, and in some places well into the eighteenth, the enclosures which clustered around the country house included not only ornamental gardens but also a range of functional and productive features and facilities, many of which had a quasi-aesthetic character. Dovecotes were, until the late 17th century, a manorial monopoly and were proudly displayed as badges of status and, therefore, considered objects of beauty; fish ponds were a prominent feature of geometric gardens;[37] orchards were a gentlemen's hobby, and areas of quiet retreat, as much as places for the production of fruit. Farmyards and barns usually lay in close proximity. At Chatsworth in Derbyshire the north front of one of the greatest Baroque houses in England looked out across a yard with barns and other farm buildings as late as 1752; the west front looked out over a rabbit warren. Production and leisure were thus inextricably intermingled, and the enclosures around a gentleman's house were a complex mixture of the ornamental, the productive, and the recreational. The traditional concentration of garden historians on the aesthetic and the horticultural serves to remove and isolate gardens and the practice of gardening from this context. But an archaeological perspective can re-affirm such connections, and we should be aware of what, to contemporaries, such multi-facetted domestic complexes represented. They signalled that their owner lived in the same world as his neighbours and tenants – was fully involved in the productive life of his estate, was at home in his 'country' - yet at the same time ate more food, and more exotic food, than they did. The gentleman's mansion was, in many ways, a yeoman's farm, writ large. It was grand, unattainable, but essentially understandable. It expressed superiority, yet not intellectual or cultural exclusion. If we focus only on ornamental gardens, and on the artistic, philosophical, and literary influences on their design, we miss this wider range of meanings expressed in the surroundings of the mansion, meanings drawn from the real world of work, labour, and food production. And we also miss the significance of the changes affected by the new landscape style of Capability Brown in the middle decades of the 18th century.

THE ESTATE LANDSCAPE: CHRONOLOGIES AND TRANSFORMATIONS

The core and periphery of the estate landscape were thus interconnected in complex ways but the character of these connections changed over time. So too did the character of the estate more generally, and its development - in England at least - can for convenience (and with considerable over-simplification) be divided into three broad phases, to each of which a number of specific research questions pertains.

We may define an initial phase, running from the early 16th to the early 18th century. In terms of mansions and gardens this has probably received more attention from archaeologists, especially excavators, than later periods. Particularly important has been studies of the conversion of monastic houses into country houses in the aftermath of the Dissolution;[38] social and ideological interpretations of Renaissance architecture;[39] and the excavation and earthwork surveys of a number of designed landscapes, such as that discussed by Paul Everson in this volume (pp.113-128). Some of the most important outstanding questions concern the rate of change across the whole period, the extent of continuity and the points of discontinuity in stylistic development. How far, for example, were the kinds of grammar of design employed in medieval designed landscapes replaced, in the course of the 16th century, by new 'Renaissance' ideas; and how far, conversely, did the real break in landscape design, like that in country house architecture (with the effective demise of single pile houses), come in the 1660s? More important perhaps is the question of how far the wider estate landscape was manipulated aesthetically in this period or, more accurately, how this increased over time. Here too it is possible to see a break, or at least an intensification of activity, in the period after the 1660s with, for example the proliferation of avenues and other planting across the countryside. On a priori grounds it seems plausible that large-scale planting, and similar interventions, were limited by the existence of customary tenure and common rights, and only became common with the spread of enclosure and the development of leaseholds, but this is a hypothesis which requires rigorous testing. The effective triumph of landed property against the arbitrary power of the Crown in the later 17th century did not in itself create the landed estate or these new institutional forms, but it must have given encouragement to their further development. Extensive landscaping beyond the core of mansion, garden and park presumably represents the archaeological signal of the emergence of the true landed estate, and this was, indeed, the key feature of this phase. This was not simply a question of the steady migration of land up the social scale, with the demise of the small owner. 16th-century lawyers and topographers described landed properties, in effect, as collections of rights and incomes; by the mid 18th century, an estate was a block of owned and controlled land.

A second phase spans, roughly, the middle and later decades of the 18th century. Broadly Palladian, and subsequently Neoclassical, forms of architecture were universal for mansions, and to some extent the design of their grounds mirrored this. Gardens became simpler, less geometric in character and under designers like William Kent evoked Italianate landscapes and might include sophisticated iconographic schemes. Formal structure was now removed from the walls of the mansion, together with the various productive features in which the gentry had once delighted. In the classic landscapes of Capability Brown and his contemporaries the house stood 'free of walls'. Shrubberies and informal gardens or pleasure grounds were retained to one side of the main façade but the principal setting for the mansion was now a park, more manicured in appearance than the deer parks of previous centuries. Some of the significance of this particular change can, perhaps, be understood quite easily in terms of contemporary social developments, especially the development of the 'consumer society'.[40] In a world of fashionable consumption, superior resources of production were no longer a major badge of status. At the same time, there was a growing emphasis on privacy at the estate core. The mansion was increasingly isolated within the park, perimeter belts proliferated and the numbers of roads and footpaths closed or diverted soared, especially following legal changes in 1773. All this manifested the growing gulf that was emerging between the gentry and the wider community. Society was now primarily organised along class lines – horizontally stratified, rather than vertically integrated through ties of obligation, deference and local or regional identity.[41] The landscape park reflected the increasing consolidation of the upper ranks of society into a single social group, 'the polite': comprising, in Girouard's words, 'the people who owned and ran the country'.[42]

Indeed, the new landscapes served to clarify the boundaries of this group, at a time of expanding economic production and increasing social mobility. The growing middle classes made elaborate gardens – the business of gardening, like other forms of consumption, expanded considerably in this period. As a result, gardens in themselves were no longer significant markers of social status and they thus played a subsidiary role in the country house landscape. The park became the principal setting for the house because it was a form of design which, by definition, those outside the ranks of the established elite could not emulate, for its precondition was the possession of land on a significant scale. Gardens were downgraded because they were redolent of the middle classes, just as agrarian production was rejected because it smacked of the tenant farmer. The precise chronology with which the new 'landscape' style was accepted, however, by different groups of landowners and in different regions, remains unclear and, insofar as such variations have important implications for our understanding of 18th-century society, would repay further research.

As all this happened – as the core of the estate became more overtly aesthetic, more exclusive devoted to the ostentatious consumption of leisure – the designed and the aesthetic migrated ever outwards, into the wider landscape, as plantations spread across the countryside, as flamboyant schemes of 'improvement' were instituted and farm buildings rebuilt on modern lines, and as land management was increasingly geared towards extensive leisure pursuits like fox hunting. Landed estates now dominated extensive tracts of the English countryside, as a consequence of large-scale enclosure, the successful consolidation of landed properties and the disappearance of customary tenancies.

Much of this is now well-trodden ground. Rather less well researched, especially by archaeologists, is the third main phase of estate development, spanning the early and middle decades of the 19th century. The landed estate now existed within an increasingly industrial and urban world in which the economic and political power of manufacturers, industrialists, and the middle class as a whole were increasing. Change is soon apparent in designed landscapes, in the work of the leading landscape gardener of the 1790s and early 1800s, Humphry Repton. His style was more subtle and considered than that of Brown, and thus better suited to smaller properties, the diminutive parks of those on the fringes of landed society. It was not by 'adding field to field, or by taking away hedges, or by removing roads to a distance' that the surroundings of the smaller villa or manor house were to be improved: instead, this could only be achieved by exploiting 'every circumstance of interest and beauty within our reach, and by hiding such objects as cannot be viewed with pleasure'.[43] Indeed, in his later work Repton considered the grounds of even more lowly properties, outside the category of the landed estate altogether, writing in 1816 how:

> It seldom falls to the lot of the improver to be called upon for his opinion on places of great extent ... while in the neighbourhood of every city or manufacturing town, new places as villas are daily springing up, and these, with a few acres, require all the conveniences, comforts and appendages, of larger and more sumptuous, if not more expensive places. And ... these have of late had the greatest claim to my attention.[44]

Repton's later designs show an increasing emphasis on gardens and pleasure grounds, and on placing these once more in prominent positions in the country house landscape.

At the same time, he consciously manipulated the landscape in order to emphasise not only the extent of ownership but also the paternalistic involvement of landowners in local affairs, advocating for example the creation of gaps in perimeter belts, or example, in order to dissolve social tensions.

These themes set the scene for much of the 19th century, and can be related quite clearly to the position of estate owners in an increasingly industrialised and urbanised society. The return of formal, structured gardens to prominence - gardens that grew ever more extensive and elaborate under mid-century designers like William Andrews Nesfield – signalled a cultural rapprochement with the bourgeoisie, served to affirm shared aesthetic values – a development fuelled in part, no doubt, by the increasing rate of social mobility, as larger numbers of individuals grown wealthy in the expanding commercial and industrial sectors bought, or married, into the landed class. The exploits of the 'gardener heroes' employed by the great estates – John Caie at Woburn, Donald Beaton at Shrubland Park, Joseph Paxton at Chatsworth – were eagerly consumed by middle-class readers of the burgeoning gardening press. Yet it was now, somewhat paradoxically, that the image of the estate as a self-consciously feudal and rural entity was also elaborated: indeed, contradictions and ambiguities are the distinguishing features of this third phase of the estate's development.

The majority of mansions erected in Britain after c. 1820 were thus built in some self-consciously archaic style, full-blown medieval gothic or pseudo-Jacobethan (one reason for the return of parterres and topiary in gardens was that they provided a suitable accompaniment for such architecture). 'Model' villages like Edensor near Chatsworth, or Holkham in Norfolk, clustering deferentially at the park gates, helped counter the claims from middle class radicals, that the country was ruled by an essentially selfish clique, but they also harked back to a supposed period of pre-industrial rural harmony – 'the rich man at his castle, the poor man at his gate'. The picturesque styles usually adopted for such places was mirrored, in more subdued form, by that used for the workers' cottages which were now (for the first time) widely constructed on estates, as well as for farms and farm buildings (see Silvester and Alfrey in this volume for a Welsh example of this kind of thing). Moreover, the specifically rural character of the estate was paraded as a badge of superiority and protected from urban and industrial intrusion, wrapped around the mansion as a kind of insulating blanket against modernity. In the 18th century the Earls of Essex at Cashiobury in Hertfordshire, like other contemporary landowners, had welcomed a new canal cutting through the middle of their park as an interesting addition to the prospect. But the same family vehemently opposed the construction of the London to Manchester railway in the late 1830s along the same valley, and it was routed several miles to the east, through a tunnel the construction of which cost several lives. Such hostility was widely shared, and for good reasons. 'I rejoice in it', remarked Dr Arnold famously as he watched a train draw out of Rugby, 'and think that feudality is gone for ever'. The subject as a whole would repay further study, not least because landed hostility to such overt symbols of modernity were not universal: the Sixth Duke of Devonshire, for example, worked hard to encourage the development of a line along the Derwent valley, close to Chatsworth. Indeed, while certain features of the modern world were clearly shunned by 19th-century landowners, and while their chosen styles of architecture, both for their mansions, and for farms, cottages and model villages, were determinedly archaic, their estates also proudly displayed an easy familiarity with the latest technology. Although few estates could boast structures to rival Paxton's Great Conservatory at Chatsworth, flamboyant glasshouses and complex heating systems could be found in the kitchen gardens of most country houses. In the mansion itself, gas lighting was standard by the middle years of the century (many country houses had their own gas works and retorts) and by the end of the century electric lighting was beginning to appear.[45] The attitudes of the landed class to science and modernity were thus complex and ambivalent, reflecting their ambiguous and uncertain position in the modern world. This is indeed a richly textured archaeology, which we have hardly begun to examine.

CONCLUSION

Post-medieval archaeologists need to work in association with scholars from other disciplines but can nevertheless make their own distinctive contribution to the study of estate landscape not only in terms of practices and techniques – excavation, field survey etc – but also, and perhaps especially, in terms of theory and perspective. In the short space available I have been able to address only a handful of the issues to which they might usefully turn their attention – I have for example said nothing about gender and space, 'inhabitation', or attitudes to the natural world. There is a vast field of enquiry out there, and the papers presented in this volume point the way, showing clearly the benefits of a specifically archaeological approach to this key subject.

NOTES

1. Clemenson 1982; Rawding 1992; Daniels & Seymour 1990.
2. Everson & Williamson 1998; West 1999; Johnson 1999; Aston 1978; Pattison 1998; Brown 1991; Taylor 1983; Currie & Locock 1991; Dix, Soden & Hylton 1995; Williamson 1998.
3. Clemenson 1982, 7-9.
4. Williamson 1995, 12-15.
5. Beckett 1984 & 1986.
6. Short 1992a; Thirsk 1987 & 1992.
7. Thirsk 1987; Short 1992b, 23-8.
8. Young 1771, Vol 2, 1.
9. Williamson 2003.
10. Hughes 1982; Neave 1993.
11. Holderness 1972; Short 1992b.
12. Such as Banks 1988; see also Way 2000.
13. Neave 1993.
14. Williamson 1998, 132-4.
15. Rackham 2004.
16. Habbakuk 1953; Clay 1985; Mingay 1989.
17. Mingay 1989.
18. Cannadine 1977, 77-97; Pearson 1983, 210-14.
19. e.g. Leone 1995.
20. Orser 1999, 280.
21. Williamson 1998; Williamson 2004.
22. Barnwell 1998; Wade Martins 2002.
23. Gregory 2005.
24. Wade Martins & Williamson 1999a, 192.
25. See also Wade Martins & Williamson 1999a, 67-9.
26. Woodside & Crow 1999, 82-3.
27. Bettey 1999; Bowie 1987; Cutting & Cummings 1999.
28. Smith 1806.
29. Wade Martins & Williamson 1999b, 205-6.
30. Wade Martins & Williamson 1999b, 206-9.
31. Clemenson 1982, 74-91; Rawding 1992; Fuller 1976.
32. Lawrence 1801, 100.
33. Whateley 1770, 1, 164-5.
34. Finch 2004; see also Carr 1976.
35. Williamson 1995, 119-24.
36. Daniels 1988.
37. See Currie 1990.
38. Howard 2003.
39. Johnson 1999.
40. MacKendrick, Plumb & Brewer 1982.

41. Williamson 1995, 100-118.
42. Girouard 1990, 76-7.
43. Williamson 1995, 154-9.
44. Repton 1816, 69.
45. Girouard 1978, 250-1, 268.

BIBLIOGRAPHY

Aston, M. 1978, 'Gardens and earthworks at Hardington and Low Ham', *Proceedings of the Somerset Archaeological & Natural History Society* 122, 11-28.

Banks, S. J. 1988, 'Nineteenth-century scandal or twentieth-century model? A new look at open and close parishes', *Economic History Review* 41, 51-73.

Barnwell, P. 1998, 'An extra dimension? Lincolnshire farm buildings as historical evidence', *Agricultural History Review* 46, 1.

Beckett, J. V. 1984, 'The pattern of landownership in England and Wales 1660-1880', *Economic History Review* 38, 1-22.

Beckett, J. V. 1986, *The Aristocracy in England 1660-1914*, Oxford: Blackwell.

Bettey, J. H. 1999, 'The development of water meadows in the southern counties', in Cook & Williamson 1999, 175-195.

Bowie, G. 1987, 'Water meadows in Wessex: a re-evaluation for the period 1640-1850'. *Agricultural History Review* 35, 151-8.

Brown, A. E. (ed.) 1991, *Garden Archaeology*, London: Council for British Archaeology.

Cannadine, D. 1977, 'The landowner as millionaire: the finances of the Dukes of Devonshire c. 1800-c. 1926', *Agricultural History Review* 25:2, 77-97.

Carr, R. 1976, *English Fox Hunting: a History*, London: Weidenfeld & Nicholson.

Clay, C. 1985, 'Landlords and estate management in England', in Thirsk 1985, 119-251.

Clemenson, H. 1982, *English Country Houses and Landed Estates*, London: Croom Helm.

Cook, H. & Williamson, T. (eds) 1999, *Water Management in the English Landscape: field, marsh and meadow*, Edinburgh: Edinburgh University Press.

Cosgrove, D. & Daniels, S. (eds) 1988, *The Iconography of Landscape*, Cambridge: Cambridge University Press.

Currie, C. K. 1990, 'Fish ponds as garden features', *Garden History* 18:1, 22-33.

Currie, C. K. & Locock, M. 1991, 'An evaluation of archaeological techniques used at Castle Bromwich Hall, 1989-90', *Garden History* 19:2, 77-99.

Cutting, R. & Cummings, I. 1999, 'Water meadows: their form, operation, and plant ecology', in Cook & Williamson 1999, 157-178.

Daniels, S. 1988, 'The political iconography of woodland in later eighteenth-century England', in Cosgrove & Daniels 1988, 51-72.

Daniels, S. & Seymour, S. 1990, 'Landscape design and the idea of improvement 1730-1900', in Dodgshon & Butlin 1990, 488-520.

Dix, B., Soden, I., & Hylton, T. 1985, 'Kirby Hall and its gardens: excavations in 1987-94', *Archaeological Journal* 152, 291-380.

Dodgshon, R. A. & Butlin, R. A. 1990, *An Historical Geography of England and Wales*, 2nd edn, London: Academic Press.

Everson, P. & Williamson, T. 1998, 'Gardens and designed landscapes', in Everson & Williamson 1998, 139-65.

Everson, P. & Williamson, T. (eds) 1998, *The Archaeology of Landscape*, Manchester: Manchester University Press.

Finch, J. 2004, '"Grass, grass, grass": fox-hunting and the creation of the modern landscape', *Landscapes* 5:2, 41-50.

Fuller, H. 1976, 'Landownership and the Lindsey landscape', *Annals of the Association of American Geographers* 66, 45-64.

Gaimster, D. & Gilchrist, R. (eds) 2003, *The Archaeology of Reformation 1480-1580*, Leeds: Maney.

Girouard, M. 1978, *Life in the English Country House*, London: Yale University Press.

Girouard, M. 1990, *The English Town*, London: Yale University Press.

Gregory, J. 2005, 'Mapping improvement: reshaping rural landscapes in the eighteenth century', *Landscapes* 6:1, 62-82.

Habbakuk, H. J. 1953, 'Economic functions of English landowners in the seventeenth and eighteenth centuries', *Explorations in Entrepreneurial History* 6, 92-102.

Holderness, B. A. 1972, '"Open" and "close" parishes in England in the eighteenth and nineteenth centuries', *Agricultural History Review* 20:2, 126-39.

Howard, M. 2003, 'Recycling the monastic fabric: beyond the act of Dissolution', in Gaimster & Gilchrist 2003, 221-34.

Hughes, M. F. 1982, 'Emparking and the desertion of settlements in Hampshire', *Medieval Settlement Research Group Annual Report* 30, 37.

Johnson, M. 1999, 'Reconstructing castles and refashioning identities in Renaissance England', in Tarlow & West 1999, 69-87.

Kirby, T. & Oosthuizen, S. (eds) 2000, *An Atlas of Cambridgeshire and Huntingdonshire History*, Cambridge: Anglia Polytechnic University.

Lawrence, J. 1801, *The Modern Land Steward*, London.

Leone, M. 1995, 'A historical archaeology of capitalism', *American Anthropologist* 97, 251-68.

MacKendrick, N., Plumb, J. & Brewer, J. 1982, *The Birth of a Consumer Society*, London: Europa.

Mingay, G. E. 1989, 'Agricultural productivity and agricultural society in eighteenth-century England', *Research in Economic History*, Supplement 5, 31-47.

Neave, S. 1993, 'Rural settlement contraction in the East Riding of Yorkshire between the mid seventeenth and mid eighteenth centuries', *Agricultural History Review* 41:2, 124-36.

Orser, C. 1999, 'Negotiating our "familiar" past', in Tarlow & West 1999, 273-85.

Pattison, P. (ed.) 1998, *There by Design: field archaeology in parks and gardens,* London: Royal Commission on the Historical Monuments of England.

Pearson, J. 1983, *Stags and Serpents: a history of the Cavendish family and the Dukes of Devonshire*, London: Methuen.

Rackham, O. 2004, 'Pre-existing trees and woods in country house parks', *Landscapes* 5:2, 1-15.

Rawding, C. 1992, 'Society and place in nineteenth-century north Lincolnshire', *Rural History: Economy, Society, Culture* 3:1, 59-85.

Repton, H. 1816, *Fragments on the Theory and Practice of Landscape Gardening*, London.

Short, B. 1992a, 'The evolution of contrasting communities within rural England', in Short 1992, 19-43.

Short, B. (ed.) 1992b, *The English Rural Community: Image and Analysis*, Cambridge: Cambridge University Press.

Smith, W. 1806, *Observations on the Utility, Form, and Management of Water Meadows*, Norwich.

Tarlow, S. & West, S. (eds) *The Familiar Past? Archaeologies of later historical Britain*, London: Routledge.

Taylor, C. 1983, *The Archaeology of Gardens*, Princes Risborough: Shire.

Thirsk, J. (ed.) 1985, *The Agrarian History of England and Wales*, Vol. 2.1, 1640-1750, Cambridge: Cambridge University Press.

Thirsk, J. 1987, *England's Agricultural Regions and Agrarian History 1500-1750*, London: MacMillan.

Thirsk, J. 1992, 'English rural communities: structures, regularities, and change in the sixteenth and seventeenth centuries', in Short 1992b, 44-61.

Wade Martins, S. 2002, *The English Model Farm: building the agricultural ideal 1700-1914*, Macclesfield: Windgather.

Wade Martins, S. & Williamson, T. 1999a, *Roots of Change: farming and the landscape in East Anglia 1700-1870*, Exeter: British Agricultural History Society.

Wade Martins, S. & Williamson, T. 1999b, 'Inappropriate technology? The history of floating in the north and east of England', in Cook & Williamson 1999, 196-209.

Way, T. 2000, 'Open and close parishes', in Kirby & Oosthuizen 2000, 65-6.

West, S. 1999, 'Social space and the English country house', in Tarlow & West 1999, 103-122.
Whateley, T. 1770, *Observations on Modern Gardening*, London.
Williamson, T. 2003, *The Transformation of Rural England: farming and the landscape 1700-1870*, Exeter: Exeter University Press.
Williamson, 2004, 'Designed landscapes: the regional dimension', *Landscapes* 5:2, 16-24.
Williamson, T. 1995, *Polite Landscapes: Gardens and Society in Eighteenth-Century England*, Stroud: Sutton.
Williamson, T. 1998, *The Archaeology of the Landscape park: garden design in Norfolk, England, c. 1680-1840*, Oxford: British Archaeological Reports.
Woodside, R. & Crow, J. 1999, *Hadrian's Wall: an historic landscape*, London: National Trust.
Young, A. 1771, *The Farmer's Tour Through the East of England*, 4 Volumes, London.

Part One

Landscapes & Improvement
———————————

Pallas, Flora and Ceres: Landscape Priorities and Improvement on the Castle Howard estate, 1699-1880

By JONATHAN FINCH

This paper addresses the relationship between the ornamental and the productive landscape through the development of the Castle Howard landscape in North Yorkshire (UK). Rather than treating the two forms of landscape as separate entities, it is argued they were conceived together by their owners. Furthermore, they were constrained and supported by the same social and economic considerations. By considering the elements together it will be shown that an understanding of the integration or transformation of earlier landscape features can inform and deepen our understanding of the meanings attached to the landscape and the manner in which they were experienced in the past.

Castle Howard is the Baroque mansion built in the Howardian Hills of North Yorkshire by the third Earl of Carlisle during the first quarter of the 18th century, to designs by Sir John Vanbrugh, and now widely recognised as one of the masterpieces of English architectural and landscape design, alongside Chatsworth and Blenheim from the same period. It sits at the centre of an exceptional landscape featuring formal lakes, fountains, terraces and temples, which largely survived the zeal for informal 'Brownian' parks in the second half of the 18th century, although the grounds have continued to evolve and change. By the 19th century the surrounding estate extended to just over 13,000 acres with a further 65,510 acres elsewhere, principally around the family's other seat at Naworth in Cumbria, making the Howards one of the most important landowning families in the north of England.[1]

Despite being a rare survival, the grounds have received less attention from scholars than the house[2], yet it is clear that they developed closely together, as one of the period's most important writers on designing country seats advised: 'When you first begin to build, and make Gardens, the Gardener and Builder ought to go Hand in Hand, and to consult together'.[3] The ornamental landscape was envisaged and laid out on a grand scale in the French style from the outset, with compartments, such as the ornamental wilderness and parterre to the south, designed to provoke different reactions and sensations through statuary, planting, and waterworks, all set within a structured framework of avenues, rides, and woodlands. One of the important dynamics enshrined within it was the relationship between the designed or ornamental landscape around the house and the wider productive,

LEFT
Figure 1. The south front of Castle Howard with the figures of Pallas (centre), Flora (right) and Ceres (left) on the pediment.

BELOW
Figure 2. The view from the south front at Castle Howard across the south terrace, remodelled by W.A. Nesfield in the early 1850s when the Atlas fountain was added. Beyond on St Anne's Hill is the pyramid (1728) that contains a bust of the third Earl's ancestor Lord William Howard, and beyond that the agricultural fields around Welburn.

agricultural landscape of the estate. That relationship formed a persistent theme within landscape writing of the early 18th century, particularly for Stephen Switzer, who has already been quoted, and at Castle Howard the designed element reached beyond the bastion walls that defined the inner core of grounds surrounding the house. A triumvirate of goddesses – Pallas, who was associated with the virtuous art of building, Flora with her cornucopia of flowers, and Ceres with a sheaf of corn – stand on the south pediment looking out over the south terrace (Fig. 1), towards the villages and fields of Bulmer and Welburn, (Fig. 2), suggesting that architecture, gardens and agriculture were seen as the three prime elements within the estate landscape.[4] Furthermore, it was the wider landscape that articulated some of the most important developments within the estate over the two and a half centuries after the designed landscape was established; a period when relatively few modifications were effected within the designed core, and so when histories of Castle Howard tend to draw to an abrupt end. In order to understand the Castle Howard landscape, therefore, one has to understand how the landscape has changed, and in order to do that, one has to engage with the changing priorities and management strategies of the Castle Howard estate.

When Charles Howard, third Earl of Carlisle first contemplated turning the relatively bleak and declining village of Henderskelfe (Fig. 3), with its fire-ravaged castle, into a Baroque mansion with a suitably grand formal landscape, he approached the most revered pair of designers in the country. William Talman provided plans for the house, and his frequent associate George London, the royal gardener and owner of the Brompton nurseries, supplied designs for the grounds. However, Talman was soon passed over by Carlisle who turned instead to the untried dramatist, ex-soldier and fellow Kit-Kat Club member, Sir John Vanbrugh and his associate Nicholas Hawksmoor. Carlisle also rejected London's formal plans for the grounds, but it is less clear who was responsible for the new and more innovative designs, but the particular praise that the third Earl attracts in *Ichnographia Rustica* particularly for the alternate design of Ray Wood, has led to speculation that Switzer himself may have been involved.[5]

Histories tracing the development of the landscape at Castle Howard tend to work out from the architectural heart of the building itself to, on the west side, the kitchen garden, begun at the same time as the house, and on the eastern side, into Ray Wood, which will be discussed in more detail below. The next addition was the obelisk that marked the crossing of the two main (though not axial) avenues, which was raised in 1714, and was originally conceived as a celebration of Marlborough's victories in Europe (see Fig. 4 for layout).[6] Constructed slightly out of 'true', the three-dimensional mass of the obelisk is apparent from any of the four approaches. Its meaning was changed in 1731 when a second large inscription panel, this time in English, was added to the western face commemorating the planting campaigns of the third Earl and expressing confidence in the longevity of the Carlisle pedigree. South of the obelisk on the main avenue, the Pyramid Gate was built in 1719, and again carries a dated commemorative inscription.[7] From either side of the gate, mock-fortification walls, complete with bastions, extend beyond the field of view, giving the impression of a formidable defensive curtain wall through the clever use of the local topography. The wall was built in the 1720s and became an important feature of the Castle Howard landscape, mirrored by an inner bastioned ha-ha around the core

Figure 3. Detail of the Henderskelfe map from 1694 showing the village clustered around the castle in the centre. To the left, the corner of Ray Wood can be seen with fish ponds to the north. Reproduced with the kind permission of the Hon. Simon Howard.

ornamental grounds.[8] At one corner of this inner wall, on a substantial bastion, the Temple of Diana[9] was added at the eastern end of the terrace walk between 1724-29 to designs by Vanbrugh. In 1735 an open rotunda by Hawksmoor, which became known as the Temple of Venus, was completed at the north-eastern corner of Ray Wood. This was also located on a protruding bastion on the inner bastion wall, to the north of the Temple of Diana which stood at the south-eastern corner of the wood.

In 1728, between the completion of the two temples, a pyramid was added to a small ridge known as St Anne's Hill, visible from the south front of the house, but beyond the ornamental core (see Fig. 2). Within the pyramid there is a large bust of Carlisle's Tudor ancestor Lord William Howard, with an inscription recording the 'grateful Remembrance' of the third Earl. Between 1728 and 1732 an outer boundary was finally defined across the approach avenue, with the addition of the Carrmire Gate, below and in front of the Pyramid Gate and bastion walls (Fig. 5).[10] The pedimented gateway is flanked by two short lengths of castellated wall each terminated by a gothic turret, complete with ornamental cruciform arrow-slits. Unlike the bastion wall beyond, there was no attempt here to disguise the limited extent of the wall, giving the structure a theatrical rather than a martial character.

Figure 4. Detail of the Castle Howard landscape, 1727, showing the formal layout. The bastion wall links the Pyramid Gate at the bottom left to the formal grounds to the south of the house, returning to the north of the house through Ray Wood. The formal avenues cross to the west of the house. Reproduced with the kind permission of the Hon. Simon Howard.

The final architectural addition or 'outwork' to the landscape was the mausoleum, designed by Hawksmoor and begun in 1731, but not finished until 1742, after the death of both its patron and architect.

This chronological and patron-orientated development, with its focus on the ornamental landscape, buildings and architects, fails to convey how these elements combined to create a coherent landscape scheme that brought together both architectural and natural elements, or the impact these had upon the visitor approaching Castle Howard along the avenue. The main approach began from the York/Scarborough Road with the Whitwell Road bringing the visitor directly to Exclamation Gate on the edge of the first of a number of ridges that define the topography of the estate (Fig. 6). The gate itself framed an uninterrupted view north to the house and the ornamental landscape, about two miles away. It is from this position that one can best understand Horace Walpole's description of the Arcadian landscape:

> 'Nobody had informed me I should see a palace, a town, a fortified city, temples on high places, woods worthy of being each a metropolis of the Druids, vales connected to hills by other woods, the noblest

lawn in the world fenced by half the horizon, and a mausoleum that would tempt one to be buried alive'[11]

His choice of words is interesting since it is quite distinct from the vocabulary used by modern landscape or garden historians. They provide an insight into how elite audiences imagined designed landscapes as fantastic and populated places rather than analysing their elements in search for architectural precedents and teleological chronologies.

Having arrived at a topographical vantage point that afforded the best view over the landscape ensemble, the road turned to the right, and joined the beginning of the processional avenue that traversed a series ridges and valleys as it headed north through the two curtain walls of the Carrmire and Pyramid Gates. Once through the Carrmire Gate, the topography of dips and climbs animated the obelisk, the tip of which was visible through the archway of the pyramid gate, in what might be interpreted as a phallic and overtly sexual combination. As mentioned above, the obelisk marks the crossing of the two main avenues: the approach avenue continues north until it emerges above the Vale of Pickering with views across to the North York Moors, whilst the other avenue crosses it east to the north front of the house and beyond to the summit of Ray Wood, and west, into the deer park. The fact that the two structuring axes are not aligned upon the house itself is an indication that the landscape design was departing from conventional French models which were usually associated with flat and even terrain, very different to the topography around Castle Howard. The disposition of the axial routes also raises questions about the position and significance of several elements within the landscape. Such is the scale and impact of the avenue, it is easy to miss the emphasis it is given by the topography and the surrounding planting; yet the landscape context was absolutely crucial to the initial choice of the site and how the grounds developed, as well as the experience of encountering the various elements placed within it.[12]

Garden historians have identified the third Earl of Carlisle's rejection of plans drawn up by George London for Ray Wood, which stands on a small prominence immediately to the east of the house and at the end of the east-west avenue, as a seminal 'moment' in the evolution of the Castle Howard landscape, and indeed, of English garden design more generally. London had submitted a fashionable formal plan of radiating paths cut through the wood from a central point, but instead Carlisle created a scheme of irregular, meandering paths that connected a number of clearings or 'cabinets' with summerhouses, statues and fountains. To Switzer the result displayed the 'more natural and Promiscuous disposition' of Nature's beauties, in a similar manner to the early naturalistic and serpentine elements of Lord Cobham's landscape at Stowe (Bucks).[13] Both are championed as important turning points in the development of English landscape gardening, and both were sites where Vanbrugh worked.

However, the implicit decision to preserve an existing 'natural' landscape feature is perhaps a more important aspect of the change in design. Ray Wood was an important element within the existing landscape of Henderskelfe before it attracted the attention of the third Earl. It has been suggested that all traces of the medieval and early-modern landscape, including the late 17th-century manor house or castle, the medieval church,

Figure 5. The view along the approach avenue showing the Carrmire Gate, with the road rising to the Pyramid Gate beyond, with the mature trees of the deer park behind the bastion wall on the horizon.

Figure 6. The view framed by Exclamation Gate looking north towards Castle Howard and the designed landscape. This was the first view visitors got of the house, its landscape and ornamental buildings.

Figure 7. Castle Howard from the north, with Ray Wood to the left dominating the horizon. The lake in the foreground was fashioned from medieval fishponds and irrigation within the deer park during the last quarter of the 18th century.

and the remaining village, were erased in the path of Carlisle's Baroque juggernaut. The significance accorded to Ray Wood suggests a more complex relationship with the existing landscape, and its survival may indicate that the site of the new house was chosen at least in part because of its relationship to 'natural' elements of the antecedent landscape that continued to contribute meaning to the new ornamental grounds.

A late 17th-century map of Henderskelfe (see Fig. 3), before the landscape was transformed, shows a village with a number of empty and engrossed tofts, suggesting that the settlement had been in gradual decline, probably since the late 15th century. Even the 'castle' seems to have evolved within the street plan, since its adjoining closes respect the back lane to the north and that to the south caused the street to be diverted. The map also shows an agricultural landscape of small enclosures, with names such as 'Coneygarth', 'Sheepgarth', and 'East Moors', confirming that the ridge was an area of poor soil put over to sheep farming and rabbits.[14]

Three features dominated Henderskelfe: the castle in the centre of the settlement, Ray Wood to the east, and a deer park to the west. All were situated on the ridge and the mature trees on either side of the castle must have presented a distinguished profile from the north and south (Fig. 7). A 16th century survey suggests that both Ray Wood and the deer park contained mature oak trees over a hundred years old, but two centuries later Ray

Wood was described as being predominantly beech.[15] Most of the historic planting in Ray Wood was felled in the 1940s, but subsequent replanting means that the area is once more covered with maturing woodland, whilst ancient oaks from the deer park still survive, now stranded in the car park, to the west of John Carr's late 18th-century stable block. The preservation of mature woodland and parkland on either side of the new house, and the inscription on the obelisk, demonstrate how important trees and woodland were within the early 18th-century landscape. The considerable extent of deforestation during the civil wars, fifty years earlier, had given political consequence to woodland and arboriculture, and John Evelyn's *Sylva* (1664) was a post-Revolutionary plea for confident investment in a stable political future.[16] It is likely therefore that the hundred acres of mature woodland within the demesne of Henderskelfe was an important consideration for Carlisle, and may have determined the position of his new mansion.[17]

If the woodland was an asset, other aspects of the working landscape came in for immediate change. From his arrival at Castle Howard, the third Earl set about a systematic campaign to convert much of the arable land to permanent pasture. One of the earliest visitors to record their impressions was John Tracy Atkyns who noted that 'it was a very barren piece of ground, the greatest part of it warren, but by enclosing a number of acres at a time…and burning it, and laying it down with grass seeds he has improv'd it greatly'.[18] Scraps of ridge and furrow, such as that to the east of Ray Wood overlooked by the bastion walls and temples (Fig. 8), indicate that the closes depicted on the 17th-century map of

Figure 8. The view from the north-west towards the Temple of Diana (Temple of the Four Winds) and Ray Wood overlooking preserved ridge and furrow beneath the bastion wall.

Henderskelfe (see Fig. 3) were the result of late 15th or 16th-century piecemeal enclosure of an open-field system. In contrast to the enclosed landscape of Henderskelfe, Ganthorpe, and Coneysthorpe at the heart of the estate, however, the landscape to the north, into the Vale of Pickering, and to the south, towards the villages of Bulmer and Welburn, was one of open-fields and common grazing at the beginning of the 18th century.

The survival of the open-fields in Bulmer and Welburn is significant because for the first fifty years after the completion of the ornamental landscape, visitors to Castle Howard would have approached the Carrmire Gate at the beginning of the processional avenue, across a functioning 'medieval' open-field system. The impact of the mock-medieval wall with its turrets and castellations would have been intensified by the open expanse of agricultural land giving it greater prominence in the landscape, and because of the association between the open-fields and the feudal past. Behind the Carrmire Gate the land rose sharply to the impressive bastion walls, defending the wooded ridge of the deer park, and contrasting the sylvan landscape – the 'metropolis of the Druids' – punctuated by temples and pyramids, with the mundane agricultural landscapes below (see Fig 5).

Open-field systems were seen as an impediment to improvement in the 18th-century landscape. The ideal estate landscape was extensive, compact, contiguous, and entirely enclosed.[19] The realisation of that ideal both created and then displayed the landowner's control over the land, free from historic legal and tenurial constraints, free to increase rents and productivity through the unopposed imposition of a single agricultural regime. By association, therefore, the survival of open-field systems must have represented a very different landscape and by the late 18th century, agricultural reformers were explicit about the degenerate and unpatriotic influence such archaic farming had upon its population. Perhaps such associations guided the ideas of visitors approaching Castle Howard. The use of the open-field system to create a dramatic prelude to the wooded interior of the designed landscape was clearly quite deliberate, and was reflected in the architectural vocabulary used by Vanbrugh and Hawksmoor. The defended, enclosed and wooded landscape with its temples and pyramids reflected a civilised, ordered and stable society that, crucially, integrated worthy aspects of the inherited landscape – the wood and parkland. The unenclosed open-fields, on the other hand, resisted the progress wrought by enlightened aristocratic patronage and demonstrated communities clinging to the outmoded and untenable systems of the feudal past.[20] It is worth pointing out that that the larger open-field systems were so entrenched in communal systems of husbandry that many remained immune to the 'improving' landlord until the process of parliamentary enclosure rationalised procedures in favour of the larger landowners. However, it is the discerning attitude to different elements within the historic landscape that is important to understand during the creation of the Castle Howard landscape, and in order to understand the subsequent landscape changes through the 18th and 19th centuries.

The Howard family and the Castle Howard estate do not figure prominently in histories of agricultural transformation during the late 18th and 19th centuries. The Howards were not involved in the same campaigns of large-scale agricultural improvement associated with some Yorkshire landowners, such as the Sykes of Sledmere on the Wolds of the East Riding, for example. It would still be wrong, however, to assume that there was little change on the estate over the same period, even though the famous agricultural commentators, such as Arthur Young, were unusually quiet about the role of the estate in the region's agricultural renaissance, in contrast to their outspoken distaste for the unfashionable architecture of the house and garden buildings, which Young described as 'all so heavy and clumsy in stile as to be perfectly disgusting'. The landscape feature of note for Young was still the 'beauty of the woods that surround [the house] almost every side. These are truly magnificent; they are extensive, very well designed, and as they in general hang on the sides of the hills, have a noble effect from whatever point they are viewed'.[21] Here again the mature woodland worked in combination with the topography to impress the discerning visitor, whilst the formal gardens were not mentioned.

The push towards greater pastoralism that had begun in the early 18th century continued. The open-fields of Bulmer and Welburn were enclosed by act of parliament in 1779 (Fig. 9), part of a wave of enclosure awards across the estate, including the large villages of Terrington (1779) and Amotherby (1777).[22] The costs accrued were substantial, with the solicitor's bill alone totalling over £360 at Bulmer in 1779, and with the buying, growing, planting, and weeding of hawthorn a prominent expense, as was the amount spent on the roads. The road leading to the Carrmire Gate was straightened, as was the road from Bulmer to Welburn that crosses it. Neither secured much agricultural advantage, but both enhanced the processional approach. Agriculturally, enclosure facilitated a shift towards a mixed farming regime as the subsequent estate accounts record repairs to barns

Figure 9. The former open-fields of Bulmer showing characteristic features of late 18th century enclosure: large rectilinear fields, hawthorn hedges with regularly spaced oak trees.

and cowsheds being built, but they do not describe a radical transformation of the farming landscape. Parliamentary enclosure was clearly welcomed as a tool with which to sweep away the open-field systems, to end and to renegotiate tenancies, but it does not stand out within the estate correspondence as part of a powerful, wider, social process as it was on estates where 'improvement' was a real engine for change.

It might be tempting, therefore, to suggest that the vogue for agricultural improvement largely passed Castle Howard by. However, there was a radical change of tack in 1824 with the appointment of James Loch as superintendent of the estate. It is difficult to convey the influence Loch had at the height of his career: he was the most prominent barrister-auditor of his day, 'the king of auditors', educated in the rationalist milieu surrounding Edinburgh University and influenced by Adam Smith, he was engaged by many other great landowning families to supervise canals, railways, and mines as well as farms up and down the country.[23] He became most widely known for ruthlessly carrying through the sustained programme of Highland clearances for the Sutherland family from 1812.[24] His own account of improvements on the estates was published in 1820, and as well as including a treatise on drainage, it set out two tenets that underpinned his practical policies: the wisdom and necessity of improvements, and the pursuit of improvement was a duty as much as a business.[25] Loch's appointment saw a radical reorganisation of the Castle Howard estate administration, including the installation of John Henderson in 1826, one of Loch's employees, in the estate office as steward to oversee the changes on the ground,

Figure 10. Graph showing the changing flock composition at Castle Howard 1826-1835.

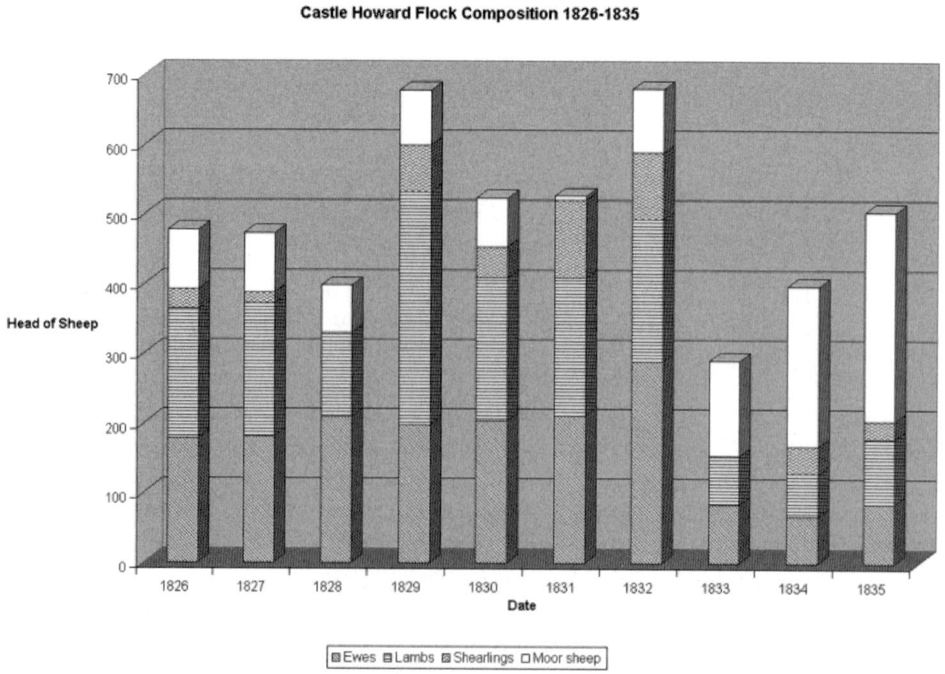

and the sub-heading 'Permanent Improvements' introduced into the estate accounts for the first time in 1828.[26] Investment was also evident in the continued programme of large-scale tree planting on the estate, with oaks and 'American Forest Trees' (probably spruce and fir) bought in their thousands to supplement and replace the existing mature stands and plantations.

In 1829 expenditure on the demesne saw a threefold increase compared to three years earlier. The expenditure was targeted on two main areas of capital investment: renovating selected farms and on drainage and irrigation. Nearly £300 of the £407 8s 7d spent on permanent improvements in 1828 was spent on drainage and irrigation, including a hefty £260 to Anthony Sutton who superintended the construction of new water meadows and carried out general irrigation work.[27] Sutton is listed as working on irrigating meadows at Terrington, Fryton, Slingsby, Hovingham Moor, and Wath, whilst water meadows are explicitly mentioned at Gaterley Farm (Henderskelfe), Charles Tate's farm in Mowthorpe, and at Stittenham Beck, where a sluice was constructed for the Bulmer water meadow. 'Draining stones' were bought to create free draining channels in underdraining irrigation systems, with more expensive draining tiles and pipes for the water meadows.[28] The net result of these improvements upon the landscape cannot have been hard to appreciate: hay production, for example, went from 80 tonnes in 1826 to 470 tonnes five years later, whilst the estate encouraged tenants to put land down to permanent pasture by offering to pay for the grass seed.

Figure 11. Graph showing the changing herd composition at Castle Howard 1826-1835.

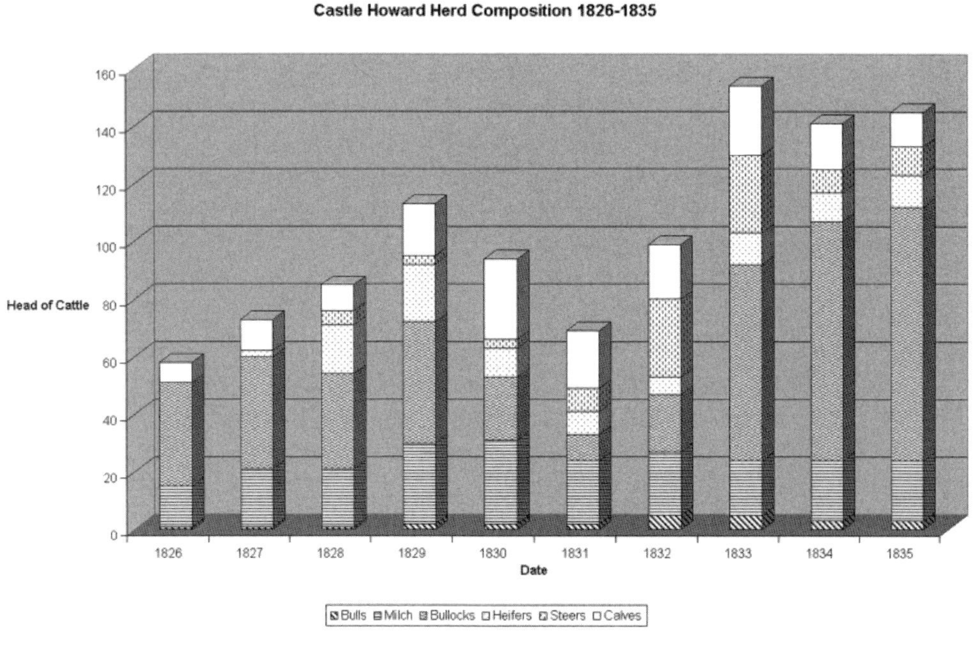

The importance of drainage within the portfolio of 19th century estate management is well documented, but the longer-term viability of the expensively constructed water meadows has recently been questioned.[29] The advantages they offered to tenants charged with maintaining them do not seem to have been universally recognised. In the winter of 1833, Henderson was already writing sternly to a tenant, Mr Thomas Freer of Ganthorpe: 'I am sorry to have again to notice the state of your water meadow. It is Lord Carlisle's determination to have the irrigation persevered in – it is only therefore left for you to say whether you will or will not comply with his wishes'.[30] The changes in the agricultural regime that the drainage and water meadows were designed to support, however, do seem to have been achieved.

Analysis of the relevant stock accounts for the period reveals that the sheep flock, which had been growing through the late 18th century, was radically cut back in 1833 (Fig. 10). As numbers started to rise again it becomes apparent that the composition of the flock had changed with a strong and increasing bias towards 'moor sheep' – the hardy sheep common in West Yorkshire that thrived on meagre soil – rather than ewes and lambs. The same analysis of the cattle herd reveals a similar transformation, also from 1833 (Fig. 11).[31] It might be expected from reading contemporary authors such as William Marshall, that the improvement would have been to create a profitable dairy herd, but the figures demonstrate that the expansion was among the head of bullocks in the herd, suggesting beef production, whereas the dairy herd remained stable in numbers during the early 19th century. The change in agricultural regime during 1833 is further illustrated by advertisements in the

Figure 12. Graph showing expenditure on cottage building within the Castle Howard estate 1868-1879.

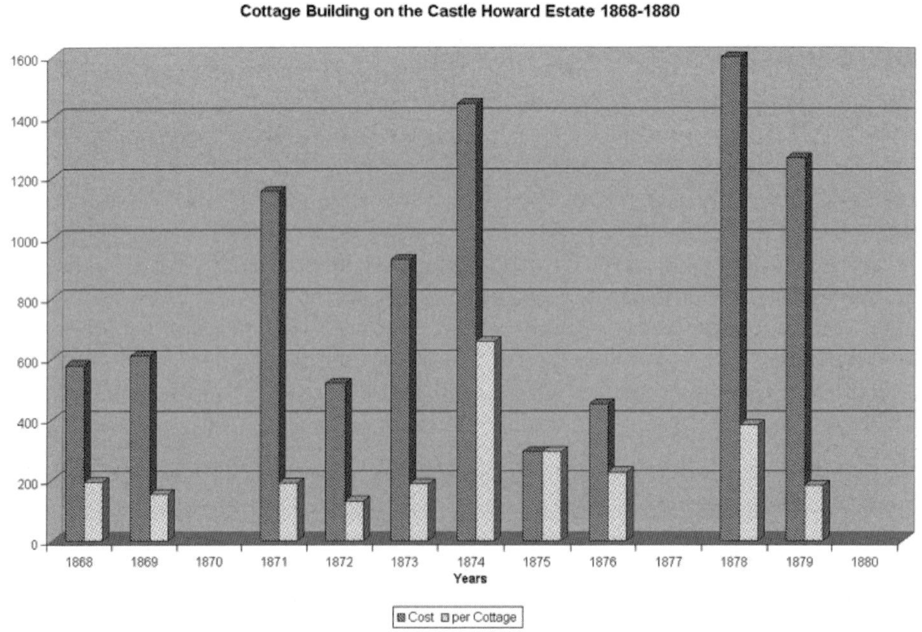

York newspapers for an auction at Castle Howard Inn on Tuesday 3rd December 1833, which saw the sale of the old stock with 70-80 'Fat Bullocks' and between 50-60 'fat Scotch Wethers' going under the hammer.[32]

By the 1840s and 50s it is apparent that Henderson, and Loch until his death in 1855, had made considerable headway. The sixth Earl reported to Loch that the sub-soil plough had only been partially successful due to deep clay underlying some fields; a new threshing machine from Beverley implement-maker Mr Crosskill broke down; the 'highly ingenious' Bell's oat harvester also purchased from Crosskill worked 'prettily', 'but it is entirely baffled whenever the corn is laid, and is besides at all times an immense effort for the horses so we consider it impractical'.[33] Lord Morpeth experimented with fertilizer made from sulphuric acid and salt.[34] By May 1858, Henderson could boast that the estate was second-to-none in its agricultural practice, especially in the quality of its stock, and employed new implements such as double-mould ploughs and drills for the cultivation of turnips.[35] All of these changes must have had an impact on the farm buildings as much as the landscape itself. Park Farm, built on the site of the former hunting lodge within the old deer park, was subject to considerable expenditure in the late 1820s. Money was also spent on the farm at Gaterley to the east, which acted as the demesne farm in the 18th century, but there was no great 'show piece', no model farm similar to those found on many aristocratic estates at the beginning of the 19th century.[36]

Apart from the absence of a model farm, the reorganisation of the Castle Howard estate fits neatly into established narratives about the 'Whig Improvements' reaping the reward of investments made during the last quarter of the 18th century.[37] However, the agricultural regime was instigated at a particular and critical moment for the Castle Howard estate as Frederick, the fifth Earl of Carlisle, had run up enormous debts and the estate was in considerable financial difficulties as a result. Loch had run the Sutherland estates for George Howard's friend, the marquess of Stafford, and his arrival just a year before the fifth Earl died suggests that measures were already in hand to turn the family finances around. The late 1820s were consequently marked by a tight economic regime designed to pay off the late Earl's debts. Income was closely examined with rents raised whenever possible, and every department of the household and estate had to justify its expenditure. Loch wrote to Henderson 'the question I have to decide is whether the present establishment can be kept up at all – and every possible shilling must be saved. So you must neither think of a new water closet nor new gilding'.[38] Loch queried everything down to the number of workmen in the house and the supply of tea to the servants: 'a great abuse – I never heard of footmen getting tea, nor housemaids, laundry maids or kitchen maids – the still room maids I am more doubtful about and will enquire into'.[39] The financial pressure had material manifestations in the labour-intensive kitchen gardens just as it did elsewhere on the estate:

'Lord Carlisle has agreed that all that part of the Garden which is orchard shall be laid down to grass… every reduction must be made that can be, let me know how much more the Garden ground may be reduced and still provide vegetables for the family. Report also what possible reduction can be made in the Stables, Game and Park Establishments…This must be done with the most vigorous hand possible'[40]

Only when the inherited financial burdens had been eased could substantial investment in the estate landscape be contemplated. Investment in buildings, and on cottages in particular, had to wait until the second half of the 19th century. Nationally, the main burst of investment in cottage provision on estates appears to have taken place in the third quarter of the century, with the decade 1865-75 being the busiest period.[41] Activity on the Castle Howard estate began rather earlier in the 1850s, however, after the seventh Earl of Carlisle took a personal interest in the estate buildings. In the winter of 1854/55, Carlisle toured the main estate villages including Terrington and Slingsby, demanding of Henderson why Widow Goodwill wasn't a member of the Coal club, reporting which roofs were in disrepair, and whether a young local lad who married a girl brought down from the Howard's Naworth estate in Cumberland, might be found a job as a mason. Henderson appears to have been both overwhelmed and relieved in his patron's new-found interest:

'Sometime in 1845…Lord Carlisle began to take a greater interest in the management of the estate and in the social condition of the resident population than he had previously done'[42]

It marked the beginning of a concerted campaign of estate improvement that included demolishing sub-standard cottages to make room for more commodious dwellings. The accounts show that expenditure continued to rise throughout the late 19th century despite rising costs, peaking in 1878 (Fig. 12). Over the 1870s as a whole some £9,500 was spent on 53 cottages, lodges, a reading room and a school-house in the six core villages.[43] In 1874, £316 was spent on cottages in Coneysthorpe and Terrington, with a further £528 spent on Ryehills farmhouse.[44] By 1883 there was a detailed inventory of the estate cottages right across the estate listing rent, tenant, number of bedrooms, occupation and remarks about the condition of the property. An undated, but probably slightly earlier, survey records that there were 315 estate cottages in the seven core townships, accommodating 1,267 inmates. Fifty-seven percent (177) were deemed to be in good repair, 15% (47) were only 'fair', whilst 29% (90) were in bad repair or were damp. Furthermore, whilst the vast majority were tiled (69%), a fifth (63) were still thatched.[45] Alongside what might be considered the essential repairs and rebuilding, Carlisle had an eye for the aesthetics of estate settlements, writing to Henderson in 1855 that he had, 'been over Slingsby, which I think on the whole presents a more gratifying appearance than any of the other villages', whilst in Terrington Carlisle proposed creating a well or 'humble fountain' instead of the 'unwholesome small round pond'.[46]

On the eve of the agricultural depression in the 1870s investment in the capital improvement of the estate and in its landscape appears to have been at an historic high. After the troubles of the 1820s, and having averted a catastrophic decline, the estate seems to have been less exposed to either personal mismanagement or national economic fluctuations. The gardens had missed the substantial remodelling so often imposed on large formal layouts in the late 18th century, and the early 19th century saw minor rather than wholesale change. Only in the 1850s did Nesfield remodel the south parterre, only for it to be simplified again, to save money, in the 1890s.[47] Expenditure of the gardens as a whole in the 1870s did not rise much beyond the restrained levels of the late 1820s, and was overshadowed by spending on the mansion itself, where the sumptuous High Victorian chapel was being created in the west wing.[48] However, the hundreds of pounds being spent on cottages and farmhouses in the mid-1870s were themselves put into perspective by the £2007 spent on the new 'conservatory' for the rejuvenated kitchen garden in 1874.[49]

The aim of this short paper has been to demonstrate that the interpretation of the wider, productive, estate landscape and the designed, ornamental landscape need to be integrated. By studying a single landscape over a time period that extends beyond its initial design phase, but which also recognises the importance of antecedent landscape features within it, we gain a much deeper understanding of the decisions being made, and the factors influencing future development. The increasing impact of global politics, be it in the fluctuating grain prices of the Napoleonic era when Europe was engulfed by war, or the influx of American tree species after the War of Independence, is manifest in the changing shades of the Yorkshire landscape. As archaeologists we cannot afford to treat aspects of the landscape in isolation, particularly when there is ample evidence from the period that patrons and visitors were unlikely to make such distinctions. The ornamental and productive landscapes maintained a dialogue with each other and both had to respond to the same economic, social, familial and political contexts. They were also conceived together within the over-arching ethos or ideology of the responsibilities attendant on landownership, and therefore embedded within the contemporary attitudes to democracy, justice and social welfare, as well as business and profit. By studying both, we not only come closer to the perceptions of the patrons, visitors, and estate workers who experienced the landscape in the past, we also stand to reach more complex and nuanced understandings of the landscape in both the past and the present.

ACKNOWLEDGEMENTS

I would like to thank David Gent for his comments on a draft version of this paper, particularly for his insights into the Howard family and references from the 1840s. I would also like to thank Dr Christopher Ridgway, the curator at Castle Howard, and Alison Brisby for their help and advice.

NOTES

1. Bateman 1883; CH/F5/98.
2. For the building see: Beard 1986; Downes 1966, 1969, 1977; Lees Milne 1970; Saumarez Smith 1997; Worsley 1995. For the gardens see: Eyres et al 1989; Hunt 1986; Hussey 1967.
3. Switzer 1742, 154.
4. Saumarez Smith 1997, 66.
5. The other possible candidate is Arthur Capel who created the woodland garden at Cassiobury (Herts) see Lancaster forthcoming Phd; Switzer 1742, 198; Hussey 1967, 119 and 125; Saumarez Smith 1997, 33-35
6. Saumarez Smith 1997, 130-32.
7. The wings were added to either side of the arch in 1756 to provide an inn for visitors.
8. Tatlioglu 2005.
9. Now called the Temple of the Four Winds.
10. The area was known as the Carrmire Gate before the architectural 'gate' was erected, as it refers to a gate within the open field system. Thus the Bulmer enclosure records state that 'Every oxgang has two Beast Gates in Oxpasture and one Carrmire Gate. The Gates belonging to the Common Balks are stocked by Thos Coverdale' CH/D2.
11. Walpole 1772, 72-3.
12. The choice of site for the house is also *contra* Switzer who advises against exposed sites; Switzer 1742, 12.
13. Atkyns made the comparison in 1732 and it has been repeated subsequently by garden historians.

14. CH/P1/2; Saumarez Smith 1997, 8.
15. CH/F4/14/3; Atkyns 1732, 23.
16. Daniels 1988; Williamson 2000, 17.
17. CH/F4/14/3.
18. Atkyns 1732, 25-26.
19. Williamson 2000, 16.
20. See Williamson 2000, 19.
21. Young 1771, 2: 47.
22. CH/D2; English 1985.
23. Spring 1963, 88-96.
24. Richards 1973; DNB.
25. Loch 1820; Spring 1963, 91.
26. CH/F6/2, March 14th 1827.
27. CH/F5/5/3.
28. E.g. CH/F5/5/4.
29. Phillips 1989; Spring 1963, 115-20; Wade Martins 2004; Williamson 2002; Cook and Williamson 2007.
30. CH/F5/2/2 Feb 26 1833.
31. CH/F5/48.
32. CH/F5/2/2.
33. CH/F6/3, November 12th 1841; F5/2/3; CH/J19/8/31 September 8th 1854.
34. CH/J19/8/1, October 15th 1843 and December 27th 1843.
35. CH/F5/3, May 5th 1858.
36. Wade Martins 2002.
37. Wade Martins 2004; Williamson 2002.
38. CH/F6/2 May 11th 1827; February 7th 1827. Mrs Flinn the housekeeper was dismissed as a result although the fact that she was 'personally disagreeable to her Ladyship' seems to have been the underlying issue, CH/F6/2 March 19th 1827.
39. CH/F6/2 April 4th 1827.
40. CH/F6/2 May 3rd 1827.
41. Clemenson 1982, 86-91
42. CH/F5/98 February 27th 1854.
43. CH/F5/81.
44. CH/F5/12/15.
45. CH/F5/83/1 and /2.
46. CH/F5/98.
47. Ridgway 1996a.
48. Pevsner 1966, 114.
49. CH/F5/12/15.

BIBLIOGRAPHY

Bateman, J. 1883 [1971], *The Great Landowners of Great Britain and Ireland*, 4th ed., Leicester: Leicester University Press.
Beard, G. 1986, *The Work of John Vanbrugh*, London: Batsford
Clemenson, H. 1982, *English Country Houses and Landed Estates*, London: Croom Helm
Cook, H. & Williamson, T. (eds) 2007, *Water Meadows. History, Ecology and Conservation*, Windgather Press: Macclesfield.
Cosgrove, D. & Daniels, S. (eds) *The Iconography of Landscape*, Cambridge: Cambridge University Press.
Daniels, S. 1988, 'The Political Iconography of Woodland in later Georgian England' in Cosgrove and Daniels 1988, 43-82.
Dictionary of National Biography.
Downes, K. 1966, *English Baroque Architecture*, London: A. Zwemmer.
Downes, K. 1969 *Hawksmoor*, Cambridge Mass.: MIT Press.
Downes, K. 1977 *Vanbrugh*, London: A. Zwemmer.
English, B. 1985, *Yorkshire Enclosure Records*, Hull: University of Hull.
Eyres, P. et. al 1989, *Castle Howard: Landscape of Epic Poetry*, Leeds: New Arcadian Press.
Hunt, J. D. 1986, *Garden and Grove. The Italian Renaissance Garden in the English Imagination, 1600-1750*, London: J. M. Dent & Sons.
Hussey, C. 1967, *English Gardens and Landscapes 1700-1750*, London: Country Life.
Lees-Milne, J. 1970, *English Country Houses. Baroque, 1685-1715*, London: Country Life.
Loch, J. 1820, *An Account of the Improvements on the Estates of the Marquess of Stafford*, London: Longman, Hurst, Rees, Orme and Brown.
Pevsner, N. 1966, *Yorkshire the North Riding*, The Buildings of England Series, Harmondsworth: Penguin.
Phillips, A. D. M. 1989, *The Underdraining of Farmland in England during the Nineteenth Century*, Cambridge: Cambridge University Press.
Richards, E. 1973, *The Leviathan of Wealth: the Sutherland fortune in the Industrial Revolution*, London; Routledge.

Ridgway, C. 1996a *'Design and Restoration at Castle Howard'* in Ridgeway 1996b, 39-52.
Ridgway, C. 1996b *William Andrews Nesfield (1794-1881), Victorian Landscape Architect*, York: IAAS.
Ridgway, C. & Williams, R. 2000, (eds) *Sir John Vanbrugh and Landscape Architecture in Baroque England 1690-1730*, Stroud: Sutton Publishing.
Saumarez Smith, C. 1997, *The Building of Castle Howard*, London: Pimlico.
Spring, D. 1963, *The English Landed Estate in the Nineteenth Century: its administration*, Maryland: John Hopkins Press.
Switzer, S. 1742, *Ichnographia Rustica: or, the nobleman, gentleman, and gardener's recreation*, 3 vols, 2nd edition, London.
Wade Martins, S. 2004, *Farmers, Landlords and Landscapes. Rural Britain, 1720-1870*, Macclesfield: Windgather Press.
Walpole, H. 1772 [1928], 'Journals of Visits to Country Seats', ed. Paget Toynbee, *Walpole Society*, 16, 72-3.
Williamson, T. 2000, 'Estate Management and Landscape Design' in Ridgway & Williams 2000, 12-30.
Williamson, T. 2002, *The Transformation of Rural England. Farming and the Landscape 1700-1870*, Exeter: University of Exeter Press.
Worsley, G. 1995 *Classical Architecture in Britain, the Heroic Age*, New Haven: Yale University Press.
Young, A. 1771 [1967] *A Six Months Tour through the North of England*, 4 vols New York: Augustus M. Kelly.

UNPUBLISHED SOURCES

Atkyns, J. A. 1732, 'Iter Borealis or the Northern Expedition', Yale Center for British Art, MS Atkyns 1, fols. 15-26.
Lancaster, D. forthcoming, 'The Landscape and 'Interiorscape' of the Eighteenth-Century Country House' unpublished PhD research, University of York.
Tatlioglu, T. 2005, 'Garden Party or Siege?: the role of martial architecture in the designed landscapes of the late-seventeenth and eighteenth centuries' unpublished MA dissertation, University of York.
CH/D2/1-12 Parish of Bulmer, Papers relating to inclosure proceedings 1775-1777
CH/F4/14/3 Surveys and Valuations, Survey of Yorkhire Estate 1562.
CH/F5/2/2 John Henderson's Letter Book 1830-1834
CH/F5/2/3 John Henderson's Letter Book 1835-1839
CH/F5/3 James Loch's correspondence with members of the Howard family
CH/F5/5/3 Annual Accounts, Castle Howard 1828.
CH/F5/5/4 Annual Accounts, Castle Howard 1829.
CH/F5/12/15 Estate Improvements Account 1874.
CH/F5/48 Valuation of Demesne Farm Stock 1828-1831
CH/F5/81 Expenditure on new cottages since 1868
CH/F5/83/1 Survey of cottages on Castle Howard Estate, nd.
CH/F5/83/2 Survey of cottages: an examination of cottages in each village 1883.
CH/F5/98 An analytical account of the population on the Castle Howard estate 1845.
CH/F6/2 James Loch's correspondence to stewards and others 1823-1838
CH/F6/3 James Loch's correspondence with 6th Earl of Carlisle and other members of the family, during the 1823-1850s.
CH/J19/8/31 Diary of the 7th Earl of Carlisle.
CH/P1/2 Map of Henderskelfe 1694
CH/P1/4 Map of Castle Howard 1727

ABBREVIATIONS
CH Castle Howard Estate Archives
DNB Dictionary of National Biography

Vaynor: A Landscape and its Buildings in the Severn Valley

By ROBERT SILVESTER and JUDITH ALFREY

The Vaynor estate, one of several gentry estates in the upper Severn Valley in east Wales, had its origins in the 14th century, but achieves tangible form only with increasing documentation in the mid 17th century. It is likely that there has been a house on the site of the present hall since the later Middle Ages, and an adjacent deer park, too. During the 18th century, successive owners, some of them absentee, continued to accumulate, and occasionally dispense with, estate holdings spread across nine parishes, but from the early 19th century there was a gradual consolidation within the estate which peaked in the 1870s. This consolidation in turn permitted modifications to the layout of both the park and the farmed estate. The building stock on the estate was of traditional form in the 18th century, but 19th-century restoration work introduced a new architectural character, to be seen both in the village of Berriew, adjacent to Vaynor Park, and in the outlying farms, and also a move towards agricultural improvement. Throughout the period from the mid-18th century, right up to the present, Vaynor has been a dynamic estate, surviving and thriving whilst some at least of its neighbours have failed.

Landed estates, or at least the mansions and parks that formed their centres, were not ubiquitous in post-medieval Wales. The seats of the gentry in the main lay within the main river valleys, although the estates might extend into the remote and sparsely occupied uplands.[1] Many Welsh estates had fluctuating histories, not least because of their uncertain passage from one generation to the next, particularly from the late 17th century onwards. In Geraint Jenkins' memorable phase, the gentry of many Welsh counties were 'stricken by the[ir] prevailing propensity to biological failure'.[2] As gentry families disappeared, so did many estates. It has been estimated that 40% of the estates in Montgomeryshire vanished between 1690 and 1760, and overall only 23 of the 132 estates (i.e. less than 20%) that were in existence at the end of the 17th century survived as dynamic entities with resident owners to 1810.[3]

In Wales, with the exception of a handful of notable examples, landed estate studies have advanced at a much slower pace than in England. This is not to claim that the topic has been totally neglected, rather that it has been the preserve of historians rather than archaeologists and landscape historians.[4] Now, however, for each Welsh county there are the descriptive texts in Cadw's recently completed Historic Parks and Gardens Register.[5] It provides a broad guide to the estates that still survive in some form, but analysis and an understanding of the wider estate context is largely absent from the Register.

It is against this far from static backdrop that we can examine one surviving estate, that of Vaynor (Fig. 1) in what historically was Montgomeryshire, but is now part of modern Powys. The wide upper Severn Valley signals the divide between the rolling eastern hills of this central portion of the Welsh borderland and the lower and generally more fertile lands of the Shropshire plain. Not surprisingly, to the south of Welshpool, landed estates mark its course, frequently established on the western flanks of the valley, but revealing very varied histories. Vaynor lies in Berriew and in the same parish were two further estates, Glansevern and Garthmyl. The former emerged only just before 1800, as the home of the lawyer, Arthur Davies Owen, and the centre of an estate that extended ultimately to nearly 4500 acres; when it was sold by the last of the Owen family in 1950 it consisted of little more than 120 acres.[6] Garthmyl originated in the later 17th century if not before, but the estate extending to nearly 8000 acres was broken up in 1857.[7] To these can be added Gregynog in the hills to the west of the Severn Valley, a case where the demise of the Blayney family in the late 18th century was not paralleled by a decline in the estate. The estate on the death of Arthur Blayney in 1795 covered 7,727 acres, but by 1888 it had been enlarged to 18,000 acres.[8] After this it went into decline, and when Gregynog was bequeathed to the University of Wales in 1963 it came with no more than 750 acres. Further north was Trefnant which went under in the early 19th century because of the landowning family's heavy debts[9], and the greatest of the Severn Valley estates, Powis Castle, the vast holdings of which stretched across Montgomeryshire and western Shropshire and into other counties as well. On the

Figure 1. The wooded landscape of Vaynor. The main house surrounded by its parkland lies in the distance, with the home farm including the walled garden in the foreground. Copyright: Clywd-Pwys Archaeological Trust.

opposite side of the valley was Leighton Hall which appears to have had its origins in the 16th century but came to prominence only in the 19th century when it was acquired by the Liverpool industrialist, John Naylor (Fig. 2).[10]

Whilst many of the estates in the middle Severn Valley have gone through a cycle of expansion and contraction, Vaynor's continued development reflects a different history. From the 16th century it passed from family to family, not by purchase, but through inheritance, albeit not in a direct family line. Eight different families involving eighteen different owners have been at Vaynor since the 1570s. But almost inevitably we know more about the families at Vaynor over the last five centuries than we do about the place itself. 19th-century antiquaries delighted in pedigrees, less so the physical entities of the estates themselves, and it is symptomatic of the general approach to landed estates that, when in 1977 an article was published in the county journal, ostensibly on the subject of Vaynor, the author devoted the entire article to a discussion of the families who had occupied it. All commentary on Vaynor itself, as park and estate, was confined to footnotes.[11]

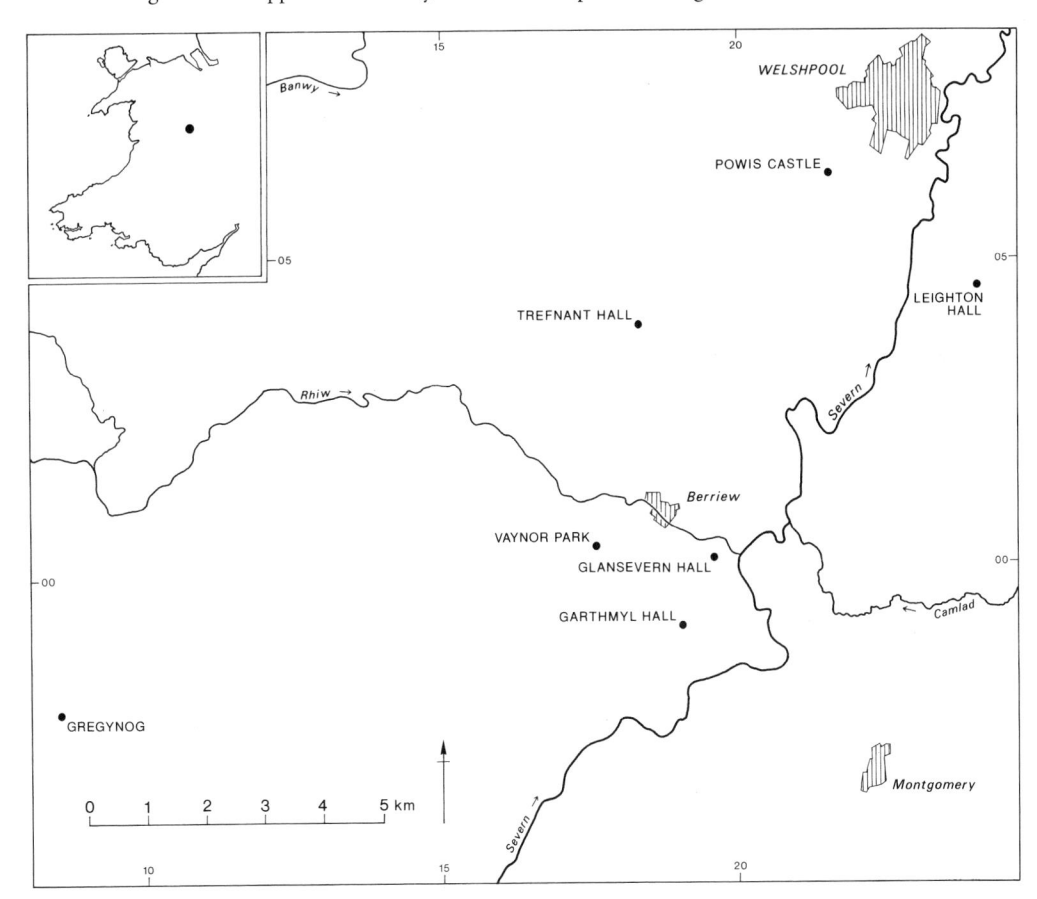

Figure 2. The upper Severn Valley, south of Welshpool, showing the main landed estates

Vaynor as a demesne centre has been in existence since at least the 14th century and if, as is generally assumed, the present hall is on the same site as its predecessors, the ridge end that it occupied would have provided a degree of protection in the unsettled periods of the Middle Ages. As the centre of an estate Vaynor first takes on tangible form in late Tudor times, and sporadic records survive for the next two hundred years. But it was only when Robert Moxon and Thomas Staunton acquired control of the estate after 1755 that the records become fuller and include a full estate survey commissioned in 1764.[12]

THE HOUSE AND PARK

It is not easy to appreciate the setting of Vaynor. The hills on the west side of the Severn tend to run off the main valley in a series of long ridges. The house occupies the end of one such ridge at what is almost the highest point in the park and from this knoll the ground falls away in all directions except to the west - the location, as already noted, is almost a defensible one. Though Vaynor lies on the western edge of the Severn Valley, the house effectively turns its back on these lowlands, and from this direction its privacy is maintained by woodland. Only rarely, for instance, is there a glimpse of it from the lane to the south. Landscaping would never have been necessary at Vaynor, such are the natural folds and ridges of its grounds. And the estate maps that survive reveal that its landscape has always been heavily wooded.

When first depicted on a map of 1746[13] Vaynor comprised a hall with ancillary buildings, a semi-formal garden and what had once been a hop yard but by then had become an orchard, to the south-east of the house. A generally rectangular park of just under 180 acres spread across the undulating ridges running to the north of the house. There are hints of parkland design on this map, in particular several avenues of trees, although none of them is focused on the house itself, and indeed there may be a degree of cartographic licence here, for on the later estate survey map of 1764 no convincing trace of such avenues can be discerned.

That there was a park at Vaynor long before the preparation of that first estate map in the mid-18th century is certain. A continuous park pale was shown on John Probert's map of 1764 and this conforms exactly with the park as drawn eighteen years earlier. However, a substantial boundary bank remains in place at the east end of the park and can also be traced intermittently on its north side. Broadly, this follows the same line as the pale, except towards the southern end of the eastern perimeter where there are equivocal indications that it adopted a divergent line before fading out in the wood pasture of the later park. This appears to be the physical remnant of a medieval deer park at Vaynor. Clearly associated with the park was the keeper's lodge. Shown on the 18th-century maps as a standing structure accompanied by a small fenced enclosure, but now only visible as a platform, this was the only building in the park other than Vaynor Hall itself. A single small lake lay to the south.

Robert Moxon was generally content to utilise and perhaps exploit his unexpected inheritance from a distance, his home being at Woodford in Essex.[14] Although he occasionally became involved in small-scale land exchanges that rationalised the open fields of Berriew, it is unlikely that Vaynor changed much during his ownership. The demesne that included the park was let to a local farmer, and a diarist in 1793 noted the 'old deserted park with a staring red ugly house upon a hill wherein a tenant resides. The park has abounded with fine timber, of which yet, much remains; but all is in wild disorder'.[15] The tenant in question was the Reverend Edward Owen, who leased the main house, a summer house, the stables and garden and the bowling green which lay to the south of the house. He seems also to have been a relative of Arthur Davies Owen who was establishing the neighbouring mansion and estate of Glansevern.

Only when the Winders inherited Vaynor at the beginning of the 19th century was there identifiable change. The deer park was still in existence in 1814[16], but by then was already undergoing a re-design. Part of its western pale had been uprooted to enlarge the parkland area. On the south, too, further fields were integrated into the park, and a number of these extensions reveal relict cultivation ridges, a rarity in the medieval park. The whole of the pale had been swept away by the mid-19th century. Previously the approach to Vaynor Hall had been through fields from the south, but now a new road swept through the park, a lodge at its junction with the public road out of Berriew, and the drive itself following a sinuous course that emphasised the exceptional setting of the hall. No longer did Vaynor sit on the perimeter of its park: it was now encompassed by a buffer zone of woodland and pasture between it and the surrounding farmed lands in a broader yet in a sense more ill-defined and expansive setting. Further pools were created in the park, and by the mid-19th century well-defined clumps of trees lay to the north and east of the house, but by the end of the 19th century many of these had been integrated into a more general spread of deciduous woodland.[17] Thus during the course of the century the deer park gave way to the landscape park, but the changes were not fundamental. As with many other Welsh parks the natural landscape was such that extensive landscape design was not necessary.[18]

THE ESTATE

In 1764, the earliest date at which the extent of the Vaynor estate can be gauged, it extended to 5030 acres.[19] It was dispersed across nine parishes, although unlike the vast Powis Castle to the north, it was at least restricted to the county of Montgomeryshire. The full details of how this geographically disparate estate was put together remain a mystery. Some of the outlying lands such as those in Llanwnog, nearly 20km higher up the Severn Valley had been in the estate since at least the 16th century and probably long before[20], while a marriage settlement of 1633 reveals land on the far side of the Severn in Churchstoke, and even impinging slightly into Shropshire at Castlewright and Aston.[21] Successive members of the Devereux family, one of whom became Viscount Hereford in 1700, accumulated holdings on a piecemeal and indiscriminate basis: the small holding known as Black Pullets in Castlewright was purchased in 1698 and the Court House holding in Churchstoke was acquired in 1705; Blackwood in Berriew was purchased in 1709 and other lands in Berriew townships were added in the second decade of the 18th century. While these acquisitions may imply a degree of deliberate engrossment in selected areas, other purchases reveal a more opportunistic approach as with the lands around Llwynybrain in Llanwyddelan obtained from a debt-ridden squire soon after 1706,[22] and the distant Forest of Trefeglwys, 25km from Vaynor about the same time.

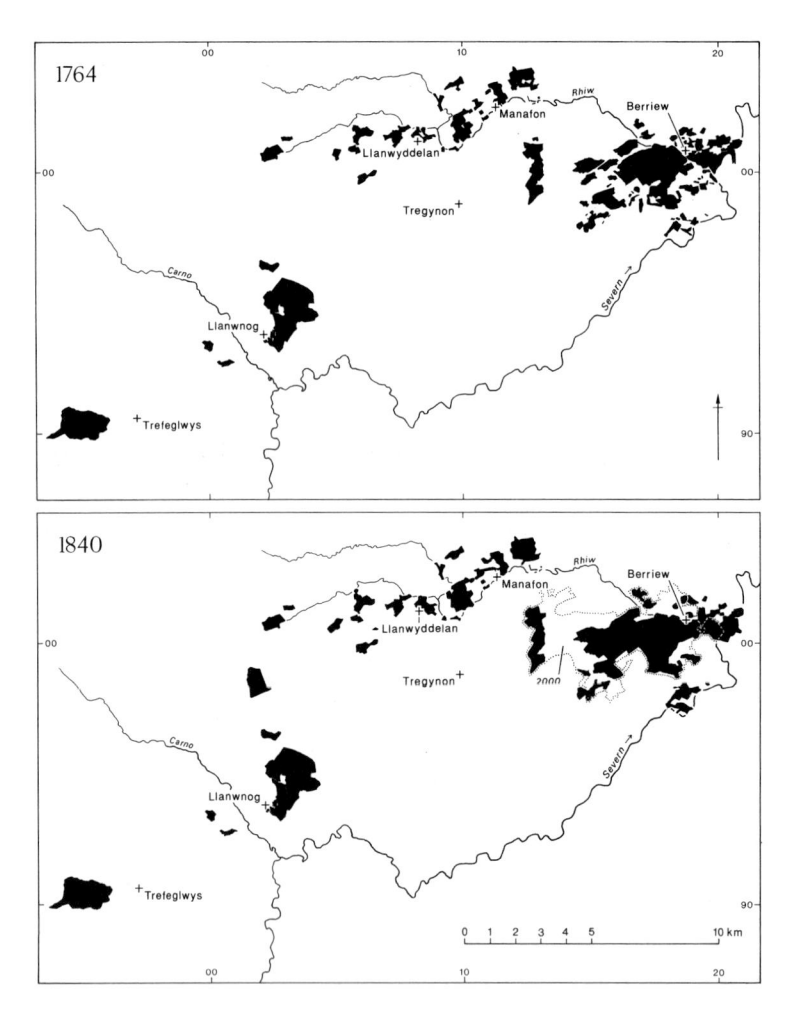

LEFT
Figure 3. The enlargement and consolidation of the Vaynor Estate between 1764 and 1840. The modern boundary of the estate is depicted as a pecked line on the map of 1840.

Yet land was also sold. Robert Moxon realised the value of some of his newly acquired landed assets in 1773 when he dispensed with all his holdings on the east side of the Severn in Forden and Churchstoke, some 230 acres, to the Countess of Powis for £9,500.[23] Significantly perhaps, John Probert who had prepared the survey and valuation of the Vaynor Estate for Moxon in 1764 was now the land agent for the Countess of Powis and was instrumental in negotiating and perhaps instigating the purchase. Indeed, even a spirit of altruism may have developed. South of the River Rhiw, Vaynor owned rather scattered holdings but close enough to Vaynor to have formed an integral part of the consolidation. Yet at the end of the 18th century, Robert Moxon's heir, John Moxon, sold some of this land beside the river to Arthur Davies Owen, enabling him to create his own park and gardens at Glansevern.[24]

Vaynor in the later 18th century oversaw a disparate estate. There was the Berriew demesne and groups of farms that were effectively satellites to it, there were sporadic strips in the open fields of Berriew beside the Severn, intermittent holdings around some of the villages further west such as Manafon, Llanwyddelan and Llanwnog, some isolated hill farms and the unenclosed Forest of Trefeglwys. Vaynor was not a medieval manorial holding, fragmented by the dispersal of lands, but the product of largely haphazard purchase and acquisition. It is not only the distribution pattern of the land that reveals this characteristic. One of the more prevalent attributes of long-established manorial holdings in eastern Wales was the control over local (and sometimes not so local) commons and waste. These open areas were frequent and lay not only in the uplands but also survived within the farmed lowlands, as Probert's maps reveal. By the later 18th century they were prized and exploitable commodities, as contemporary surveys indicate. Yet with the exception of the recently acquired Forest of Trefeglwys, Vaynor appears not to have controlled a single common, even though virtually every one of its tenants had rights on some nearby unenclosed grazing. The commons were in the possession of much longer established estates that held manorial lordships.[25]

Consolidation is a term encountered regularly in the secondary literature relating to gentry estates of this period, and from the early 19th century onwards successive owners of Vaynor focused at least some of their energies on enlarging the estate (Fig. 3). Initially, at least, the term consolidation may not be apposite: existing holdings across the whole estate were enlarged as opportunities arose, often by the addition of just one field. Sale and exchange were the main agents of change. Thus when the commons of Llanwyddelan and Dwyrhiw were enclosed in 1805-7, one relatively small piece in each was purchased.[26] But as the 19th century progressed, a more systematic approach to the estate can be observed, in marked contrast to what had occurred before. When the Clive estate was sold in 1828 some land in Berriew was bought by the heirs to Vaynor and likewise the dispersal at auction in 1857 of the Garthmyl Estate benefited neighbouring Vaynor. This estate extended to over 7900 acres, much of it distant in the hill parishes of western Montgomeryshire, but Lyon Winder purchased only 36 acres of it, all of it lying contiguous to Vaynor. Fourteen years later on a totally different scale, the outlying holdings in Manafon and Llanwyddelan were sold off en bloc, nearly 1200 acres, and the proceeds were used in 1873 to purchase Stingwern, closer to the core holding of Vaynor.[27]

On a much smaller scale, small plots of only a few acres were exchanged with neighbouring landowners, as agreements were reached to rationalise holdings, particularly in the open fields; in one instance the exchange was of no more than five perches to even out irregularities in adjacent fields.[28] In 1849 a farm in the adjacent parish of Manafon was exchanged for one in the home parish of Berriew, and interestingly it was not only the owner of Vaynor who was a signatory, but also his brother and sister, both of whom, in later years, were to inherit the estate.[29]

From all of this emerged a much more cohesive estate pruned back to three parishes, centred around Vaynor itself and extending by the later 19th century to approximately 5157 acres, little different in size from the 5030 acres mapped by Probert more than a century earlier. Vaynor in 1873 was ranked just outside the largest one hundred estates in Wales at the time of the New Domesday Book.[30]

Thus during the last quarter of the 18th century and more so throughout the 19th century, the Vaynor Estate changed at what can be termed the macro-level. It changed, too, at the micro-level. Elements of its landscape underwent gradual transformation. Such changes had in a sense been presaged in 1764 by Probert who was not only a surveyor but also that somewhat rarer breed, a valuer. His survey notes where farms could profitably be amalgamated or 'layed down', but to what extent Robert Moxon took this advice cannot be known; we do not even know whether in the late 18th century there was a land agent at Vaynor.

Improvements to the efficiency and agricultural productivity of an estate may well manifest themselves in accounts and rentals[31], yet the minor physical alterations to the pattern of the landscape rarely merit mention in the archives. Exceptional, solely because it needed the approval of local justices of the peace, was the re-routing of the highway from Berriew westwards to Bettws in 1791. The old lane beyond Vaynor Park was stopped up for two miles and a new road further south was agreed and documented at the Quarter Sessions,[32] a better road no doubt but one that also enhanced the privacy and control of the Vaynor owners over their estate. Nor can the importance of timber to the estate be understated[33], and in one instance in the mid-19th century Vaynor land was exchanged for the timber provided by a mature oak tree standing in a field near Berriew.[34] Generally, however, modifications went unremarked, yet it is evident that changes did occur throughout the 19th century, in some holdings on a considerable scale. While the Moxons as absentee owners may not have been too concerned about improvements to the estate, it is clear that in the half century that followed Probert's survey, some holdings had their field systems modified. In particular the network of small and irregular fields around the farm at Lower Park immediately to the west of Vaynor Park was redesigned. Fundamental alterations such as this were rare, but in the second half of the 19th century, there were widespread changes to the lands around Vaynor. Sinuous field boundaries were replaced by straight ones, established to define more regularly sized enclosures; old lanes were abandoned and at least one new thoroughfare away from the park was established, several cottages were removed, new plantations were created, and the meadows beside the river Rhiw, formerly large open tracts which probably functioned in common, were divided and enclosed. Some of these changes may have followed directly on from the continuing consolidation of the estate around Berriew, yet there can be no doubt that it was the immediate environs of the Park that underwent deliberate and perhaps systematic alteration, considerably more fundamental than anything seen in any of the outlying holdings. And it was not only the modified agrarian landscape that reveals the guiding hand of successive generations at Vaynor but also the building stock.

BUILDINGS IN THE 19th-CENTURY LANDSCAPE

The 19th-century architectural landscape of the Severn valley was dominated by the large landed estates. The big players – Powys Castle, Leighton Hall and Gregynog – were major patrons of architecture with a high impact on the shape of the rural landscape, both literally and in the social and economic structures underlying it. On a smaller scale, the Vaynor estate also re-shaped its landscape, and in the process created a distinctive rural architecture of its own.

As noted above, Vaynor is an old estate with a long pedigree. The house, now rather obscured by the woodland of its park, is sited on an eminence, occupied since at least the late 15th century when a poem celebrated an earlier house 'built on top of a hill, above 3 districts.... Its smoke could be seen from Anglesey Chester and Glamorgan'.[35]

This long history is important: it helps to define the character of later change. The early house of oak and stone was rebuilt, probably c. 1640, in the newer materials of brick and slate. Although it was remodelled again in the later 17th century and early 18th century, it was essentially as a 17th-century house that it came, by indirect inheritance, into the hands of the Winder family at the end of the 18th century. In the mid 19th century, John Winder Lyon Winder employed the architect Thomas Penson to remodel and extend the house yet again. He did this in such a way as to 'intensify the 17th-century character of the house'.[36] This may stand as a theme for work undertaken elsewhere on the estate, where, in the spirit of the Picturesque, the decorative potential of historical styles was exploited to aesthetic effect, lending distinctive character to what was essentially a campaign of modernisation and improvement.

LEFT
Figure 4. Picturesque character in Berriew, showing the architectural signature of the estate. a) Blacksmith's shop Berriew (above) and b) cottages in Berriew (below)

If the mansion of Vaynor itself was old and in need of upgrading in the 19th century, so were many of its farms. The farms (of varying acreages, though with several which were quite large by Welsh standards) were mainly apparently long-established holdings, and in many cases, 17th- or 18th-century building dates may be assumed. Certainly, the detailed account in Probert's survey of 1764 describes a building stock which is resolutely traditional: timber with clay or plaster walls, boarding to farm-buildings, and thatched roofs. Whilst some were described as 'old', the survey makes it clear that others were more recent constructions. The fact that repairs specified in the survey were often also for re-thatching and the replacement of timbers etc. makes it clear that (notwithstanding the much earlier use of brick and slate for the mansion itself), locally sourced materials and traditional techniques remained in active use for lesser houses and their farm-buildings, until the latter part of the 18th century at least.

Traditional practices pertained not just in construction, but also in layout and planning: the 18th-century record portrays farmsteads set out in linear fashion, with significant farm-buildings in a single range with the house. This arrangement survives in some few instances but was abandoned in 19th-century work elsewhere, when semi-formalised yards or at least a clear separation of house from farm-buildings became much more common.

Much of the interest of Vaynor lies in the fact that it was not apparently undertaking extensive new building, but rather adapting what it had. It is fortunate that this process is well documented, from the detailed descriptions of the 18th-century building stock, to the high survival rate of the buildings themselves, reinforced, in some cases, by a series of plans and specifications for restoration work in the mid-19th century.[37] It is clear that even where the buildings themselves had traditional origins, 19th-century work introduced a wholly new architectural character to the estate.

DOMESTIC ARCHITECTURE

In the village of Berriew the mixture of old and new is clearly displayed. Here, there was some honest new building in the earlier 19th century, mainly in brick. Other buildings look superficially traditional, but were in fact extensively re-worked under the auspices of the estate. A good example is the old smithy, which is dated 1774, though it was re-ordered in the mid-19th century, acquiring the strong character of an estate cottage. The conspicuous black and white work - some of which is painted on brick - for which the village is celebrated almost certainly reflects a new, picturesque aesthetic: in 1830 the village was described with reference to the colour white.[38] More detailed hallmarks of change are the chimneys, the chamfered brickwork window surrounds, little timber hood moulds, gable-end windows and fretted bargeboards. These same features occur on other farms and cottages on the estate, and form part of its architectural signature (Fig. 4).

Documented alterations at several farmhouses in the mid-19th century permit a closer examination of the process of change.[39] Some seem to have been inherently practical, in line with contemporary ideals for the clearer separation of working and domestic space. At one farm - Cefn Dreboeth - the first floor was modified to create more bedrooms including a servants' room, and the ground floor was given a separate entrance hall (formerly a pantry), with a dairy added at the rear. Plans for Dollas (1858) show the creation of more working areas (the addition of pantry and cellar, provision of a larger dairy, and back-kitchen), a separate entrance and new parlour; clearer separation of living and working accommodation, including detaching the house from its farm buildings. On a much smaller scale, the farm-cottage of Mount Pleasant (not now extant) was also modified (in 1859) to create three bedrooms and a passage upstairs – drawings show how this was to be achieved by raising the height of the eaves. The farmhouse at Pandy may also have been re-organised: it was certainly extended, but the characteristic Vaynor axial brick chimney stack and the gable-end windows in the earlier house, may indicate a more radical re-ordering. These features display the stylistic hallmarks which have already been noted in the village of Berriew.

The same signature is clear at the small, isolated cottage called Pen-y-parc, for which plans of 1846 survive. The drawings show that the building started life as a lobby-entry cottage with a doorway against the single gable-end chimney, and a single dormer in the roof. In the alterations, the chimney was removed, and an axial stack inserted (presumably to provide heat for both the ground-floor rooms, but at the cost of a reduced floor area), and windows were added in the gable end. Two dormers replaced the single dormer, perhaps indicating that the upstairs space was subdivided for the first time, and a central door in a prettily finished porch was added. Pen-y-parc had been a large farm (81 acres) in 1840[40] - perhaps this re-modelling work was the first stage in its evolution from farmhouse to the cottage which it is now (Fig. 5).

These and other changes to the dwellings are all more-or-less radical. Some of the traditional elements recorded in 1764 have been lost: there is, for example, no thatch in the area now, though it was the ubiquitous roof material in the 18th century. In its place

LEFT
Figure 5. Pen-y-parc, Berriew. A small vernacular farmhouse transformed into a picturesque cottage.

came slate. And whereas in 1764, the houses were mostly described as being of timber, with plaster or clay walls, they are now all piebald, with black timbering, and white painted brick in-fill. The chimneys are also mostly 19th-century brickwork, and several were relocated in re-ordering work. They form the most striking feature of the estate's 19th-century aesthetic, with their tall clustered shafts rising from massive bases. At Pen-y-parc, the 1846 plans specify that this 'stack of chimnies' should be the same as at the stables at Vaynor', presumably a reference to the 17th-century work there. In its 19th-century incarnation, the form was also used on the gate lodge designed by Thomas Penson in 1843.[41]

Other notable changes in style included the introduction of improved lighting by inserting windows in gable ends; most joinery detail is also 19th-century, with windows to a standardised design, and decidedly decorative barge-boards – not a feature of traditional building. These repeated motifs are a reminder that as patrons of building, estates had the wherewithal to build in multiples, producing, presumably in their own workshops, stock components. Estates could also afford to pay for the import of building materials – here most obviously, the roofing slate. Perhaps this came via the Montgomery Canal, which had been constructed from the Ellesmere Canal near Llanymynech to Garthmyl between 1794-1797 and was subsequently extended to Newtown.[42] The bricks which were used in new cottage building, on some of the farms, and as in-fill and under-pinning for the timber framing may not have travelled quite so far (their source is not known), but as a manufactured material they represented significant expense.

There is a very strong picturesque aesthetic in these remodelled buildings, and a strong estate signature. They have been transformed from genuinely vernacular buildings, to picturesque cottages on an improving estate. Change on this scale suggests more than just concern for the appearance of things, however: it seems likely that this building work is evidence for structural change on the farms themselves – enlargement or contraction, perhaps; significant new investment, certainly.

CHANGE ON THE FARMS

Another major theme of 19th-century rural life was agricultural improvement. In many areas of Wales, most farm-buildings were built after c. 1800. Much of this work was sponsored by the landed estates, and the Severn Valley area was no exception. The Gregynog estate had been at the forefront of agricultural improvement in the late 18th century under the benign management of Arthur Blayney (and was to be so again in the 1870s during its ownership by the fourth Lord Sudeley).[43] The Leighton estate, developed by John Naylor from 1849, provided the most spectacular example in the region[44], but on a more self-effacing scale. Vaynor's farms also document this process of change. Here once again, is a mixture of new building, and re-working an existing building stock.

The earliest documented example of change on the estate is on a farm called Coed Tafol. Its farm-buildings were completely rebuilt in 1837-8.[45] The brick barn (comprising barn floor and two corn bays) with stable and granary, the single storey, brick and timber cattle shed with rear feeding passage or bin, and the calves cot grouped around the fold yard, have all survived. What they replaced were timber buildings with boarded walls and thatched roofs which had been described as 'good' in 1764. The new buildings lack the showy character of some estate farms, but their rational layout shows the application of contemporary good practice.

The emphasis on farm-yard layout is certainly an important characteristic of 19th-century agricultural improvement. As we have seen, a linear arrangement had characterised farm layout in the 18th century, but agricultural improvers set great store by the enclosed yard, which enabled dung to be efficiently collected. Vaynor applied these principles on several of its farms. Dollas, for example, was one of the larger farms on the estate (192 acres in 1840), and in 1764, adjoining the 'old and inconvenient house' were five bays of timber buildings including a barn, and two other ranges comprising stable, cattle shed and wain house.[46] Now, a barn with storeyed end bays, and the stable range at right-angles to it, are at first sight traditional in character (timber-framed on brick plinths), but appear to be of mid-19th-century date; the Tithe map records the earlier, conjoined, layout. They form two sides of an enclosed yard, to which a secondary cattle yard was added, its plans dated 1852. Again, the buildings themselves are not flamboyant – they are modest brick constructions - but they suggest greatly enhanced accommodation, and their meticulous planning, several versions of which are recorded in documents, shows a nice rationalism.

That the estate was interested in the issue of farm planning is also revealed in undated plans for a model farm. This appears never to have been built, but would have been an ambitious affair including a large octagonal enclosed yard. Perhaps this was derived from a pattern-book prototype.

Even where whole new yards were not provided, there was significant investment in new building. The little farmstead of Bronsquilfa, for example, was provided with a new range of farm-buildings in 1856, comprising a cowhouse for ten cows, a calf house and a lofted haystore. There was already a stable of two stalls and two pigsties, but they have not apparently survived. Bronsquilfa had been a 110-acre farm in 1840, but these modest buildings seem inconsistent with such a substantial acreage, perhaps indicating some reorganisation of holdings on the estate. In the new building work, there was no provision for a barn, suggesting that the farm may have been re-established as a specialist small-holding

The new brick buildings here have an unassuming architectural character, but some signature detailing such as the use of chamfered brick surrounds to the windows. This detail can also be seen at Pandy. This farm had been acquired by the estate some time between 1764 and 1840, and was the subject of considerable building work. Here new buildings were added to an existing barn in 1857, in a mixture of timber and brick construction. They comprised a cart-house, granary, turnip house, stable, and a secondary brick range, probably used for stock. The earlier barn at right-angles to the house is a timber-framed and weather-boarded building, but the brick which underpins it, and the slate roof, suggest major investment in the 19th century. Apparently traditional construction on other farms may also belie the extent of new building in the 19th century: in farm-buildings at least, new modes of building (using brick and slate) did not entirely supplant the active maintenance of traditional techniques in timber-framing and weather-boarding.

BUILDINGS AND SOCIETY

Buildings afford us a glimpse of the social landscape of the estate. At the apex was the mansion itself, but the farms themselves display a clear hierarchy, ranging from substantial gentry farms to tiny small-holdings. The cottages clustered in the village of Berriew introduce another dimension – here presumably, were the craftsmen and tradesmen integral to an agricultural community. Then, scattered across the estate, the landless agricultural labourers have left their trace, in cottages which lack the agricultural out-buildings of the farms and small-holdings. After farms, cottage-building was one of the great subjects of estate patronage in the 19th century, spurred perhaps by the criticism of agricultural commentators surveying the rural scene during the Napoleonic wars.[47] Pre-19th-century cottages are rare indeed. Across Wales, there was a marked shift in responsibility for providing homes for labourers, with landlords increasingly undertaking this work themselves. Two aspects of this stand out: on the one hand, a concern to ameliorate conditions by increased investment in building, and on the other, the establishment of a tighter control over the building process, and over rural settlement and land use more generally. Both of these may be seen at Vaynor.

At Cefn Garthmyl, there is a tiny cottage on a small plot of land which did not belong to the estate in 1840. The building bears the strong hallmark of the estate now, but its diminutive proportions suggest that it may have originated as a self-built 'squatter' cottage. Close by, a pair of much more substantial brick cottages were built on a virgin site in 1855, in a picturesque idiom. The difference in accommodation is quite marked, but the reconstruction of the small cottage shows the estate in a process of rationalising its holdings and assuming control over anomalous free-holdings caught up in its consolidated acreages. To the north of the estate, the Tithe survey recorded areas with the haphazard scatter of small plots and cottages typical of encroachment. These have all vanished, presumably in a similar process of rationalising land management. The landscape of the estate is still characterised by dispersed settlement, but what remains is something of an edited sequence, though there are still occasional ruins to suggest a once much more populated landscape.

CONCLUSIONS

How typical was Vaynor of the estates in the borderland of England and Wales through which the Severn passed? It was far from bring the largest, lying immediately outside the top ten Montgomeryshire estates when ranked in size in 1873. Its park did not have the attention of a Jones, a Repton or even an Emes, and was not festooned with parkland features, although limited works enhanced the setting of the hall in its parkland. It benefited little from the enclosure of the commons, unlike such neighbouring estates as Gregynog[48], nor was mineral wealth much in evidence.[49]

But what is clear is that Vaynor was a dynamic estate, and that despite absentee owners in the 18th century and the diarist's disdainful words in 1793, it was never static. Nor was the emphasis of successive owners solely on the immediate surroundings, the parkland, but it was the estate as a whole that developed. It was never a high-profile estate, yet it was propelled throughout the 19th century and into the 20th century, by its resident owners, whose care and good management, seemingly without the assistance of land agents, oversaw its consolidation whilst contemporary estates foundered. In the modification and sometimes rationalisation of its agrarian landscape and in the development of its own distinctive building tradition, Vaynor may well be typical, but this must remain an assumption until comparative studies of similar estates in the region are conducted. Certainly, however, it provides first-hand evidence for the management of the rural landscape.

The example of Vaynor, too, reveals the active intervention of an estate in the management of its building stock in the 19th century, showing the reach of the estate, and concomitantly, the degree to which the landscape of building was renewed. It reveals something of the economic organisation and, indeed reorganisation, of the land during the 19th century, and a glimpse of the social hierarchy that sustained it. Above all, though, the story of Vaynor is of interest for the light it sheds onto the development of rural architecture during the 19th century. Through repair and maintenance and even in some new work, traditional practices had survived at least into the late 18th century. The programme of work inaugurated in the mid-19th century introduced new materials – brick and slate – and using them, together with a new aesthetic vocabulary, re-shaped its vernacular inheritance to create a new image of rural building.

ACKNOWLEDGEMENTS

Without the help and co-operation of William Corbett-Winder, Esq, this study would not have been possible. He made accessible papers and drawings still held at Vaynor Hall, including the 1764 survey and allowed us unfettered access to the estate. Our thanks too, to the staff at the National Library of Wales in Aberystwyth who provided access to other Vaynor Papers now lodged there.

NOTES

1. See for instance Howell 1986, 3.
2. Jenkins 1987, 264.
3. Humphreys 1996, 99.
4. See for instance the various works by David Howell, particularly Howell 1977 & 1986 and in Hughes et al 1977.
5. Cadw 1999.
6. HMSO 1874; Cadw 1999, 83.
7. NLW/Vaynor Park/71.
8. Morgan 1977, 27; Howell 1977, 43.
9. Silvester 2001, 166.
10. Cadw 1999, 129.
11. Pinhorn 1977.
12. See Silvester 2001, 170. The full survey of 1764 by John Probert is at Vaynor Hall. Probert's notebooks for the survey are in the National Library of Wales archived as Powis Castle 16711 and Powis Castle 17256. An abstract of the 1764 valuation of the Vaynor lands is archived as Powis Castle 16966.
13. The Colledge map, prepared for Price Devereux, 10th Viscount Hereford, has been bound into the Vaynor survey of 1764.
14. Pinhorn 1977, 37.
15. Andrews 1936, iii, 239-97.
16. NLW/Vaynor Park/8.
17. Berriew Tithe Map (1st class) of 1840.
18. See, for example, Howell 1986, 180.
19. Vaynor Estate Survey of 1764. The lands in several parishes on the east side of the Severn cannot be mapped because of the removal of the relevant maps from the atlas when these lands were sold on in 1773.
20. NLW/Vaynor Park/595.
21. NLW/Vaynor Park/599.
22. Humphreys 1996, 112.
23. NLW/Vaynor Park/625.
24. The creation and growth of a completely new gentry estate at Glansevern in the years after 1800 raises interesting questions about how Arthur Davies Owen

was able to achieve this in a relatively short space of time. It is hoped to devote a future paper to the subject.

25. Compare with Howell 1986, 51 for the situation in south-western Wales.
26. NLW/Vaynor Park/721,
27. NLW/Vaynor Park/130; Vaynor Park/1028,
28. NLW/Vaynor Park/138,
29. NLW/Vaynor Park/713-16,
30. HMSO 1874.
31. See, for instance, Howell 1977, 46.
32. NLW/Vaynor Park/160-1.
33. From 1764, the woodlands on the estate were carefully husbanded by the successive families that owned Vaynor. The timber crops were individually valued and it is not only John Probert's recommendations that indicate this. Even today the woodlands are an integral and important part of the estate.
34. NLW/Vaynor Park/271.
35. The poem by Guto'r Glyn praised the new house built by Edward ap Hywel ab Ieuan Llwyd and his wife Gwenllian, on top of a hill. It was higher than Owain Glyndwr's house at Sycharth in Denbighshire and as high as Beeston Castle in Cheshire. Its smoke could be seen from distant parts, and must have thereby emphasised the lavish hospitality at Vaynor. Derived from Pinhorn 1977, 33.
36. Haslam 1977, 46.
37. Private collection; NLW/Vaynor Park/334-5.
38. 'The village presents a cheerful and pleasing appearance, containing several good houses and neat white-washed cottages' (Lewis, 1833).
39. Private collection.
40. NLW, Berriew Tithe Survey, 1840.
41. Private collection.
42. Hughes, 1981, 9.
43. Blayney, seeing that labourers were migrating, 'resolved to render them more attached to his neighbourhood by building for them not only convenient but elegant houses and offices, and annexing land to each sufficient for the keeping of a cow, some two, and some even more, at very easy rents' (Davies 1815, 82). The fourth Lord Sudeley pioneered the use of concrete on the estate – the mansion itself was rebuilt in it, and it was also used for the construction of farm houses and buildings as well as cottages on the estate (Haslam 1979, 201).
44. Haslam, 1979, 117.
45. 'An account of building and repairs done upon the Montgomeryshire estate from Lady day 1837 to Lady day 1838'. The entry for Coed Tafol records 'the entire new outbuildings consisting of barn floor, two corn bays, carthouse, stable, ties for 18 cattle, calves kit, hay bay, granary and shed over barn door, the fold yard levelled and formed with new gates put up and a new fence round the stack yard which was also levelled' (NLW/Vaynor Park/335).
46. Survey of 1764 by John Probert: Private Collection.
47. For example, Davies 1815.
48. There is little evidence that the owners of Vaynor benefited from the widespread enclosures of the later 18th century and 19th century in Montgomeryshire. In 1806 Joseph Lyon did purchase newly enclosed land, but on a small-scale only: some 120 acres in Llanllugan and Llanwyddelan (NLW/Vaynor Park/721). Some of the open field strips on the Severn Valley floor were probably amalgamated to produce large units but this will have been through private rather than parliamentary enclosure and again cannot have been on any scale. Gregynog on the other hand was creating tenant farms on its newly enclosed commons in Montgomeryshire (Hughes et al 1977, 7).
49. During the 17th and 18th centuries Welsh landowners exploited the mineral resources, supposed and real on their lands. Vaynor was probably unlucky. Unlike for example Garthmyl and Powis Castle their lands so close to the Severn valley offered little potential in this respect. There is a single reference (NLW/Vaynor Park/328) to a one-year lease for searching for minerals on the land at Trefeglwys, perhaps the best that they could hope for. That this was as late as 1850 implies a level of desperate optimism on the part of the leasees.

BIBLIOGRAPHY

Andrews, C. B. 1936, *The Torrington Diaries of the Honourable John Byng*, London: Eyre & Spottiswoode.
Cadw, 1999, Powys. *Register of Landscapes, Parks and Gardens of Special Historic Interest in Wales; Part 1: Parks and Gardens*, Cardiff: Cadw.
Davies, W. 1815, *The Agriculture and Domestic Economy of North Wales*, London: Board of Agriculture.
Haslam, R. 1977, 'A note on the architecture of Vaynor Park'. *Montgomery Collections* 65, 43-46.
Haslam, R. 1979, *The Buildings of Wales, Powys*, London: Penguin.
Howell, D. W. 1977, *Land and People in 19th–Century Wales*, London: Routledge & Kegan Paul.
Howell, D. W. 1986, *Patriarchs & Parasites. The Gentry of South-West Wales in the 18th Century*, Cardiff: University of Wales Press.

HSMO, 1874, *Return of Owners of Land, 1872-3*. Volume II. London.
Hughes, G. T., Morgan, P. & Thomas J. G. (eds) 1977, *Gregynog*, Cardiff: University of Wales Press.
Hughes, S. 1981, *The Archaeology of the Montgomery Canal*, Aberystwyth: RCAHMW.
Humphreys, M. 1996, *The Crisis of Community. Montgomeryshire 1680-1815*, Cardiff: University of Wales Press.
Jenkins, G. H. 1987, *The Foundations of Modern Wales, 1642-1780*, Oxford: Clarendon Press.
Lewis, S. 1833, *Topographical Dictionary of Wales*, London: S. Lewis & Co.
Morgan, P. 1977, 'The Blayney period', in Hughes et al 1977, 25-41.
Pinhorn, M. 1977, 'Vaynor, Berriew, Montgomeryshire', *Montgomery Collections* 65, 32-42.
Silvester, R. J. 2001, 'John Probert and the map of Trefnant township', *Montgomery Collections* 89, 163-78.

UNPUBLISHED SOURCES
National Library of Wales: Berriew Tithe Map and Apportionment, 1840.
National Library of Wales: Powis Castle 16711, 16966, 17256.
National Library of Wales: Vaynor Park 8, 71, 130, 138, 160-1, 271, 328, 334-5, 595, 599, 625, 713-6, 721, 1028.

ABBREVIATIONS
NLW National Library of Wales.
HMSO Her Majesty's Stationery Office.

Fields, Property, and Agricultural Innovation in Late Medieval and Early Modern South-West England

By SAM TURNER

This paper presents a preliminary overview of certain changing aspects of the agricultural landscape in the English counties of Devon and Cornwall during the later medieval and early modern period. This region in the far south-west of Britain provides a good opportunity to consider such developments since much of the landscape here was already enclosed before AD c. 1400, and so contrasts between medieval and later field patterns can often be clearly observed. The paper suggests that some agricultural practices characteristic of the post-medieval period in other parts of Britain can be detected during the late medieval period in the south-west, and that the physical alterations to the region's agricultural landscape during this period reflect changing social and ideological conditions, in particular the growing power of an emerging class of independent landholders over their estates.

'Here begynneth a ryght frutefull mater: and hath to name the boke of surveyeng and improvmentes'.[1]

The Bronze Age reaves of Dartmoor and the related field systems found elsewhere in southern England have become well-known symbols of Bronze Age people's ability to plan their landscapes.[2] The reaves were laid out with magnificent precision over distances of many miles, and they ignore intervening topographical features like river valleys with quite stunning boldness. Running north-east across Holne Moor, for example, the parallel reaves appear to stop where the moorland plunges into the valley of the River Dart, only to re-appear climbing up the opposing hillside on the same alignment to the summit of Corndon Down around 2km distant.[3] Oliver Rackham has called such field systems 'mindless' because of the way they march uncompromisingly across the landscape.[4] Although it is clear what Rackham means, the metaphor is rather unfortunate. These fields have been deliberately planned and carefully marked out, and perhaps more importantly they seem to have wider aims: to create order in the landscape, and perhaps to structure the lives of the people living and working in it.

The straight lines of the Bronze Age field patterns are strongly reminiscent of other episodes of landscape re-organisation in Britain and further afield. There are Roman field-systems with semi-regular grid plans in Britain, for example in Essex, Wiltshire, Somerset, and even perhaps in east Devon,[5] but the regular, straight-sided Roman fields created through centuriation in the Po valley or parts of Provence are justifiably the most famous.

During the Roman period, the goal of surveying and re-structuring the landscape in this way seems commonly to have been '...the ambition of intensifying production, above all through the possibility of supplying external markets'.[6]

A similar motivation lay behind much later landscape re-structuring after the European Enlightenment, not only in the north, but also in Mediterranean countries like Italy and Greece.[7] In south-west England the pinnacle of achievement (in terms of surveyed field systems) was surely reached in the 18th and 19th centuries. On Stockland Hill in Devon, for example, over 1200 hectares of almost entirely straight-sided fields were imposed on a previously open heathland in the mid-19th century. Like the large-scale regular enclosures of the later 18th century made on Dartmoor by Sir Thomas Tyrwhit[8] or the massive 19th-century improvements of the Knight family on Exmoor,[9] the aim of these enclosures was to make the barren heath and moorland fruitful. These fields represent order and agricultural efficiency imposed upon the former wilderness, and they are very much the product of the social and political movements of their time. They unambiguously reflect the power of members of the social elite to design and create new landscapes and, as in the Roman examples or Fitzherbert's Boke,[10] the surveying and ordering of the land is clearly linked to production for a market and the creation of profit.

One problem facing us is to establish how the Bronze Age reaves were planned. Were they the product of direct elite control over the landscape, or did they result from coordinated communal action? Andrew Fleming has suggested that we should not necessarily confine our interpretations to 'top down' or 'bottom up' planning: the reaves might, for instance, be the result of communal organisation and forward planning in response to centralised demands for tribute.[11] This might be suggested by the junctions between sections within the parallel reaves, where it appears that different groups of reave builders (who perhaps lived in nearby roundhouses) were unable to make their respective sections of boundary meet up exactly, creating a slight dog-leg effect. However, even if these regular landscapes were not directly imposed by the will of a single ruler, administrator or landowner, they all clearly subscribe to centrally defined models of how the landscape should be organised. As a group, they exhibit a great degree of planning and artificiality; they are surely landscapes that are the product of what we might reasonably call top-down societies.

It is implicit in this discussion that whilst landscapes are created and re-shaped by the people who live and work in them, both the people and the land are in a recursive relationship, so that they affect one another.[12] Since pre-existing boundaries and patterns of organisation are always physically present at the beginning of periods of change, it is important to consider the development of landscapes over a fairly long period of time. My paper will take the form of a preliminary look at the late medieval and early modern fields of Devon and Cornwall. A long-term perspective is particularly important here since many practices that latterly proved influential in other parts of the country were developed in the region over several centuries. The agricultural landscape of the south-west provides an opportunity to investigate how the countryside was changed by an emerging social elite and how, over time, their innovations influenced the practices of an increasingly wide cross-section of the population.

During the middle ages there were some distinctive differences between the south-west and other areas of Britain, but there were also similarities. Whilst the region was home to some unusual and locally distinctive forms of social structure – for example, servile customary tenure in some places, [13] or large numbers of free tenants[14] – the overall scene of manors and tenants is broadly recognisable when compared to that found elsewhere in southern England. A degree of similarity between Devon and Cornwall and other parts of the country can even be found in the organisation of the agricultural landscape: for example, during the earlier part of the middle ages it seems that the great majority of fields in the region were divided up into strips[15] in a similar way to those in the large open fields of the 'Central Province'.[16]

Perhaps the most significant difference between the south-western fields and either medieval fields elsewhere or the distinctively regular, straight-sided fields of the Bronze Age or the 18th and 19th centuries is the scale of the human landscape. In physical terms, the region is dominated by rolling hills that are dissected by steep valleys, and the broken character of the landform must have contributed in some way to the development of a highly dispersed settlement pattern. This pattern is of great antiquity in both Devon and Cornwall:[17] place-name evidence suggests that in Cornwall at least, it took shape between the 6th and 10th centuries AD.[18] In an agricultural landscape, virtually every settlement would have had farmland attached to it, and it seems likely that the general outline of some of the region's fields have changed little since the pre-Conquest period.[19] This medieval

Figure 1. Luppitt, east Devon. The sinuous boundaries of the medieval fields on the valley-sides contrast with the later post-medieval and modern enclosures on the ridge of Luppitt Common beyond. Photo: Sam Turner, November 2005.

landscape was small-scale and intimately detailed with different landscape resources lying side-by-side, often intermixed in complex patterns.[20] It would be rash to argue that since the medieval landscape of the south-west lacked the rigid, surveyed organisation of Roman or Bronze-Age fields, medieval society it must also have lacked strong leaders; though related, the form of monuments or landscapes does not correlate in a simple way to ideology or social structure. Nevertheless, fields were commonly small and their boundaries sinuous or irregular: the organisational virtues of straight lines seem to have been wholly unappreciated. It seems that the priorities of medieval people before the beginnings of capitalism were fundamentally different to those afterwards; neither the majority of the population nor the landscape was geared towards the creation of profit:

> 'On peasant farms work intensity was handicapped by a sub-optimal ratio of labour to land, with much consequent under-employment of labour.'[21]

The unpredictable sinuous boundaries and lack of large-scale organisation suggest that before the 15th century the individual landlords and tenants who created the fields were not guided by a central ideology that had something definitive to say about how people should organise their fields. Perhaps the social elite took less interest in how rent or tax was physically produced during the middle ages than later – as long as the required amount turned up on time.[22] The economic imperative to produce more and more, so dominant in recent centuries, was less of a driving force then; this may be reflected, for example, in the way rents due on many medieval Cornish freeholdings changed little over long periods of time.[23] For various reasons, the imperative to create rigidly ordered landscapes was largely absent in south-west England throughout most of the middle ages (Fig. 1).

There is a long history of enclosure in the South-West, though the enclosed landscape has developed at different rates in different places. Parts of the region's fieldscape has been enclosed since prehistory, and medieval farmers incorporated earlier land divisions into their own field systems both in upland and lowland areas.[24] As mentioned above, the outer limits of the fields of many medieval settlements may have been bounded from the outset. Harold Fox has identified the consolidation of strips in the open fields from 13th-century documents relating to east Devon,[25] and through his many studies has traced the differential progress of enclosure and the development of farming *pays* in the south-western landscape.[26] Based on the evidence of documentary sources, he has argued that certain areas were subject to intensive episodes of enclosure earlier than others. For example, the part of east Devon around Axminster was largely enclosed in the 13th and 14th centuries as it developed an increasingly pastoral economy; the coastal south South Hams, on the other hand, which maintained the arable basis of its economy well into the early modern period, was mostly enclosed between the 14th and 16th/17th centuries.[27] In other areas, for example those with relatively large populations of non-agricultural workers like west Cornwall, numerous open strip fields remained unenclosed at the beginning of the 18th century.[28]

Linked to this developing regionalism was increasing participation in the markets that gathered momentum from the 13th century onwards. Fox has shown, for example, how from the 14th century areas of north Devon were able to rear livestock for sale, only growing enough arable crops for their own consumption.[29] During the same period there was a gradual increase in empty tenements in these areas; elsewhere in Britain this may reflect the active eviction of tenants by landlords,[30] but in Devon and Cornwall it is generally regarded as a consequence of long-term changes in tenurial customs that resulted in part from continuing population decline during the 14th century.[31] Many hamlets, whose origins probably lay before the Norman conquest, dwindled to individual farmsteads; their holdings were subsequently engrossed by tenants able to occupy the available land.[32] In many areas the result seems to have been that fewer people were in possession of more land, and that they were increasingly involved in specialised production for external markets under their own initiative: '…within their several enclosures both lord and tenants could do as they pleased.'[33]

Increasing commercial activity based on agricultural products seems to have resulted in a growing appreciation of the value of land as a commodity in its own right, reflected in an

Figure 2. Manuscript map dating to 1603-8 showing land in Halberton, north-east Devon. The map was made to provide evidence in a dispute about rights over the water supply, and it vividly illustrates the importance attached to watering the hillside meadows at this date. Reproduced by kind permission of Devon Record Office, DRO 6065Z/E1.

increasingly active property market.[34] Fox has suggested that flexible farming practices such as convertible husbandry may have helped ease the transition to less labour-intensive forms of production despite the drastic decline in population of the late medieval period. Under this system, individual cropping units were kept under arable for a few years before being returned to grass for a long rest; if the area of a holding increased, the time between arable crops in each field could just be extended.[35] Convertible husbandry has a long history in Devon and Cornwall; far from being an innovation of the late medieval period, there is good evidence that it was practiced in the 13th century and strong indications that its origins lie much earlier.[36] The system was clearly recognised by 16th century observers such as Hooker,[37] Norden,[38] and Carew[39] who described beat-burning, the process whereby the grassland was broken and prepared to be sown. Though it was not limited to the south-western counties in the middle ages, as 'Denshiring' or Devonshiring, convertible husbandry appears to have influenced regions of England further east during the early modern period.[40]

Other south-western practices linked to the improvement of agricultural land were taken up elsewhere in the 17th centuries and later. Watermeadows, for example, are most commonly associated with the central Wessex counties of Dorset, Wiltshire and Hampshire. During the 17th and 18th centuries large and very complicated systems of small leats and channels were created in river valleys like the Avon near Salisbury (Wiltshire) to carry the water regularly across the meadows and hence increase the amount of early grass available to the region's great sheep flocks.[41] Whilst the flow of natural flood-waters across the meadowland was probably artificially controlled to a limited extent in medieval central Wessex,[42] it is possible that the origins of systems with leats and channels lie further to the west. Fox notes a reference to cleaning out the *rivuli* of a meadow in an early 15th-century source,[43] and Hooker's description in his *Synopsis Chorographical* shows that by the 16th century there were fairly complicated systems that involved the use of agricultural chemicals:

> '…but if theire growndes be higher then theire greatest industrie is howe to conveye some runninge ryll or streme of water into it…if the waters be standinge pooles and a hungrye water they do amende the same by castinge donge and lyme into it and this they do sturre with a staffe and so carye it throughe the growndes and medowes.'[44]

This is entirely in tune with the kind of practices advocated in the first quarter of the 16th century by the preeminent early advocate of agricultural improvement in Britain, the surveyor Fitzherbert:

> 'But specially that water that cometh out of a towne from every mannes mydding or donghyll is best and wyll make the medowes moost rankest.'[45]

In his description Hooker mentions two kinds of watermeadows, those that lie on the valley bottom and those, like the ones described above, with channels to convey the water onto the hillsides. Contemporary map evidence shows that highly developed examples of both were well established in Devon by the end of the 16th century. A map of Haccombe in south Devon shows meadows of the first kind. This document is of great interest, not least because it depicts one of the best examples of a deserted village known in Devon, a settlement that has now been completely lost (on the surface) to 18th-century landscaping and 20th century ploughing.[46] Both to the north-west and south-east of the former village, the map depicts complicated systems of leats for watering the valley-bottom meadows. A second map, dating to between 1603 and 1608, shows channels near Moorstone Barton in east Devon controlled by a system of sluices taking water from a main stream and distributing it across neighbouring fields.[47] The map, a particularly elaborate example, was made to provide evidence in a dispute about rights over the water supply, and it vividly illustrates the importance attached to watering the hillside meadows at this date (Fig. 2). The channels of these meadows probably represent an early stage in the development of 'catch-meadows', otherwise known as 'catchwater' or 'catchwork' meadows, or 'field-gutter' systems, which went on to become extremely widespread in south and mid-Devon and elsewhere during the later post-medieval period.[48]

Further distinctive practices related to the improvement of farmland that were noted by 16th-century writers on south-west England include the application of dung, sand, and marl.[49] An agricultural chemical whose use proved particularly influential in the later post-medieval period was lime.[50] Lime was produced by burning limestone and used to improve crop yields by reducing soil acidity and thereby increasing the efficacy of organic fertilizers.[51] Fitzherbert commented on its usefulness in 1523, although he did not say where he had seen it applied:

> 'And in many countreis where plentie of lyme stonne is the husbandes do bren the lymestonne with wode and secole [coal] and make lyme therof: and do set it upon their landes as they do their dong and do sprede it in lyke maner, the whiche they calle moche better than dong.'[52]

Lime was produced for use in buildings during the middle ages, and a limekiln is even referred to in a 9th-century charter boundary clause from south Devon,[53] so it remains a possibility that it had a long history of use for agriculture.[54] However, it seems that the 16th century was the period when its popularity began to increase more quickly; Havinden lists a series of references from the later 16th and early 17th centuries[55] and when Hooker published his *Synopsis Chorographical* in 1599 he described the use of lime as if it was then quite widespread.[56] One of the earlier references occurs in a manuscript map of the 1540s depicting the area around the parish church at Buckfastleigh,[57] which stands on a prominent limestone hill above the River Dart. West of the church, the map marks a quarry 'for the kyngs tennts to bill there howysys and to marlee there grounde to bring forth corne.' The local geology makes it improbable that marl (as understood in the modern sense) was available here,[58] and the reference seems likely to indicate limestone for burning. This interpretation is further supported by Hooker's passage on lime:

> 'In some places there be greate Rockes and Quaries of stone called marle and of which stone the best lyme is made…'[59]

The Buckfastleigh map may have been commissioned by Sir Thomas Dennis who acquired the land there from the King after the dissolution of Buckfast Abbey.[60] It is interesting to note the possibility of the monastery's involvement with an innovative agricultural technique during the later middle ages that proved so influential in post-medieval agricultural improvement.

Techniques like the use of watermeadows and the application of new fertilizers were increasingly employed to improve the profitability of land from the 15th century onwards, and they were linked both to developing regional economies and to the growing appreciation of land as a commodity in its own right.[61] Fitzherbert's *Boke of Surveyeng and Improvmentes* makes an explicit link between new agricultural technologies and increases in productivity. It is also clear about the relationship between consolidating and enclosing holdings and creating greater profits.[62] The growth in the number of surveyors and maps during the 16th century and the improvement of survey techniques and instruments are one indication of the increasing importance of the measurement and quantification of property: '…rising rents made imperative the clearest and most accurate delineation of estate and farm boundaries.'[63] In addition, the possession of land itself became an important indicator of an individual's status; it provided a growing class of merchants, lawyers, minor gentry and yeoman farmers with the opportunity to climb through the social ranks.[64]

Changes in the landscape of Devon and Cornwall at around this time can be interpreted as a result of these economic, social and ideological changes. Since much of Devon and Cornwall was enclosed before the middle of the 15th century, it is possible to compare medieval and later enclosures side-by-side in many places. Harold Fox has drawn attention to the contrast between the fields around Axminster, enclosed mainly in the 13th and 14th centuries, and later enclosures in the South Hams around Stoke Fleming and Slapton.[65] The main difference between newly created fields of the 15th – 17th centuries and earlier medieval examples seems to be the increasing regularity of their boundaries and the tendency to impose new divisions on the landscape rather than to follow the lines established by earlier farmers.

At Buckfastleigh, the schematic manuscript map of the mid 16th-century depicts the fields surrounding the church and notes the rents payable to the landowner for each. One is called 'Bromeparke…in the whiche iii closys'; the lack of individual names for these three fields both in the map and in a slightly earlier document[66] suggests this was probably a recent division effected by the new landowner Sir Thomas Dennis to increase the value of his rents. The boundaries of the three closes, which survive almost intact to the present day, are markedly straighter even than those of the earlier monastic demesne fields into which they have been inserted. Thomas Dennis was a prominent figure in 16th-century Devon who had used his influence to acquire significant estates after the Dissolution.[67] Another of his new estates was the manor of Crediton Great Park which he held from the 1540s to the 1590s. It had formerly been a park in the possession of the Bishop of Exeter, but by the time it was mapped in the 1590s by John Norden it had been divided into the patchwork of farms that still survive today.[68] Their boundaries have changed little since the late 16th century and compared to the medieval strip-enclosures that are common in the surrounding area they are extremely straight and regular. The fields in the old Park also tend to be held in discrete blocks around the individual farmsteads, as opposed to the holdings in the medieval strips-enclosures which are intermixed between neighbours.[69] Written documents, when related to later post-medieval map evidence or surviving landscapes, provide evidence for further examples of systematic and regular enclosure of demesne land for leasing in the late medieval and early post-medieval periods. At Bishop's Clyst, for example, Alcock has traced the sub-division of the demesne fields into smallish, straight-sided closes during the 16th and 17th centuries.[70] Until their recent destruction by ploughing and the creation of the new Devon County Showground, it seems vestiges of ridge-and-furrow cultivation may have been visible in some of these fields. Alcock noted that it was hard to tell whether the new boundaries followed the line of the ridge-and-furrow, although the straightness of the boundaries suggests they probably did not.[71] It seems more likely that this is an example of the transformation of a medieval landscape of open arable fields into one of regular stock-rearing enclosures. Similar divisions were made in the demesne of other east Devon manors like the former fields of Newenham Abbey at approximately the same time.[72] It seems likely that the layout of farms with straight-sided fields such as Eastpark and Westpark either side of Iddesleigh, or Weekpark near Week (Burrington) could have resulted from similar processes.

Sarah Child has recently discussed an early 17th-century dispute between the two farmers of East and West Backstone (Rackenford) which shows how the common arable of a small hamlet was divided into several fields during the 16th century.[73] Indeed, it was not just the demesnes of major landlords and aristocrats that were seeing new, more regular enclosures at this time; it was also the lands of less prominent men ranging from merchants and lawyers who had recently bought their properties to the lords of small manors and the descendants of medieval freeholders, those who together made up Hoskins' emerging 'squirearchy'.[74] Re-organising their estates into more regular enclosures could have been a way of expressing their rights of ownership; power to alter and improve their lands might have emphasised their growing status (Fig. 3).

Figure 3. Typical 'barton' fields around Straightgate Farm, Ottery St Mary (Devon). Photo: Sam Turner, November 2005.

All over the map of Devon and Cornwall there are farms whose names include the element 'Barton'.[75] A few of these are bartons in the Anglo-Saxon sense as used elsewhere in England, that is to say the *bere-tūn* or 'barley farm' dependent on a nearby multiple estate centre,[76] and a few others are bartons in the later medieval sense, 'a grange situated in an outlying part of the manor.'[77] However, most represent a distinctive local usage that appears to have developed during the later middle ages and early modern period. The editors of *The Place-Names of Devon* do not discuss them on the grounds that they are not place-names 'proper', but have rather been added to earlier medieval names.[78] Nevertheless they are important for a discussion of the early modern agricultural landscape. Finberg notes that from the 14th century they probably signify the home farm of a manor, and suggests that barton '…may first have acquired this meaning through deliberate withdrawal of the magnates [from the open fields with intermixed arable] into ring-fenced manor farms.'[79] 'That part of the demesne,' wrote Carew in the late-16th or early-17th century 'which appertaineth to the lord's dwelling-house they call his barton, or berton.'[80] With the passage of time it seems the name was increasingly applied to the farms of other types of landholder who had also consolidated their holdings into compact blocks - not only manorial lords,

Figure 4. One of Hoskins' bartons: Acland Barton, near Barnstaple (Devon). 1st edition OS 1:2,500 map, 1888-90. Map reproduced by kind permission of Landmark. © and database right Crown copyright and Landmark Information Group Ltd (all rights reserved 2007).

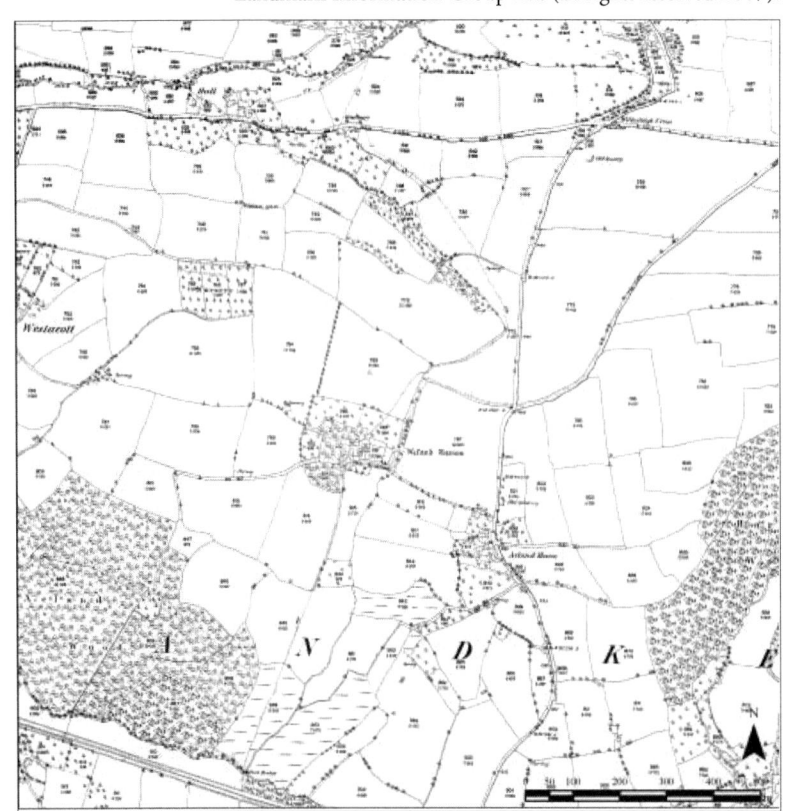

but also prosperous yeomen farmers; some parishes and manors contained many more than one such 'barton' farm by the 17th or 18th centuries.

Hoskins pointed out that many of the barton farms are the sites of surviving late medieval and early modern farmhouses and sometimes other buildings, and suggested they were associated with a major phase of rebuilding.[81] Recent work on the landscape history of the two counties has also suggested that bartons are often associated with a characteristically regular arrangement of fields.[82] Whilst such fields are not laid out with perfectly surveyed straight boundaries like those characteristic of 18th- and 19th-century enclosure, they are normally larger and almost always more regular than those in surrounding holdings, with gently sinuous but almost straight boundaries. At Cotehele in east Cornwall, for example, the present fields were enclosed from deer parks perhaps in the 17th century.[83] The large regular fields around the house and its gardens provide a stark contrast to the tiny strip-enclosures around the neighbouring hamlets of Harrowbarrow, Metherell, Albaston and Bohetherick. Notably regular fields surround all the farms in Devon with barton-names discussed by Hoskins: at Acland Barton (Landkey, Fig. 4), Honiton Barton (South Molton), Shapcott Barton (Knowstone), Rashleigh Barton (Wembworthy), Bury Barton (Lapford), Colleton Barton (Chulmleigh), Upcott Barton (Cheriton Fitzpaine) and Westcott Barton (Marwood). In Cornwall, there are good examples at Earth Barton (Saltash), Trebartha Barton (North Hill), Haye Barton (St Ive), Bodrugan Barton (St Goran) or Trenowth Barton (Ladock) (Figs 5 & 6).

It might be objected that the barton fields owe their regular form to their origins as medieval manorial demesne. However, this seems unlikely on a number of grounds. Firstly, not all manors or indeed even all parishes in Devon and Cornwall contain areas of 'barton fields'; so for example there are no clear examples in Farway in east Devon, even though there are in the neighbouring parishes of Offwell (Colwell Barton) and Widworthy (Sutton Barton). Secondly, it is not clear that medieval freeholdings can necessarily be expected to have had less regular fields than those of bond tenants.[84] In fact there are many well-established farms with solid medieval pedigrees as manorial centres or freeholdings that do not have 'barton'-type fields. A good example is Moorstone Barton, which was Morston Howse on the early 17th-century map (discussed above in connection with watermeadows), Moriston in 1242, and probably Morin in 1086.[85] The fields around the Barton here are distinctly irregular and look as though they have been enclosed directly from strip-fields and open cropping units. Thirdly, there were other types of fields created in the 15th and 16th centuries that lack the regularity of 'barton' fields: the ring-fence farms of Bodmin Moor,[86] for example, or the enclosure from woodland and heath undertaken round the margins of Axminster.[87] Finally, archaeological evidence is also beginning to suggest periods of re-organisation around barton farms. For example, at Charlestown Barton, a late 16th-century house in Charles (north Devon), recent work in advance of quarrying included large-scale geophysical survey. The results indicated that the present 'barton'-type fields may have replaced medieval strip cultivation on a different alignment.[88] These considerations all suggest that rather than being the result of a more-or-less random process of development from open medieval strip fields or medieval enclosures, decisions were actively taken about the most appropriate way to lay out the regular new 'barton' fields.

Agricultural enclosure has a long history in south-west England. It is now clear that the area of farmed land was not expanded steadily and gradually between the post-Roman period and the 19th century by pioneering enclosure from the 'waste'; instead, field systems have a complex history with many remodellings and innovations that involved both the re-use of old boundaries, the creation of new ones, and fluctuations in the area cultivated from prehistory to the present.[89] During the late medieval and early modern period, such alterations commonly occurred within the area that had been under cultivation (or otherwise enclosed) during the middle ages. In general, field systems created or remodelled at this time were increasingly regular with straighter boundaries and larger areas than their medieval predecessors; they seem to have been the result of deliberate decisions by their creators who wanted both to 'improve' and quantify their estates and to demonstrate their power over them. In this respect these locally distinctive field patterns were linked to wider national and international developments. They were the result not only of changing agricultural practices, but also of changing social structures and perceptions of the value of land; like the new farmhouses, gardens and agricultural buildings created in the same period they are a

Figure 5. Earth Barton, Saltash (Cornwall), its relatively regular fields contrasting with those of its neighbours. 1st edition OS 1:10,560 map, 1867-96. Map reproduced by kind permission of Landmark. © and database right Crown copyright and Landmark Information Group Ltd (all rights reserved 2007).

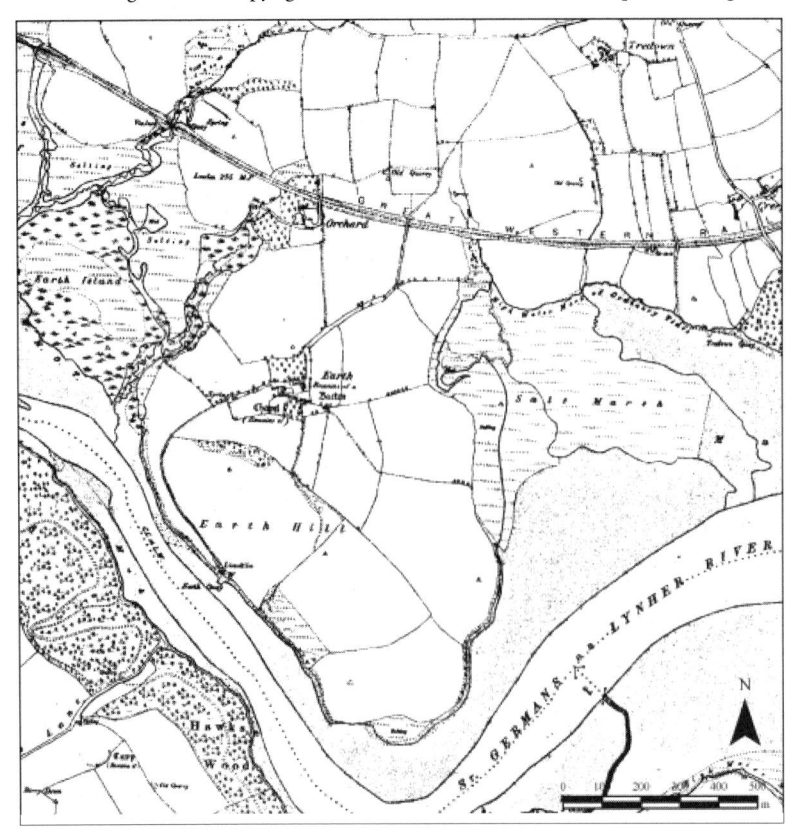

material expression of the ambitions and aspirations of a class of people whose control over their estates gave them increasing power to participate at a regional and national scale.[90]

Just as the use of watermeadows or lime in agriculture increased steadily from the 16th century into the later post-medieval period, so did the regularity of enclosures associated with settlements across the social scale. Whilst this growing regularity clearly reflects national and international trends, it is nevertheless true that it finds its antecedents in the local late- and early post-medieval landscape. The tiny regular fields of a small 17th century farm like Little Comfort (Rackenford),[91] which overlie and only partially re-use earlier medieval hedgebanks, or the straight, surveyed boundaries that are ubiquitous within 18th- and 19th-century miners' smallholdings[92] are later expressions of the same movement: the desire and need for profit, the valuation of land as a commodity in itself, and the individual esteem owing to those who controlled it.

Figure 6. Bodrugan Barton, Goran (Cornwall). 1st edition OS 1:10,560 map, 1888-91. Map reproduced by kind permission of Landmark. © and database right Crown copyright and Landmark Information Group Ltd (all rights reserved 2007).

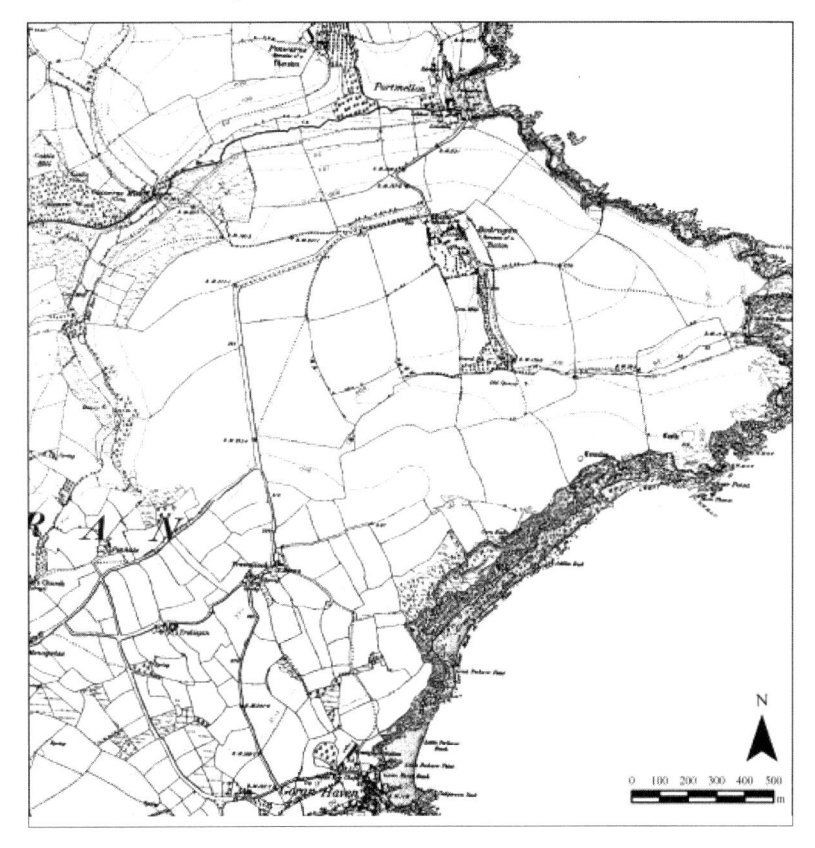

NOTES

1. Fitzherbert 1974, frontispiece.
2. Fleming 1988.
3. Gerrard 1997, 115.
4. Rackham 1986, 156.
5. Rackham 1986, 159-161; Walters 2001, 136; Rippon 2000; Weddell et al. 1993.
6. Horden & Purcell 2000, 285.
7. Rackham 2003.
8. Fletcher & Dunn 1999.
9. Orwin et al. 1997.
10. note 1, above.
11. Fleming 1994, 65.
12. Knapp & Ashmore 1999: 20-21; Altenberg 2003.
13. Fryde 1996, 209-219.
14. Hoskins 1954, 78-79; Hull 1971, xxvi-xxxi.
15. Finberg 1969a; Herring 2006.
16. Roberts & Wrathmell 2000.
17. Fox 1989, 41-42.
18. Padel 1985; Turner 2003.
19. As suggested, for example, by the solution proposed in Herring & Hooke 1993 to the Anglo-Saxon boundary clause of Trerice (Cornwall).
20. Fox & Padel 2000; Williamson 2002, 118.
21. Campbell 2000, 309.
22. Williamson & Bellamy 1987, 40-41.
23. Though this was not the case for customary tenants: Fox & Padel 2000, lii-lxvii.
24. Johnson & Rose 1994; Fleming & Ralph 1982; Johns & Herring 1996.
25. Fox 1972, 115-116; see also Flatrès 1949.
26. Fox 1975, 1989, 1991a, 1991b, 1991c, 1995, 1999; Fox & Padel 2000.
27. Fox 1972; Fox 1975.
28. Fox & Padel 2000, lxxxii-lxxxiii.
29. Fox 1995, 128-131.
30. Allen 1992, 37-55.
31. e.g. leasing and splitting up of demesnes and movement into unoccupied tenements: Dyer 1997; Fox 1989; Fox 1991a.
32. Fox 1983; Fox 1989; Dyer 1997.
33. Finberg 1951, 103.
34. Fox 1989, 45; Dyer 2002, 360-361.
35. Fox 1991b, 309.
36. Finberg 1951, 108-109; Fox 1991b; Fyfe 2006.
37. Blake 1915, 343.
38. Norden 1966, 17-18.
39. Carew 1953, 101-102.
40. Williamson 2002, 108-109; Wade Martins & Williamson 1999a, 1-7; Fox 1991b, 310.
41. Bettey 1999, 179-181.
42. Bettey 1973, 13-15.
43. Fox 1991b, 315-316.
44. Blake 1915, 344.
45. Fitzherbert 1974, Cap xxv. Fitzherbert does not specify where he has observed the practices he describes, though Cook 1994, 61 notes 'catchwork' systems in Herefordshire in the 16th century.
46. Ravenhill & Rowe 2002, 224-226; the map is in a private collection but is partly reproduced by Gray 2003, 122; see Haccombe parish file, Devon Historic Environment Record (held by Devon County Council, Exeter); see also Fox 1972, 123 for a probable early 16th-century example near Axminster.
47. DRO, 6065Z/E1 (formerly DRO G13); Ravenhill & Rowe 2000, 29-31.
48. Bettey 1999; Turner 2004; see also Wade Martins & Williamson 1999b.
49. Carew 1953; Blake 1915.
50. Williamson 2002.
51. Havinden 1974.
52. Fitzherbert 1974, Cap xxxiiii.
53. Hooke 1994, 105-112.
54. Havinden 1974, 111; 133 n.30.
55. Havinden 1974, 113-115.
56. Blake 1915, 343-344.
57. NA, SC 12/2/39, partially transcribed in Beer 1981.
58. Dr Roger Taylor, pers. comm. 2002.
59. Blake 1915, 343. See also Havinden 1974, 114 for vernacular use of the terms 'marrell' and 'marble.'
60. Youings 1955, no.12.
61. Delano-Smith & Kain 1999, 116-124.
62. Fitzherbert 1974, Cap xli.
63. Delano-Smith & Kain 1999, 121-122.
64. Blake 1915, 340-341; Hoskins 1952; Hoskins 1954, 79-87; Fox 1991a, 174; Harley 1983, 30-31; Delano-Smith & Kain 1999, 122.
65. Fox 1972.
66. NA, SC 12/2/39; Youings 1955, no.12.
67. Hoskins 1954, 84.
68. DRO, 1660A/add4/E1. The surviving version is a 19th century copy: Ravenhill & Rowe 2000, 16-17.
69. For east Devon examples, see Fox 1972, 107-108.
70. Alcock 1974.
71. DHER, SX99SE/87. Alcock 1974, 124; 171 n.37.
72. Fox 1972, 120.
73. Child 2001.
74. Hoskins 1954, 76-87.
75. Hoskins 1966a.
76. Faith 1997; e.g. Barton (St Marychurch), Gover et al. 1932, 519.
77. Mawer 1924, 5.
78. Gover et al. 1932, 674.

79. Finberg 1951, 49.
80. Carew 1953, 122.
81. Hoskins 1966a.
82. In particular English Heritage's Historic Landscape Characterisation projects, undertaken by Peter Herring and colleagues at Cornwall County Council (Herring 1998) and by Devon County Council's Archaeology Service.
83. Carew (1953, 183) described Cotehele as '… appurtenanced with the necessaries of wood, water, fishing, parks, and mills' though since 'park' is the local term for an enclosed field it is not entirely clear what he meant; see Pett 1998. Medieval deerparks at nearby Kerrybullock (Pittman 1990, 39-43) and at Crediton (above, n.68) were put to productive agricultural use (including enclosure) during the 16th century; see Pett 1998, 256-260, for other examples of deerpark development.
84. Herring 1986, vol 2, 139-146; see Brandon 1979; Austin 1985, 73-75, for discussion.
85. Gover et al. 1932, 549; Thorn & Thorn 1985, 51.14.
86. Herring 1986, vol 2, 177-181.
87. Fox 1972.
88. Humphreys 2004.
89. Hoskins 1954; cf. Hoskins 1963; Fox 1989, n.4.
90. Aston & Bettey 1998.
91. Gover et al. 1932, 341.
92. Herring 1998; Herring & Giles forthcoming.

BIBLIOGRAPHY

Abulafia, D. (ed.) 2003, *The Mediterranean in History*, London: Thames & Hudson.
Alcock, N. 1974, 'Fields and farms in an east Devon parish' *Transactions of the Devonshire Association* 107, 93-172.
Allen, R. 1992, *Enclosure and the Yeoman. The Agricultural Development of the South Midland 1450 – 1850*, Oxford: Oxford University Press.
Altenberg, K. 2003, *Experiencing Landscapes*, Stockholm: Almqvist & Wiksell International.
Ashmore, W. & Knapp, B. (eds) 1999, *Archaeologies of Landscape: Contemporary Perspectives*, Oxford: Blackwell.
Aston, M. & Bettey, J. 1998, 'The post-medieval landscape c. 1540-1700: the drive for profit and the desire for status' in Everson & Williamson 1998, 117-138.
Austin, D. 1985, 'Dartmoor and the upland village of the south-west of England' in Hooke 1985, 71-79.
Beer, E. 1981, *Buckfastleigh Remembered*, Plymouth: PDS Printers.
Beresford, G. 1979, 'Three deserted medieval settlements on Dartmoor: a report on the late E Marie Minter's excavations', *Medieval Archaeology* 23, 98-158.
Bettey, J. 1973, 'Sheep, enclosures and watermeadows in Dorset agriculture in the sixteenth and seventeenth centuries' in Havinden 1973, 9-18.
Bettey, J. 1999, 'The development of water meadows in the southern counties' in Cook & Williamson 1999, 179-195.
Blake, W. 1915, 'Hooker's Synopsis Chorographical of Devonshire', *Transactions of the Devonshire Association* 47, 334-348.
Brandon, P. 1979, 'Appendix: the medieval fields', in Beresford 1979, 150-152.
Campbell, B. 2000, *English Seigniorial Agriculture 1250 – 1450*, Cambridge: Cambridge University Press.
Carew, R. 1953, *The Survey of Cornwall*, (ed. F. Halliday), London: Andrew Melrose.
Carver, M. (ed.) 2003, *The Cross Goes North: Processes of Conversion in Northern Europe, AD 300 – 1300*, York: York Medieval Press.
Chalklin, C. & Havinden, M. (eds) 1974, *Rural Change & Urban Growth 1500 – 1800*, London: Longman.
Child, S. 2001, 'Devon fields enclosed and regretted: a seventeenth century argument among north Devon farmers', *The Devon Historian* 62, 22-25.
Cook, H. 1994, 'Field-scale water management in southern England to AD 1900', *Landscape History* 16, 53-66.
Cook, H. & Williamson, T. (eds) 1999, *Water Management in the English Landscape: Field, Marsh and Meadow*, Edinburgh: Edinburgh University Press.
Delano-Smith, C. & Kain, R. 1999, *English Maps: a History*, London: British Library.

Dyer, C. 1997, 'Peasants and farmers: rural settlements and landscapes in an age of transition' in Gaimster & Stamper 1997, 61-76.
Dyer, C. 2002, *Making a Living in the Middle Ages. The People of Britain 850-1520*, New Haven: Yale University Press.
Ellis, P. (ed.) 2001, *Roman Wiltshire and After. Papers in Honour of Ken Annable*, Devizes: Wiltshire Archaeological & Natural History Society.
Everson, P. & Williamson, T. (eds) 1998, *The Archaeology of Landscape*, Manchester: Manchester University Press.
Faith, R. 1997, *The English Peasantry and the Growth of Lordship*, London: Leicester University Press.
Finberg, H. 1951, *Tavistock Abbey. A Study in the Social and Economic History of Devon*, Cambridge: Cambridge University Press.
Finberg, H. 1969a, 'The open field in Devon' in Finberg 1969b, 129-151.
Finberg, H. 1969b, *West-Country Historical Studies*, Newton Abbot: David & Charles.
Fitzherbert, 1974, *The Boke of Surveying and Improvements, London 1523*, reprinted Amsterdam: Theatrum Orbis Terrarum.
Flatrès, P. 1949, 'La structure agraire ancienne du Devon et du Cornwall et les enclôtures des XIIIe et XIVe siècles', *Annales de Bretagne* 56, 130-134.
Fleming, A. 1988, *The Dartmoor Reaves*, London: Batsford.
Fleming, A. 1994, 'The reaves reviewed', *Devon Archaeological Society Proceedings* 52, 63-74.
Fleming, A. & Ralph, N. 1982, 'Medieval settlement and land use on Holne Moor, Dartmoor: the landscape evidence', *Medieval Archaeology* 26, 101-137.
Fletcher, M. & Dunn, C. 1999, 'The evolution and changing perceptions of a moorland landscape' in Pattison (eds) 1999, 129-134.
Fox, H. 1972, 'Field systems of east and south Devon, part 1: east Devon', *Transactions of the Devonshire Association* 104, 81-135.
Fox, H. 1975, 'The chronology of enclosure and economic development in medieval Devon', *Economic History Review*, 2nd series, 27:2, 181-202.
Fox, H. 1983, 'Contraction: desertion and dwindling of dispersed settlement in a Devon parish', *Annual Report of the Medieval Village Research Group* 31, 40-42.
Fox, H. 1989, 'Peasant farmers, patterns of settlement and pays: transformations in the landscapes of Devon and Cornwall during the later middle ages' in Higham 1989, 41-73.
Fox, H. 1991a, 'The occupation of the land: Devon and Cornwall' in Miller 1991, 152-174.
Fox, H. 1991b, 'Farming practice and techniques: Devon and Cornwall' in Miller 1991, 303-323.
Fox, H. 1991c, 'Tenant farming and tenant farmers' in Miller 1991, 722-743.
Fox, H. 1995, 'Servants, cottagers and tied cottages during the later middle ages: towards a regional dimension', *Rural History* 6:2, 125-154.
Fox, H. 1999, 'Medieval farming and rural settlement' in Kain & Ravenhill 1999, 273-280
Fox, H. & Padel, O. 2000, *The Cornish Lands of the Arundells of Lanherne, Fourteenth to Sixteenth Centuries*, Devon & Cornwall Record Society, New Series 41 (for 1998), Exeter: D&CRS.
Fryde, E. 1996, *Peasants and Landlords in Later Medieval England*, Stroud: Sutton.
Fyfe, R. 2006, 'Palaeoenvironmental perspectives on medieval landscape development' in Turner 2006, 10-23.
Gaimster, D. & Stamper, P. 1997, *The Age of Transition: the Archaeology of English Culture 1400-1600*, Society for Post-Medieval Archaeology Monograph 15, Oxford: Oxbow Books.
Gerrard, S. 1997, *Dartmoor*, London: Batsford/English Heritage.
Gover, J., Mawer, A. & Stenton, F. 1932, *The Place-Names of Devon*, English Place-Name Society, Vol. 9 (2 vols.), Cambridge: Cambridge University Press.
Gray, T. 2003, *Lost Devon: Creation, Change and Destruction over 500 Years*, Exeter: Mint Press.
Harley, J. 1983, 'Meaning and ambiguity in Tudor cartography' in Tyack 1983, 22-45.
Havinden, M. (ed.) 1973, *Husbandry and Marketing in the South West*, Exeter Papers in Economic History 8, Exeter: University of Exeter.
Havinden, M. 1974, 'Lime as a means of agricultural improvement: the Devon example' in Chalklin &

Havinden 1974, 104-134.
Herring, P. 1998, *Cornwall's Historic Landscape: Presenting a Method of Historic Landscape Character Assessment*, Truro: Cornwall Archaeological Unit.
Herring, P. 2006, 'Cornish strip fields' in Turner 2006, 44-77.
Herring, P. & Giles, C. forthcoming, 'Agriculture' in Herring et al. forthcoming.
Herring, P. & Hooke, D. 1993, 'Interrogating Anglo-Saxons in St Dennis', *Cornish Archaeology* 32, 67-75.
Herring, P., Sharpe, A. & Smith, J. (eds) forthcoming, *Bodmin Moor: an Archaeological Survey. Vol. 2: The Post-Medieval and Industrial Landscapes*, London: English Heritage & Cornwall Archaeological Unit.
Higham, R. (ed.) 1989, *Landscape and Townscape in the South West*, Exeter: University of Exeter Press.
Hooke, D. (ed.) 1985, *Medieval Villages: a Review of Current Work*, Oxford: Oxford University Committee for Archaeology.
Hooke, D. 1994, *Pre-Conquest Charter-Bounds of Devon and Cornwall*, Woodbridge: Boydell.
Horden, P. & Purcell, N. 2000, *The Corrupting Sea. A Study of Mediterranean History*, Oxford: Blackwell.
Hoskins, W. 1952, 'The estates of the Caroline gentry' in Hoskins & Finberg 1952, 334-365.
Hoskins, W. 1954, *Devon*, London: Collins.
Hoskins, W. 1963, *Provincial England*. London: Macmillan.
Hoskins, W. 1966a, 'Some old Devon bartons' in Hoskins 1966b, 30-44.
Hoskins, W. 1966b, *Old Devon*, London: Pan Books.
Hoskins, W. & Finberg, H. 1952, *Devonshire Studies*, London: Jonathon Cape.
Hull, P. 1971, *The Caption of Seisin of the Duchy of Cornwall (1337)*, Devon & Cornwall Record Society, New Series 17, Torquay: D&CRS.
Johnson, N. & Rose, P. 1994, *Bodmin Moor: an Archaeological Survey. Vol. 1: The Human Landscape to c. 1800*, London: English Heritage.
Johns, C. & Herring, P. 1996, *St Keverne Historic Landscape Assessment*, Truro: Cornwall Archaeological Unit.
Kain, R. & Ravenhill, W. (eds) 1999, *Historical Atlas of South-West England*, Exeter: University of Exeter Press.
Knapp, B. & Ashmore, W. 1999, 'Archaeological landscapes: constructed, conceptualized, ideational' in Ashmore & Knapp 1999, 1-30.
Mawer, A. 1924, *The Chief Elements Used in English Place-Names*, English Place-Name Society, Vol. 1 Pt 2, Cambridge: Cambridge University Press.
Miller, E. (ed.) 1991, *The Agrarian History of England and Wales*, Vol. III, 1348-1500, Cambridge: Cambridge University Press.
Norden, J. 1966, *Speculi Britanniae Pars: a Topographical and Historical Description of Cornwall*, Newcastle: Frank Graham.
Orwin, C., Sellick, R. & Bonham-Carter, V. 1997, *The Reclamation of Exmoor Forest*, Tiverton: Exmoor Books.
Padel, O. 1985, *Cornish Place-Name Elements*, Nottingham: English Place-Name Society Vols. 56-7.
Pattison, P., Field, D. & Ainsworth, S. (eds) 1999, *Patterns of the Past: Essays in Landscape Archaeology for Christopher Taylor*, Oxford: Oxbow Books.
Pett, D. 1998, *The Parks and Gardens of Cornwall*, Penzance: Alison Hodge.
Pittman, S. 1990, *Kerrybullock: the Evolution of the Royal Deer Park in Stoke Climsland*, Stoke Climsland: Stoke Climsland Parish Archive.
Rackham, O. 1986, *The History of the Countryside*, London: Dent.
Rackham, O. 2003, 'The physical setting' in Abulafia 2003, 33-65.
Ravenhill, M. & Rowe, M. 2000, *Early Devon Maps*, Exeter: Friends of Devon's Archives.
Ravenhill, M. & Rowe, M. (eds) 2002, *Devon Maps and Map-Makers: Manuscript Maps before 1840*, 2 vols., Devon & Cornwall Record Society, New Series 43, Exeter: D&CRS.
Rippon, S. 2000, 'The Romano-British exploitation of coastal wetlands: survey and excavation on the North Somerset Levels, 1993–7', *Britannia* 31, 69-200.
Roberts, B. & Wrathmell, S. 2000, *An Atlas of Rural Settlement in England*, London: English Heritage.
Thorn, C. & Thorn, F. (eds) 1985, *Domesday Book 9*: Devon, 2 vols., Chichester: Phillimore.
Turner, S. 2003, 'Making a Christian landscape: early medieval Cornwall' in Carver 2003, 171-194.

Turner, S. 2004, 'The changing ancient landscape: south-west England c. 1700-1900', *Landscapes* 5, 18-34.

Turner, S. (ed.) 2006, *Medieval Devon and Cornwall: Shaping an Ancient Countryside*, Macclesfield: Windgather Press.

Tyack, S. (ed.) 1983, *English Map-Making 1500-1650*, London: British Library.

Wade Martins, S. & Williamson, T. 1999a, *Roots of Change: Farming and the Landscape in East Anglia, c. 1700-1870*, London: British Agricultural History Society.

Wade Martins, S. & Williamson, T. 1999b, 'Inappropriate technology? The history of 'floating' in the north and east of England' in Cook & Williamson 1999, 196-209.

Walters, B. 2001, 'A perspective on the social order of Roman villas in Wiltshire' in Ellis 2001, 127-146.

Weddell, P., Reed, S. & Simpson, S. 1993, 'Excavation of the Exeter-Dorchester Roman road at the River Yarty and the Roman fort ditch and settlement site at Woodbury, near Axminster', *Devon Archaeological Society Proceedings* 51, 33-133.

Williamson, T. 2002, *The Transformation of Rural England. Farming and the Landscape 1700-1870*, Exeter: University of Exeter Press.

Williamson, T. & Bellamy, L. 1987, *Property and Landscape. A Social History of Land Ownership and the English Countryside*, London: George Philip.

Youings, J. 1955, *Devon Monastic Lands: Calendar of Particulars for Grants 1536 – 1558*, Devon & Cornwall Record Society, New Series 1, Torquay: D&CRS.

UNPUBLISHED SOURCES

Devon Historic Environment Record, Haccombe parish file.

Devon Historic Environment Record, SX 99SE/87.

Devon Record Office, 1660A/add4/E1, manuscript map of Crediton, Devon.

Devon Record Office, 6065Z/E1 (formerly DRO G13), manuscript map of part of Halberton, Devon.

The National Archives, SC 12/2/39, manuscript map of part of Buckfastleigh, Devon.

Herring, P. 1986, 'An exercise in landscape history. Pre-Norman and medieval Brown Willy and Bodmin Moor, Cornwall', 3 vols, unpublished MPhil thesis, University of Sheffield.

Humphreys, C. 2004, Charlestown Barton, Charles, Devon, unpublished report held by Devon Historic Environment Record, Devon County Council.

ABBREVIATIONS

DHER Devon Historic Environment Record.
DRO Devon Record Office.
NA The National Archives.

Part Two

Landscapes & Material Culture
———————————

Estate Landscapes and the Cult of the Ruin: A Lesson of Spatial Transformation in Rural Ireland

By CHARLES E. ORSER, JR.

Landscapes are seldom designed merely to be functional. In addition to serving a practical purpose, landscapes also express symbolic messages. Archaeology can assist in landscape interpretation, particularly in cases where the design and construction sequence over time is unclear. Excavation at Tanzyfort House in County Sligo, Ireland, reveals the importance of symbolic interpretation as an aid to excavation analysis, and highlights the significance of the Cult of the Ruin to the late 17th- and 18th-century gentry.

INTRODUCTION

Archaeologists who investigate the modern era, and indeed other periods of history as well, have long understood the importance of examining landscapes and the structures they contain as symbolic expressions. Symbolically-focussed studies began to appear in earnest by the early 1990s, and analyses incorporating symbolic dimensions are commonplace in today's archaeology. Archaeologists of the modern world have presented examples in such diverse locales as a 19th-century Canadian fur-trading fort and 16th-century English dwellings. Such research demonstrates empirically the pivotal role that the conscious and unconscious symbolic expressions of buildings and landscapes can play in affecting and indeed structuring social relations.[1]

The archaeologist's symbolic understanding of a building, a structure, or an entire landscape is typically presented as part of an analytical interpretation. Archaeologists tend to appreciate the symbolic aspects of a landscape and its integral elements as a feature of ascribing meaning within the sociohistorical context in which it was situated. As Matthew Johnson notes, the goal of such analysis is to allow archaeologists to grasp some measure of both the social relations constantly being recreated in the landscape and to understand simultaneously the worldview of the landscape's creators and users.[2] Archaeologists today widely accept such reasonable logic. Archaeological interpretation should proceed multidimensionally, recognizing that human-built landscapes and their various features can have multiple, layered meanings that are situationally sensitive and temporally mutable. Less frequently, however, does an archaeologist's symbolic interpretation and the practical aspects of excavation align in such a way that the symbolic interpretation actually helps to explain the archaeological features discovered during the excavation process.

This paper presents information from the late 17th- and 18th-century demesne of the Coopers, a gentry family living in County Sligo, Ireland. The goal is to show how the symbolic interpretation of features discovered during the excavation at their first home helps to explain the visual transformation of the structure within the recreated elite landscape. An associated goal is to illustrate how this interpretation leads to understanding the sequence of transformative building activity on the estate.

THE COOPERSHILL ESTATE

The Elizabethan English took their concept of the demesne to Ireland as part of a comprehensive colonialization scheme. English power had destroyed and replaced Gaelic authority by the 18th century, and so Anglo-Irish landholders could cease their construction of defensive dwellings, even as they continued to surround their demesnes with high walls, some of which contained corner turrets as defensive vestiges.[3]

At the height of their presence, demesnes covered over 5% of Ireland.[4] Demesnes, as places reserved for the sole use of the landed gentry, were invented landscapes created as part of a larger process of 'improvement'. Improvement schemes, being firmly rooted in Enlightenment philosophy, incorporated concepts of transformation for both people and places.[5] Demesne walls provided physical and visual barriers from the outside, and offered a tangible reaffirmation of the social gulf separating those living inside (usually elite, English, Protestant) from those living outside (usually non-elite, Irish, Catholic).[6]

The designers of Irish demesnes began by attempting to duplicate the English landscape, but by the early 18th century most of them had adopted as less-formal, more open 'parkland' style.[7] Most Irish estates remained largely intact until the passage of land reform measures in the late 19th and early 20th centuries caused their subdivision. Some estate owners were able to retain their estates, either in part or in whole, and their descendants continue to hold these estates today.[8] The Coopershill Estate, though reduced in size from its original extent, retains its demesne and is still owned by the family responsible for its creation.

The Coopershill Estate is located in southeastern County Sligo in the Republic of Ireland, near Riverstown. The first identifiable Cooper in the region was Edward Cooper, an officer with Sir Charles Coote's dragoons in the mid-17th century.[9] Like many English officers serving in Ireland, Cooper received land instead of payment for his military service. County Sligo, though not officially planted by English undertakers, was home to about 140 English families by 1641.[10] The Cooper's main residence in County Sligo was Markree Castle, often called 'Mercury', a huge tract still renowned today for its crenelated mansion and Gothic gates, its stately trees, and its famous 19th-century observatory.[11]

The connection between the Coopers of Markree and those at the Coopershill Estate is largely unknown. Edward Cooper may have descended from the Coopers of Thurgarton, Nottinghamshire. He had two brothers, Thomas and George, and the Coopers of Coopershill likely descended from George.[12] Records indicate that a George Cooper of Drumadderilohan leased the original Coopershill Estate—then called 'Lisbrislan', 'Tanzyhill,' or 'Tanzyfort'—from Arthur Cooper of Markree on 25 March 1684.[13] George Cooper, his wife Jane, and their son Arthur and his wife Sarah were likely the inhabitants of Tanzyfort House, the first elite dwelling on the estate and the subject of archaeological research during the summers of 2003 and 2004.

The land use history of the Coopershill Estate is complex and convoluted, with various plots being sold, mortgaged, and leased through time. Most of the tenant farmers associated with the estate paid their rents to the Markree Estate, though some also paid rents to Coopershill. In any case, the Tanzyfort (or variously 'Tansyfort') property came into being as a discretely-named estate in the late 17th century. In 1684, the initial lease lists the Tanzyfort property as 'the quarter of the land of Lisbrislan'. This document provides the first clear reference to Tanzyfort as a discrete spatial entity. An indenture document dated 18 August 1716 mentions 'William Cooper of Lisbrislan als [alias] Tanzyhill.'[14] The co-occurrence of the words 'Tanzyhill' [Tanzyfort] with 'Lisbrislan' is significant because the word 'Tanzyfort' is likely a direct English rendering of the Irish 'Lisbrislan'. In Irish Gaelic '*lios*' means 'fairy fort' and '*brislein*' means 'white tansy'.[15] An earthen ringfort is indeed situated on the demesne not far from the Coopers' 17th- and 18th-century dwelling called Tanzyfort House. In the 18th century, country people commonly associated ringforts with fairy communities,[16] so the derivation of the name 'Tanzyfort' seems reasonable within the local context.

A parchment map dated 1760 indicates that Tanzyfort House was surrounded by a 67.5 ha demesne that included 31 fields, each one identified by function. Richard Feely, the draughtsman, depicts the house in lot 26, identified as the 'Garden & liberty about the House'. The fields adjacent to the house's yard are named 'Kitchen Garden', 'Farm Yard', 'Orchard', and 'Horse Park'. Feely shows the road to Sligo Town running in front of the house[17], and the Unshin River meandering behind it (Fig. 1). He depicts two additional

Figure 1. A portion of Richard Feely's map of 1760. (Courtesy of Brian and Lindy O'Hara, Coopershill Papers.)

structures further up the road west of the main house in a 'Farm Yard'.[18] One of these stone structures still stands as a shell, and is referred to as 'the barn'.

The precise design of the Tanzyfort House cannot be determined from Feely's map alone. He draws it as a central block with two-and-a-half storeys and four chimneys. Adjacent on one side are two one-and-a-half storey additions, each of which has a single chimney. The larger building has a central door, three windows, and two gables, while the two additions each have a central door and one gable. He does not show the presence of any outbuildings or support structures in the vicinity.

The veracity of Feely's drawing is unknown, and it may merely constitute an imaginative rendering. The still-standing ruins, however, indicate that Tanzyfort House was an L-shaped, stone building. The interior floor space totalled 155.5m^2 divided into two rooms. A 'front hall', running east-west, contained 91.4m^2, and a 'kitchen', extending north-south, encompassed 64.1m^2 (Fig. 2). The building's walls, averaging about 1m thick and between 2.4 and c. 20m tall, were composed of randomly-placed rubble covered with lime plaster rendering. When inhabited, the house undoubtedly had multiple gables and thick chimneys, following the construction conventions of the time and in keeping with Feely's drawing.[19] Excavation finds indicate that the interior probably contained decorative stucco moulding, and that the building had been covered with heavy stone roofing tiles.

L-shaped houses were common in late 17th-century Ireland.[20] Castle Baldwin, located just south of the Coopershill Estate in Ballinafad, constitutes a roughly similar, extant

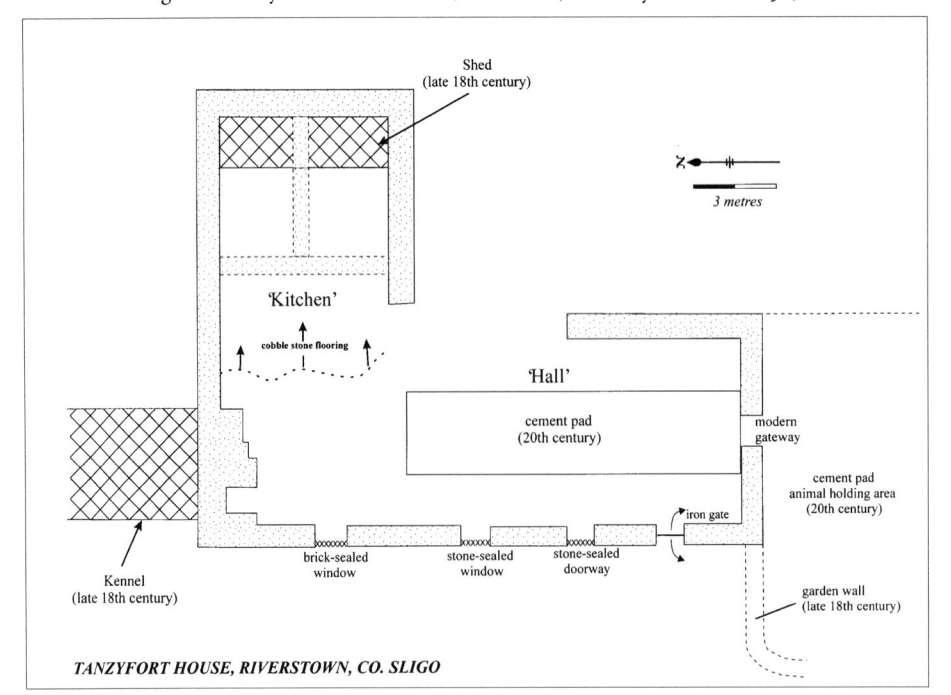

Figure 2. Tanzyfort House remains, 2003-04. (Drawn by C. E. Orser, Jr.)

example.[21] Here, however, the body of the L is much larger that the extension, which is actually a stairway projection. This building, earlier in date than Tanzyfort House, is more properly described as a semi-fortified house because of its thick walls, firing loops, and the presence of a machicoulis over the door. As such, it probably represents an antecedent model of Tanzyfort's design. Killincarrig House in County Wicklow is almost identical to Tanzyfort House.[22] This house has the same L-shaped design and measures 153.3m^2 in interior space. Like Tanzyfort House, Killincarrig House was also oriented with its front wall facing west. Killincarrig House had two-and-a-half storeys, three fireplaces, a single entrance, several mullioned windows, and defensive firing loopholes on the ground floor. One clear difference between this house and Tanzyfort House is the location of the stair projection. The builders of Killincarrig House put the stairs on the west-faced wall, whereas the designers of Tanzyfort House installed their stairs on the north-facing wall.

A combination of archaeological and documentary research indicates that the Coopers inhabited Tanzyfort House from c. 1684 to 1781. Beginning around 1755, they contracted for the construction of a new house. County Clare architect Francis Bindon was contracted to design the Cooper's new house, the still extant Georgian mansion called Coopershill House. Bindon situated the house on a hill about 200m almost due north of Tanzyfort House (Fig. 3). The visual power of the new mansion has never been lost on visitors to the estate. One early 19th-century observer described the house as 'superbly fine', while a late 19th-century local historian favourably compared its strength and size to the pyramids at Cheops. Today's independent tourist literature still extols of the architectural quality of this house and its beautifully-kept demesne.[23]

Coopershill House, like most estate mansions, was never simply a functional residence for the Cooper family. Its residents imbued the house with symbolic meanings that were intended to distinguish it from Tanzyfort House. They designed the new, grander, and larger house as 'conceputalized space' or as a 'representation of space' intended to mediate between space as lived and space as perceived.[24] This reinvention of the dwelling house transformed the essentially colonial space of the Tanzyfort House into a form of spatial practice that rested on the foundation of late Stuart and early Hanoverian rule. The need to establish Tanzyfort House had been effected within a carefully designed myth of Gaelic savagery, in which the struggle between in-migrating, Protestant Englishman and indigenous, Catholic Gael occurred, in one dimension, as a battle over space. The earliest days in the life of Tanzyfort House was part of a larger material/conceptual transformation that was rooted and expressed in the landscape.[25]

The symbolic aspects of Coopershill House derived from two sources, both of which distinguished it from the earlier, more vernacular Tanzyfort House. Its commanding location was far different from the situation of the earlier house. The builders of Tanzyfort House had placed it on the main road to Sligo in a wet, low area on land adjacent to the slow-moving Unshin River. The position of the new house on a hill certainly signified strength and power, but it also made the house susceptible to good breezes and a direct view of the surrounding countryside. The position of the new house also made it possible for the designers to run the looping main road to the house directly past the deer park.[26] The position of the house, the road along the deer park, and the associated outbuildings all

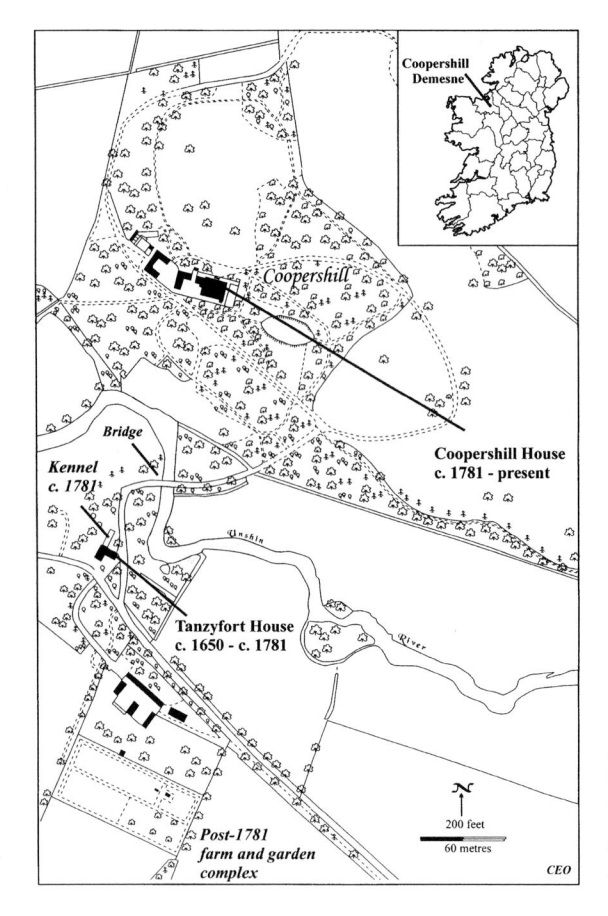

LEFT
Figure 3. Residential core of the Coopershill Demesne. (Drawn by C. E. Orser, Jr., adapted from the 1911 Ordnance Survey map.)

helped to promote the strength and authority of the house's owners. At the same time, the remade estate expressed genteel beauty and refinement.

The name 'Coopershill House' also carried a double meaning that would have been understood by the Coopers and recognized by their educated visitors. The name had an undoubted practical meaning to be sure. The house was commissioned and inhabited by a family named Cooper, and it was situated on a hill owned by them. The name 'Coopershill' is on one level thus merely descriptive, signifying the 'Coopers' house on the hill'. But the name also carries a deeper, more philosophical meaning that would have been acknowledged by all well-read English men and women in the late 18th century. The name 'Coopershill' would have evoked the poem of the same name by Dublin-born John Denham, first published in 1642. In this early topographical poem, Denham drew a stark contrast between the environments of the city and the country.[27] He directed his comments toward Britain and its New World colonies, but the Coopers, as an English family seeking to create a new landscape in a colonized environment, would undoubtedly have understood the poem's more profound significance.[28] The Coopers, in their effort to create a remarkable landscape from land that was not originally theirs, would have appreciated Denham's observation that colonial power 'Finds wealth where 'tis, bestows it where it wants'.

The transformation of the Coopershill Estate in the late 18th century thus inculcated both practical and ideological elements. As prominent County Sligo residents - living across the island from Dublin's dynamic urbanity - the Coopers desired the grand material/conceptual surroundings of their class, just as they also sought to use their name to evoke the genteel sentiments expressed in topographical poetry. The transformation of their estate was surely intended for their own senses of well-being and success. Moreover, their created landscape was also designed as a pedagogical tool intended to educate both the locals who lived outside the estate walls, and all visitors who entered the estate regardless of class affiliation.[29] Their ability to impress members of their own class would have an especially important role in maintaining their place in genteel society.[30] The Coopers, like the vast number of their fellow 18th-century landowners, understood that land was the key to wealth and power, but few owners 'had much to boast about in the way of ancient lineage'.[31] Given their paucity of historical depth in the countryside, most of the landed gentry had to create the trappings of an ancient lineage. The estate demesne was an obvious place to pursue this project.

At about the same time that the builders were raising Coopershill House, they were also engaged in considerable construction projects elsewhere on the estate. The construction of a bridge over the Unshin River made the location of Coopershill House possible. Prior to the construction of the bridge, which was viewed then as it is today as a considerable feat of engineering, all settlement on the estate was south of the river. With the completion of the bridge, the estate's buildings and plantings could extend to both sides of the river, thus greatly expanding the surface area of the demesne. Other notable constructions were the erection of a walled, formal garden and farm complex (both located south of Tanzyfort House) and a kennel (see Fig. 3). The location of the kennel was the most curious construction on the estate because of its proximity to Tanzyfort House. The interpretation of the kennel's placement held the key to understanding the conscious transformation of Tanzyfort House into a purely symbolic structure after c. 1781.

THE KENNEL

The building referred to as the kennel, which is still standing though no longer used as intended, measures 4.6m wide and 14m long. Feely does not show this building on his map of 1760, and no documents have yet been identified to provide a firm date for its construction. All evidence suggests, however, that the building is roughly contemporaneous with the Coopershill mansion.

The designer of the kennel had it built as a two-storied, gabled building with a slate roof. In 2003-04 it contained one mullioned window (probably robbed from Tanzyfort House), and other windows and door openings, all framed in brick. Its walls consist of randomly-placed stones similar to those of Tanzyfort House. Unlike the house, however, its randomly-set courses were separated by parallel courses, one small, flat stone thick. The distance between the parallel stone courses was approximately 33cm. This method of wall construction was duplicated on a curving garden wall that was extended westward from the west wall of Tanzyfort House. At some point after the house was abandoned, probably in the 20th century, a door had been cut through its south wall to allow movement between the interior of the ruined house and the enclosed garden space. The walled garden was used in living memory as an animal-holding pen after inoculation, which was administered inside the Tanzyfort House ruin on a 20th-century cement pad (see Fig. 2).

The presence of a kennel on a refurbished elite estate in late 18th-century Ireland is not surprising. Fox and stag hunting were common pursuits of the landed gentry, and the expense of keeping a pack of hounds in the 1780s, though high at £80 annually, was a useful mark of breeding and prestige.[32] In fact, in the early 19th century, Sir Jonah Barrington described one category of the gentry he met in Galway, as the 'half-mounted gentlemen': 'squireens with unpolished boots, hunting on good horses which jumped well but were never groomed'.[33] The Coopers were also engaged in hunting, and the Coopershill hounds were renowned throughout County Sligo.[34]

Thus, the presence of a kennel on the redesigned Coopershill Estate is unremarkable. What is surprising about the kennel, however, is its placement. The architect in charge of designing the landscape in the 1760-80 era had the entire demesne in which to situate it, but chose to place it through the north wall of the old Tanzyfort House (Fig. 4). This construction allowed the builders to re-use the Tanzyfort House stairs, but forced them to rebuild a section of the north wall of the house because they had to remove it in order to construct the kennel's south wall. Excavation along the interior wall of the house fully documented this sequence of destruction, construction, and reconstruction. Given that the designers of the estate landscape had the entire demesne in which to construct the kennel, why did they choose to place it, not simply near Tanzyfort House, but actually through its northern wall? The location is perplexing from our present vantage point because of the increased expenditure required to rebuild the old wall. The builders would have had to

Figure 4. Axonometric sketch of Tanzyfort House and kennel (Tanzyfort, right; kennel, left). The walls of Tanzyfort House have been extended upward to exaggerate its appearance relative to the kennel. (Drawn by Christine C. Orser).

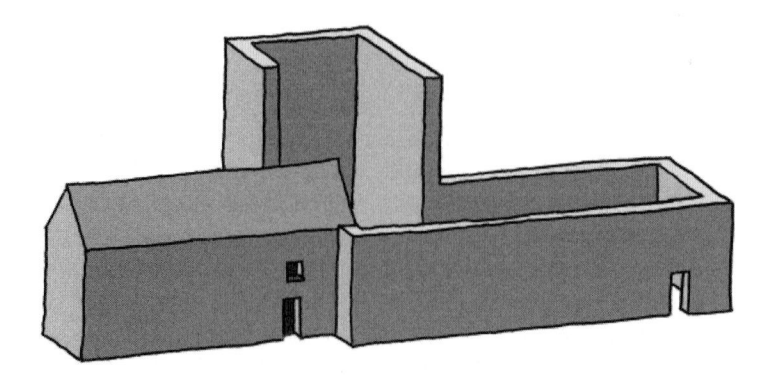

dismantle an existing two-and-a-half-storey, stone wall merely to reuse a one-hundred-year old set of stairs. Could they not have constructed another stairway elsewhere?

One possible explanation for the placement of the kennel may rest with the re-routing of the local roads. Local tradition contends, and the 1760 map confirms, that Tanzyfort House was situated to face the old road to Sligo Town. With the redesign of the demesne in the late 18th century, this road was rerouted to run past the demesne walls rather than through it. People travelling on the main road no longer passed Tanzyfort House. A new road, intended purely for estate use, extended from the main gate, along a tree-lined avenue, across the Unshin River bridge, and looped up to the front steps of the Georgian mansion. This road was located behind Tanzyfort House, but in front of the kennel, which faced the new road. The old road to Sligo simply became one of many roads within the demesne.

This explanation, though useful in part, does not adequately explain why the builders pushed the south, gable-end wall of the kennel through the north wall of Tanzyfort House. After all, they could have built the kennel anywhere on the estate without going to the trouble of having to dismantle part of Tanzyfort House. They had built the walled, formal garden and the farm complex about 80m south-east of the House; they could have built the kennel anywhere in the same area. Fortunately, excavation answered questions about the estate designers' desire to place the kennel through the wall of Tanzyfort House.

EXCAVATION AND INTERPRETATION

Prior to beginning the excavation in 2003, an obvious depression could be observed in front of (west) of the Tanzyfort House ruin. Roughly triangular in shape, its southernmost edge was adjacent to the back wall of the kennel (Fig. 5). Geophysicist Kevin Barton, from Landscape & Geophysical Services and Sligo Institute of Technology, conducted a thorough topographic survey of this area and documented that the depression measured about 25m east-west, about 16m north-south, and was approximately 1m deep. Excavation inside the depression revealed that it contained a large amount of rock rubble and an artefact collection that include a mix of objects that post-date the mid-17th century. The datable artefacts included a lead cloth baling seal reading '[D]UBLIN 1718' and 18th-century Queen's ware pattern creamware. Also present in the same contexts, however, were early 19th-century mocha and annular banded pearlwares. None of the family members currently resident on the estate could recall any excavation in this area of the property, and thus no immediate explanation for the depression could be devised. Excavation inside the Tanzyfort House ruin the following summer, however, provided an explanation for the depression.

While clearing leaf clutter in the ruin at the end of the 2003 field season, excavators discovered a cobble-stone floor inside the projection termed the 'kitchen'. The cobble was compact, uniform, and neatly laid. Clearing the entire surface of the 'kitchen' the following summer revealed that the flooring extended throughout the entire surface of the 'kitchen' floor, and terminated in a broken manner inside the house adjacent to the kennel projection (see Fig. 2). An initial interpretation suggested that the builders of the kennel had destroyed the western edge of the cobbled floor when they were raising the kennel. In other words, the heavy construction required to build the substantial walls of the kennel caused the old

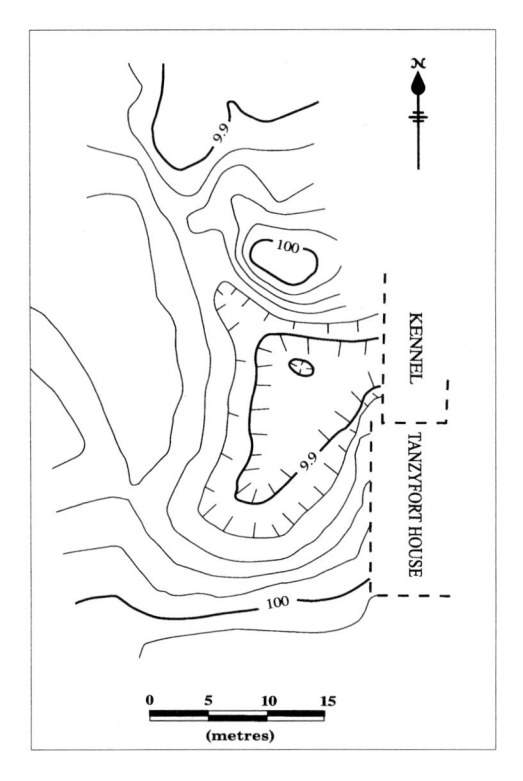

LEFT
Figure 5. Topography of Tanzyfort House yard. (Drawn by C. E. Orser, Jr., adapted from map by Kevin Barton, Landscape & Geophysical Services.)

flooring adjacent to its new walls to be uprooted. Excavation revealed, however, that the cobbles were contemporaneous with the kennel and not with Tanzyfort House.

Beneath the cobbled floor inside Tanzyfort House excavators discovered a two-room cellar. Its walls, like those of the house itself, were lime-plastered. The two rooms were roughly equal in size and were formed by a stone wall running east-west, parallel to the outside walls of the house (see Fig. 2). The northern room measured 2.60m wide and the southern room, 2.56m wide. The length of the two rooms was approximately 5m long. The cellar's length could only be estimated because of the presence of a shed built inside the house ruin, against the interior eastern wall of the 'kitchen'. The wall running north-south, perpendicular to the house walls, was formed of cut stone with only one clean face, that facing the cellar interior. The western wall of the cellar (running parallel to the front wall of the house) appeared to have been built into a clay embankment. The builders of Tanzyfort House had obviously dug the hole for the cellar into the area's natural clay and then constructed the cellar wall against the created berm. The other interior-facing walls of the cellar (the interior dividing wall and the two inside walls of the house) were also lime plastered. Excavation revealed that the two cellar walls were c. 45cm wide and 165cm deep. The floor of the cellar was composed of hard-packed clay, and the cellar walls had been placed directly on the clay surface rather than extending into it. The artefacts inside the cellar were 18th century in date, and the cellar was clearly an original feature of Tanzyfort House.

The discovery of the cellar under the cobbled floor of the 'kitchen' illuminates much about Tanzyfort House. In fact, the key to unravelling the history of the house rests mostly with understanding its post-occupation usage. The presence of the cellar underneath the original floor of the house meant that the reuse of the building's interior required special attention by the designers of the reconstituted estate demesne.

After 1781, when the Coopers moved into their grand Coopershill mansion up the hill, any adaptive reuse of Tanzyfort House meant that the cellar rooms had to be filled to stabilize the area. At some point during the reformulation of the demesne, someone—perhaps Cooper, Bindon, or a family member—must have realized that the 'kitchen' area of the old ruin, which today still resembles the shell of a much-earlier tower house, could function as an enclosed yard for the kennel. They would simply need to fill in the two rooms of the cellar and cover it over with a cobble-stone floor. A shed could then be built against the inside wall of the old house, and the riding equipment needed for hunting could be kept there, near the hounds and the huntsman. Local tradition contends that the huntsman lived in the top floor of the kennel. The dirt needed to fill the cellar could be taken from the front of the old house, because this area was now behind the kennel, out of sight of any visitors to the estate riding up the road to Coopershill House.

To make these changes in and around Tanzyfort House, the builders had to dismantle the front wall of the old house before the cellar could be filled. This procedure makes abundant sense, but why reconstruct the walls of the house after they were finished filling in the cellar? One practical reason might have been simply to hide the excavated depression from visitors. Another more provocative interpretation, however, rests upon taking into account the genteel ideology that was integral to estate design and presentation. From a purely practical standpoint, the Coopers had no need to rebuild the Tanzyfort House ruin. If they wished to hide the deep excavation needed to fill the cellar, they simply could have used soil taken from elsewhere to level the depression, or build a garden wall much like the one they had constructed adjacent to the south wall of the house. Instead, they instructed their builders to perform the difficult task of constructing a wall that now contains an open doorway, one window sealed with stone, one window sealed with brick, and a doorway sealed with stone. The open doorway has a cambered, brick arch, and the sealed windows have brick relieving arches and the sealed doorway has a crenellation above it. These features represent considerable foresight and labour, so why did the owners decide against leaving the house as a dismantled ruin? The most compelling reason for the builders to go through the difficulty represented by the front wall of the house probably rests with their dedication to the evocative power of the Cult of the Ruin.

Many late 18th-century estate owners sought to transform their estate grounds through the introduction of trees, shrubs, hedges, and decorative flowers, and so examples of the science of dendrology abound.[35] For example, from the summer to the spring of 1811-12, Lord Kenmare at Killarney had over 1,200,000 species planted on his estate. His conscious effort to remake a tiny piece of the English landscape in Ireland was expressed florally in that many of the saplings were in fact cuttings from trees then growing in England.[36] Other large landowners followed suit. When visiting Strokestown Park House in County Roscommon, Arthur Young noted in the late 18th century that the trees planted on the estate were 'the finest woods I ever saw'. A bill dated October 1841 substantiates the seriousness of the Strokestown planting programme: the owner of the estate purchased 2,100 trees, shrubs, and seedlings on a single day.[37] As Finola O'Kane demonstrates in rich detail, many elite estate owners took seriously the transformation of their landscapes through the careful use of greenery, both indigenous and imported.[38]

The linkage between carefully-planted estate fields and grand mansions provides a spatial example of the Diderot Effect. The Diderot Effect is a concept scholars of consumption use to explain a people's urge to surround themselves with material things that are basically complementary. According to anthropologist Grant McCracken, individuals acquire material things based on a concept of cultural consistency, so that the individual meanings of the various components create an 'object code' that is contextually uniform.[39] Georgian mansions and consciously-planted yards and fields constitute a cultural consistency that made sense for Ireland's landed gentry.

The Coopers also conscientiously practiced the science of dendrology at Coopershill and experienced the Diderot Effect. By 1802, the 'quality of the grounds' was a recognizably notable feature of the demesne.[40] Receipts for the period 1782-91, just when the estate was being transformed to the height of its Georgian grandeur, indicate that the Coopers purchased hundreds ash, elm, sycamore, oak, fir, pine, beech, yew, and lime for their estate.[41] Records indicate that some of the new vegetation was planted around the Tanzyfort House ruin. But the greenery surrounding Tanzyfort House was only a supporting player to the drama embedded within the creation of the Cult of the Ruin on the estate. The ruin itself had to be refashioned.

When the workers rebuilt the first storey of the west wall of Tanzyfort House they put a vertical stone coping on its top surface. This simple decorative treatment, in addition to the decorative window and door treatments over the sealed openings, transmitted their plan to recreate the house as ritual ground dedicated to the Cult of the Ruin. Their goal was to remake the house into 'calcified ritual',[42] to reproduce the house as part of a programme of spatial architectonics[43] that encompassed all elements of the reconstituted landscape around their Georgian mansion. The bridge, the walled formal garden, the farm buildings, the kennel - all built of solid stone - and the roads and the yards were all carefully included as part of an integrated whole that would be greater then its individual parts.

Clearly, one goal of the Coopershill Estate architects in transforming the vernacular Lisbrislan-Tanzyfort property was to create a picturesque and romantic image. The Tanzyfort ruin constituted an important example of the 'dialectics of decay'[44] within this recreated landscape. Their ultimate goal was to employ the ruin to promote a sense of antiquity and continuity on the estate. They could effectively use the introduced trees, shrubs, and bushes along with the conspicuously unplanted fields to facilitate a sense of growth, regeneration, and expansive space. The introduction of hundreds of new plants helped to mediate between present and future. In the present, the greenery evinced the Coopers' ability to purchase such non-essentials; as growing, living things, the plants also predicted the Cooper's future presence on the land. Both assessments were correct. The Coopers, though occasionally beset with financial difficulties like many of their fellow estate owners, did have the economic capital needed to purchase plants, many of which were exotic for Ireland. Equally significant, many of these plants continue to grow on the estate today. The demesne today does not retain its late 18th-century size, but it continues to constitute a sizable, grand space, much of which is still notable for its floral beauty.

The ability to demonstrate financial wealth in the present and the luxury to look optimistically to the future was only two-thirds of the landed gentry's temporal worldview. To be truly successful, they also had to look to the past, to be mindful of the years that had gone before. Settlers living in locales their ancestors had not indigenously occupied often discovered that they had to create a sense of their own history. On the reinvented Coopershill Estate, the Tanzyfort House ruin could perfectly serve the needs of providing a sense of nostalgic antiquity, longevity, and temporal stability.

The use of antiquity to express such qualities on the estates of the gentry extended at least to the early 18th century, when playwright-turned-architect John Vanbrugh expressed the symbolic advantage of preserving ancient buildings on the demesnes of the gentry. He noted that some buildings have the ability to provide 'more lively and pleasing Reflections (than History without their Aid can do) On the Persons who have inhabited them.' He believed that structures with historical durability have the power to evoke the 'Remarkable things' that had occurred in them and the 'extraordinary Occasions' involved in their erection.[45] In cases where history 'Stands in need of Assistance' it was perfectly acceptable for architects to rely on their refined sensibilities and to construct historically evocative ruins on an estate. In keeping with this idea, architects ordered both the careful renovation of existing buildings and the construction of sham ruins. The earliest sham ruins in Ireland appeared in 1724 at Castle Ward in County Down.[46] Other examples appear throughout the countryside, including at Strokestown Park House in County Roscommon, where a 'medieval church' was constructed some distance behind the house but in view from the ballroom's bay windows. An especially pertinent example of a sham construction appears at Glin Castle in County Limerick. Architects here built walls of completely fabricated castles complete with crenelations. To instil historicity to the structure, the builders blocked the windows in the new walls with stones to imply long reuse over time.[47] The men who rebuilt the front wall of Tanzyfort House used the same technique, though in both stone and brick.[48] The appearance of the two materials implied a long history for the structure, and materially expressed the 'social life of ruins'.[49]

CONCLUSION

The late 18th-century transformation of Tanzyfort House in Count Sligo, Ireland, provides a useful case study of the intertwined aspects of landscape practicality and symbolic practice. In many cases archaeologists investigating landscape meaning have no need to excavate the places they study. Standing ruins and relict landscape features can often provide information abundant enough for analysis and interpretation. At Tanzyfort House, however, the lack of excavation would never have provided clues to its transformational history. First built within a landscape that had been contested by colonialism and conquest, Tanzyfort House was relatively simple in design, but functional and different enough from the surrounding countryside to transmit important messages about the Cooper family's presence in the area.

Its stone walls and roofing tiles, chimneys, and named fields worked in concert to promote the house and its inhabitants as tenacious residents of the region. By the late 18th century, when other large landowners throughout Ireland were remaking their estate landscapes, the quasi-vernacular character of Tanzyfort House was no longer adequate. To maintain their social position and to publicize their standing, the Coopers had to have a new dwelling, a grand Georgian mansion constructed on a hill. As this house was being raised, the Diderot Effect took over, and the rest of the estate had to be remade as well to conform to the genteel effect of the new mansion. Part of the refashioning process involved Tanzyfort House.

The transformation of Tanzyfort House from a useless, old ruin to a nostalgic, meaningful expression of longevity involved rebuilding its front wall. The new front wall would be designed in an almost purely decorative manner with coping stones and sealed openings. The decorative treatments stated the symbolic associations between social standing and landscape presentation. As important as Tanzyfort House was within the ideological structure of the Cult of the Ruin, it was never merely decorative. The house always retained a functional element, even as it was reconstituted. The location of the kennel, through the wall of the house, meant that late 18th- and 19th-century huntsmen could use its interior as a starting point for their genteel, country activities. The conflation of elite social practice and inanimate space also served the needs of the symbolic reinvention of the Coopershill Estate.

ACKNOWLEDGEMENTS

The research reported here was conducted during the terms of excavation licence 03E0925 granted by the National Monuments Section of the Heritage and Planning Division of the Department of the Environment, Heritage, and Local Government.
We deeply appreciate the kindness shown during the course of this research by Brian O'Hara and Lindy O'Hara (owners of Coopershill House), and Tim O'Hara, Jane O'Hara, and Mark O'Hara (owners of Tanzyfort House). We also acknowledge the warm support of the dedicated men and women of Sligo Folk Park in Riverstown, including Hugh and Doreen Kelly, John Taylor, Michael Tuohy, and Paul Quinn. Others who assisted by offering advice or ideas were Kevin Barton, Colm Donnelly, Norman Hammond, Matthew Johnson, Derek Warfield, Eamon Grennan, Kieran O'Conor, Elizabeth Scott, and Donald Heldman. We also thank Janice Orser, Stephen Brighton, Katherine Hull, Michelle Charest, Julie Richko, and all the students who participated in the excavations.

NOTES

1. Monks 1992; Johnson 1993.
2. Johnson 1993, 180.
3. Dickson 2000, 22.
4. Reeves-Smyth 1997a, 549.
5. Orser 2005, 394-6.
6. Aalen 1989, 108.
7. Busteed 2000, 20.
8. Malins & Bowe 1980; Reeves-Smyth 1997b, 205.
9. Coopers of Markree 1935.
10. O'Rorke 1878, 152; O'Dowd 1991, 103.
11. O'Rorke 1890, I, 17; McTernan 1994, 17, 2000, 63-4.
12. Charest 2005, 87.
13. Cooper Papers, D.4031/B/1.
14. Cooper Papers, D.4031/A/1.
15. MacBain 1982; Charest 2005, 107.
16. Crofton Croker 1824, 80.
17. Tanzyfort House is shown near the road in Taylor 1783, 64.

18. See Orser 2006, 26.
19. Gailey 1987, 91-2.
20. Craig 1982, 129-33.
21. Craig 1976, 56; MacLysaght 1969, 96; Waterman 1961, 273.
22. Leask 1961, 246.
23. McParlan 1802, 8; O'Rorke 1890, II, 253; Collins 1993, 368.
24. Lefebvre 1991, 38-9.
25. After Sluyter 2002.
26. Orser 2006, 29.
27. Banks 1928, 333-50.
28. Johnson 1996, 92, 2007, 14; Spencer 1973, 58.
29. Orser 2006.
30. Connolly 1992, 63.
31. McConville 2001, 126.
32. Barnard 2004, 247.
33. Trench 1997, 83.
34. Wood-Martin 1892, 388.
35. O'Kane 2004.
36. Malins & Knight of Glin 1976, 190.
37. Young 1780, 184; Orser 1996, 149.
38. O'Kane 2004.
39. McCracken 1990, 118-29; Orser 2004, 169.
40. McParlan 1802, 8.
41. Cooper Papers, D.4031/E/7.
42. After Comer 1996, 22.
43. After Lefebvre 1991, 169-228.
44. Lang 1997.
45. Hunt &Willis 1975, 120-21.
46. Howley 1993, 106.
47. Ibid, 110.
48. Orser 2006, 30.
49. McGregor 2005.

BIBLIOGRAPHY

Aalen, F. 1989, 'Imprint of the past', in Gillmor (ed.) 1989, 83-119.
Aalen, F. H. A., Whelan & Stout (eds) 1997, *Atlas of the Irish Rural Landscape*, Cork: Cork University Press.
Banks, T. H. (ed.) 1928, *The Poetical Works of Sir John Denham*, New Haven: Yale University Press.
Barnard, T. 2004, *Making the Grand Figure: Lives and Possessions in Ireland, 1641-1770*, New Haven: Yale University Press.
Busteed, M. 2000, 'The practice of improvement in the Irish context: the Castle Caldwell estate in County Fermanagh in the second half of the eighteenth century', *Irish Geography* 33, 15-36.
Collins, A. (ed.) 1993, *Fodor's 93 Ireland*, New York: Fodor's Travel.
Comer, D. C. 1996, *Ritual Ground: Bent's Old Fort, World Formation, and the Annexation of the Southwest*, Berkeley: University of California Press.
Connolly, S. J. 1992, *Religion, Law, and Power: The Making of Protestant Ireland, 1660-1760*, Oxford: Clarendon.
Craig, M. 1976, *Classic Irish Houses of the Middle Size*, London: Architectural Press.
Craig, M. 1982, *The Architecture of Ireland from the Earliest Times to 1880*, London: B. T. Batsford.
Crofton Croker, T. 1824, *Researches in the South of Ireland*, London: John Murray.
Dickson, D. 2000, *New Foundations: Ireland, 1660-1800*, 2nd ed. Dublin: Irish Academic Press.
Foster, J. W. (ed.) 1997, *Nature in Ireland: A Scientific and Cultural History*, Dublin: Lilliput Press.
Gailey, A. 1987, 'Changes in Irish rural housing, 1600-1900,' in O'Flanagan, Ferguson & Whelan (eds) 1987, 86-103.
Gillmor, D. (ed.) 1989, *The Irish Countryside: Landscape, Wildlife, History, People*, Dublin: Wolfhound Press.
Howley, J. 1993, *The Follies and Garden Buildings of Ireland*, New Haven: Yale University Press.
Hunt, J. D. & Willis, P. (eds) 1975, *The Genius of the Place: The English Landscape Garden, 1620-1820*, London: Paul Elek.
Johnson, M. 1993, *Housing Culture: Traditional Architecture in an English Landscape*, Washington, D.C.: Smithsonian Institution Press.
Johnson, M. 1996, *An Archaeology of Capitalism*, Oxford: Blackwell.
Johnson, M. 2007, *Ideas of Landscape*. Malden, MA: Blackwell.
Jope, E. M. (ed.) 1961, *Studies in Building History: Essays in Recognition of the Work of B. H. St. J. O'Neil*, London: Odhams Press.
Lang, K. 1997, 'The dialectics of decay: rereading the Kantian subject', *Art Bulletin* 79, 413-439.

Leask, H. G. 1961, 'Early seventeenth-century houses in Ireland,' in Jope (ed.) 1961, 243-50.
Lefebvre, H. 1991, *The Production of Space*, D. Nicholson-Smith (trans.). Oxford: Blackwell.
MacBain, A. 1982, *An Etymological Dictionary of the Gaelic Language*, Glasgow: Gairm Publishers. <http://www.ceantar.org/Dicts/MB2/mb05.html#brisg> accessed January 2006.
MacLysaght, E. 1969, *Irish Life in the Seventeenth Century*, 2nd ed., Shannon: Irish University Press.
McConville, M. 2001, *Ascendancy to Oblivion: The Story of the Anglo-Irish*, London: Phoenix Press.
McCracken, G. 1990, *Culture and Consumption: New Approaches to the Symbolic Character of Consumer Goods and Activities*, Bloomington: Indiana University Press.
McGregor, J. 2005, ' The social life of ruins: sites of memory and the politics of a Zimbabwean periphery', *Journal of Historical Geography* 31: 316-37.
McParlan, J. 1802, *Statistical Survey of the County of Sligo with Observations on the Means of Improvement: Drawn up in the Year 1801, for the Consideration, and Under the Direction of the Dublin Society*, Dublin: Graisberry & Campbell.
McTernan, J. C. (ed.) 1994, *Sligo: Sources of Local History*, New ed., Sligo: Sligo County Library.
McTernan, J. C. (ed.) 2000, *A Sligo Miscellany: A Chronicle of People, Places, and Events of Other Days*, Sligo: Avena.
Malins, E. & The Knight of Glin, 1976, *Lost Demesnes: Irish Landscape Gardening, 1660-1845*, London: Barrie & Jenkins.
Malins, E. & Bowe, P. 1980, *Irish Gardens and Demesnes from 1830*, New York: Rizzoli.
Monks, G. G. 1992, 'Architectural symbolism and non-verbal communication at Upper Fort Garry', *Historical Archaeology* 26:2, 37-57.
O'Dowd, M. 1991, *Power, Politics, and Land: Early Modern Sligo, 1568-1688*, Belfast: Institute of Irish Studies, Queen's University.
O'Flanagan, P., Ferguson, P. & Whelan, K. (eds) 1987, *Rural Ireland, 1600-1900: Modernisation and Change*, Cork: Cork University Press.
O'Kane, F. 2004, *Landscape Design in Eighteenth-Century Ireland: Mixing Foreign Trees with the Natives*, Cork: Cork University Press.
O'Rorke, T. 1878, *History, Antiquities, and Present State of the Parishes of Ballysadare and Kilvarnet, in the County of Sligo*, Dublin: James Duffy & Sons.
O'Rorke, T. 1890, *The History of Sligo: Town and County*, 2 vols., Dublin: James Duffy & Sons.
Orser, C. E., Jr. 1996, *A Historical Archaeology of the Modern World*, New York: Plenum.
Orser, C. E., Jr. 2004, *Race and Practice in Archaeological Interpretation*, Philadelphia: University of Pennsylvania Press.
Orser, C. E., Jr. 2005, 'Symbolic violence, resistance and the vectors of improvement in early nineteenth-century Ireland', *World Archaeology* 37: 392-407.
Orser, C. E., Jr. 2006. 'Symbolic violence and landscape pedagogy: an illustration from the Irish countryside.' *Historical Archaeology* 40:2, 20-36.
Reeves-Symth, T. 1997a, 'The natural history of demesnes', in Foster (ed.) 1997, 549-72.
Reeves-Symth, T. 1997b, 'Demesnes', in Aalen, Whelan & Stout (eds) 1997, 197-205.
Sluyter, A. 2002, *Colonialism and Landscape: Postcolonial Theory and Applications*, Lanham, MD: Rowman & Littlefield.
Spencer, J. B. 1973, *Heroic Nature: Ideal Landscapes in English Poetry from Marvell to Thomson*, Evanston: Northwestern University Press.
Taylor, G. 1783, *Taylor and Skinner's Maps of the Roads of Ireland, Surveyed in 1777 and Corrected Down to 1783*, 2nd ed., London: T. Longman.
Trench, C. C. 1997, *Grace's Card: Irish Catholic Landlords, 1690-1800*, Cork: Mercier.
Waterman, D. M. 1961, 'Some Irish seventeenth-century houses and their architectural ancestry,' in Jope (ed.) 1961, 251-74.
Wood-Martin, W. G. 1892, *History of Sligo, County and Town, Volume III*, Dublin: Hodges, Figgis.
Young, A. 1780, *A Tour of Ireland with General Observations on the Present State of That Kingdom made in the Years 1776, 1777, and 1778*, London: T. Cadell & J. Dodsley.

UNPUBLISHED SOURCES

Charest, M. 2005, 'Faded Receipts and Buried Walls: A Historical Archaeological Investigation of the Material Culture and Identity of the Cooper Family of Riverstown, County Sligo, Ireland', Unpublished master's thesis, Illinois State University, Normal.

Coopers of Markree. 1935, Cooper's of Markree: Sketch of Family History. Unpublished mss., Item 230. Sligo Folk Park, Riverstown.

Cooper Papers. Coopershill House, Riverstown, County Sligo, Ireland.

'Animated Prospect' – An 18th-century Kiln at 'the Pottery House in the Old Park', Dunster, Somerset

By DAVID DAWSON & OLIVER KENT

Henry Fownes Luttrell was one those 18th-century landowners for whom populating the landscape with temples, ornamental bridges, grottoes and other follies provided a scene too tranquil to his taste. Archaeological evidence from Dunster suggests that he sought to 'animate' the prospect from Dunster Castle by building a pottery works as an integral part of his scheme. The investigation of the kiln from this pottery, recently purchased and repaired by Exmoor National Park, and probably the earliest surviving substantially intact pottery kiln in Britain, is the central subject of this paper.

INTRODUCTION

The town of Dunster lies 3.3km. south-east of the seaside resort and harbour of Minehead and 1.4km. from the present coastline. It is situated on rising ground where the foothills of Exmoor meet the coastal plain (Fig. 1). At the foot of the town on its own prominent hill known as the Tor and overlooking the valley of the river Avill is Dunster Castle. The view of the castle across the Old Park from the railway and modern road (A39) is still used in tourism advertising as an icon of the romantic landscape of west Somerset. The lime-washed pottery kiln can be glimpsed on the right hand of this classic view, partially concealed by vegetation.

The kiln is situated at SS99244385 on the crest of a knoll, 44m. above OS datum, and to the rear of the Luttrell Arms Hotel formerly a town house of the abbots of Cleeve. The plot of land on which the kiln stands adjoins and overlooks the Old Park and appears to have been dug away on the north to accommodate the later 19th-century outbuildings of the hotel leaving the kiln perched on top of a retaining wall. Nothing survives above ground of any other buildings associated with the pottery. The ground around the kiln seems to have been raised by about 0.75m. at some time after these buildings were removed, burying the lower part of the kiln including the firebox openings.

In 1989, this structure was inspected at the request of the local historian, Hilary Binding, and the authors were able to confirm its identification as a pottery kiln. It is marked as 'Old Pottery Kiln' on the 1888 (with additions in 1938) 6 inch to the mile OS sheet XXXV SW. It is reported in 1894 as a 'very ancient and rather ruinous kiln, called

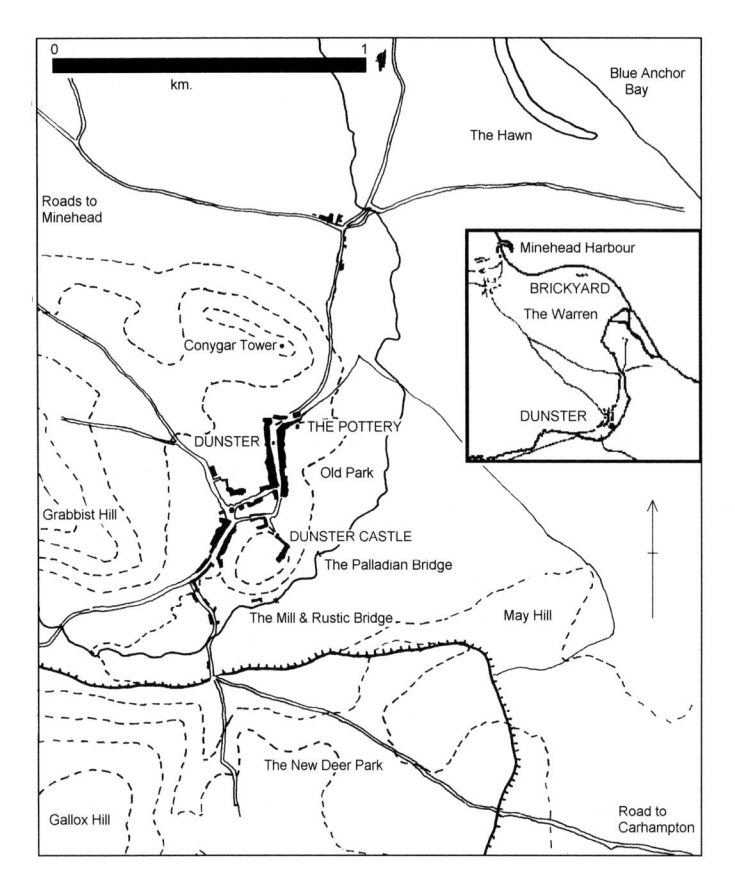

LEFT
Figure 1. Location map
(David & Tim Dawson).

locally the "bell house".'[1] To understand what kind of kiln it was, Trust House Forte kindly gave permission for the ivy and brambles to be cleared, the standing structure to be surveyed and the western half of the floor to be excavated to reveal one firebox and half the under floor structure. Following the purchase of the kiln by Exmoor National Park and during its repair over the winter and spring of 1999/2000, the eastern half of the substructure was also excavated. No attempt was made to remove build-up outside the kiln or to locate the pottery buildings.

THE POTTERY HOUSE IN THE OLD PARK

The conclusion that the pottery was unusual in its conception was prompted by its location. It is situated on a knoll south of the old road that once led from the high end of the town to Dunster Hawn, the former haven for Dunster, and to the Warren, an area of flat ill-drained land between the Hawn and Minehead. By the 18th century, the Hawn was long separated from the sea by a bar of shingle and its function replaced by a more sheltered harbour protected by a 17th-century breakwater at the foot of Bowhead Hill at Minehead.[2] The knoll is not an appropriate location to secure ease of access to any of the raw materials required in pottery-making, particularly water, clay and fuel. There is no readily available source of water on the site. Coal would have had to be carted up from Minehead harbour. Clay in the form of red-firing clays from the Mercia mudstones was in plentiful supply from the pits of the estate brickyard at the Warren (now the site of Butlins) but again had to be carted up hill to the pottery. It has been suggested that there was an intention in 1758 to establish the pottery at this much more convenient location on the coastal plain. However the estate papers make it clear that in 1759 work started on building the pottery on its knoll in full view of the castle (Fig. 2).

The concept is admirably recorded in the panoramic painting commissioned from William Tomkins in 1768.[3] This prospect of the town, castle and park from the south-east currently hangs on the main staircase of the present castle. It depicts the castle, since remodelled by Anthony Salvin in 1868-1872 to make it appear even more romantic, in its strikingly prominent situation facing down the valley of the river Avill and beyond up the Bristol Channel towards Steep Holm. May Hill encloses the scene to the east and the singular outline of Conygar Hill to the west. The pottery house (Fig. 3) lies in almost direct line of sight from the castle to the tower on Conygar Hill. Today, the dog-toothed rim of the kiln seemingly echoes the crenellated parapet of the tower.

The historical context is much illuminated by the survival of the meticulous accounts insisted on of his agent, George Gale, by Henry Fownes Lutterell.[4] Henry Fownes had acquired the name and estates of the Luttrells by marriage in 1747 to his cousin, Margaret, on condition that he was resident at Dunster for at least six months of every year.[5] He set about improving the estate by employing the artist, Richard Phelps, to remodel the landscape round the house, starting with levelling part of the Tor (the castle motte) for a bowling green. The succession of works that followed included the Pottery House in the Old Deer Park in 1759, the tower on Conygar Hill, completed in 1770, the remodelling of the bridge over the Avill in 1774, the creation of the New Deer Park stocked from Marshwood in 1775 and the repair and remodelling of the grist mill from 1779 to 1782. The degree of Henry Fownes's personal involvement is indicated in a letter from George Gale of 15 June 1779 concerning the rebuilding of the mill and insisting that, 'The Mill and houses being

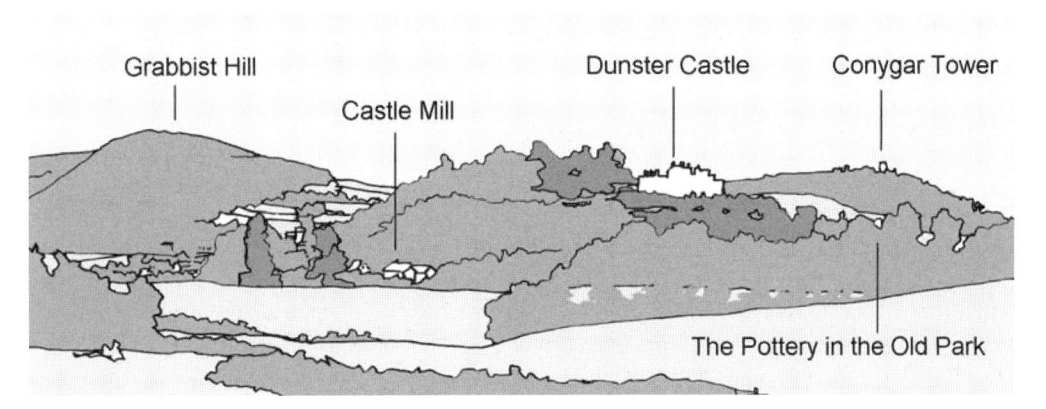

Figure 2. Panorama of the castle from the New Deer Park in 2003 (Oliver Kent).

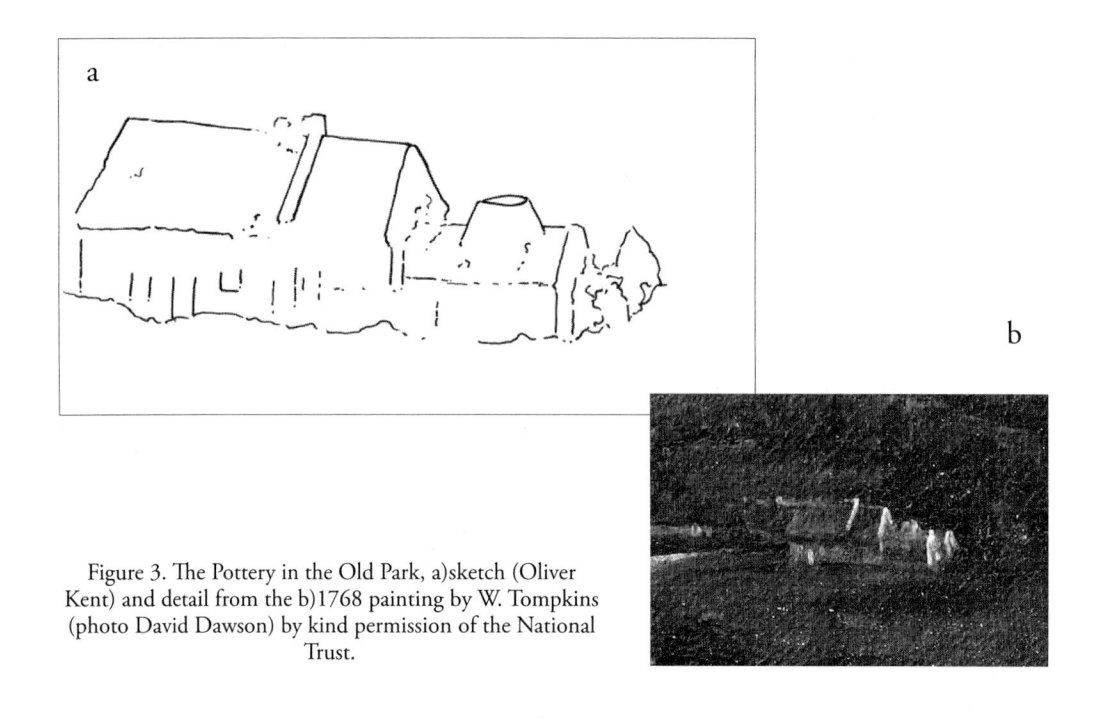

Figure 3. The Pottery in the Old Park, a) sketch (Oliver Kent) and detail from the b) 1768 painting by W. Tompkins (photo David Dawson) by kind permission of the National Trust.

in full view of the Park &c. is the reason Mr. L. expects any alterations made shall be done uniform & therefore ..... it be agreeable to his liking.'[6]

A pottery might seem to be an odd choice of structure to incorporate in the landscape programme. George Gale's meticulous accounts faithfully record what happened but not why. It can be conjectured that building the pottery on that site would offer the opportunity of adding the dramatic element of fire to a prospect with a superabundance of the other three elements of air, earth and water. Perhaps Luttrell envisaged the evening flickering glow of flame from the top of the kiln in its weekly firing adding to the movement of the stately procession of lights from shipping in the Bristol Channel. Was it perhaps a precocious example of the later 18th-century awakening to the visual excitement that fire and industry offered as portrayed in the work of painters such as Joseph Wright of Derby[7] and Philippe Jacques de Loutherbourg?[8] Horace Walpole in his *Essay on Modern Gardening* of 1785 notes that: 'Men tire of experience that is obvious to few spectators……. The Doric portico, the Palladian Bridge, the Gothic Ruin, the Chinese Pagoda, that surprise the stranger, soon lose their charms to their surfeited master…. Prospect, animated prospect, is the theatre that will always be the most frequented'.[9] The pottery is evidence that a person of substance like Henry Fownes Luttrell, who is known to have been a man of the new age, could appreciate industrial activity as an essential element of the 'picturesque' and 'sublime'.[10]

There is a further piece of evidence that the kiln was appreciated as a landscape feature. As will be discussed below the pottery went out of use by the time that Salvin's rebuilding of the castle started in 1868. Whilst the Pottery House was cleared away, the kiln was left standing in full view from the principal rooms on the east side of the remodelled castle. It remained in use doubling up as a place for storing the hotel's garden furniture and as an ornament to the park until 1989.

DESCRIPTION OF THE KILN

The kiln, a simple updraught kiln, is substantially complete (Fig. 4). It consists of a substructure with two fireboxes and a domed ware chamber supporting a squat conical structure that performs the function of a chimney. The substructure and ware chamber are contained within a cylindrical structure 3m. in diameter and 3m. high built of local sandstone rubble and lined with local red brick. The walls are 0.9m. thick. The doorway, also lined in brick, is 1.26m. wide but the sill has been cut away to create a full height of 1.69m. The ware chamber is vaulted in local red brick laid end-on in concentric courses to form a low segmental dome. Holes to create the updraught have been left by omitting individual bricks. The original ware chamber floor appears to have been removed when the doorway was lowered to the present external ground-level and a new floor of beaten earth laid upon potsherds and broken roof tiles infilling the substructure. This was excavated to reveal two arched fireboxes on opposite sides of the kiln and a substructure of three roughly circular concentric flues of brick to distribute the heat under the original floor (Fig. 4). The firebox on the western side had been filled a mixture of rubble and transfer-printed wares and blocked from the outside by several layers of zigzag Bridgwater roof-tiles lent over the fire mouth. The firebox on the eastern side had been bricked up to the thickness of the wall. One firebar, a simple bar of wrought iron survived *in situ* in this firebox though badly distorted. This has been identified as part of a flattened out wheel strake. A meltdown of the flue brickwork, so severe that it probably happened during the last firing, had blocked the openings of the flues on the north side of the lefthand (west) firebox.

Surmounting the ware chamber is a partly ruined brick cone or chimney. It survives to a height of 1 5 m. but was probably about 2m. tall when first built. It is built of local brick horizontally laid and corbelled in. Four arched openings give access to the interior of the cone so that the draw of heat through the holes in the vault of the ware chamber could be adjusted during the firing. It was clear that the whole of the outside of the chimney had been rendered and finished.

Weathering for a pitched roof survives in the kiln wall above both fireboxes indicating the kiln was set in a single storey building to project slightly more on the south side to allow clear access to the door.

THE FINDS

The finds are deposited with Somerset County Museums Service and can be studied citing accession numbers 42/1989 and 68/2000. They all derive from the infill of the substructure and fall into three broad categories: 1) ware produced on the site, mostly recovered from the infill of the flues; 2) broken roof-tile and debris such as clinker and clay pipes, all used to infill the flues and the eastern firebox; 3) transfer-printed ware and other ceramics from the filling of the western firebox.

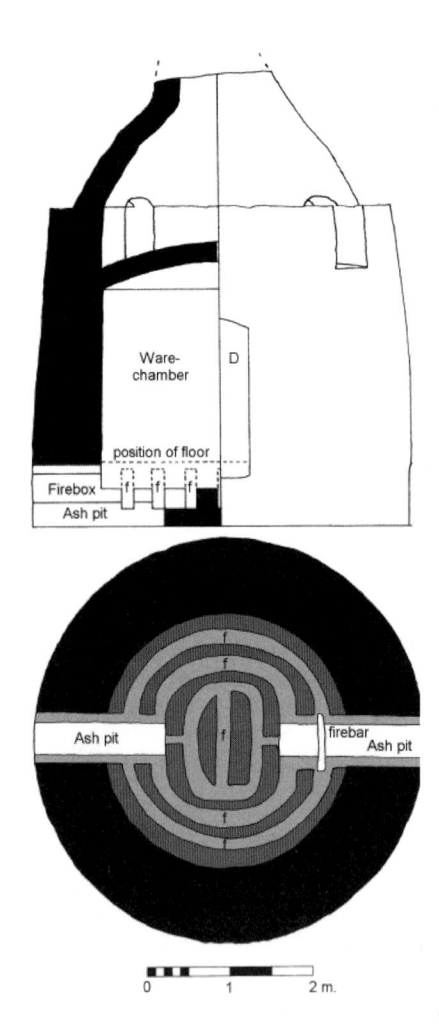

LEFT
Figure 4. Section and plan of the kiln: D = doorway, f = flue (David and Tim Dawson).

1. Wares produced on site

A small proportion of the ware found was green and covered with pink unfired lead glaze. Other vessels were severely under-fired and crumbly to the touch. This material is rarely found amongst kiln waste and its survival suggests that it was shovelled in when the pottery workshops were being cleared and survives because the environment in which it is buried has remained roofed and well drained. The presence of such raw and under-fired glazed material, which under normal conditions of burial would break down, may explain the high incidence of free lead on so many kiln sites. Slightly fewer than 40% of the sherds were waste for other reasons – over-firing, breakages, etc. It is reasonable to assume that all were made on this particular site.

The fabric is a sandy red in its soft-fired oxidised state tending to hard gritty buff its reoxidised state. The plain lead glaze fires brown oxidised to dark green reoxidised.[11] The

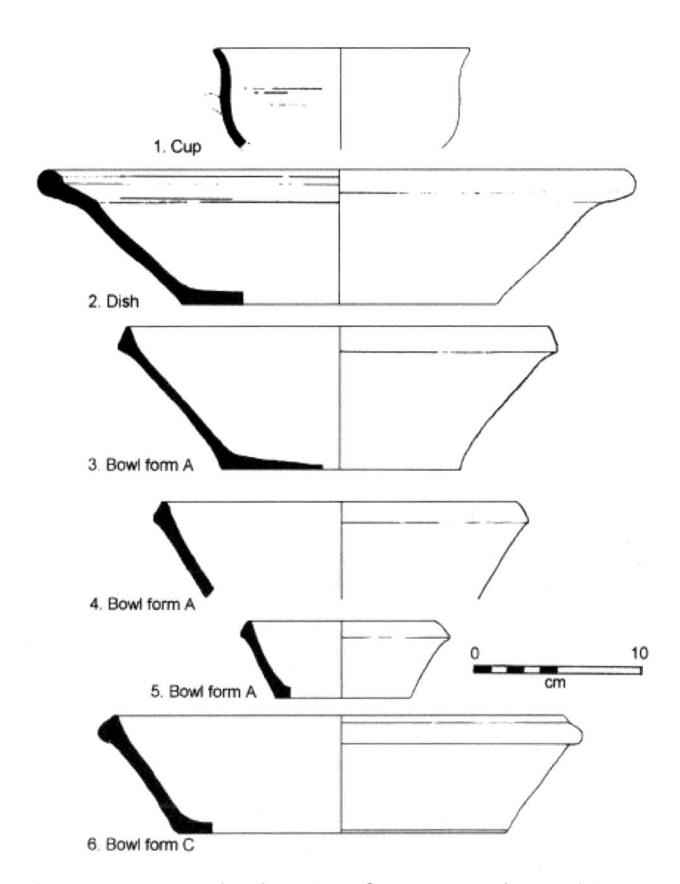

RIGHT
Figure 5. Wares produced on the site, numbers 1-6.© the authors

clay most probably derives from the extensive nearby deposits of Mercia mudstone (Keuper Marl) and alluvial clays. The glaze is applied to the inside of the ware and wiped off at the rim unless otherwise stated.

Forms have been drawn where it has been possible to reconstruct them.

Jugs

The evidence is extremely fragmentary. The rim and pulled spout compares with the normal 18th-century North Devon form.[12] A minimum of seven handles survive. All have been pulled on the pot with a central thumbed groove.

Cups (Fig. 5.1): minimum two, maximum four vessels.

Stubs of small pulled handles and projecting foot, compare the form of Bristol yellowware double-handled cups.[13]

Dish (Fig. 5.2): maximum and minimum of four vessels.

Bowl form A – a distinctive group.

Three sizes are represented: large (Fig. 5.3) one vessel, medium (Fig. 5.4) one vessel and small (Fig. 5.5) one vessel.

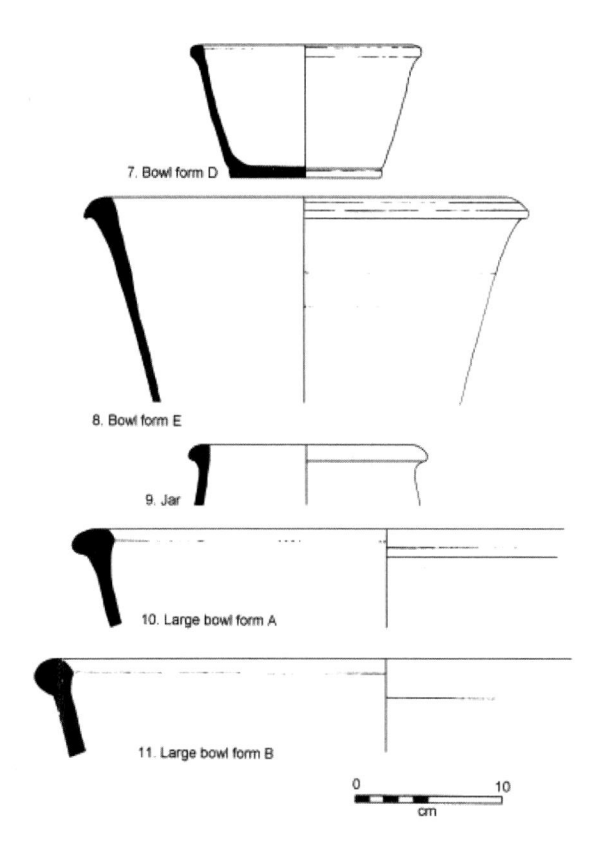

LEFT
Figure 6. Wares produced on the site, numbers 7-11. © the authors

Bowl form B: minimum two, maximum three vessels – rim form similar to C.
Bowl form C (Fig. 5.6): minimum four, maximum seven vessels.
Bowl form D (Fig. 6.7): minimum five, maximum seven vessels.
Bowl form E (Fig. 6.8): minimum five, maximum eight vessels.
Jar (Fig. 6.9): one vessel.
Large bowl form A – hammer-headed (Fig. 6.10): minimum seven: maximum eleven vessels.
Large bowl form B – rounded rim (Fig. 6.11): one vessel.
Large bowl form C – rounded rim with pouring spout (Fig. 7.12): one vessel.
Very large bowl (Fig. 7.13): minimum four, maximum five vessels.
The rim is reinforced with an applied strip. The thumb-marks are rather hesitant compared with similar wares from elsewhere in Somerset. There are two sizes of vessel represented.
In addition, there are two complete plus a minimum of two or a maximum of four lug handles which may be associated with this form. They have been pulled on the pot and applied tightly to the side of the vessel (Fig. 7.14).
Corners of an unidentified four-sided vessel (Fig. 7.15): Five survive.

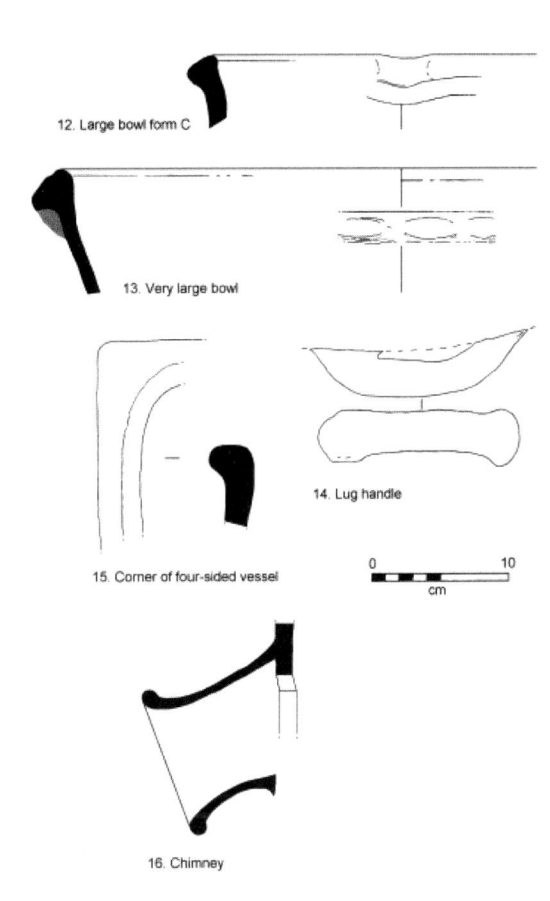

RIGHT
Figure 7. Wares produced on the site, numbers 12-16. © the authors

- 12. Large bowl form C
- 13. Very large bowl
- 14. Lug handle
- 15. Corner of four-sided vessel
- 16. Chimney

2. Building debris

Roof-tiles

Both broken flat tiles and pantiles were used in the filling of the substructure. Most were weathered and appear to have been available from the dismantling of the adjoining pottery buildings. The breaks are unworn and shapes irregular as if freshly broken. Some fragments of both types of tile show glaze dribbles and the occasional scar as evidence of their use as kiln furniture.

Chimneys (Fig. 7.15)

Some sherds have been used as kiln setters with one sherd having the clear scar and shadow of the rim of a small 70mm. diameter cup. The form is very fragmentary. To a thrown probably tapering cylinder, thrown cylindrical vents have been applied at an angle to improve the updraught.[14] So similar is the fabric to the rest of the wares, there remains a possibility that the chimneys were also made on this site rather than at the brickyard down in the marsh.

3. Transfer-printed and other wares

The blocking of the west firebox is discreet from the filling of the rest of the substructure and may be slightly later. Three pieces of transfer-printed ware are marked: one impressed PHILLIPS LONGPORT and a Staffordshire knot, a mark used from 1834 until the firm closed in 1848; a blue transfer print SPODE used from 1805 and possibly after the sale of the company to Copeland and Garrett in 1833; and COPELAND & GARRETT, late SPODE, used in the period 1833 to 1847.[15] The complete assemblage also includes Mocha, Bristol slipware and Somerset trailed slipware.

THE CONSTRUCTION OF THE KILN

There is no direct archaeological evidence to date the construction of the kiln. The location, outline and appearance of the present structure so well matches the kiln with a conical chimney projecting from a low single-storey building depicted on the Tomkins painting of 1768 that it is reasonable to assume that the kiln has survived from that date. Further the estate papers deposited the Somerset Record Office (DD/L) by the Luttrell family provide detailed information about this kiln and its pottery, particularly its inception. References in the general account tally with a remarkable document entitled, 'Pottery Account Current' and endorsed, 'G Gales Acct of the Pottery Settled 4th Nov: 1763' (transcribed as Appendix 1). It is a remarkably complete account of the commission agreed with Ruth Mogg from 1759 to the death of her husband, John, in November 1760. The couple had evidently responded to an advertisement placed in the *Western Flying Post* for 5th February, 1759:

> 'Wanted, At a New Yard set up near Minehead in Somerset, a Person that understands making and burning (with Welch Coals) Bricks, Tyles, and other Goods, and can undertake the whole Management of a Brick and Tyle Yard. Also a good Hand for making Panty'e. And Also is wanted, a person that can undertake making and burning of all sorts of Coarse Pottery Ware. Any sober Person, well qualified for either of the said business, and who can produce a good Character, shall have confident Employ, and great Encouragement - Application may be made to George Gale, at Dunster in the said County.'[16]

The advertisement clearly refers to two distinct businesses: the estate brickyard in the Warren and the pottery. From the payment in September 1759 to Francis Strong for carpentry work 'about the Pottery House in the Old Park, Dunster' it is clear that these businesses were located in two different places. Work on the pottery seems to have been started by James Saunders 'the potter' who received payments in May 1759 for 'work done by himself & Man.' Apart from the carpentry work paid for in September and November 1759, there were payments for 'Lyme used in Building the Kiln, etc.' in November 1759 and for mason's work 'about Building the Kiln' and blacksmith's work 'done for the Pottery' in September 1760. In the general accounts are references to payments made on January 3 1760 for sawing 'board for flooring the Pottery House in the Park' and March 27 for 'Drawing 100 rope of Stones from Coniger for building the Pottery Kiln & House'.[17] In the final reckoning in December 1760, John and Ruth Mogg are credited for '15 days Work directing & helping put the House & things in Order to go forward Work' and for 'loss time afterwards in directing the Masons about Building the Kiln – and for preparing the clay & making Arches to go round the bottom of the Kiln – and repairing the bottom of the Kiln 3 times.' Some of the payments may have been made in retrospect for the pottery seems to have been in production by November 1759 when there is a record of 'making goods for burning in the first kiln.'

Taken all the evidence together, we seem to have a new project, the Pottery House in the Old Park, started by James Saunders early in 1759 but substantially designed and built under the supervision of John and Ruth Mogg of Bristol using the resources that the estate could command.

THE END OF THE POTTERY

The archaeological evidence for the date the kiln was taken out of use consists of two phases. The considerable amounts of green and waste pottery as well as building debris used in filling the substructure and lowering the floor and threshold of the door suggests a rapid change probably involving the clearance and demolition of the rest of the pottery buildings. No diagnostic material could be found that could suggest a more refined date than the first half of the 19th century. The blocking of the west firebox was distinct from this activity and was characterised by the use of dark soil and a quantity of Staffordshire wares. The marks on these wares indicate that this was not before 1834 and may have been some time after 1848. The use of spare Bridgwater zigzag tiles to complete the blocking, tiles identical to those used to roof the range of outhouses alongside the 'new' road to Dunster Marsh and to the new coastal road, suggest that these works were part of the remodelling of the Luttrell Arms in the mid 19th century. The raising of the ground around the kiln may well have been intended to conceal the roofline of the new range of buildings from the castle whilst preserving the kiln as a prominent landmark. With its modifications the kiln entered a new lease of life as a shed for the hotel gardens.

KILN TECHNOLOGY

There is no evidence from the documentation that either Henry Fownes Luttrell or his agent, George Gale, were particularly interested in what the pottery made other than 'Coarse Pottery Ware' or in the design of kiln. They might well have expected the latest in technological design by securing the services of an experienced potter from Bristol, then a major pottery-making centre. A potter from one of the more rural redware potteries, such as John Norris, 'a potter coming from Crock Street [at Donyatt, Somerset] to take work' to succeed the Moggs in 1761, might have built a less sophisticated and visually less interesting design of kiln in the form of an open cylinder of the kind that was later converted to a closed kiln at Ewenny.[18] From a thorough examination of the structure of the existing kiln it is clear that, apart from rebuilds and repairs to the substructure, the essential fabric of the kiln was built as a complete unit.

This simple type of kiln with two fireboxes, domed ware-chamber and conical chimney sitting directly on the walls of the ware chamber might excite little comment in a country pottery of the late 19th century. Examples are recorded from Winchcombe (Gloucs.),

Fremington (Devon) and Poling (Sussex).[19] Larger coal-fired cousins with up to eight fireboxes are known elsewhere in the West Country, such as the example preserved at East Quay, Bridgwater, where the type is colloquially known as a 'pinnacle' or 'pinny' kiln.[20] However, as noted above, this may not have been the situation in the mid 18th century when the simpler small open-topped cylindrical kiln may have been more commonly found in country areas.[21]

The purpose of the cone is to act as a chimney which increases the draw of air though the kiln. Given that the ware chamber at Dunster is lined and vaulted with ordinary brick, not high-firing firebrick, the normal ceiling temperature cannot have been higher than about 1000°C, a temperature more than adequate for firing glazed red earthenware. The fireboxes are grated, that is designed to burn coal, presumably the 'Welch coal' referred to in the advertisement. Updraught kilns are difficult to heat evenly, cooling towards the top and limited in width by the reach of the flame into the centre. This tends to result in a preference for small designs, their internal width approximately equal to their height. The increased draw induced by the chimney would encourage flame and heat through a suitable network of flues under the ware chamber floor and through to the top of the ware chamber to produce a more even distribution of heat. This characteristic may be important in a kiln fired with coal, a fuel which burns with a shorter flame length than wood.

The interesting point raised by the design of kiln commissioned by Luttrell is how up to date was it for its time? Unfortunately no record of John and Ruth Mogg has been found to associate them with the pottery industry in Bristol. Indeed aside from the reference to them 'coming down from Bristol' there is nothing to connect them with the city. Evidently they must have been familiar with this design of kiln which may have been developed to be a commonplace in an urban setting by this date.[22] There is a surprising dearth of direct evidence for the form of kilns used in ordinary earthenware making in the early to mid 18th century. For this reason alone the Dunster kiln, a relatively sophisticated coal-firing design, is a significant survivor.[23]

CONCLUSION

The contractual relationship between Henry Fownes Luttrell and the Moggs illuminates a particular circumstance. In 1759 a pottery is built to produce coarse red earthenware. The estate engages the expert services of a potter and his wife to supervise its construction and then to do the making and selling. The estate also provides the resources of labour and materials required in construction, it assembles all the raw materials for making – clay, coal and even lead ore for making glaze. All the work is accounted for in detail to and by the estate agent. Above all the estate provides a site – not a site convenient for making pottery but a site in full view of the castle, an integral part of an evolving scheme to landscape the valley of the Avill. The documentary evidence implies that as a business the pottery was not a success and was eventually closed, but the kiln was preserved as a prominent part of the landscape of the park.[24]

ACKNOWLEDGEMENTS

The authors wish to thank to Hilary Binding, Trust House Forte Ltd. and the then manager of the Luttrell Arms for facilitating the initial investigation; Mark Clitheroe and Rob Wilson-North of Exmoor National Park for facilitating the second stage; Sarah Pennal, their conservator, for her enthusiasm and co-operation, the National Trust for access to Dunster Castle and for permission to publish the detail of the Tompkins' painting, Brian Murless for sharing his extensive knowledge of the clay industries of Somerset, colleagues at Somerset County Museums Service and at the Somerset Record Office, David Bromwich of the Somerset Studies Library and to Tim Dawson, Benjamin Kent, Paul Rees, Bill Stebbing and Amy Sutcliffe for assisting with the excavation and survey. We all owe a debt of gratitude to Exmoor National Park for purchasing the kiln to preserve it for posterity and to their conservator, Sarah Pennal, for her outstanding work.

NOTES

1. Barrett 1894, 326.
2. Minehead breakwater was finished in 1616 at the expense of George Luttrell (Farr 1954, 144).
3. The painting in oils on canvas is signed and dated 'W. Tomkins 1768' and attributed to William Tomkins ARA 1730-92 (National Trust DC/P/34).
4. SRO DD/L.
5. National Trust 1999, 51.
6. Capps [1980], 4.
7. For example sketches of Bristol, South Wales and Coalbrookdale 1786 and 1800 (Tate Britain: Turner Bequest).
8. For example his painting entitled, Coalbrookdale by Night, 1800, which has become an icon for the Industrial Revolution.
9. Fleming & Gore 1979, 144.
10. See Briggs 1979, 12-13.
11. For a description and discussion of the processes of oxidation, reduction and reoxidation see Dawson & Kent 1999.
12. Compare for example the North Devon jugs in the Barton collection in Somerset County Museums Service.
13. As described in Barton 1961, 164-168.
14. Examples of this form of chimney can be found still in use at places along the west Somerset and north Devon coast such as Minehead, Porlock and Lynmouth, particularly on buildings located below steeply rising ground.
15. Dating from Sussman 1979, 8-9.
16. See Warren 1997, 121.
17. SRO DD/L 1/4/12 Account Current March 1759 to Christmas 1760.
18. SRO DD/L 1/4/12 Pottery Account Current; Lewis 1982, 50-51.
19. Wheeler 1998, 47; McGarva 2000, 91 & 99.
20. David Dawson as one-time curator of the Somerset Brick & Tile Museum recorded extensive use of this term when discussing with local people their experiences of working in the industry.
21. Brears 1971, 148; Dawson & Kent 1999, 168; McGarva 2000, 90-93.
22. There is evidence of contemporary high-firing kilns of this type see the drawings of Worcester (1752), Plymouth (1770) and those by François Joseph Bélanger (c. 1768-1771) cited by Young 1999 and the discussion in Green 1999, 21-28. Much of the visual evidence cited to support the assumption that such earthenware kilns were commonplace in the 18th century tends to be of later misattributed 19th-century origin, see for example Baker 1991 plates 1, 2, 7 & 9.
23. For a full discussion of Dunster and the kiln evidence cited here in the context of our understanding of pottery kiln development in Britain in the post-medieval and later period, see Dawson & Kent forthcoming.
24. The accounts suggest that none of the hired potters lasted very long at Dunster. The lack of shop sales for 1761-1762 suggests work was at a stand. The estate was advertising for a potter again in Felix Farley's Bristol Journal, for Feb 18th and 25th 1775, 'A POTTERY-WORK to be LETT, WHERE is exceeding good CLAY and FUEL, plenty for making the COARSE-WARE, situate near several Towns, and above 20 Miles Distance from any other work of the Kind.' The Dunster Castle Park is in the care of the National Trust and is freely accessible. The kiln, now a scheduled ancient monument, has been reincorporated into the park and is to be found behind the present Exmoor National Park Visitor Centre and is a short walk from the main car park.

BIBLIOGRAPHY

Atkinson, M. (ed.) 1997, *Exmoor's Industrial Archaeology*, Tiverton: Halsgrove Books.

Barrett, C. R. B. 1894, *Somersetshire: Highways, Byways and Waterways*, London: Bliss, Sands and Foster.

Baker, D. 1991, *Potworks: the industrial architecture of the Staffordshire Potteries*, London: Royal Commission on the Historical Monument of England.

Barton, K. J. 1961, 'Some Evidence for Two Types of Pottery Manufactured in Bristol in the Early Eighteenth Century,' *Transactions of the Bristol & Gloucestershire Archaeological Soc.* **80**, 160-168.

Brears, P. C. D. 1971, *The English Country Pottery, its history and techniques*, Newton Abbot: David & Charles.

Briggs, A. 1979, *Iron Bridge to Crystal Palace: Impact and Images of the Industrial Revolution*, London: Thames and Hudson.

Capps, A. [1980], *Dunster Watermill*, Dunster: Arthur Capps.

Dawson, D. & Kent, O. 1999, 'Reduction Fired Low-Temperature Ceramics' *Post-Medieval Archaeology* **33**, 164-178.

Dawson, D. and Kent, O. forthcoming, 'The development of the bottle kiln in pottery manufacture,' in forthcoming *Industrial Processes* monograph.

Farr, G. 1954, *Somerset Harbours*, London: Chistopher Johnson.

Fleming, L. & Gore, A. 1979, *The English Garden*, London: Michael Joseph.

Green, C. 1999, *John Dwight's Fulham Pottery: Excavations 1971-79*, London: English Heritage.

Lewis, J. M. 1982, *The Ewenny Potteries*, Cardiff: National Museum of Wales.

McGarva, A. 2000, *Country Pottery: Traditional Earthenware of Britain*, London: A. & C.Black.

National Trust, 1999, *Dunster Castle*, Somerset, London: National Trust.

Sussman, L. 1979, *Spode/Copeland Transfer-Printed Patterns found at 20 Hudson's Bay Company Sites*, Quebec: Canadian Historic Sites Occasional Papers in Archaeology and History, **22**.

Warren, D. 1997, 'Miscellaneous Industries: Bricks, Tiles and Pottery' in Atkinson 1997, 119-121.

Wheeler, G. 1998, *Winchcombe Pottery: The Cardew-Finch Tradition*. Cheltenham: White Cockade.

Young, H. 1999, 'Evidence for Wood and Coal Firing and the Designs of Kilns in the 18th-century English Porcelain Industry', *English Ceramic Circle Transactions* **17**:1, 1-14.

UNPUBLISHED SOURCES

Somerset Record Office Luttrell Papers SRO DD/L

SRO DD/L 1/4/12 'Account Current March 1759 to Christmas 1760'.

SRO DD/L 1/4/12 'Pottery Account Current' (transcribed below as Appendix 1).

SRO DD/L 1/31/30 part 2 'Dr John Mogg. Potter Decd. In Account Current to Henry Fownes Luttrell' (transcribed below in Appendix 2).

ABBREVIATIONS

SRO Somerset Record Office

Appendix 1.

The Luttrell Estate Account for the 'Pottery in the Old Park,' Dunster. 1758-1763.
This account is drawn up on two sheets of paper folded and sewn to make an eight page book. It is an almost completely self-contained record of the pottery's early years and sits alongside others for the various projects underway at this time including the establishment of a brickworks at the Warren near Minehead and the extensive alterations to the park. Although, as might be expected, the project did not cover its costs during this initial setting up period, this account minimises the apparent loss. Several bills for construction costs are entered in the general accounts for these years but are not mentioned in this document (see Appendix 2).

Pottery Account Current [front cover]

[endorsed] G Gales Acct of the Pottery Settled 4th Nov: 1763 [back cover]
[pp. 1/2] Dr .. Geo. Gale in Acct. Current about the Pottery Ware to H J Fownes Luttrell Esq.
[p.1]

1759			£ s d
Novr 13th		To Cash reced of Several People for Pottery Goods sold	0: 8: 3
16		To Cash of Ruth Mogg for Goods sold in the Shop	0:19: 1
23d		To more Do. of Do…. for Do.	0: 7: 8
Decr 28th		To more Do. of Do…. for Do.	1: 7: 6
Jany 1760		To more Do. of Do…. for Do.	1: 6: 10½
Feby 8th		To more Do. of Do …. for Do.	0:13: 1½
		To Do… of Mrs Waye for Goods sold her	0: 3: 1½
22d		To more Do. of Ruth Mogg for Goods sold in the Shop	0:17: 0
March 13th		To Do.. of George Squiers for Goods	0: 5: 6
April 5th		To Do … of Henry Strong for Do.	1: 0: 6
11th		To more Do. of Ruth Mogg for Goods Sold in the Shop	4:13: 0
May 7th		To more Do. of Do …. for Do.	1:1: 0
24th		To more Do. of Do. … for Do.	2: 4: 0
		To more Do. of a Shopkeeper for Goods	0: 2: 0
25th		To Do … of Mrs Mow for Goods	0: 14: 0
		To Do … of Henry Strong for Do.	0: 15: 0
		To Do … of Barbara Stonnings for Do.	0: 15: 8
		To Do … of Richard Hobs for Do.	0: 11: 3
		To Do … of a Stranger for Do.	0: 11: 0
		To Do … of Thomas Baker for Do.	1: 8: 0
		To Do … of John Lake .. for Do.	1: 7: 8
June 30th		To more Do. of Ruth Mogg for Goods sold in the Shop	2: 10: 0
July 30th		To more Do. of Do …. for Do.	2: 10: 0
Sepr 17th		To Do … of John Burge for Do.	0: 10: 9
19th		To Do … of Mrs Mow for Goods	0: 14: 0
25th		To Do … of Ruth Mogg for Goods sold in the Shop	3: 0: 0
Oct 9th		To Do … of John Burge for Goods	1: 2: 6
Oct 10th		To Do … of John Lakey for Do.	1: 2: 0
		To Do … of Rich. Hobbs for Do.	0: 4: 0
		To Do … of Barbara Stonnings for Do.	0: 5: 6
		To Do … of Mrs Mow for Do.	0: 7: 0

	Carried Over	33: 16:11½
[p.3]		
	Dr…. Same …Brought Over	33: 16:11½
1760		
Octr 15th	To Cash of Henry Strong for Goods sold him	0: 2: 0
30th	To Do.. of Ruth Mogg for Goods sold in the shop	2: 10: 0
Novr 21st	To Do.. of Willm. Popham for Goods	0: 3: 0
26th	To Do … of Thomas Baker for Do.	0: 3: 6
	To Do … of Ruth Mogg for Goods sold in the Shop	2: 10: 0
Decr 20th	To Do … of Do …. for Do.	2: 10: 6
1761		
Jany 24th	To Do … of Do …. for Do.	0: 16: 0
31	To Do … of Do …. for Do.	1: 0: 4¾
Decr 25	To Cash for Goods sold since in the Shop since R. Mogg went away	2: 10: 0
1762		
Decr 24th	To Cash reced for Goods Sold in the Shop since Xmas last	4: 10: 0
	Balance	50: 12: 4¼
		28: 17:10¼
		79: 10: 2½

[p.2]		
P Contra is		
1758		£ s d
Octr 2d	By paid Willm. Taylor for diging & throwing out Clay to be Carried to Minehead Key for making Earthen Ware	0: 5: 0
1759		
May 16th	By paid Jas. Saunders the potter on Acct for work done by himself & man	0:10: 6
26th	By pd. Do… more on Account for Do.	1:1: 0
Sepr 30th	By pd. Frans. Strong's Bill for Carptrs. work about the pottery house in the Old Park at Dunster	1: 3: 0
	By pd. Wm. Elworthy's Bill for Do.	0:16: 8
Octr 8th	By pd. Capt. Harrison for 7c.weight of Lead Oar he Bot. in Bristol at 11s. p hundred 3:17: 0 By pd. him also for 6 Bags to put the Oar in 2/4 & for freight at 3/6 0:5:10	4: 2:10
Novr 5th	By pd. John Ingram for bring of the 7cwt. Of Lead Oar from Minehead Key	0: 1: 9
8th	By pd. Geo: Grinslade's Bill for Lyme used abt. Building the Kiln &ca.	5:19: 0
13th	By pd. for a ffile for the potter's use 6d. & for a Broom 1½	0: 0: 7½
	By pd. Wm. Elworthy's Bill for Carprs.work about the House	0:15: 4
1760		
Jany 8th	By pd. Mary Baker's Bill for Sieve's &ca. for the Potter	0: 2: 9
March 21	By pd. Capt. Harrison for 5c. of Lead Oar he bot. in Bristol	2:15: 4
Apl 14th	By pd. him for freight of it from Bristol	0: 2: 6
July 28th	By pd. Capt. Harrison for 5cwt. of Lead Oar he bot. in Bristol & freight	3: 0: 6

Sepr 29th	By pd. Wm. Rawle's Bill for Mason's work about Building the Kiln	8:13: 1
	By pd. Eliz.a Lucas's Bill for Blacksmith's work done for the Pottery	3: 9: 7
Decr 20th	By Cash now and at Diverse times before to John Mogg the Potter and his Wife on Account towards Goods made and Burnt by him as by Account Current of particulars	46: 1: 0
	Carried Over	£79: 0: 5½

[p.4]

1761	Per Contra is Brought Over	£79:0:5½
Jany 3d	By paid Eliza.Hancock for Carriage of 5 hundd. of Lead Oar from Minehead to Dunster last August	0: 1: 3
Feby 10th	By paid the Craze's for making 3 hundreds of Potters wood @ 2s.p.hund.	0: 6: 0
June 30th	By gave James Norris a Potter towards his Expenses in coming from Crock Street to take the work	0: 2: 6
		79:10: 2½
		28: 17:10¼

[p.3-4]
Dunster Castle 4th Novr. 1763
Examined and Settled the beforegoing Accounts and I do hearby acknowledge – to have received from the Said Henry Fownes Luttrell Esq. the Sum of Twenty eight pounds Seventeen Shills. & ten pence being the full Balance thereof – [ ] All vouchers relating Thereto being delivered up – (Errors Excepted) [signed] F. G Gale

Appendix 2.

The Wages of and Advances to John and Ruth Mogg 1759–60 as recorded in the Accounts of the Luttrell Estate, Dunster by George Gale.

[p.1]
[p 1-2] Dr ... John Mogg. Potter Decd. in Account Currt. to Henry Fownes Luttrell Esq. is @

1759		**£ s d**
Augt 27th	To Cash to his Wife, of Geo: Gale on Account	1:16: 0
Novr 20th	To more Do.........of Do.	4:12: 0
Decr 20th	To more Do.........of Do.	3:12: 0
1760		
Feb 9th	To more Do.........of Do.	4: 0: 0
Apl 5th	To more Do.........of Do.	4: 0: 0
May 24th	To more Do.........of Do.	2: 0: 0:
Sepr 25th	To more Do.........of Do.	8: 0: 0
Novr 20th	To more Do.........of Do.	6: 0: 0
Decr 20th	To more Do.........of Do.	12: 1: 0
		£46:1: 0

NB all the above is Chd in G. Gales, Pottery Acct Currt to Mr .Luttrell

[p.2]

			£ s d
1759			
Novr 1st		By making Goods for burning in the first Kiln	3: 2: 1
1760			
Feby		By Do................Do................ the second	2: 1: 7
April		By Do................Do................ the third	2: 3: 3½
May		By Do................Do................ the fourth	2: 3: 7½
June		& By Do.............Do................ the fifth	1: 4: 9½
July		& By Do.............Do................ the sixth	1:14: 7
Octr		& By Do.............Do................ the seventh	2:12: 0
		& By Diging the Clay, Setting, Burning and Drawing the Kilns of Goods 1:10: 0 pr Kiln	10:10: 0
Decr		& By making Goods which is not burn't	1:15: 5
			27: 7: 4½
		By Expenses coming down from Bristol	1: 0: 0
		By 15 days Work directing [& h]elping to put the House & things in order to go to Work - at [1/6] per day	1: 2: 6
		By lost time afterwards in dir[ect]ing the Masons about Building the Kiln - and for preparing the [clay] & making Arches to go round the bottom of the Kiln - and repa[ir]ing the bottom of the Kiln 3 times	1: 0: 0
		By 2 days Work for himself & wife in Sorting, Chiping, Stoping Cracks and Packing away each Kiln of Goods at 2/3 per day for 14 days	1:11: 6
		By loss time about delivering & packing Goods Sold to people in the Wholesale way	0: 9: 7½
			32:11: 0
		By a present, by way of Gratuity, from sd. Mr.Luttrell	1: 10: 0
			34: 1: 0
		Ballance due	12: 0: 0
			46: 1: 0

Dunster 27th Jany 1760 Settled and adjusted the above accounts and I do hereby acknowledge myself to be Indebted to said Henry Fownes Luttrell Esq. the above mentioned the Balance of Twelve Pounds, which I do promise to pay to him, or to his order, on demand as witness my hand

[signed] Ruth Mogg
Witness [signed] G Gale

Reflecting a Stance: Establishing a Position; Moving Beyond Description and Function in Designed Estate Landscapes?

By PAUL EVERSON

This paper is about the opportunities and propriety of reading meaning - in the form of political and religious affiliation - in combinations of field evidence of 16th- and 17th-century designed estate landscapes. It presents two case studies of limited archaeological fieldwork – at Wyeford in Hampshire and Chesterton in Warwickshire – and uses them to explore such possibilities, incidentally drawing together evidence for quietist practices that are especially visible archaeologically in fishing gardens of various forms. It proposes that such readings are not only a part of good archaeological practice, but necessarily influence the objectives of any investigations of such sites and resulting understanding.

INTRODUCTION

It is widely acknowledged – and even something taught in basic historical courses on the early modern period – that buildings can commonly be understood not solely in terms of aesthetic taste and functional practicality, but also as reflecting ideological viewpoints. Some would indeed claim that it is through recognition and exploration of just those values in buildings that architectural history can make one of its most significant contributions to wider cultural history. [1] For the 16th and 17th centuries, it is not difficult to cite familiar examples, where this is uncontroversially the case. They would include Sir Thomas Tresham's remarkable series of buildings in Northamptonshire – notably the Triangular Lodge at Rushton and the so-called New Bield at Lyveden – through which he affirmed his belief in the Old Faith at the end of the 16th century. [2] Or Sir Robert Shirley's church of Holy Trinity at Staunton Harold, which again – under the Commonwealth - asserted through its architectural form and detailing an adherence contrary to the prevailing temper.[3]

Rushton Lodge was very much part of a landscape, in the distinctive form of a rabbit warren, which itself carried symbolic meanings (to do with the role of the rabbit as an image of the human soul) that were closely integrated with those of the building itself. [4] Lyveden New Bield, too, is but one component of an extensive, structured landscape, where work to date has concentrated on recording and description at the expense of thought about the integrated and no doubt complex meaning of the whole. [5] Modern theoretical writing in archaeology and landscape studies does indeed urge that similar agendas can be read in landscapes and in the created contexts that surround and structure the experience of buildings as in buildings themselves.[6] In any individual case, the field evidence is inevitably and differently limited; and there may be debate about the confidence and emphasis of interpretation offered. In the case of Sir Henry Lee's late 16th-century mansion at Quarrendon near Aylesbury, for example, there are extensive, impressive earthworks, but no standing survival of the main house and effectively no visual record.[7] One might take the view that the imaginative leap from the observed contrast in the earthworks - between elaborate formal gardens on its one side and the equally contrived 'natural' parkland landscape on the other - to the speculation that there may have been a similar architectural contrast between one side of the house and the other is no more than that – empty speculation. One might furthermore feel sceptical of the identification of the contrasting parts of the layout with two contrasting religious outlooks: the one (as the published report proposes) has a set of almshouses integrated within it and uses that emblem of Protestant charity as the module and measure for its geometry, the other – through a set of warren mounds that nail the skyline - deploys the image of the rabbit with its significance for the Old Faith. The further implication that the contrasting elements of this exceptional layout may also be capable of reading as public and private and /or as gendered landscapes, with explicit links to Sir Henry Lee on the one hand, and to his wife Mary Paget, the daughter of Queen Mary's privy councillor and lord privy seal and sister of notoriously recusant brothers, on the other, may be further than most would want to go. But in principle a gendered reading of such landscape contexts, and perhaps especially of formal gardens, must surely be an additional and apposite aspect of current interest in the reconstruction of the architectural spaces in early modern buildings occupied by men and women, and through that their domestic relations. [8] The fact that interpretation is debatable, and worthy of debate, does not undermine but rather reinforces the importance of our signposting the potential of the material evidence we routinely handle, by bringing forward insights for discussion.

So, it is my view that it is with an awareness of this sort of multi-layered approach that we should be aspiring to discuss elite and estate landscapes. And it is my experience that specific instances repeatedly offer opportunities to do so. In support and elaboration of this assertion, I offer a couple of examples of recent fieldwork within my experience – not so much sought, but stumbled on for quite unconnected practical reasons. Neither is fully worked up, but they may illustrate opportunities available at quite parochial levels and promote discussion about approaches to these sorts of elite landscapes.

WYEFORD FARM, PAMBER, HAMPSHIRE

At Wyeford within the bounds of the former Pamber Forest in northern Hampshire, there is a house of some complexity and pretensions, situated within a regular, rectangular moat.[9] Surrounding earthwork features, principally water-holding and water management features of one sort or another, have conventionally been interpreted as medieval fishponds going with a medieval moat. When we examine and plan them carefully (Fig. 1), they form a coherent and purposeful grouping of ponds and basins and their supply leats on three sides of the moated house. On the west, up-slope of the moat, the principal feature is a small lake – now dry – perhaps with ornamental islands; on the north side, there is a curious pond with a long narrow axial peninsular; and on the south-east side there survives as elaborate

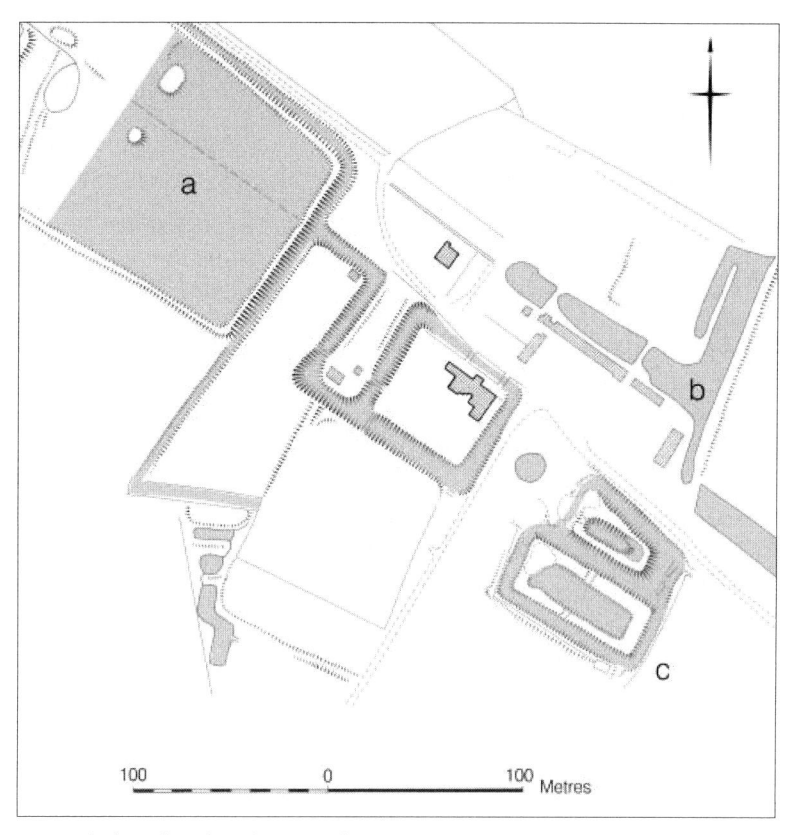

Figure 1. Surveyed plan of earthworks at Wyeford, Hampshire; original at 1:2500, with water features reinstated. *a)* lake and ornamental islands, *b)* pond with peninsular, *c)* basins with walks (© English Heritage).

earthworks a pair of basins of different configuration, with walks. The approach, now from the east, may originally have been from the south.

This is clearly a garden layout, closely integrated with a house within the moat and perhaps of the mid 17th century. More specifically, it is the sort of watery or 'fishing' garden that I have previously suggested is specifically associated with the concept of quietism in Puritan eschatological thought.[10] They formed, that is, a distinctive and sometimes dominant part of the role of gardens as places of proper rest and contemplation, undertaken to aid the renewal (*renovatio*) or re-creation of moral virtue. We know of beautifully articulated archaeological examples of this in the water gardens at Tackley in Oxfordshire and those at Old Madeley Manor in Staffordshire, just to name a couple that have been systematically investigated and published.[11] The most obvious context is supplied by literary analogues. That includes the poetry of Andrew Marvell:

> Annihilating all that's made
> To a green thought in a green shade.

Or, of Cromwell's emergence to dynamic public action:

> ... from his private gardens, where
> He lived reservèd and austere
> (As if his highest plot
> To plant the bergamot) [12]

Izaak Walton's *The Compleat Angler*, too, may be a practical handbook on fishing, but its subtitle, '*the contemplative man's recreation*', shows it at the same time to be a quietist tract. And the poetry of Walton's close friend and co-author, Charles Cotton, is full of its own brand of quietist sentiment closely bound up with fishing, in poems such as 'The Angler's Ballad', 'To my dear and most worthy Friend, Mr Isaac Walton' or 'The Retirement'.

> Farewell thou busie World, and may
> We never meet again;
> Here I can eat, and sleep, and pray,
> And do more good in one short day,
> Than he who his whole Age out wears
> Upon the most conspicuous Theaters,
> Where nought but Vice and Vanity do reign. [13]

The underlying ideology is clearly articulated by Lady Grace Mildmay, daughter of Sir Henry Sherrington of Lacock Abbey, in describing the daily activities and 'works of myne owne invention' of her strictly Puritan upbringing in her journal.

> All which varietie did greatly recreate my mynde; for I thought of nothing else but that I was doing in every particular one of these exercises. And, though I was but meanly furnished to be excellent in any one of these exercises, yet they did me good, inasmuch as I found myselfe that God wrought with me in all. [14]

Such quietist behaviour, promoting the re-creation of the mind and awareness of God's purpose for the individual, did not automatically or inevitably include fishing, especially for the women whose diaries and journals afford especially direct and vivid contemporary evidence. Yet neither was it confined to needlework and drawing, singing and playing an instrument. Anne Savage, who in 1533 bore the train of Anne Boleyn at her marriage to Henry VIII, later in life as the second wife of Thomas, Lord Berkeley was known 'betimes in Winter and Somer mornings to make her walkes to visit her stable, barnes, day house, pultry, swinetroughs, and the like'. [15] And the sternly Puritan Lady Margaret Hoby, whose diary was itself an exercise in religious discipline, actually did have the practice of going 'afishinge' at her home at Hackness in North Yorkshire.[16]

This exercise evidently used the chain of ponds along the River Derwent to the west of the Hoby manor house, which (as it is alleged) were inherited from the Whitby Abbey's ancient estate at Hackness, and (more certainly) were later transformed into the emparked and ornamental lake that now occupies their site. Some of these times, Lady Hoby – perhaps more fully and accurately – 'walked abroad to se fishe taken' or 'walked a fisshinge with a friend that came to me for that purpose' or was part of a family group who 'all went abroad to take the aire and to fishe'.

If it was actually Sir Thomas rather than Lady Hoby who principally fished for recreation at Hackness between his assertive bursts of activity aimed at discomforting his delinquently recusant neighbours, so too did the even more famous, severe Puritan man of action and regicide, Colonel John Hutchinson, at Owthorpe in Nottinghamshire half a century later. When Hutchinson retreated from the world in the wake of the Civil War, alienated from both sides of the great quarrel in his rigorous ideological outlook, his domestic regime had many hallmarks of a quietist outlook. He

> ... liv'd with all imaginable retirednesse att home, and because his active spiritt could not be idle nor very sordidly employ'd, tooke up his time in opening springs and planting trees and dressing his plantations; and these were his recreations, wherein he reliev'd many poore labourers when they wanted worke. [17]

In the 1650s, before his persecution, imprisonment and death in 1664, Hutchinson created a detached garden based on a set of fishponds at Owthorpe. These lie some 500m to the north-east of the contemporary house – built plainly also by Hutchinson, ' att home whereof he was the best ornament' – and linked to its immediate garden by a formal access way, quite in the manner of the detached water garden at Tackley. Here, the series of ponds are of linear form and arranged in parallel blocks that may reflect their creation out of the

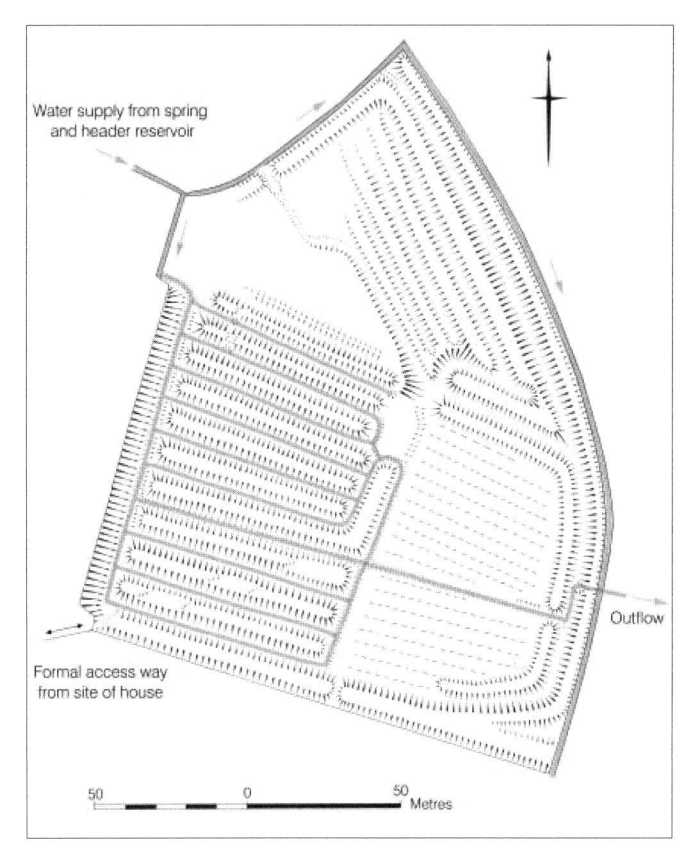

LEFT
Figure 2. Plan of fishponds and other earthworks at Fishpond Wood, Owthorpe, Nottinghamshire (re-drawn and published by courtesy of C. Salisbury).

pattern of pre-existing open-field furlongs (Fig. 2); but limited excavation has revealed the care and quality of their original construction and they have a water supply carefully regulated by ponds or reservoirs occupying the springs up the slope, in the manner also found in the archaeology of Old Madeley Manor, Staffs.[18] The house was pulled down in 1825, and its site and immediate surrounds lie, poorly understood, in improved pasture; but the adjacent church of St Margaret notably owes its form to Colonel Hutchinson's era,[19] and the layout of the village and enclosure of the wider landscape reflect the impact of this 17th-century estate, about whose ideological interests we know unusually much.

If such elaborate and ornamental manipulation of water for fishing as a gentleman's recreation is archaeologically the most accessible and distinctive marker of the quietist ideology, and the Puritan tradition of thought where it most readily found a place, it may be too simplistic to suppose that this was necessarily and exclusively so. Charles Cotton, Walton's co-author and 'half-brother-in-law' to Hutchinson, expressed his Royalist sympathies boldly and integrated the quietist exercise of fishing closely with that viewpoint.

> Whilst we sit and fish
> We do pray as we wish,
> For long life to our King James the Second;
> Honest Anglers then may,
> Or they've very foul play,
> With the best of good Subjects be reckon'd. [20]

His fishing house survives on the Dove at Beresford in Staffordshire, with its dedication 'PISCATORIBUS / SACRUM / 1674' and Artisan Mannerist detailing; and, whatever field evidence remains of the site and setting of Beresford Hall itself (pulled down in 1856), a backdrop is provided by woodland originally of Cotton's own planting.[21] Similarly, and not far away, the walled, compartmented garden layout at Snitterton Hall in Derbyshire (which survives part as ruins part earthworks) also incorporates an angled fishpond and fishing house located at the angle. Its owner was a royalist colonel, John Milward, who was related to Izaak Walton and who linked his own initials with Walton's over one of the gateways between the garden compartments.[22] The garden's heyday under the Commonwealth was as a place of organised leisure of a gentleman scholar whose particular interest in plants is reflected in the carved decoration of the entrance;[23] when Milward became politically active again at the Restoration, it was evidently put aside in favour of his other interests. Again, at Hunstanton Hall in Norfolk, the octagonal temple on an octagonal island in an octagonal moat or lake afforded Sir Hamon le Strange – no friend of Cromwell's – a location of retreat within an elaborately watery layout, between his pamphleteering and stirring ineffective revolts against the Commonwealth.[24] Nevertheless, the Protestant cast was dominant in 17th-century quietism, and its continuing special relevance may find a later expression in the sabbath walks and designed landscape effects created under Quaker influence at Ironbridge and referred to elsewhere in the volume.[25]

The archaeological evidence for such post-medieval fishing gardens may be even more widespread than an initial cast suggests. It may include not only complexes of ponds, conventionally thought medieval but which stand out for their unusually formal layout and relationship to a nearby garden plan or house site. An example is the complex at Kettleby near Brigg in Lincolnshire, which may have formed a set of initials referring to the early 17th-century owner, Sir Robert Tyrwhitt. [26] But it may also extend to at least some of the many fishponds that are conspicuously the most coherent surviving field remains on former monastic sites. As such, they would form an aspect of the conversion of monasteries to secular mansions – now established as an archaeological commonplace.[27] Candidates, almost at random, might be the splendid fishpond complex at Kirkstead Abbey in Lincolnshire, where ranks of parallel long ponds offer a surprisingly close formal analogy to Owthorpe, or ponds and walks of similar configuration at the site of Coxford Priory in Norfolk; [28] or Leez Priory in Essex, occupied as a country mansion by Lord Rich and his successors, where not only are there extensive fishponds visible but a so-called Fishing Hut. [29]

At Wyeford, the house contemporary with the watery layout is frustratingly partial in its survival, and what there is has not been adequately investigated. But in part at least it comprises an east wing in brick with fine Artisan Mannerist detailing (Fig. 3). This ought, presumably, to belong to the 1630s, '40s or '50s. The remainder of the house has been rebuilt in the early years of the 20th century, though (without internal investigation) it may be that the fabric cloaks something earlier or at least perpetuates an older footprint. Certainly, it cannot be simplistically presumed that the Artisan Mannerist parts are the survival of a whole house in this style. Perhaps even its form argues against that, and in favour of a hypothesis that it represents either an added wing or even a stylish casing of an existing element of an old house of extended, rambling form.

What is certain, however, is that the fashionable detailing is most prominently located, both in relation to the access to the property (whether from the east or south), and in relationship to the most elaborate parts of the garden layout – and those most clearly designed for perambulation, namely the basins and walks to the east.

LEFT
Figure 3. Wyeford, Hampshire; east range of the house (photo P. Everson).

Artisan Mannerist building of this sort belongs characteristically to the period of the Commonwealth, and its adoption and spread has been associated (e.g. by no less an authority than Sir John Summerson) especially with the temper and outlook of those with a firmly Puritan leaning.[30] The manor of Wyeford was owned at the turn of the 16th century by Sir Edmund Ludlow, whose established family residence was at Maiden Bradley in Wiltshire. It passed to the assertively Puritan and republican Henry Ludlow (in 1625), and thence into the hands (in 1639) of his son - Edmund Ludlow, Lieutenant General of the Horse in the army of the Commonwealth, regicide and the most prominently doctrinaire republican of the age.[31] The Ludlows may therefore have been authors/ instigators of the works we see at Wyeford. But already by 1641 Ludlow had passed the manor to Joseph Blagrave, close kin to another regicide and subsequent political exile, Daniel Blagrave. Joseph's inclination was to philosophy and astronomy rather than to politics, though - like all the Blagrave clan that was firmly rooted in and near to Reading – his religion was staunchly nonconformist.[32] Whichever of this likeminded grouping was responsible, the context for the building and its distinctive form of designed setting seems clearly to be that politically and religiously committed milieu. What was created, both in the building and in the garden setting and in their combination, can be read as having badged and symbolised the affiliations of their creators, as well as underpinning the practice of their philosophical stance.

CHESTERTON, WARWICKSHIRE

My second case is at Chesterton in Warwickshire. The dominant resident family here, since the 14th century, were the Peytos or Petos. Just as Edmund Ludlow first made a reputation for himself by obstinately enduring a siege of Wardour Castle for Parliament in 1643, so too Sir Edward Peto (d. 1643) successfully defended Warwick Castle for Parliament. But

Figure 4. Chesterton House, Warwickshire, demolished 1802; south elevation of Edward Peto's mansion, begun 1659, as drawn by the Reverend Thomas Ward (British Library, Add. MS 29264).

not a century earlier there was a Cardinal in the family, William Peto who died in 1558 in circumstances (he was pelted with stones by a derisive London mob and died shortly after, allegedly of the injuries he received) that gave the account preserved in the traditions of his Franciscan brethren the savour of martyrdom.[33]

In the church of St Giles at Chesterton, there is a splendid sequence of Peto monuments of the end of the 16th and much of the 17th century, grouped tidily at the west end of the nave. Outside, in the centre of the north side of the large rectangular churchyard, an exceptionally interesting free-standing gateway with pilasters and intermittent rustication of moulded, cut and rubbed brick stands as the most obvious remnant of an elaborate house and garden layout. Many years ago, Howard Colvin, in a characteristically elegant and authoritative essay, took this archway and the Peto tombs – one of them a product of Nicholas Stone's London workshop (1639) and the second by his son John Stone (1643) – as the springboard for an exploration of the architectural affiliations of the lost mid 17th-century house of Petos at Chesterton, which was pulled down in 1802, and of the buildings appurtenant to it.[34] For the designed and estate landscape at Chesterton is made up of a series of elements that are now all too easily viewed as discrete items, but actually repay understanding in their interrelationships as part of a single whole. What Edward Peto, son of the defender of Warwick Castle of the same name, created in the final years of the 1650s - just too late for the transformation to be noticed in Dugdale's Warwickshire, first published in 1656 - comprised structures and features that included:

- The site of the lost mansion, whose construction was set in train by Edward Peto, but was incomplete at his death in 1658 and was completed by his widow, Elizabeth, in fulfilment of his strictest and most explicit instructions to do so. We know its precise location and footprint from geophysical prospection[35] and the ambitious design of its south elevation from early drawings (Fig. 4).

- A curious lodge located on high ground several hundred metres north-west of the house and within its direct sight. It stood alongside a small copse, now removed, that may have resulted from or concealed an associated ornamental feature.

- The famous 17th-century windmill, whose circular plan and openwork ground-floor arcade of six arches have caused speculation that it was built in origin as some form of observatory or eye-catcher. (As with the watermill, below, the two ideas are not necessarily in conflict, of course.) It occupies high land and was certainly intended to be seen from the mansion, while at the same time it stood as a landmark of the Peto estate for all those moving through the lower ground to the south-west, including travellers on the Fosse Way. Views from its enclosed upper floors were extremely circumscribed by there being only two substantial windows, and those side-by-side looking downslope into the estate and in the direction of approach from the outside world from the south-west.

- An equally stylish watermill of a period with the main house.

- The church of St Giles itself, which has clearly been a feature in this designed landscape and has been re-made for that role. The south façade, for example, has been given an ashlared uniformity with fenestration of generically Perpendicular type. It is conventionally said to be of later 15th- or 16th-century date, but it could in itself be rather later. Dugdale speaks, for example, of a south aisle, which there clearly is not now.[36] The tower, too - said to be of c. 1600 – has the appearance of an eye-catching addition of a type, and perhaps with detailing, more suitable to the 18th century.

- A layout of earthworks lying north, east and west of the church, and incorporating the rectangular churchyard in its orthogonal configuration. Labelled 'The Hop Yard' on early maps, the most obvious features were formerly categorised and protected as a medieval manorial moat and fishponds. They are (rather) all best understood as formal garden remains, including substantial terraced walks, a cut-and-fill levelled core and elaborate water features that include the ornamental moated island, aka medieval moat.

There is early mapping available for the site. [37] But in practice these features are clearly part of a whole, and are visually and conceptually interlinked in the landscape.

From the site of the house, the view of the church on its low ridge and formal garden complex forming a foreground is artfully contrived (Fig. 5). There is every indication – though the details of this have not been worked out by close investigation – that the physical appearance of the church itself was 'constructed' in relation to the designed landscape. Messages were being given both to the insider and to the outside observer. An apparently contemporary painted sundial over the south porch of the church reinforced just such a

Figure 5. Formal garden remains and church of St Giles at Chesterton, viewed from the north-west (photo P. Everson).

message with the admonition, 'See and be gone about your business'. Undoubtedly the windmill held comparably diverse meanings for those observing it from within the estate and from without, as its very prominent location clearly made it susceptible to. And no doubt there are there are other linkages not yet explored.

As a piece of designed landscape based on a long-established landed estate, therefore, Chesterton has considerable interest and considerable potential. And that interest apparently lies not least – though certainly not solely – in the stylistic or art historical issue of the date when a design of this sort appears to be originated. But the heart of the matter must necessarily lie in the house that Edward Peto set out to construct as the centre-piece of the whole thing, and which he was so concerned should be completed despite the intervention of his own death. Colvin's architectural analysis teases out the close dependence of the design of the south elevation of Chesterton House on Inigo Jones's Banqueting House in Whitehall, and its comparative fidelity to that model. 'Its dependence on the Banqueting House is obvious, and shows how faithfully John Stone followed the Palladian formulas which his father had learned from Inigo Jones.' At one level, of course, that has to do – as Colvin, Pevsner and others spell out with secure assurance – with the Peto family's connexions with the London workshop of Nicholas and John Stone and their patronage. But what we might be inclined to ask – as archaeologists interested in reading the archaeology of designed landscapes– is what significance there is in the fact that, in the late 1650s, Edward Peto set about building in rural Warwickshire a house whose unmistakable, dominant and explicit reference was to the Banqueting House in Whitehall. What was he doing running up a house that was not only stylish, but actually evoked one of the most prominent emblems of the royalist cause and a symbol of the martyred king (Fig. 6) Is this a case of 'establishing a position', in this instance in the context of changing political circumstances and the prospect of the restoration of the monarchy, against whom a previous generation had fought? Might this have been a reason for Edward Peto's anxiety that the task begun by him was completed precisely as it was conceived?

If this seems commonsensically implausible in 'jumping the gun' in the uncertain agenda of restoring the monarchy in England, it might be remembered that no less a personage than Edward Montagu – pillar of the Parliamentary cause, who served Cromwell as colonel, general-at-sea and holder of many offices of state – went home to Hinchingbrooke House for Christmas 1658, there to greet his latest new-born son and to name the boy Charles. This striking gesture for a prominent anti-royalist came only a couple months after the death of Oliver Cromwell at the beginning of September 1658. It followed even more closely on Montagu's declarations of support and loyalty for Richard Cromwell as his father's successor, and long before he entertained messengers from Charles when in the Baltic in summer 1659, when first – as he assured Samuel Pepys – he converted to the king's cause.[38] His earlier 'Commonwealth' children were named Jemima 1646, Paulina 1649, Anne 1653, Oliver 1653, John 1655: Charles was followed by Catherine 1661 and James 1664.

At all events, this has to be a question that matters. In fact, it is fundamental to what ought to come out of any purposeful programme of work at Chesterton. For if we bring forward a reading of the core house in this way, it provides a framework of thinking that inevitably influences the understanding we might draw from all the other elements in this

LEFT
Figure 6. Contemporary print of the execution of Charles I in Whitehall.

landscape. Most certainly and perhaps most obviously it affects any reading of the recasting of the church. Its influence extends even to the earthworks. For what prompted fieldwork at Chesterton at the end of 2002 was the practical circumstance that rabbit burrowing was throwing up large quantities of late medieval window glass from the allegedly medieval moat within the earthworks.[39] English Heritage's Centre for Archaeology mounted an assessment excavation and the agency's field staff supported that initiative by offering an understanding of the site context. This re-interpreted the earthworks – previously categorised as medieval moat and settlement remains - as part of a formal garden layout of late 16th- or 17th-century type. But Chesterton was known to Dugdale in the early to mid 1650s for its old hall with a big oriel window packed with heraldic glass and for its church with family monuments grouped in the chancel and south aisle.[40] Edward Peto's programme evidently recast this utterly and completely – obliterating the old manor house and re-inventing the church. In such radical circumstances, the embedding of a mass of window glass in the construction of garden features – indeed the recycling of any of the (presumably very considerable) quantities of *spolia* and 'rubbish' – might be an act with its own symbolic significance, on which the archaeological deposit might be expected to throw some light.[41]

Interestingly, the garden compartment immediately west of the churchyard contains a series of low mounds, which seem most plausibly interpreted as 'pillow mounds'. That is, there is a small warren forming a component of the garden. Those of us who have found propositions about the archaeology of the rabbit and its symbolism for adherents to the Old Faith interesting and persuasive [42] will find that feature and its prominent location adjacent to the church in the direction of approach a relevant additional signal in reading this landscape. Those sceptical of such approaches must find the remains bizarre and (presumably) may continue to attempt to interpret them - as they have been hitherto within an earlier theoretical framework - as settlement tofts of a putative deserted settlement called 'Church End' rather than as garden remains at all.[43]

If we still doubt the prevalence and purpose of symbolism in garden and estate landscapes in this era, an encounter with the elaborate detail of the layout conceived and executed by William Lawrence at Shurdington in Gloucestershire in the last quarter of the 17th century is quite salutary. In that case we have his own commentary on it, and a near-contemporary Kip view to illustrate it; yet, as Lawrence says himself, 'the design appears not to the world unless I turn the key'.[44] Nevertheless, though the precise, personal significance may have been problematic to access, this garden of mourning and family piety was articulated with quite conventional imagery and classical allusion, and (most tellingly) the fact that it should carry significance was clearly unexceptional.

The expectation that archaeological approaches will engage with such meanings has to be part of a developed agenda for this sphere of study, therefore. It applies to both the overtly designed elements and the wider productive landscape of estates, to large and small, to architectural and archaeological components. In a scholarly world which reminds us that Hampton Court was 'envisioned as Camelot-on-Thames presided over by the Tudor reincarnation of King Arthur and his knights' and – even more strikingly - was preserved by king and Commonwealth alike as a monument to the ruler who had laid low the pope and given the bible in English to his subjects, a lack of alertness to such matters surely will not do.[45]

The landscapes discussed here are products of a particular age. It was one where issues of religion and politics were at the forefront of people's minds, as much as were status and ancestry. Such landscapes would have looked old-fashioned in the 18th century, or perhaps rather less meaningful – just as at a greater remove (not solely of time and fashion but of religious awareness) they are problematic for us to 'read', except by intellectual effort. It is certainly not that other, later times lacked symbolic landscapes, just that their frames of reference on the whole were different. After the Restoration and the recreation of an aristocratic society, gentlemen no longer built in the way they had before, and their emphasis shifted to adopt the court/ aristocratic style. The example at Chesterton, though rooted in the religious past, in other ways (including its transformation of an extensive landscape) points the way forward to this change. Even if the 18th-century house and landscape was very different from that of the early 17th century, it was just as symbolic, just as much 'reflecting a stance'. Only at this time it was more one of social emulation aligned with high society, rather than with a particular political and religious affiliation.[46]

ACKNOWLEDGEMENTS

This paper draws on fieldwork shared with Mark Bowden, ideas emanating from discussions with David Stocker and Paul Barnwell, and interest expressed at the conference especially by Paul Belford and David Cranstone. The late Chris Salisbury has been generous with information about Owthorpe, Deb Cunliffe redrew the plans with her customary expertise.

NOTES

1. Fernie 2003.
2. Isham 1964; Pevsner 1973, 300-1, 400-2.
3. Pevsner 1984, 390-1; Cooper 1999, 30-34, 37 gathers and references further examples.
4. Stocker & Stocker 1996.
5. Brown & Taylor 1973; for recent work by the National Trust see articles by Mark Newman in the National Trust Annual Archaeological Review for 2000-2001 and 2001-2002, available on-line at <http://www.nationaltrust.org.uk/main/w-ar3-k-emid.pdf > and <http://www.nationaltrust.org.uk/main/w-ar4-j-emid.pdf >; and for the garden restoration programme, with its strictly functional mindset, <http://www.nationaltrust.org.uk/main/w-vh/w-visits/w-findaplace/w-lyvedennewbield/w-lyvedennewbield-garden/w-lyvedennewbield-garden-restoration.htm > [last accessed February 2007].
6. e.g. Cosgrove & Daniels 1988.
7. Everson 2001.
8. e.g. Laurence 2003.
9. Bowden 2003.
10. Everson & Williamson 1998b, 147-50.
11. Whittle & Taylor 1994.
12. Stocker 1986, especially 124-64.
13. Buxton 1958, 48; this is the first stanza of "The Retirement. Stanzes Irreguliers to Mr Izaak Walton'.
14. Weigall 1911. This is perhaps a more ideologically informed formulation than the generically pious daily round usefully characterised (e.g.) by Laurence 2002.
15. Quoted by Meads 1930, 46 and fn. 138.
16. Moody 1998, 84, 85, 87, 101, 214; Meads 1930, ad locc.
17. Sutherland 1973, especially 206, 207-8, 216, 239.
18. Firth 1916, 84-5; 87. These well-preserved remains in Fishpond Wood are being managed and studied by Dr Chris Salisbury and his colleagues of the Owthorpe History and Archaeology Society and the Friends of Fishpond Wood, to whom I owe thanks for information and permission to reproduce a re-drawn version of their plan.
19. Pevsner 1979, 285.
20. Buxton 1958, 35; this is the last verse of 'The Angler's Ballad'.
21. NMR, Ordnance Survey Record Cards, SK 15 NW 4 & 5.
22. Worsley 1992; Henning 1983, III, 68.
23. Mowl & Earnshaw 1995, 221-2.
24. Mowl & Earnshaw 1995, 222-3; Williamson 1998, 252-3.
25. See Mullett 2002, especially 198-209, for evidence of contemplative quietism continuing into the 18th century and its relationship to traditional characterisations of the Puritan work ethic.
26. Everson, Taylor & Dunn 1991, 70-1 and frontispiece.
27. Gaimster & Gilchrist 2003, thematic section on 'Dissolution landscapes and secular power'.
28. Tuck 1993; and for the emblematic care with which this monastery was treated as a result of its involvement in the Lincolnshire Rising, see Everson & Stocker 2003; forthcoming.
29. Pevsner 1965, 265-7.
30. Summerson 1963, 89-98.
31. DNB xii, 255-61; Henning 1983, 779-80; Firth 1894.
32. DNB ii, 618-20.
33. Salzman 1949, 42-7; DNB xv, 974-5.
34. Colvin 1999b.
35. Adams 2002.
36. Dugdale 1730, especially 479-82 describing the Peto monuments in their earlier locations on the south side of the chancel, in the chancel and in the south aisle of the church.
37. BL, Add. MS 29264, reproduced in Adams 2002.
38. Tomalin 2003, 73, 75, 108.
39. Reilly, Jennings & Brook 2002; Reilly 2003.
40. Dugdale 1730, 474-6.
41. See, for example, Pam Graves's discussion of the window glass from the destruction phase at St Andrew's Priory at York - Graves 2000, 462-4.
42. Stocker & Stocker 1996.
43. Bond 1982, 151-2 and Fig 7.1.
44. Sinclair 1994, especially 138-47; Allen 1984; Kingsley 1989, 96-8.
45. Thurley 2003a; reviewed by Roy Strong in the Evening Standard, 23 February 2004. See also Thurley 2003b, where other possible examples of such emblematic fossilisation are explored.
46. This shift, though expressed in different terms, is discussed by Cooper 1999, 19-51, and its widespread impact effectively defines the end limit of his study.

BIBLIOGRAPHY

Allen, B. 1984, 'Paradise in Gloucestershire', *Country Life* 19 July 1984, 194-6.
Bond, C. J. 1982, 'Deserted medieval villages in Warwickshire and Worcestershire', in Slater & Jarvis 1982, 147-71.
Brown, A. E. & Taylor, C. 1973, 'The gardens at Lyveden, Northamptonshire', *Archaeological Journal* 129, 154-60.
Buxton, J. 1958, *Poems of Charles Cotton*, London: The Muses' Library.
Colvin, H. 1999a, *Essays in English Architectural History*, New Haven (Ct.) & London: Yale University Press.
Colvin, H. 1999b, 'Chesterton House, Warwickshire', in Colvin 1999a, 179-90.
Cooper, N. 1999, *Houses of the Gentry 1480 – 1680*, New Haven (Ct.) & London: Yale University Press.
Cosgrove, D. & Daniels, S. 1988, *The iconography of landscape: essays on the symbolic representation, design and use of past environments*, Cambridge: Cambridge University Press.
Dugdale, W. 1730, *The Antiquities of Warwickshire,* 2nd edn revised W. Thomas, London: J. Osborn & T. Longman.
Everson, P. 2001, 'Peasants, peers and graziers: the landscape of Quarrendon, Buckinghamshire, interpreted', *Records of Buckinghamshire* 41, 1-45.
Everson, P. & Stocker, D. 2003, 'The archaeology of vice-regality: Charles Brandon's brief rule in Lincolnshire', in Gaimster & Gilchrist 2003, 145-58.
Everson, P. & Stocker, D. forthcoming, 'Masters of Kirkstead: hunting for salvation', in McNeill forthcoming.
Everson, P. & Williamson, T. (eds) 1998a, *The Archaeology of Landscape*, Manchester: Manchester University Press.
Everson, P. & Williamson, T. 1998b, 'Gardens and designed landscapes', in Everson & Williamson 1998b, 139-65.
Everson, P. L., Taylor, C. C. & Dunn, C. J. 1991, *Change and Continuity: rural settlement in north-west Lincolnshire*, London: HMSO.
Fernie, E. 2003, 'History and Architectural History', *Transactions of the Royal Historical Society* 13, 199-206.
Firth, C. H. 1894, *The Memoirs of Edmund Ludlow, Lieutenant-General of the Horse in the army of the Commonwealth of England, 1625-1672*, Oxford: Clarendon Press.
Firth, J. B. 1916, *Highways and Byways in Nottinghamshire*, London: Macmillan.
Gaimster, D. & Gilchrist, R. (eds) 2003, *The Archaeology of Reformation 1480-1580*, Society for Post-Medieval Archaeology Monograph 1, Leeds: Maneys.
Graves, C. P. 2000, *The Window Glass of the Order of St Gilbert of Sempringham: a York-based study*, The Archaeology of York 11/3, York: Council for British Archaeology.
Henning, B. D. 1983, *History of Parliament. The House of Commons 1660-1690*, London: Secker & Warburg.
Isham, G. 1964, 'Sir Thomas Tresham and his Buildings', *Reports and Papers of Northamptonshire Antiquarian Society* 65, 23-33.
Kingsley, N. 1989, *The Country Houses of Gloucestershire. Volume 1 1500-1660*, Cheltenham: author.
Laurence, A. 2002, 'Daniel's practice: the daily round of godly women in seventeenth-century England', in Swanson 2002, 173-83.
Laurence, A. 2003, 'Women using building in seventeenth-century England: a question of sources?', *Transactions of the Royal Historical Society* 13, 293-303.
McNeill, J. (ed.) forthcoming, *Art and Architecture in Kings Lynn and the Fens*, Transactions of the British Archaeological Association's 2005 Conference at Kings Lynn.
Meads, D. M. (ed.) 1930, *Diary of Lady Margaret Hoby 1599-1605*, London: Routledge.
Moody, J. (ed.) 1998, *The Private Life of an Elizabethan Lady. The diary of Lady Margaret Hoby 1599-1605*, Stroud : Sutton.
Mowl, T. & Earnshaw, B. 1995, *Architecture without Kings. The rise of puritan classicism under Cromwell*, Manchester: Manchester University Press.
Mullett, M. A. 2002, 'Catholic and Quaker attitudes to work, rest, and play in seventeenth- and eighteenth-century England', in Swanson 2002, 185-209.

Pevsner, N. 1965, *Essex*, 2nd edn revised by Enid Radcliffe, Harmondsworth: Penguin.
Pevsner, N. 1973, *Northamptonshire*, 2nd edn revised by Bridget Cherry, Harmondsworth: Penguin.
Pevsner, N. 1979, *Nottinghamshire*, 2nd edn revised by Elizabeth Williamson, Harmondsworth: Penguin.
Pevsner, N. 1984, *Leicestershire and Rutland*, 2nd edn revised by Elizabeth Williamson, Harmondsworth: Penguin.
Reilly, S. 2003, 'Chesterton Moat, Warwickshire: mitigation of rabbit damage', *English Heritage Centre for Archaeology News* 5, 2-3.
Salzman, L. F. (ed.) 1949, *Victoria County History of Warwickshire, Volume 5*, London: Oxford University Press.
Sinclair, I. (ed.) 1994, *The Pyramid and the Urn. The life and letters of a Restoration squire: William Lawrence of Shurdington, 1636-1697*, Stroud: Sutton.
Slater, T. R. & Jarvis, P. J. (eds) 1982, *Field and Forest, an historical geography of Warwickshire and Worcestershire*, Norwich: Geo Books.
Stocker, D. & Stocker, M. 1996, 'Sacred Profanity: the theology of rabbit breeding and symbolic landscape of the warren', *World Archaeology* 28:2, 264-72.
Stocker, M. 1986, *Apocalyptic Marvell: the Second Coming in seventeenth century poetry*, Brighton: Harvester.
Summerson, J. 1963, *Architecture in Britain 1530 to 1830*, Harmondsworth: Penguin.
Sutherland, J. (ed.) 1973, *Lucy Hutchinson's Memoirs of the life of John Hutchinson, with the fragment of an autobiography of Mrs Hutchinson*, London: Oxford University Press.
Swanson, R. N. (ed.) 2002, *The Use and Abuse of Time in Christian History, Studies in Church History 37*, Woodbridge: Boydell.
Thurley, S. 2003a, *Hampton Court: a social and architectural history*, New Haven (Ct.) & London: Yale University Press.
Thurley, S. 2003b, 'The Early Stuarts and Hampton Court', *History Today* 1 November 2003, 16-20.
Tomalin, C. 2003, *Samuel Pepys: the unequalled self*, London: Penguin.
Walton, I. 1985, *The Compleat Angler*, Harmondsworth: Penguin.
Weigall, R. 1911, 'An Elizabethan gentlewoman', *Quarterly Review* 215, 119-38.
Whittle, E. & Taylor, C. C. 1994, 'The early seventeenth-century gardens of Tackley, Oxfordshire', *Garden History* 22:1, 37-64.
Williamson, T. 1998, *The Archaeology of the Landscape Park. Garden design in Norfolk, England, c. 1680-1840*, British Archaeological Reports British Series 268, Oxford: Archaeopress.
Worsley, G. 1992, 'Snitterton Hall, Derbyshire', *Country Life* 5 March 1992, 68-71.

UNPUBLISHED SOURCES
British Library, Add. MS 29264
National Monuments Record, Ordnance Survey Record Cards, SK 15 NW 4 & 5

Adams, D. 2002, 'Landscape Project at Peyto Mansion, Chesterton, Warwickshire: Project W1201-EFM Peyto Mansion, Chesterton Geophysical Survey April 2001-2', unpublished report of work by the Warwickshire Archaeology Research Team.
Bowden, M. 2003, 'Wyeford Farm, Pamber, Hampshire: Level 2 Archaeological Survey', English Heritage Archaeological Investigation Reports Series 5/2003.
Reilly, S., Jennings, S. & Brook, E. 2002, 'Evaluation at Chesterton Moat, Warwickshire: interim report', English Heritage Centre for Archaeology Project Number 3590, unpublished report.
Tuck, C. 1993, 'Field Survey Report: Kirkstead Abbey fishponds', unpublished RCHME report (National Monuments Record archive number 947582).

ABBREVIATIONS
BL The British Library
NMR National Monuments Record Officer, Swindon

Thomas Jefferson's Landscape of Retirement

By BARBARA J. HEATH

Archaeologists working in the United States middle-Atlantic region have analysed landscapes as tools of capitalist social relations, purveyors of religious ideology, or containers of memory. This paper uses the formal landscape of Poplar Forest—Thomas Jefferson's retirement retreat in Bedford County, Virginia—as a case study of one man's interaction with place. Weaving narratives of Anglo-Saxon history and classical antiquity with family ties and personal experience, Jefferson created a retirement villa that affirmed his position as a model statesman for the new nation and became a material expression of his ideals for a new national identity.

INTRODUCTION

The archaeology of American garden and estate landscapes has blossomed in the last 25 years, encompassing a variety of theoretical perspectives. While much work continues to be driven by restoration and is largely descriptive, a growing body of more anthropologically- or historically-oriented research is emerging. In the middle-Atlantic region of the United States, many scholars have argued that owners of urban and plantation landscapes expressed, maintained, and legitimised their positions of power within society through the manipulation of geometry, the apparent control of natural phenomena, the mastery of exotic plants, and the creation of lines of sight that facilitated surveillance or enhanced views.[1] Others have found religious ideals expressed in garden design and plant materials, while still others have approached gardens and broader landscapes as containers of memory, where important residues of the past are preserved, recontextualised, and commemorated by succeeding generations.[2]

This paper examines the bond between landscape and memory at Poplar Forest—the Bedford County, Virginia plantation and retirement villa of Thomas Jefferson (Fig. 1). My approach draws on the work of anthropologists, geographers, historians, and philosophers who see place - the culturally constructed tapestry of location, environment, experience, and remembrance - as a setting for social action and a reservoir of memory.[3] Individuals assign meaning to space on their own terms so that place becomes a structuring agent for personal experience. Movement between places, in the words of Christopher Tilley, is 'intimately related to the formation of biographies and social relationships.'[4] While individuals create personal histories from places, layers of meaning accumulate through the actions of multiple people acting within them. Thus, historical memory of place is at once personal and collective.

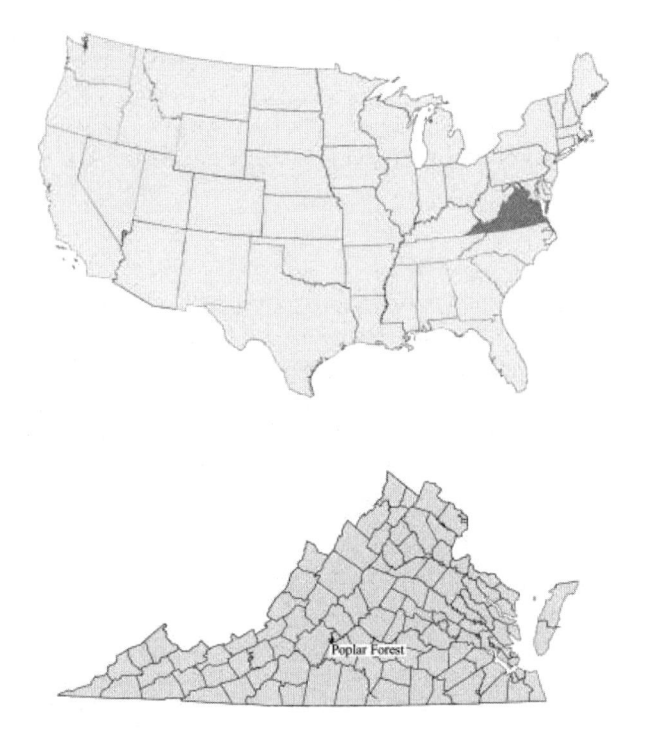

LEFT
Figure 1. Poplar Forest: location map based on 2000 US Census Maps (drawn by author).

Identity and memory can be approached through the analysis of landscape and other more portable forms of material culture contained within it. Landscapes capture the physicality of place in the interrelationships of elements such as buildings, roads, gardens, landform, and vegetation. When approached through close readings of ever-broadening circles of context, these features, together with more portable artefacts, are physical reminders of complex and changing interrelationships bound up in place. Both landscapes and objects embody and reflect processes enacted by or acting upon the individuals that created them and the wider societies of which they were a part.

Thomas Jefferson's well-documented life and well-preserved properties at Poplar Forest and his home estate of Monticello make it possible to explore his relationship to particular landscapes in some depth. Historians have lauded Jefferson as the author of the Declaration of Independence, debated his performance as the third president of the United States, condemned him as a slave owner, and praised him as an agricultural reformer, self-taught architect and landscape designer. While there can be no doubt that his social and economic status among Virginia's elite made the creation of a retirement villa at Poplar Forest both possible and desirable, this paper seeks to move beyond an analysis of landscape based on power relations. Instead, through reconstructing and examining layers of context, it provides a richer understanding of one man's creation of and interaction with place. The Poplar Forest grounds were intensely autobiographical, allowing Jefferson one final experiment, drawing on a lifetime of reading, observation and practice, in the fine arts of gardening and architecture. More significantly, they were didactic, an important example of a grandfather's, and Founding Father's interpretation of broader notions of history, beauty, art, and democracy in post-Revolutionary America. As such, they situated this place within an imagined landscape whose idealised historical narrative often stood at odds with the physical realities of exhausted soils, years of drought, periodic neglect, and the social realities of slavery, that also shaped this landscape.

HISTORIC OVERVIEW

Today, Poplar Forest is a non-profit historic site where full-time archaeological research has been on-going since 1989. Thomas Jefferson's 53-year association with this place is the dominant story currently conveyed on the property, although other tales could be told drawing on the land's roughly 8,000 years of human habitation. A consideration of three areas in which personal and collective memory shaped and reflected Jefferson's conception of Poplar Forest during his lifetime will follow a brief outline of the documented history of the property.

In 1745, William Stith patented an approximately 1619-hectare (4000-acre) tract of land 'at the Poplar Forest.' It passed to subsequent owners without recorded improvements until attorney and entrepreneur John Wayles acquired this land nineteen years later. He expanded its boundaries and transferred enslaved Africans and African Americans to the property to produce tobacco. Under his ownership and continuing into the late 18th century, the residential and administrative core of the property lay between the north and south branches of Tomahawk Creek in an area later known as the 'old plantation.' This quarter contained at minimum an overseer's house, barn, and one or more adjoining slave quarters.[5] At his death in 1773, Wayles left 135 enslaved people and over 4451 hectares (11,000 acres) of land to his daughter Martha and her husband Thomas Jefferson. This included the Poplar Forest tract, which by that time had been enlarged to 2023 hectares (5,000 acres) and consisted of two quarter farms. In the two decades following Martha's death in 1782, Jefferson was an infrequent visitor to the property, although the enslaved labour force he continued to maintain there produced tobacco and wheat crops that constituted a significant source of income for him during this period.

As Jefferson approached retirement from the presidency, he undertook a significant reorganization of Poplar Forest, beginning with the construction of an octagonal Palladian retreat house and the creation of pleasure grounds at the centre of the property. From 1810-1823, he visited his Bedford County holdings one or more times yearly, creating a refuge from the more public life of Monticello and overseeing plantation operations. Jefferson's post-retirement alterations of Poplar Forest also extended to slave housing, agricultural reform, and other changes to the wider landscape. He continued to modify the plantation until his final visit in 1823; however, by 1816, the physical transformation of Poplar Forest from a vernacular quarter farm to a gentleman's villa was essentially complete.[6]

Grandson Francis Eppes and his wife Mary Elizabeth moved to Poplar Forest in 1823, inheriting about 435 hectares (1074.75 acres) of land at the time of Jefferson's death three years later. The remainder of the property was divided and sold to settle debts. Eppes sold his portion of the property in 1828 to neighbour William Cobbs, whose daughter Emma married Edward Hutter in 1840. Following their marriage, Hutter assumed management of the property. The Cobbs and Hutters modified the landscape during their lives to fit their vision of the appropriate use of space and in response to the needs of plantation slaves, tenants, and others. While several changes are currently recognized, others remain to be discovered and understood.[7]

Edward Hutter's son Christian acquired the property in the late 19th century and used it as a farm and a summer home for his family. Tenants and hired workers under the direction of a succession of farm managers worked throughout the year. In 1946, Christian Hutter sold Poplar Forest to the James Watts family, who refurbished the main house and revitalized the farm as a dairy operation in the ensuing years. They oversaw many changes to the landscape surrounding the house, including the break-up and sale of much of the remaining property to a developer. Yet while busily erasing the historic landscape, Watts employed a New York architectural firm to reconstruct Jeffersonian elements of the house's interior and to create a brick-walled garden using a serpentine design commonly associated with Jefferson, although not with Poplar Forest.[8]

The Watts family sold what remained of the property—about 20 hectares (50 acres) and the house—to Dr. James Johnson of North Carolina in 1980. Three years later, he sold it to the newly-formed Corporation for Jefferson's Poplar Forest. This private non-profit organization currently supports archaeological and historical research, architectural restoration, and the interpretation of the property's Jeffersonian past to the public.

JEFFERSON, POPLAR FOREST, AND MEMORY

Personal Ties, Family Memory

In the winter of 1856, sixty-year-old Ellen Randolph Coolidge paused to share memories of her famous grandfather with his biographer Henry Randall. Setting pen to paper, she conjured up an idealized view of herself 40 years earlier as a young woman, presiding as hostess over Jefferson's table.

'The first visit I ever paid with him to what afterwards became a favorite retreat, must have been I think in the summer of 1816. …Sitting with my grandfather after dinner he would not infrequently speak to me of his early years and home and friends—of his favorite sister Jane, her rare talents, her wit, her musical powers—of my grandmother whose memory he cherished with deep and tender affection. He often quoted to us her sayings and opinions, and would preface his own advice with "your grandmother would have told you," "your grandmother always said" '.[9]

At Poplar Forest, Thomas Jefferson created a place built on memory. Here he designed a retreat, modelled on the villas of antiquity and shaped by his own life experiences. Through a landscape both mental and physical, he strengthened connections with family, friends, and with the land itself. Nearing the end of his life and conscious of his mortality, he linked his own experiences with the broader stream of history.

From his childhood, Jefferson had strong personal ties to the landscape of eastern Bedford County. His father was a surveyor, mapmaker, and prosperous landowner in central Virginia. During the 1740s, Peter Jefferson worked with Joshua Fry to survey important dividing lines in northern and southern Virginia that ultimately led to the creation and publication of the first accurate map of the colony in 1751.[10] On it, Fry and Jefferson depicted the skyline of Bedford County and the series of tributaries leading into Virginia's iconic river, The James. The mountains of the Blue Ridge, each named according to individual topographic, natural, historic, or personal associations, dominate this landscape. To the southwest of Poplar Forest rise the Peaks of Otter that Jefferson believed for much of his life to be 'of a greater height, measured from their base, than any others in our country, and perhaps in North America.'[11] It was only in 1815, at age 72, that he proved himself wrong by measuring the Peaks during a visit to his Bedford County retreat.[12]

Peter Jefferson's familiarity with the area grew not only out of his experiences as a surveyor and mapmaker, but from his family's substantial landholdings in Bedford County. He acquired property along Tuckahoe and Tomahawk Creeks, and an 809 hectare (2,000 acre) tract known as The Rough a few miles north of Poplar Forest.[13] Following the elder Jefferson's death in 1757, his son Thomas inherited these lands. Peter Jefferson's brother-in-law, Thomas Turpin, was county surveyor.[14] In addition to Turpin's large landholdings adjacent to The Rough, he surveyed the boundaries and drafted the first plats of both Poplar Forest and the Judith's Creek plantation, another property that Thomas Jefferson ultimately came to inherit. The younger Jefferson is likely to have had some familiarity with the area by the 1760s, when he visited the nearby town of New London and likely toured his Bedford County estates.[15]

Thomas Jefferson's maternal ties to Poplar Forest and the surrounding countryside were even stronger. His mother, Jane Randolph Jefferson, was first cousin to Poplar Forest's patentee, William Stith, to his wife Judith, and to Peter Randolph, third owner of the property and an executor of Peter Jefferson's estate. Thomas Jefferson ultimately came to own Poplar Forest and the nearby Judith's Creek plantation through his marriage to the widow Martha Skelton. The latter parcel lay at the foot of Fleming's Mountain and along Judith's Creek, both believed to have been named for Judith Fleming, his mother's aunt.

As an old man of 77, Jefferson recorded the views of mountains visible from Poplar Forest.[16] The ridge named for his kinswoman could be seen from the front portico of the house, one of many reminders of his longstanding family ties to this place. Over the course of his lifetime, Jefferson sold much of the land he had inherited from his parents and from his father-in-law. While his decision to retain Poplar Forest and eventually to settle there has been credited to the land's fertility, the strength of family ties to the land must also have held some sway.

Jefferson intended to continue those ties into the future. As part of a marriage settlement in 1790, he gave his older daughter and son-in-law a substantial piece of land along the northwest side of the property with the hope that their children would ultimately be settled there.[17] In 1806, as construction of his retreat house was underway, he reported to friend Elizabeth Trist that 'I am preparing an occasional retreat in Bedford where I expect to settle some of my grandchildren.'[18] Finances and personal affairs precluded this course of action for all but one grandchild, Francis Eppes. With his sale of the property in 1828, nearly a century of family ties to this property, and this area, ended.

LANDSCAPE, HISTORY, AND REVOLUTION

While Peter Jefferson does not appear to have been a bookish man, he arranged a classical education for his son, who remained profoundly grateful for this opportunity for the rest of his life. While visiting Poplar Forest in the summer of his 76th year, he wrote:

> 'Among the values of classical learning, I estimate the luxury of reading the Greek and Roman authors in all the beauties of their originals…I think myself more indebted to my father for this than for all the other luxuries his cares and affections have placed within my reach; and more now than when younger, and more susceptible of delights from other sources. When the decays of age have enfeebled the useful energies of the mind, the classic pages fill up the vacuum of ennui, and become sweet composers to that rest of the grave into which we are all sooner or later to descend.' [20]

As a student at the College of William and Mary, Jefferson he studied natural philosophy under the direction of William Small and read widely in history, mathematics, and law. His personal studies also included the subjects of ancient and modern architecture, landscape design, and gardening.[21]

Jefferson adhered to the philosophy known in his time as Epicureanism, centred on a materialist world, where all knowledge grew out of nature and all phenomena could be explained through their natural material expressions. Following the lead of Francis Bacon, he subdivided the realm of knowledge into Memory (civil and natural history), Reason (moral and mathematical philosophy), and Imagination (literature, languages, music, the arts and gardening).[22] He believed that historical memory provided men with evidence of the capacity for progress and served as a caution against errors that might impede that progress. The past served as a direct model for the future.[23]

English history played a strong role in Jefferson's revolutionary ideology. He considered colonial Americans to be heirs to the legacy of Anglo-Saxon England, a society organized around elected monarchs and a parliamentary democracy. Basing his understanding of Anglo-Saxon law and culture on Roman historian Tacitus's *Germania* and on the writings of English Whig historians, Jefferson saw America's rejection of British subjugation as a natural result of her Anglo-Saxon heritage. He argued that just as the Anglo-Saxons had left Germany and created an independent, democratic society in England, so too had their descendants, the people who colonized British North America, left behind the current monarchy. In creating a new society, they no longer owed allegiance to the Crown.[24]

Jefferson's interests in the classical world and his enthusiasm for Anglo-Saxon history found unlikely expression in an unexecuted plan for Poplar Forest believed to have been drafted in 1781.[25] In June of that year, nearing the close of his term as war-time Governor of Virginia, he narrowly escaped capture by British troops who had been sent to Monticello to arrest him for treason. Jefferson gathered his family and fled to Poplar Forest, rightly convinced that he would not be pursued to this 'distant possession.' A map, believed to have been created by him during or shortly after this period of residence, depicts existing features and planned improvements to the landscape. Of interest here is Jefferson's sketch of a house, grounds, and garden along the western boundary of the property that likely represents his earliest plan for a second home on his Bedford county plantation.

The map delineates existing features of the plantation: overseer's house, barn, tobacco houses (drying barns), enclosed fields, and roads. To this Jefferson added a plan of a proposed house and its associated landscape (Fig. 2). Almost perfectly conforming to the hilltop which he described as 'a fine situation for a house,' the design he developed consisted of a 1.2 hectare (three acre) square bounded to the east by a 40.5 hectare (100 acre) fenced field and to the west by a pentagonal garden set within a larger enclosure that may have mirrored the eastern tract.

Adhering to 18th-century interpretations of classical gardens, his landscape elements drew on the geometry of the house. Jefferson sited the proposed garden and its opposing enclosure at a distance equal to two and one half times the structure's core dimension of 18.3m (60 ft). The garden's north-south dimension of 11 poles (363 ft/110.6m) mirrored the length and width of the square surrounding the house. Both fields and garden were rotated so that their corners faced the house, creating a forced perspective to the north and south.[26] The Peaks of Otter lie almost directly north of the proposed house site, and although this vista went unrecorded, these mountains would have been visible from the north portico in the winter. Jefferson noted 'vista to Candler's mountains' as dominating the eastern view, visible from the bedchambers in the house and eastern dependency through a clearing between rows of trees.

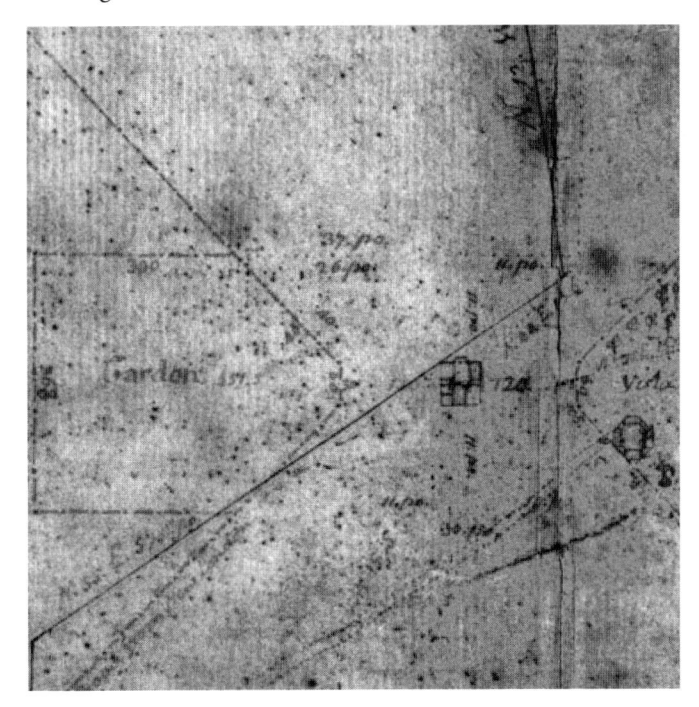

LEFT
Figure 2. Detail of Poplar Forest plan c. 1781 (courtesy of the University of Virginia, Special Collections Library).

On the reverse of the map, a more detailed drawing of the house represents a reworking of plans Jefferson had recently completed for a redesigned Governor's Palace in Williamsburg.[27] The Poplar Forest house combined a one-story, temple-form structure in the classical tradition with a more contemporary interior design. Covered, colonnaded passageways led to service rooms to the west, facing the garden, and bedchambers to the east, facing the 40.4 hectare (100 acre) enclosure (Fig. 3). Porticos defined the north and south faces of the building that apparently were meant to front on a road passing south of the structure. It is likely that Jefferson drew on the distant vistas of the mountains and the closer views of fields and woodland to complete the context of pastoralism characteristic of the Roman villas he sought to emulate with this plan.

Architectural historian Mark Wenger, who drew attention to this plan, has argued:

'…the image of the temple drew satisfying parallels between political institutions of the new order and the ancient models on which they were self-consciously patterned—Athenian democracy and the Roman Republic. The temple was fraught with moral significance as well. For Jefferson and his contemporaries, it embodied the rugged goodness of the ancients and its echo in the virtuous simplicity of American life. In the midst of nature's abundance, Americans would rediscover the rustic virtue of Athens and the Roman Republic.'[28]

Jefferson labelled the plan using Anglo-Saxon names to designate room use for the proposed dwelling, an explicit reference to that society's superior democratic traditions and his connection to them. While the functions of these spaces are domestic - wash house,

Figure 3. Plan for house at Poplar Forest with room labels in Anglo-Saxon, c. 1781. Room labels (left to right) waesc-ern (wash house), hlaefdiges-cofe (ladies' room), spraecende-cofe (parlor), bedd-cofe (bed chamber), cilda-cofe (children's room, aetende-cofe (dining room). Translations from Wenger 1999, p. 238. (courtesy of the University of Virginia, Special Collections Library).

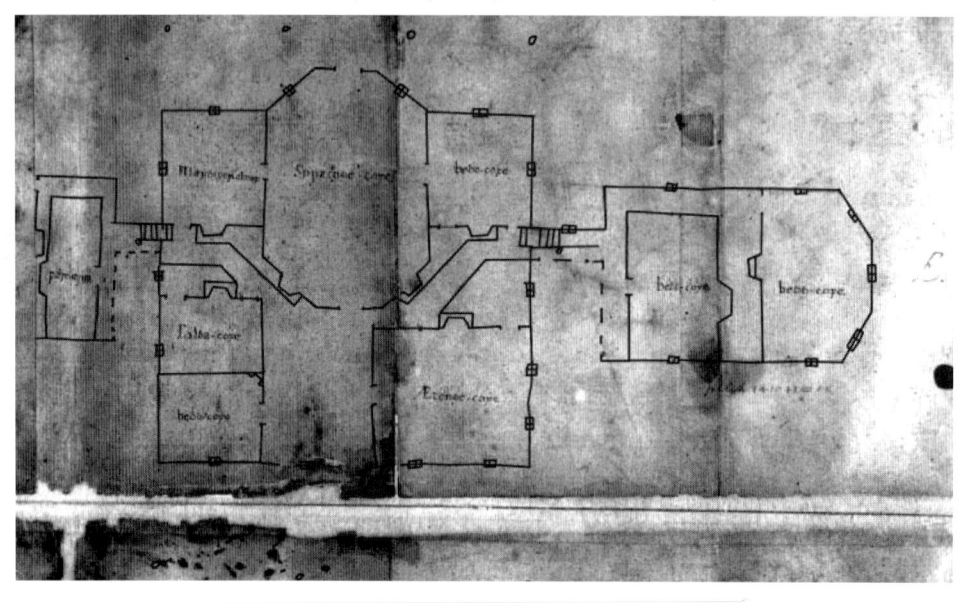

ladies' room, parlour, bedchambers, children's room and dining room - Jefferson imposed the symbolic language of revolution on this domestic design. The exterior of the house spoke of Athenian democracy and the Roman Republic, but the interior evoked America's moral right, grounded in English history, to be free.[29]

In February 1782, Jefferson sent fruit trees to Poplar Forest to plant an orchard, presumably the first step in establishing his domestic compound.[30] With the death of his wife later that year, and his removal to Paris in 1784, his plans for the house and grounds were never realized. Yet the notion of creating a retreat at Poplar Forest stayed with him, and its implementation occupied him throughout his retirement.

JEFFERSON'S RETREAT

The tension between civic action and personal retirement was a recurrent theme in elite society of 18th- and early 19th-century England and America. Throughout his life, Jefferson created places where he could periodically withdraw and frequently wrote of his desire to leave behind public service to enjoy the happiness that private life among his family, farms, and books could provide.[31] While he withdrew to Monticello as a younger man, by late middle-age that house had become a centre of activity for family and friends and a place of pilgrimage for curiosity seekers. As he planned for the end of his second term as President, Jefferson set in motion the construction of a retreat at his Bedford County plantation.[32] Poplar Forest was intended to be a private place, modelled on the villas of antiquity where virtuous statesmen retired to enjoy rural pastimes among their families and friends.[33] Jefferson described his experience there in 1811 by noting:

> 'I write to you from a place, 90 miles from Monticello, near the New London of this state, which I visit three or four times a year & stay from a fortnight to a month at a time. I have fixed myself comfortably, keep some books here, bring others occasionally, am in the solitude of a hermit, and quite at leisure to attend to my absent friends.' [34]

Situated, as he was that year, at the heart of a plantation inhabited by 57 enslaved men, women, and children, overseers and assorted other free residents, his solitude was more imagined than real. The description nevertheless makes explicit his perception of Poplar Forest as a place largely removed from the world, and supports the argument that the landscape that he designed and oversaw there had little to do with overt statements of power. Certainly such an effort would have been excessive had his primary goal been to naturalize his authority over the plantation community, a group comprised largely of people who rarely saw a brick house of any description or grounds more sophisticated than fields, woodlots, and kitchen gardens.

Between 1805-1809, hired workmen and enslaved labourers set about constructing the house and creating the 'skeleton' of the pleasure grounds by excavating a basement level and a sunken lawn perpendicular to its southern façade. From the soil removed from house and lawn, slaves built two mounds, roughly equal in diameter and height, to the east and west of the structure. While Jefferson had observed mounds in English gardens that he had visited, his decision to site them on axis with and equidistant from the house, rather than at a distance, argues against their use as vantage points. Instead, he may have used them to invoke Palladian design in an ingenious blend of architecture and landscape, where the mounds took the place of classical pavilions and *allées* of trees served as hyphens.[35]

When complete, the site was dominated by a two-story brick octagonal dwelling house set into the hillside. Porticos of the Tuscan order faced north and south, the southern supported by an arcade. The interior of the house consisted of four elongated octagonal rooms surrounding a central cube. Jefferson proportioned and ornamented the north, east, and west rooms to the Tuscan order, and selected 'the Ionic of the temple of Fortuna virilis' (the temple of Portunus) to ornament the parlour.[36] At his request, the sculptor adapted the Doric order frieze from the Baths of Diocletian, adding ox-skulls to the traditional motif of human faces, to ornament his dining room. While drawing heavily on classical precedent and Palladio's interpretation of it, the house also incorporated modern features that Jefferson had observed in France, including polished oak floors, alcove beds, triple-sash windows, and a skylight. Granddaughter Ellen Randolph Coolidge later described the house as having 'a very tasty air'.[37]

Jefferson set the house within a 24.8-hectare (61.5-acre) curtilage, 'divided it into suitable appendages for a dwelling house' and planted 'trees of use and ornament' within it.[38] An 1813 map of the property depicts a four-hectare (ten-acre) enclosure in the centre of the curtilage that hints at his further refinement of the use of space closest to his home (Fig. 4). This division of space echoes a similarly-sized enclosure bounding his childhood home at Shadwell in Albemarle County and may have formed a symbolic connection between his first and last homes.[39] The dividing and subdividing of space was further realized by the construction of a road centred on the dwelling house that encircled nearly two hectares (five acres) of pleasure grounds.

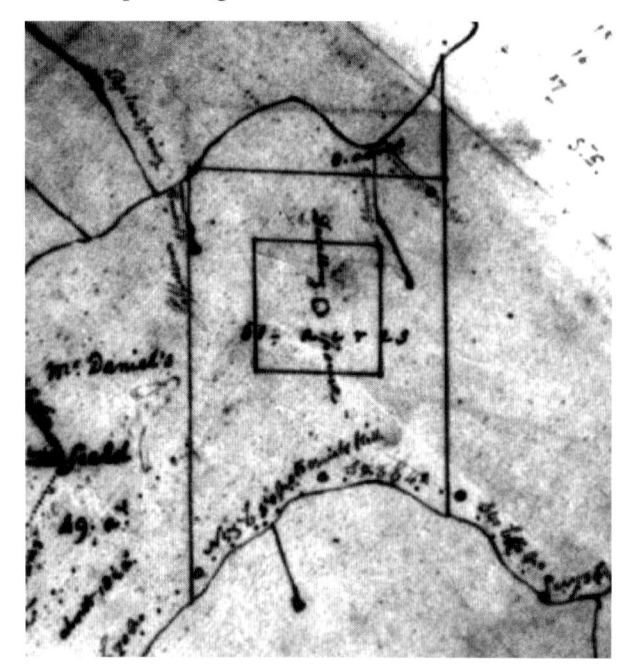

LEFT
Figure 4. Detail from 1813 survey of Poplar Forest by Joseph Slaughter (courtesy of the University of Virginia, Special Collections Library).

Elements of the landscape exhibit Jefferson's interest in contemporary and ancient gardening. While serving as Minister to France in the 1780s, he travelled extensively through Europe, becoming not only a keen observer of architectural forms, both classical and modern, but an avid visitor to gardens.[40] A tour of the most acclaimed English gardens of the 18th century led him to observe, 'The gardening in that country is the article in which it surpasses all the earth. I mean their pleasure gardening. This indeed went far beyond my ideas.'[41] Jefferson felt that parks and gardens in the English style had a place in America, 'where the noblest gardens may be made without expense. We have only to cut out the super-abundant plants.'[42]

For the gardens at Monticello, Jefferson considered creating classical elements like grottos, temples, and cascades so prominently featured at Painshill, Stowe, Hagley and other gardens that he visited. In the end, he contented himself with a pavilion located at the edge of the 1000 ft-long retaining wall for his vegetable garden.[43] At Poplar Forest, two finely finished octagonal brick privies, designed to be partially screened from view by successive plantings of weeping willows (*Salix babylonica*), paper mulberries (*Broussonetia papyrifera*), and privet (*Ligustrum sp.*), were the closest he came to garden temples.[44]

RIGHT
Figure 5. Map of South Lawn excavations showing locations of major features (adapted by author from drawing by Tim Trussell, courtesy of Thomas Jefferson's Poplar Forest).

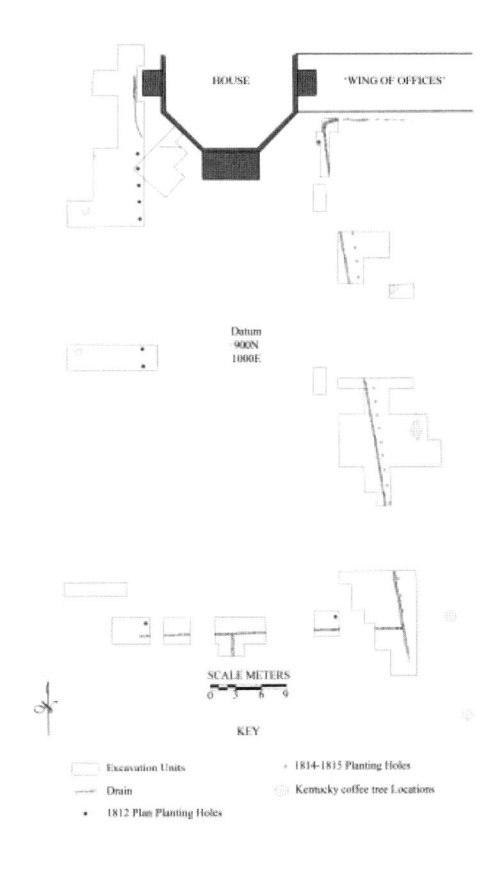

Jefferson selected common elements of the English picturesque style for his American grounds. Archaeological excavations northwest and northeast of the house have uncovered planting holes and root disturbances associated with two tree clumps as well as the remains of an oval bed where he specified the planting prickly locust (*Robinia hispida*).[45] These landscape features fit into a pre-existing grove of tulip poplars (*Liriodendron tulipifera*) that clustered along the north face of the lawn, most likely regenerating at the edge of an abandoned 18th-century tobacco field. Jefferson favoured the creation of groves in his grounds, explaining to a fellow gardener in Philadelphia, that in contrast to the 'canvas of open ground' of English landscape gardens,

> 'under the beaming, constant and almost vertical sun of Virginia shade is our Elysium…Let your ground be covered with trees of the loftiest stature. Trim up their bodies as high as the constitution & form of the tree will bear, but so as that their tops shall still unite & yield dense shade. A wood, so open below, will have nearly the appearance of open grounds.'[46]

That groves also symbolised removal from the world he made explicit on the occasion of his retirement, when he wrote, 'I shall now bury myself in the groves of Monticello, & become a mere spectator of the passing events.'[47]

At Poplar Forest, the north and south grounds were initially separated by an east-west alignment of *allées* of trees, mounds, privies, and their associated plantings. Later, the eastern *allée* was replaced by a row of service rooms attached to the main house. Jefferson referred to this addition as his 'Wing of Offices.' Archaeological excavations undertaken from 1989-1991 revealed the layout and function of these spaces.[48] While the north lawn favoured a naturalistic design, to the south the landscape took on the more geometric, orderly appearance common to gardens with Palladian or neoclassical associations. A sunken lawn dominated this more strongly geometric design.

The south lawn was the site of extensive excavations during the late 1990s. A complex of soil layers and features including an intact early 19th-century surface, individual planting holes for shrubs planted between *c.* 1812 and 1816, contemporaneous drains composed of quartz field stones, bricks, and schist, and larger disturbances resulting from the removal of Kentucky Coffee trees (*Gymnocladus dioica*) in the early 20th-century combined to tell the story of the lawn's evolving design (Fig. 5). Documents supply the rest. In 1812, Jefferson oversaw the planting of parallel rows of shrubs, placed 21.3m (70ft) apart and spaced at roughly 1.6m intervals (5.5-6 ft) at the base of the lawn's east and west banks. Evidence of the shrubs extended to a distance of 61m (200ft) south of the house, with further plantings possibly obliterated by a later garden. Given Jefferson's interest in dynamic symmetry, it is likely that he originally designed the lawn as a triple square measuring 21.3m x 64m (70ft x 210ft). Sometime between 1815 and 1817, he dramatically altered the plan, with the east bank being cut away at a 9.5 degree angle east of south and replanted to replicate that angle. The west bank and the western alignment of shrubs remained unaltered, resulting in an asymmetrical plan for the lawn that mirrored the asymmetry of the house following construction of the Wing of Offices.

Pollen and phytolith evidence recovered from soils associated with early 19th-century gardening corroborate and expand on the documentary record. An 1812 memorandum specified that lilacs (*Syringia sp.*), Rose of Sharon (*Althaea rosea*), gelder roses (*Viburnum opulus*), roses (*Rosa sp.*), and calycanthus (*Calycanthus floridus*) be planted along the lawn. With the exception of calycanthus, pollen and phytolith results supported the documents to varying degrees. Paleoethnobotanical analysis also pointed to the presence of flowering bulbs distributed throughout in the area, suggesting that one or more rows of flowers were planted at the base of the slope below the shrubs. Photographs taken in the late 19th and early 20th centuries show old Kentucky Coffee trees lining the tops of both banks in an alignment consistent with their planting sometime after the east bank was altered. A computer-aided photographic analysis of the trees, combined with the documentary evidence, supports the likelihood that these trees were part of Jefferson's redesign of this space. It now appears that the final design consisted of tiered vegetation ranging from flowers to shrubs to trees. Festicoid grasses from lawn-related contexts indicate that introduced grasses, likely planted as maintained turf, characterized the lawn's surface. Phytoliths recovered on the banks represent a variety of native grasses and weeds, suggestive of opportunistic growth and less regular maintenance of these areas.[49]

In 1813, the construction of the Wing of Offices necessitated further earthmoving. When complete, the addition consisted of four rooms set into a hillside, opening onto a covered, colonnaded walk, and roofed with a flat deck. This roof acted as an outdoor extension of the house, stretching 30.5m (100ft) east of a first floor bedroom. Jefferson ordered that soil from construction-related excavations be carted and dumped at a distance of 91.4m (300 ft). Enslaved labourers involved in this earthmoving episode, or the concurrent reshaping of the south lawn, were responsible for creating an artificial terrace that archaeologists have recently located southeast of the house. Construction-related soil was used to bury an existing structure or structures, possibly remnants of outbuildings associated with the nearby 'old plantation' complex built by Jefferson's father-in-law, which was being phased out at this time. The earlier activity area was likely replaced by pleasure grounds, with one or more new work-related structures erected outside of the four-hectare enclosure at a distance and elevation that precluded visibility from the main house.[50]

Jefferson continued to oversee modifications to the landscape until his final visit to the property in the spring of 1823 (Fig. 6). By that time, Poplar Forest had ceased to be a place of solitude, even by Jefferson's reckoning. Regular visits by neighbours, family members—especially grandchildren— and the installation of newlyweds Francis and Mary Eppes provided a limited, intimate audience for the messages embedded in this place.

Throughout his life, Jefferson believed that architecture and the arts had the ability to instruct and improve mankind, serving as models of taste and virtue. Poplar Forest became Jefferson's final material expression of beauty. Drawing on the aesthetic theories of Enlightenment philosophers, especially those of Lord Kames in his *Elements of Criticism*, Jefferson believed that harmonies of form or colour—manifested in classical and neoclassical architecture by good proportion and elegant ornamentation, and in contemporary landscape by a balance of regularity and variety—were intrinsically beautiful, able to be recognized and appreciated by all people. That which was tasteful was universally evident. Jefferson further believed that an appreciation of beauty exercised man's innate moral sense and that the regular exercise of moral feelings produced a habit of thinking and acting virtuously.[51]

Figure 6. Conjectural view of Jefferson's Poplar Forest based on archaeological findings and documents (adapted from original watercolor by Diane Johnson, courtesy of Thomas Jefferson's Poplar Forest).

After a lifetime of creating houses and gardens, Jefferson took one final opportunity to make tangible the connections between history, beauty, and virtue. While the primary audience for this lesson was his family, the strong mental connection that he drew between himself, the classical Republic, and the notion of retreat suggests that through his actions at Poplar Forest, Jefferson also saw himself in the broader context of a model statesman for the new nation. In that light, his retirement retreat became the material expression of his ideals for a new national identity.

CONCLUSIONS

The Poplar Forest of Jefferson's retirement was a complex autobiographical landscape, layered with contemporary aesthetic and historical references, Revolutionary ideology, life experiences, and family associations. The main house, inspired by Andrea Palladio's reinterpretation of ancient Roman villas, was a conspicuous symbol of Jefferson's embrace of the classical idiom in architecture.[52] Historian Colin Rowe captured the transformative qualities of Palladian design, noting, 'the ancient house is not recreated, but something far more significant is achieved: a creative nostalgia evokes a manifestation of mythical power in which the Roman and the ideal are equated,' while Carl Richard notes that 'the classics gave Jefferson a sense of identity and purpose. It enabled him to view himself as part of an ancient and noble struggle.'[53] The landscape surrounding the house melded ideas of ancient gardening with Jefferson's personal memory of modern gardens he had experienced in Europe and America.

As young Ellen Randolph sat at the table during that first visit of 1816, listening to her grandfather recall his 'early years and home and friends,' she was surrounded by more tangible representations of this landscape of memory. In the library sat Jefferson's volumes of 'Virgil, Tacitus, Caesar, Cicero, Ovid, Horace, Aesop, and Homer.'[54] The table might have been set with Ridgway plates, found in archaeological contexts associated with his household. Bordered by a neoclassical pattern of goats and cherubs that framed a series of views of Oxford College, they combined a complex series of symbols invoking the classical world, Jefferson's visit to Oxford in 1786, and his strong commitment to education, realized through his work in founding the University of Virginia a few years later. Through the window Ellen might have glimpsed the south lawn, laid out in lines of flowering shrubs of different types and opening to a view of fields and woodlands descending to a stream, a view sure to suggest 'variety among uniformity.'

This landscape, rich in memory, survived intact for less than a decade. Following Jefferson's death, the processes of change, reinvention, and recollection would transform Poplar Forest into both a commemorative landscape and the dynamic setting for new family histories.

NOTES

1. Epperson 2003, 58-77; Kryder-Reid 1994, 136, 140; Leone 1984, 371-391; Leone et al. 2005, 139, 140-142, 153-156; Leone and Shackel 1990, 153-167; Yentsch 1990, 169-170, 179-184.
2. De Cunzo et al. 1996, 96-113; King 1999, 77-105; McKee 1996, 76-87; Shackel 2003, 6-9.
3. Ryden 1993; Tilley 1994; King 1996.
4. Tilley 1994, 11.
5. Chambers 1993, 2-4; Heath 1999, 4-9.
6. Chambers 1993, 31-167; Brown 1990, 125-129.
7. Chambers 1993, 167-194; Olson 1999.
8. Chambers 1993, 195-208.
9. ViU, Ellen R. Coolidge to Henry S. Randall, February 18, 1856. The context of this quote in relation to the complete letter of which it was a part, along with subsequent letters strongly suggests that she is referring to Poplar Forest here.
10. Malone 1981a, 25-26.
11. Peden 1982, 20.
12. Peden 1982, 262, n. 7.
13. Chambers 1993, 4; Bear and Stanton 1997, 7.
14. Malone 1981a, 32.
15. Bear and Stanton 1997, 39-40.
16. Brown 1990, 129, 138.
17. By 1811, this land had passed out of the family.
18. MoSHi, Thomas Jefferson to Elizabeth Trist, April 27, 1806. He also wrote on this topic to his son-in-law. DLC Thomas Jefferson to Thomas Mann Randolph, January 17, 1809.
19. Thomas Jefferson Randolph was still selling off Poplar Forest land until 1836 as an agent of estate charged with settling debts.
20. Thomas Jefferson to John Brazier, August 24, 1819 in Lipscomb and Bergh 1904, 209; Randall 1857 (3), 346 (reprinted 1970).
21. In the 1760s and 1770s, he read widely on architecture and gardening, including Henry Home, *Lord Kames's Elements of Criticism* (Edinburgh 1762), James Gibbs's *Rules for Drawing the Several Parts of Architecture, The Builder's Dictionary* (1734), William Kent's *Designs of Inigo Jones* (1727), George Mason's *Essay on Design in Gardening* (1768), Andrea Palladio's *Quattro Libri dell'Architecttura*, Claude Perrault's *Architecture de Vitruve*, Jacob Spon's *Voyage d'Italie* (Amsterdam 1679), William Shenstone's *Works* (London, 1764), and Thomas Whately's *Observations on Modern Gardening* (1770), Beiswanger 1986, 176-177, 179.
22. Miller 1993, 23, 35-37.
23. Colbourn 1958, 57.
24. Colbourn 1958, 60-68. While his interest in Anglo-

Saxon history appears to have waned after the Revolution, he advocated teaching the language at the University of Virginia, and was discussing its merits with John Adams as late as 1820 (Thomas Jefferson to John Adams, August 15, 1820 as cited in Lipscomb and Bergh 1904, 270).
25. Wenger 1997, 238-241.
26. The plan depicts double rows of trees lining the western enclosure; however their regular 12.1m (40ft) spacing pattern does not suggest that they contributed to the effect of forced perspective.
27. Wenger 1997, 237-241; ViU, N255a.
28. Wenger 1997, 234.
29. Wenger 1997, 234.
30. Betts 1944, 94.
31. Manca 2003, 79-82; McDonald 1994, 3-5; Betts 1944, 394; DLC, Thomas Jefferson to Madame de Corgay, March 2, 1809.
32. Jefferson used the term 'retreat' to characterize his planned house while it was under construction, and favored the term 'distant possession,' which he used to describe it to nine separate correspondents between 1814-1821.
33. Brown 1990, 117-118.
34. DLC, Thomas Jefferson to Benjamin Rush, August 17, 1811.
35. Brown 1990, 127.
36. MHi, Thomas Jefferson to William Coffee, July 10, 1822.
37. Chambers 1993, 145-147; McDonald 1994, 5-6; McDonald 2002, 32; Randall 1857, 342 (reprinted 1970).
38. CsmH, Thomas Jefferson to Frances Eppes, April 18, 1813.
39. Kern 2005, 224-225.
40. Beiswanger 1986, 180; Shackelford 1995, 18, 19, 36, 39, 50-60, 65-67, 126, 151-152.
41. Thomas Jefferson to John Page 1786, as cited in Betts 1944, 111.
42. Boyd and Bryan 1956, 269.
43. Beiswanger 1986, 170-185; Kelso 1990, 11-13.
44. Betts 1944, 464-465, 549, 563.
45. Heath 1993, 49-73, 75-82. A surviving bed containing an antique rose variety and lying due north of the house may mark the location of a central bed where Jefferson instructed that 'large roses of difft. kinds' be planted; the northeast bed of 'dwarf roses' has not been located.
46. Betts 1944, 322-325.
47. Looney 2004, 24.
48. Kelso et al. 1991.
49. Because the documented shrubs are pollinated by insects, individual pollen grains were heavy in relation to wind-born pollens and produced in much smaller quantities. While these attributes posed challenges for identification using standard analytical techniques, they also allowed for identifications that were fairly location-specific. By expanding standard counts of 200 grains per sample to 1,000-2,000 grain counts, analysts were able to identify ornamentals that produce relatively small quantities of pollen. Analysis confirmed the presence of *Althaea rosea*) and Viburnum (possibly *Viburnum opulus*) along the east bank. Pollen and phytoliths from the *Oleaceae* family, which includes lilac among its members, and *Rosaceae*, which includes roses, were also found. In addition, both pollen and phytolith samples contained evidence of members of the *Liliaceae* family; with phyoliths suggesting taxa such as hyacinth or lily. Kealofer 1999; Anderson et al. 2000; Trussell 2000, 62-76; Jones 2001, 2002, Table 3; Reiley et al. 2002.
50. Heath et al. 2004, 9, 29; Heath et al. 2005, 12, 21.
51. Hafertepe 2000.
52. Brown 1990, 117-118; Malone 1981b, 17; McDonald 2000, 177-178, 191, 2002, Trussell 2000, 126-129.
53. Rowe 1976, 15; Richard 1989, 454-455.
54. Chambers 1993, 86.

BIBLIOGRAPHY

Bear, J. A. Jr. and Stanton, L. C. (eds) 1997, *Jefferson's Memorandum Books*, Vol. 1 & 2, Princeton: Princeton University Press.

Beiswanger, W. L. 1986, 'The temple in the garden: Thomas Jefferson's vision of the Monticello landscape', in Maccubbin & Martin 1986, 170-188.

Betts, E. M. (ed.) 1944, *Thomas Jefferson's garden book 1766-1824*, Philadelphia: The American Philosophical Society.

Boyd, J. P. & Bryan, M. R. (eds) 1956, *The Papers of Thomas Jefferson, March 1788 to October 1788*, vol. 13, Princeton: Princeton University Press.

Brown, C. A. 1990, 'Thomas Jefferson's Poplar Forest: the mathematics of an ideal villa', *Journal of Garden History* 10:2, 117-139.

Chambers, S. A. 1993, *Poplar Forest and Thomas Jefferson*, Forest, Virginia: The Corporation for Jefferson's Poplar Forest.

Colbourn, H. T. 1958, 'Thomas Jefferson's use of the past', *The William and Mary Quarterly* 3rd Ser., 15:1, 56-70.
De Cunzo, L., O'Malley, T., Lewis, M. J., Thomas, G. E. & Wilmanns-Wells, C. 1996, 'Father Rapp's garden at Economy: harmony society culture in microcosm', in Yamin & Bescherer Metheny 1996, 91-117.
Delle, J. A., Mrozowski, S. A. & Paynter, R. (eds) 2003, *Lines that Divide, Historical Archaeologies of Race, Class, and Gender*, Knoxville: University of Tennessee Press.
Epperson, T. W. 2003, 'Panoptic plantations, the garden sights of Thomas Jefferson and George Mason,' in Delle et al. 2003, 58-77.
Haftertepe, K. 2000, 'An inquiry into Thomas Jefferson's ideas of beauty', *The Journal of the Society of Architectural Historians* 54:1, 216-231.
Heath, B. J. 1999, *Hidden Lives, The Archaeology of Slave Life at Thomas Jefferson's Poplar Forest*, Charlottesville: University Press of Virginia.
Kelso, W. M. 1990, 'Landscape archaeology at Thomas Jefferson's Monticello', in Kelso & Most 1990, 7-22.
Kelso, W. M. & Most, R. (eds) 1990, *Earth Patterns, Essays in Landscape Archaeology*, Charlottesville: University Press of Virginia.
Kern, S. A. 2005, 'The material world of the Jeffersons at Shadwell', *The William and Mary Quarterly* 3rd Ser., 62:2, 213-242.
King, J. A. 1996, '"The transient nature of all things sublunary": romanticism, history, and ruins in nineteenth-century southern Maryland', in Yamin & Bescherer Metheny 1996, 249-272.
King, J. A. 1999, 'Landscape and the use of the past in 19th-century Virginia', in Reinhart & Sprinkle 1999, 77-109.
Kryder-Reid, E. 1994, '"As is the gardener, so is the garden": The archaeology of landscape as myth', in Shackel & Little 1994, 131-148.
Leone, M. P. 1984, 'Interpreting ideology in historical archaeology: using the rules of perspective in the William Paca garden in Annapolis, Maryland', in Orser 1996, 371-391.
Leone, M. P., Harmon, J. M. & Neuwirth, J. L. 2005, 'Perspective and surveillance in eighteenth-century Maryland gardens, including William Paca's garden on Wye Island', *Historical Archaeology* 39:4, 138-158.
Leone, M. P. & Shackel, P. 1990, 'Plane and solid geometry in colonial gardens in Annapolis, Maryland', in Kelso & Most 1990, 153-167.
Lipscomb, A. A. & Bergh, A. E. (eds) 1904, *The Writings of Thomas Jefferson*, Washington, D.C.: Thomas Jefferson Memorial Association.
Looney, J. J. (ed.) 2004, *The Papers of Thomas Jefferson, Retirement Series, March 1809 to November 1809*, vol. 1, Princeton: Princeton University Press.
Maccubbin, R. P. & Martin, P. (eds) 1986, *British and American Gardens in the Eighteenth Century*, Williamsburg, Virginia: The Colonial Williamsburg Foundation.
McDonald, T. C. 1994, Poplar Forest, synthesis of a lifetime', *Notes on the State of Poplar Forest* 2, 1-7.
McDonald, T. C. 2000, 'Constructing optimism, Thomas Jefferson's Poplar Forest', in McMurry & Adams 2000, 176-200.
McDonald, T.C. 2002, 'Thomas Jefferson's Poplar Forest, privacy restored', *Virginia Cavalcade* 51:1, 26-35.
McKee, L. 1996, 'The archaeology of Rachel's garden', in Yamin & Bescherer Metheny 1996, 70-90.
McMurry, S. & Adams A. (eds) 2000, *People, Power, Places, Perspectives in Vernacular Architecture III*, Knoxville: The University of Tennessee Press.
Malone, D. 1981a, *Jefferson the Virginian*, Boston: Little, Brown and Company.
Malone D. 1981b. *The Sage of Monticello*, Boston: Little, Brown and Company.
Manca, J. 2003, 'Cicero in America: civic duty and private happiness in Charles Willson Peale's portrait of "William Paca", *American Art* 17:1, 68-89.
Miller, C. A. 1993, *Jefferson and Nature, an Interpretation*, Baltimore: The Johns Hopkins University Press.
Orser, C. E. Jr. (ed.) 1996, *Images of the Recent Past, Readings in Historical Archaeology*, Walnut Creek: Altamira Press.
Peden, W. (ed.) 1982, *Notes on the State of Virginia*, New York: W.W. Norton & Company.

Randall, H. S. 1857, *The Life of Thomas Jefferson*. 3 vols. Reprinted 1970 by Freeport, New York: Books for Libraries Press.
Reinhart, T. R. & Sprinkle, J. H. Jr. (eds) 1999, *The Archaeology of 19th-Century Virginia*, Richmond: The Archaeological Society of Virginia, Spectrum Press.
Richard, C. J. 1989, 'A dialogue with the ancients: Thomas Jefferson and classical philosophy and history', *Journal of the Early Republic* 9, 431-455.
Rowe C. 1976, *The mathematics of the ideal villa and other essays*, Cambridge: MIT Press.
Ryden, K. C. 1993, *Mapping the Invisible Landscape: Folklore, Writing and the Sense of Place*, Iowa City: University of Iowa Press.
Shackel, P. A. 2003, 'Archaeology, memory and landscapes of conflict', *Historical Archaeology* 37:3, 3-13.
Shackel, P. A. & Little, B. J. (eds) 1994, *Historical Archaeology of the Chesapeake*, Washington, D.C.: Smithsonian Institution Press.
Shackelford, G. G. 1995, *Thomas Jefferson's Travels in Europe 1784-1789*, Baltimore: Johns Hopkins University Press.
Tilley, C. 1994, *A Phenomenology of Landscape: Places, Paths and Monument*. Oxford: Berg.
Wenger M. R. 1997, 'Jefferson's designs for remodeling the Governor's Palace', *Winterthur Portfolio* 32:4, 223-242.
Yamin, R. & Bescherer Metheny, K. (eds) 1996, *Landscape Archaeology, Reading and Interpreting the American Historical Landscape*, Knoxville: The University of Tennessee Press.
Yentsch, A. 1990, 'The Calvert orangery in Annapolis, Maryland, a horticultural symbol of power and prestige in an early eighteenth-century community', in Kelso & Most 1990, 169-187.

UNPUBLISHED SOURCES

ViU, Correspondence of Ellen Wayles Randolph Coolidge, 1810-1861, Accession #38-584, 9090, 9090-c Special Collections.
ViU, Poplar Forest. Plan of house, rooms designated in Anglo-Saxon. Survey on reverse. N255.
MoSHi, Thomas Jefferson to Elizabeth Trist, April 27, 1806.
DLC, Thomas Jefferson to Thomas Mann Randolph, January 17, 1809.
DLC, Thomas Jefferson to Madame de Corgay, March 2, 1809.
DLC, Thomas Jefferson to Benjamin Rush, August 17, 1811.
MHi, Thomas Jefferson to William Coffee, July 10, 1822.
CsmH, Thomas Jefferson to Frances W. Eppes April 18, 1813.

Anderson, S. & Brunner-Jass R. 2000, 'Pollen analysis of historic features at Thomas Jefferson's Poplar Forest estate, Bedford County, Virginia', Manuscript, Forest, Virginia: Thomas Jefferson's Poplar Forest.
Heath, B. J. 1993, 'A report on the 1992-1993 excavations: the perimeter of the house and excavations related to restoration drainage/foundation work at Poplar Forest, Forest, Virginia', Manuscript, Forest, Virginia: Thomas Jefferson's Poplar Forest.
Heath, B. J., Lichtenberger, R. M., Adams, K. W., & Paull, E. 2004, 'Poplar Forest archaeology: studies in African American life, excavations and analysis of Site A, Southeast Terrace and Site B, Southeast Curtilage, June 2003-June 2004', Manuscript, Forest, Virginia: Thomas Jefferson's Poplar Forest.
Heath, B. J., Lichtenberger, R. M., Adams, K. W., Lee, L. & Paull, E. 2005, 'Poplar Forest archaeology: studies in plantation life and landscape, excavations and analysis of Site B, Southeast Curtilage, June 2004–August 2005', Manuscript, Forest, Virginia: Thomas Jefferson's Poplar Forest.
Jones, J. 2001, 'Analysis of pollen from Poplar Forest, Virginia', Manuscript, Forest, Virginia: Thomas Jefferson's Poplar Forest.
Jones, J. 2002, 'Analysis of pollen from Poplar Forest, Virginia', Manuscript, Forest, Virginia: Thomas Jefferson's Poplar Forest.
Kealofer, L. 1999, 'The south lawn at Poplar Forest, phytolith analysis', Manuscript, Forest, Virginia: Thomas Jefferson's Poplar Forest.
Kelso, W. M., Patten, D. & Strutt, M. A. 1991, 'Poplar Forest Archaeology Research Report for NEH Grant

1990-1991, Short Version'. Manuscript, Forest, Virginia: Thomas Jefferson's Poplar Forest.

Olson, H. A. 1999, 'The changing face of Poplar Forest: exploring nineteenth-century landscape modifications', Manuscript, Forest, Virginia: Thomas Jefferson's Poplar Forest.

Rieley & Associates & Field, E. M. 2002, 'A photographic analysis of the Kentucky Coffeetrees on the south lawn at Thomas Jefferson's Poplar Forest', Manuscript, Forest, Virginia: Thomas Jefferson's Poplar Forest.

Trussell, T. 2000, 'Jefferson's villa in the garden: a report on the landscape archaeology project at Thomas Jefferson's Poplar Forest 1998-1999,' Manuscript, Forest, Virginia: Thomas Jefferson's Poplar Forest.

ABBREVIATIONS

CsmH   Henry E. Huntington Library and Art Gallery,
DLC Library of Congress
MHi Massachusetts Historical Society
MoSHi   Missouri Historical Society
ViU University of Virginia

Monuments and Memory in the Estate Landscape: Castle Howard and Sledmere

By HAROLD MYTUM

This paper examines the ways in which commemoration and remembrance were evoked in the estate landscape through the erection of monuments. Previous research on commemoration in the context of estates has tended to focus on mausolea. An archaeological perspective can place these in a local commemorative context, as exemplified here with Castle Howard and the nearby villages of Bulmer, Welburn and Conseysthorpe. Other strategies can be identified, however, as exemplified by Sledmere. Here, a series of monuments in the church, the estate village and beyond were gradually constructed to extol the virtues of successive generations. Not only were the land-owning families visible in the Sledmere commemorative landscape. Those who died in the World Wars, and particularly valued members of the household or estate workforce, could also be remembered. The monumental reminders of past people and events created a historical context for the continued working of the estate, and reinforced the ethic of loyalty to the estate, county and country.

INTRODUCTION

The estate landscape incorporates many elements, the house and its formal gardens and parkland, its agricultural fields and buildings, woodland and copses for game, housing for estate workers, and a church and churchyard for the whole population. Within this mosaic, linked by a network of footpaths, track ways and roads, inhabitants and visitors of every station made their way about their business. As they did so, they experienced a landscape full of sensations and, for many, remembrance of those then dead. Most of these memories were personal and are generally no longer accessible to us, but others were invoked through the use of monuments placed in the landscape. What memories and reactions were felt by these people would have varied over time and social context, but the monuments were certainly erected with the purpose of generating remembrance of deceased individuals. Their public nature allows some consideration of their role in social memory.[1]

For some archaeologists, emotions generated by such features could be seen as an important aspect of research,[2] but it is too easy to impose our own feelings or create stereotypical reactions that are unverifiable. In this study the monuments, their form, texts and locations are considered so that their creators' aspirations may be suggested, and their visual impact on others, at least, can be noted; these were deliberately created to evoke memory. The construction of monuments in the landscape altered the perceptions of movement and divisions of space by creating fixed points that carried associations with the past. As such the monuments formed part of the everyday life of the inhabitants, and their actions and reactions in relation to these monuments was an element in their agency, often considered biographically in terms of their own experience and that of their family and friends. They were thus active in the formulation of identities from the personal to the national.[3] It is possible to identify the existing structural features of normative cultural behaviour, explicit regulations and elite ideals and values within and against which

Figure 1. Memorials in the Castle Howard estate landscape.
A Pyramid to Lord William Howard; B Mausoleum; C Column to the 7th Earl; D Bulmer church; E Welburn Church; F Coneysthorpe cemetery.

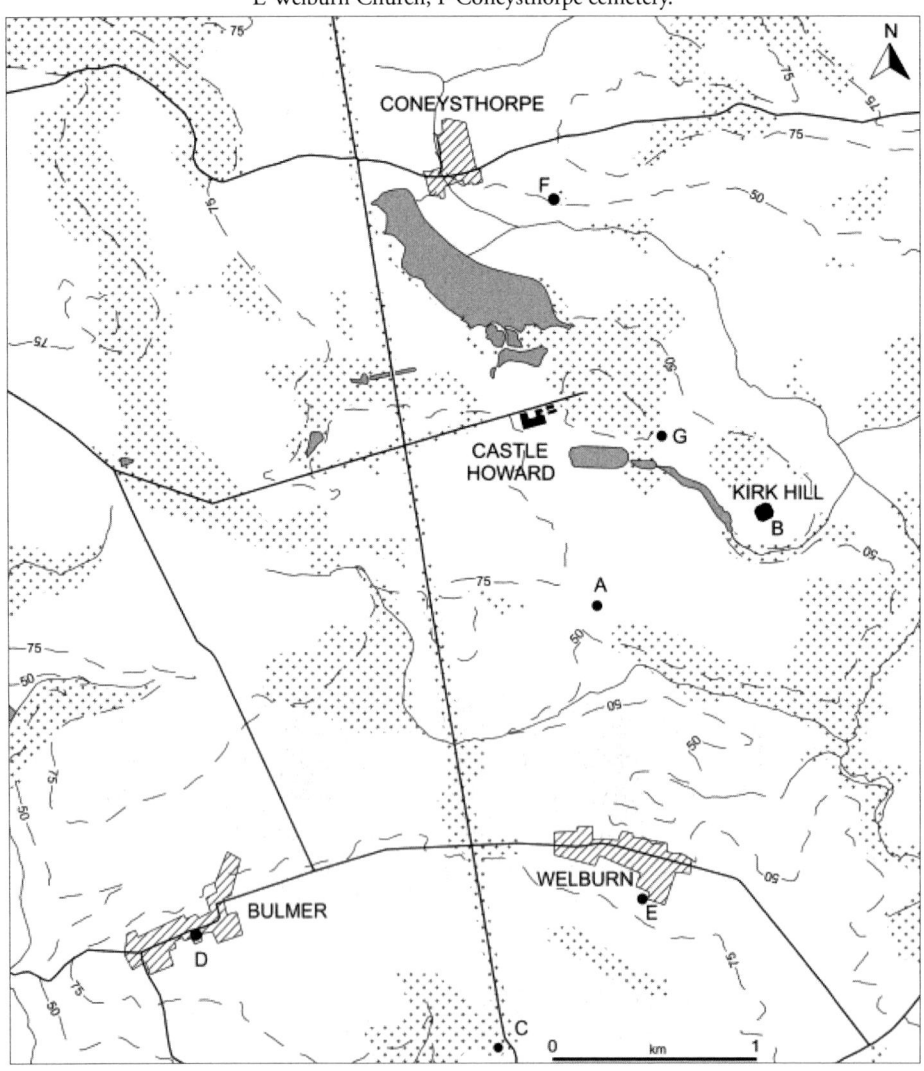

individuals of all classes could act, their agency often reinforcing but sometimes challenging the existing patterns of commemoration and the perpetuation of memory. Moreover, the placing of the monuments over the landscape allows space to be part of the medium of transmission – travelling past a number of monuments, seeing them in the distance, is also important.[4]

Many memorials were within buildings, both domestic and religious. They varied greatly from paintings and photographs to samplers and memorial cards in secular contexts,[5] and from large tombs to stained glass windows in ecclesiastical ones. These all generated memories within intimate spaces. Interesting and important though these were, they are difficult to reconstruct given the changes in internal decoration and furnishing over the generations,[6] and so only some internal church monuments are considered here. Nevertheless, the aspects outlined below would have been set against a constant pattern of other iteration and reinforcement of remembrance that came in other local contexts. Many estate owners focused commemoration only in the local church and churchyard, and here the combination of internal and external memorials can be instructive. The ownership of internal or external family vaults provided an appropriate resting place for the mortal remains,[7] and a gradual increase in the number of internal monuments could create impressive genealogies in stone. These are important and have been little studied in this regard, but are beyond the scope of the landscape theme of this study, though church and churchyard monuments are considered within the repertoire of commemorative forms in the two Yorkshire case studies discussed below, and graveyard monuments have been considered within a spatial context in a few studies.[8]

MEMORIES IN THE LANDSCAPE AND CHURCHYARD - CASTLE HOWARD MAUSOLEUM AND THE ESTATE CHURCHES, NORTH YORKSHIRE

The landscape around Castle Howard was a carefully contrived environment for contemplation and memory (Fig. 1). Here Charles Howard, the 3rd Earl of Carlisle, cleared away the medieval village of Henderskelfe and its castle, and had erected the house and gardens of which so much has been written.[9] Memories of the previous owners were thus eradicated, and Howard familial associations were promoted in their place. External commemoration was most notable with the Pyramid erected in 1728 (Fig. 1A) and celebrating the ancestor Lord William Howard, alive five generations earlier and having no association with the place. The celebrated mausoleum for the 3rd Earl and his descendants was the other major commemorative feature of the original design (Fig. 1B), prominently placed on Kirk Hill. This was subsequently augmented in 1865 by the church at Welburn, dedicated to Georgiana, wife of the 7th Earl, and a column to the 7th Earl, erected in 1869-70 on the edge of a scarp, beside the start of the approach to the house from the south (Fig. 1C).

THE MAUSOLEUM

The mausoleum (Fig. 1B) was the first burial structure erected away from the control of the English church, and had been in the mind of the earl since at least 1722.[10] Here we see the conscious action of a person disillusioned with the established church, able to challenge the accepted structure of ecclesiastical burial and commemoration. The architect Vanbrugh, and Lord Carlisle, both shared a strong anti-clerical stance and, to quote Charles Saumarez Smith, 'The mausoleum was to be an emblem of a universe that was rational, lucid and mathematical. It was to be bereft of conventional symbols of the resurrection and free from the jurisdiction of the priesthood'.[11] The mausoleum underwent a long and convoluted history of design, under Vanbrugh, Hawksmoor and Garrett, seeing the deaths of the first two architects and its commissioner Lord Carlisle, only being completed in 1745. It is not the intention here to further discuss this much-described building, but rather to note its placing within the designed landscape of Castle Howard. This allowed the integration of ancestor memory with other contemplations encouraged by the reworked landscape, planting of trees, commissioned statuary and other buildings such as the Temple of the Four Winds (Fig. 1C), from which a stunning view of the mausoleum could be obtained. The mausoleum could also be seen from many other locations on the estate; its rotunda visible above the tree-tops in many directions. The message of authority and ancestry was thus reinforced not only within the gardens but also to the population on the wider estate. It is in this light that it is important also to move from this to another, more traditional location for commemoration and monumentality and one where the estate can also be seen to have had a notable impact.

Though against the clergy and not greatly enthused by the Church of England, Lord Carlisle was aware that he could die before his long-planned mausoleum was completed. He therefore instructed that his body should be placed in the nearby Bulmer church, and it is here that some commemorative evidence survives. Two members of the Carlisle family were indeed interred within the chancel of Bulmer church but were later translated to the mausoleum after its completion. The first to be buried was the 3rd Earl, who was interred on 14th May 1738.[12] He was placed beneath an existing grave slab, and a simple inscription was placed inside the marginal late medieval text. The reuse of this earlier, relatively high status monument to Sir Ralph Bulmer,[13] one of the family that had given their name to the village, may have been deliberate, or it may have been incidental to the need to place the Earl in a prestigious location within the chancel, and thus beneath this slab. Charles, Lord Viscount Morpeth, died in 1741, and he was buried on 17th August[14] beneath a slab near the south door of the porch, again marked by a simple inscription. Both slabs were subsequently inscribed 'Removed to the Mausoleum MDCCXLV'. In the mausoleum, both were placed in loculi immediately to the right of the basement entrance; the terms loculi and basement were those used by Hawksmoor in his letters to the 3rd Earl.[15]

BULMER CHURCHYARD

Although no memorials to the Carlisles were erected at Bulmer, a surrogate form of commemoration was provided there for many generations. This was through a number of exterior memorials which overtly demonstrate a pattern of patronage which links the Carlisles to this community (Table 1). Some of the memorials were clearly paid for by the Earls or their wives, but others suggest that local families identified themselves in some way with the Castle Howard estate.

Figure 2. Memorials to Castle Howard workers in Bulmer churchyard. (clockwise from top left) a James Nicholson, groom to the 3rd Earl of Carlisle, d. 1733; b monument on the south wall of the porch to Christopher Thompson, craftsman, d. 1748; c chest tomb to Iveson Wise, butler to the 4th Earl of Carlisle, d. 1748; d Memorial in Coneysthorpe burial ground to Geoffrey and Ethel Howard, d. 1935, 1932.

The earliest external memorials date from the period of the 3rd Earl; although none of the inscriptions explicitly state Carlisle patronage, this is highly likely. The larger monuments would have been beyond the resources of those commemorated and, given the limited number of other external stone memorials at this period in graveyards in this region, all including the smaller headstones may have been produced through patronage. The earliest external memorial with a clear date is to James Nicholson, groom to the 3rd Earl for 20 years (Fig. 2a). During the 1740s some impressive monuments were erected in the graveyard, and two are worth noting as examples here. The first is a large memorial on the east side of the southern porch with a long text and Greek key pattern border. It is to Christopher Thompson who was a craftsman with long service at Castle Howard (Fig. 2b). The other is a very large chest tomb with clusters of three columns on each corner, and an inscribed southern face. This monument was erected to Iveson Wise, butler to the 4th Earl of Carlisle (Fig. 2c). Neither inscription states that the Carlisle family paid for the monuments, but this must have been the case, and so suggests a deliberate monumental investment in the churchyard for much valued retainers at the time that mausoleum was just coming into use for the family. The mausoleum was first used in 1745, and soon after these two elaborate monuments, to trusted servants who both died in 1748, were erected in the churchyard. This supports the inference that the translation of the aristocratic remains in 1745 encouraged the Howards to substitute their visibility in the Bulmer ecclesiastical locale through commissioning retainer monuments instead. The scale and size of such monuments is greater than any found in graveyards of the region at this time. The gentry were placing marble wall monuments within the church, and those successful in commerce or agriculture aspired to ledger slabs within the church or less elaborate and smaller table or chest tombs in the churchyard. Here, important and trusted servants of long standing were provided with even larger and more impressive memorials than their social superiors;

Figure 3. (Left) a Welburn church, 1865, a memorial erected by the 7th Earl of Carlisle to his mother Georgiana.

(Right) Memorials at Sledmere church; b simple Gothic revival low granite coped monument to Sir Tatton Sykes, d. 1863; c internal wall monument to Mary Kirkby and her family; d medieval style monument to Sir Mark Sykes, d. 1919.

Sacred to the Memory of the Family of Kirkby:
formerly of Cottingham, descended from Sir Robert Kirkby;
and particularly to Mary, Second Daughter and Coheiress of
Mark Kirkby Esq.r who married Richard Sykes Esq.r
and died the 14th Day of April 1714.
He was descended from the Sykeses, formerly of Sykes Dike in
Cumberland.
This Tablet is gratefully inscribed by their Descendant
Sir Chris.r Sykes Bart.
Sledmere 1795.

the 4th Earl could demonstrate his role in the estate through these features that were highly visible to all who attended the churchyard.

During the period of the 5th Earl four more monuments were erected. Some of the gravestones may have been commissioned by the Howards, or by relations of the deceased who noted their association with Castle Howard as part of their own strategies of identity; the inscriptions are not explicit regarding patronage. Another substantial chest tomb to John Turner, described as a servant, commemorated his death in 1788, and this again is a monument that is highly likely to be a gift from the Earl. Two more individuals died during the period of the 6th Earl, and twelve in the time of the 7th Earl, though many of these retainers had served several generations of the Howard family. Indeed, in the middle of the 19th century a whole cohort of long-lived servants can be identified on their memorials by their service; some of these were explicitly provided by the Earls of Carlisle (Table 1). Others, such as that to Isaac Elliot, seem to be commemorated on monuments selected by the family. It would seem that key household servants and estate employees – butlers, valets, housekeepers, grooms, gardeners and keepers - were those who were commemorated, and especially those with very long service. Some are described as friend, emphasising a relationship of special quality. Two of those who were commemorated during the time of the 8th Earl had served the Howards since the 5th Earl and presumably had a long association with the ancient church at Bulmer. Given the unstable mental state of the 8th Earl and his non-residence of Castle Howard, it is unlikely that the family was strongly associated with these memorials, though both reflect in their inscriptions long service to the Earls. The 9th Earl never cared for Castle Howard and although his wife Rosalind was involved in many local affairs, her temperament probably did not encourage devotion.[16] Only three other Bulmer memorials include any reference to Castle Howard, one mentioning the lodge as an address, the other two noting Castle Howard as the place of death. No memorials mention Castle Howard after 1910, which reflects its declining direct importance; by the late 1930s, only four indoor servants were employed at the house.[17]

Commemorative monuments thus emphasise patronage, loyalty, service and mutual respect, whilst retaining social order through choice of monument type and spatial arrangement. Some reflect actions by the country house owners, others are commissioned by the deceased and/or their relations, and actively select associations with the house and its family as part of their commemorative strategy. This was important in the 18th and 19th centuries, though the significance of the estate association waned during the latter part of the 19th century and was absent for most of the 20th century. Bulmer was unusual in the scale of the early patronage, but the later headstones mirror a wider pattern found at estate churchyards.

WELBURN CHURCH

Welburn, a Castle Howard estate village lying east of Bulmer, was until 1865 served by the Bulmer church and churchyard. In that year a new church and churchyard were completed at Welburn after several years of construction. Although ostensibly funded by public subscription the works were largely paid for by the unmarried 7th Earl of Carlisle (Fig. 3a). The church was in remembrance of his mother, Georgiana, who died in 1858, and a tablet in the tower porch states this clearly to all who enter. A memorial in the chancel, and the stained glass east window, were both contributed by Georgiana's friends. This demonstrates a later phase of patronage by the Carlisles, though here commemorating a member of the family whilst providing a new place of worship and burial. The Earl himself was commemorated by his sisters and nieces with a large brass plaque and west window after his death in 1864, before the church was completed. However, neither he nor Georgiana were buried at Welburn, and both lie within the mausoleum on the estate. Thus, Welburn provided a commemorative role for two generations of the Howards, but otherwise Welburn shows limited explicit link with the estate in its churchyard memorials.

The recording of the graveyard at Welburn has highlighted the pattern already noted at Bulmer,[18] that by the later 19th century explicit association with the estate was not a significant element in social identity as revealed on monuments (Table 2). Only two monuments link individuals to service of the Earls of Carlisle. The first was erected by Lady Taunton for David Beale who, despite being only 32 on his death, had served the 6th and 7th Earls for seventeen years. The other monument was a white marble cross, erected after the death of John Pallister in 1925, coachman and friend to four generations at Castle Howard. The most frequent mention of Castle Howard is in relation to place of death, with two individuals dying at Castle Howard, and two young males accidentally drowned in the lake in the 1890s. This is only an association through method of death, a common identifier for those who have succumbed to an unusual or early death. Two more memorials identify individuals associated with Henderskelfe, Castle Howard, and three others are linked to Castle Howard School, but none of these indicate a strong estate element, Castle Howard acting more as a simple place name. Despite the fact that many of those buried must have been employed on, or were tenants of, the estate, this was rarely seen as a significant element of their social identity. Despite the philanthropy of building the church, the links to the Howards were not emphasised in Welburn graveyard. This reflects not only the lack of interest in the estate by the later Earls but also probably the changing attitudes to such families by the local population.

The church to Georgiana was later complemented by a substantial monument to her son the 7th Earl placed in the landscape to the west (Fig. 1c). A tall column was erected in 1870,[19] set on a massive base on which four knight's helmets were placed. It is located at the southernmost point of The Stray, the long straight approach to the house from the south. Recently restored, it clearly formed part of a later 19th-century effort to contribute to the estate landscape. Both this column and the Welburn church spire were widely visible, and created new fixed points in the estate landscape that added to the 18th-century creations of the 3rd Earl.

CONEYSTHORPE

The small village church was not provided with its own graveyard when constructed in 1835,[20] but a 20th-century burial ground lies outside the village, facing the lake and with a view across it to the north front of the house. Links to the estate are not present on the gravestones, unsurprising given the 20th-century trends already observed at Bulmer and Welburn, but it is noteworthy that one of the Howards is commemorated there. Geoffrey

William Algernon Howard was the first Howard who was not an Earl of Carlisle to inherit Castle Howard. He died in 1935 and his wife, Ethel Christian, died in 1932. Their memorial is a distinctive and unusual monument, and a fine quality product of its time (Fig. 2d).

LANDSCAPE WITH MEMORIALS - SLEDMERE, EAST YORKSHIRE

The creation of mausolea such as that of Castle Howard within estate landscapes created points of remembrance that also served as aesthetically pleasing features within the countryside. Though often used far less consistently than their creators had intended, they acted as communal, familial statements of continuity and genealogy, though the details would only be known to those familiar with the family as they have no external commemorative inscriptions. Other commemorative landscapes such as that of Stow, Buckinghamshire, contained scattered monuments not only linked to Cobham by genealogy, but also politics. Its aesthetic and Whig messages attracted a great deal of attention when they were constructed,[21] and have become a popular subject for study in the renaissance of interest in garden history in the later 20th century.[22] Other landscapes also could contain a scatter of monuments, though related more traditionally back to the landowning family. A fine example of this commemorative strategy can be seen on the Sledmere on the Yorkshire Wolds where a wide range of monuments has been set up within the landscape (Fig. 4).

The Sykes family are well documented, and their archives are now housed at the Brynmor Jones Library at the University of Hull.[23] The family made its fortune in shipping, particularly with the Baltic out of Hull, and in finance. The link to Sledmere was achieved through marriage of Richard Sykes to Mary Kirkby, co-heiress to the Sledmere estates. His eldest son, also called Richard, was now much more wealthy, and so could replace the medieval manor house in 1751. He also demolished the medieval nave and chancel of the parish church close to the house, replacing them in a neo-classical design (Fig. 4A). On his death without issue in 1761, the estate passed to his brother Mark, the 1st Baronet. The Revd. Sir Mark was Rector of Roos in Holderness, East Yorkshire, and on his death in 1783 he was commemorated in All Saints church there with a fine wall monument in the church and a burial vault in the churchyard, paid for according to his will of 1781;[24] no memorial is extant from Sledmere. His son, Sir Christopher Sykes, greatly increased the family fortunes in 1770 by marrying Elizabeth Egerton of Tatton who benefited several times during her life by inheritances. The shipping and other Sykes family interests were disposed of, and instead all efforts were devoted to expanding and improving the Sledmere estate, increasing it to nearly 30,000 acres. In the 1780s Sir Christopher added two wings to the house, creating an H plan, the grounds were landscaped and the village moved to its present position.[25] Sir Christopher took a very great interest in agricultural improvement, and enclosed many areas and brought them into cultivation for the first time since the Middle Ages.

The importance of marriages and the resources they brought are acknowledged in two identical neo-classical church wall monuments in the form of sarcophogi topped with pairs of urns which were set up on the south wall of the nave (Table 3), both erected in 1795 (Fig. 3c). One commemorated the Kirkby family, and particularly Mary who married Richard Sykes; the other remembered Elizabeth Egerton who provided the second major influx of

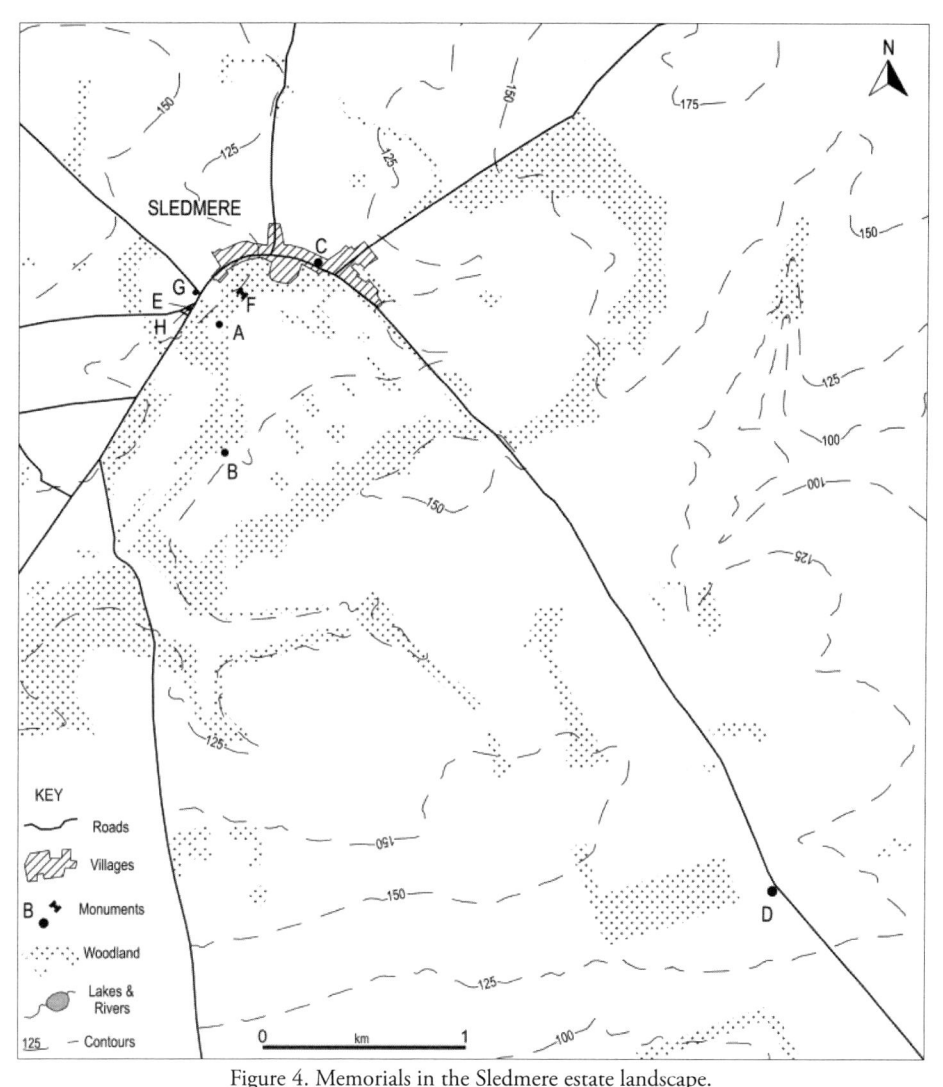

Figure 4. Memorials in the Sledmere estate landscape.
A Church; B Pet memorial; C Rotunda to Sir Christopher Sykes; D Monument to Sir Tatton Sykes, d. 1863; E Eleanor Cross and War Memorial; F Catholic chapel, Sledmere House; G Wagoners' memorial; H Bench to Sir Richard Sykes and his wife Virginia.

funds which allowed for the development of the Wolds landscape and the family fortunes via her niece Elizabeth, wife of Christopher Sykes.

The first monument within the grounds of Sledmere House was a pedestal tomb to commemorate favourite dogs of the Sykes (Fig. 4B; Fig. 5a). On the southern vertical panel an inset bronze plaque provides a long quotation from Byron extolling the dog, with another face inscribed in Latin to commemorate two dogs that died in the 1780s. The other faces have later commemorations up to the 1980s (Table 4). This monument, a feature in the parkland which also served to remember special dogs, shows intermittent use over six generations, and is another enduring and repeatedly active contribution to the landscape of memory; it is now publicly accessible with the introduction of a permissive path through the grounds.[26]

Sir Christopher's son, Sir Mark Sykes, began the tradition of family commemoration within the wider landscape when he had a monument to his father erected opposite the west lodge, and over the village well (Fig. 4C; Fig. 5b). It was built in 1840, and consists of a rotunda supported on eight Tuscan columns, and with a suitably laudatory inscription (Table 4). It would have been seen by the Sykes family members whenever they left their home, but also by the inhabitants of Sledmere as they visited the well, and by travellers through the village as it is right next to the main thoroughfare.

Sir Mark died without issue, and his brother Tatton Sykes became the 4th baronet, and devoted his time very successfully to agriculture and horse breeding and racing. The next memorial to be erected was to this Sir Tatton Sykes, who died in 1863, after 40 years running the estate. This monument was built two years later, not in the village but on the edge of the scarp off the Wolds (Fig. 4D; Fig. 5c). It was positioned where an old green lane that ran along the escarpment cut across the road (now the B1252) which ran down into the small town of Driffield 8 km away, and as such was visible to passers by. It was, however, also intended to be a landscape feature, its 37m-high Gothic style spire visible for considerable distances.[27] Set within a square moat, but approachable across a small bridge from the road, the monument may be unfinished as only two panels are carved, though in an undistinguished manner. One shows Sir Tatton Sykes mounted on a horse, indicating one of his major interests (Fig. 5d); the other depicts a plough, tree and cottages testifying to his agricultural concerns. The monument was paid for by public subscription, and cost c. £5,000.[28] An inscription on the monument records that it was erected by his friends and grateful tenants (Table 4). Sir Tatton Sykes was buried in the churchyard, his grave marked by a simple Gothic revival low granite coped monument, typical of the time (Fig. 4A; Fig. 3b). The estate was taken over by Sir Tatton Sykes Junior, 5th baronet, who continued to manage his enormous Wolds estates, and who is best remembered for his widespread construction and rebuilding of churches in the area, many by Street and all in Gothic revival style. The church contained no memorial to Sir Tatton Sykes until the early 20th century, when his grandson Henry had a wall monument commissioned in a style that matched another Sir Tatton Sykes, 5th baronet (see below).

Subsequent memorials were erected within the village itself. In 1893 Sir Tatton Sykes, 5th baronet, rebuilt the church in a Gothic revival style by Temple Moor, incorporating the surviving medieval tower (Fig.4A). The existing wall monuments were retained and re-erected, though all lost their dark backing slates, perhaps to make them less obviously neo-classical in their new setting. This is likely to have been part of the motivation since those with the classical figural sculpture (those to Sir Mark Sykes and his wife Henrietta)

OPPOSITE Figure 5. (Clockwise from top left) Memorials in the Sledmere estate landscapes a) Pet memorial in the grounds of Sledmere House; b) Rotunda over the village well, erected by Sir Tatton Sykes in 1840; c) Moated monument to Sir Tatton Sykes to the southeast of the village; a general view; d) detail of one of the panels.

HIC JACENT
SILVIA FIDELIS
5 MAY 1785
Æ 10
ET
SUAVIS JULIA
5 NOV 1788
Æ 7

were placed in the relative obscurity of the tower. Opposite the church an Eleanor Cross (Fig.4E), also designed by Temple Moore and largely based on the surviving medieval example at Hardingstone, Northamptonshire, was built in 1895.[29] Despite recent research on this memorial by Banbury, the reasons for its erection by Sir Tatton Sykes (and indeed the choice of monument form) remain uncertain. It may, however, been meant to represent the culmination of the rejuvenation, in Gothic revival style, of the area achieved through ecclesiastical investment in the rebuilding of six churches, and the significant restoration of another ten. It also provided an eye-catching pointer to the largely hidden church which is set back from the road and obscured within woodland. The Eleanor Cross was thus placed near the road at the western approach to the village, and at a junction where the road from Malton via North Grimston joined the road that swept around the Sledmere House and Park.

The function of this memorial has since been extended. Sir Mark Sykes, the 6th baronet, a noted expert in Middle Eastern affairs and commissioner of the noted Turkish room in the house, used the Eleanor Cross as a basis for one of his First World War memorials. Unfairly described as comical by Pevsner,[30] it was transformed by the addition of memorial brasses within the blind arcading, each with designs heavily inspired by 13th- and 14th-century brasses (Fig. 6c). This unusual form of commemoration makes them of particular interest, and they have been subject to two detailed studies[31] though no comment has been made about the arrangement of the brasses on the monument, nor of its place within a wider commemorative setting on the Sledmere estate.

The Eleanor cross was modified in two ways by Sir Mark in its conversion to the role of memorial. The central mullions of the tracery on sides of the lowest tier of the cross where a large brass was placed, and the open books in relief on alternate sides, were all removed to make a smooth surface for the brasses. In addition, the original coats of arms were removed from the existing shields by cutting them back, and appropriate heraldry selected by Sir Mark was painted onto them.[32] Whilst an art-historical perspective sees this as 'spoiling' the Temple Moore creation, an archaeological interpretation can emphasise the recreation of meaning and material re-working of the monument in a more positive light. Indeed, given that no one seems to understand the reason for the Eleanor Cross in the first place, these modifications and additions gave it a clear social role for the first time. Banbury seems surprised that there was no criticism of the use of the cross for this purpose and its adaptation by Sir Mark,[33] suggesting that it was therefore seen as a privately owned feature. It could equally have been seen as part of a tradition of Sykes benefaction; this was after all an estate village where public and estate identities would have been blurred. Here a publicly visible monument could be appropriately turned to a new and in contemporary terms highly potent feature in the landscape. That this was carried out on a Gothic style monument, and continuing this theme, has been the matter of some art-historical debate.

Girouard had noted that Sir Mark 'retained many of the elements of the knight errant' and it is contended that these designs, largely made by Sir Mark himself before his death from influenza in 1919, were highly suited to his chivalric inclinations.[34] An interesting figure, he has been subject of two biographies,[35] and many of his papers have been deposited in Hull. With so much known of his life and interests, it is possible to understand his choice of chivalric themes on the brasses. However, the effects of the First World War in finally crushing those last remnants of such attitudes, with the terrible conditions and slaughter of the conflict, today make them seem an inappropriate vehicle for remembrance. Nevertheless, it would seem that neither the families of the bereaved nor the wider community considered them inappropriate at the time.[36] Indeed, the correspondence with some of the bereaved families that survives indicates no such concern, and indeed the presence of the Archbishop of York to hold a commemorative service on 8th July 1918 for all of the 5th Yorkshire regiment, and to unveil the brass to Lieut. Col. James Mortimer,[37] all suggest a pride in this adaptation.[38]

The monument is more personal than most war memorials, and has not only personalised portraiture for the figures but also appropriate symbols and at times lengthy citations regarding their civilian roles and military achievements.[39] The letters between Sir Mark and both Dora, the widow of Lieut. Col. James Mortimer, and Dorothy, widow of Major Harold Brown, all point to a deep concern with portraying the likeness of the deceased.[40] Photographs and life sketches were used to ensure accuracy, and at all stages the family was consulted to ensure a satisfactory likeness and appropriate associated symbolism. The commissioning of the firm T. J. Gawthorp & Son that was well acquainted with medieval brasses and interested in medieval technique[41] shows Sir Mark's commitment to an effective medieval style. Whilst evidence only survives for those families that were paying for the brasses, it would seem that this concern was applied to all. Unlike war memorials erected under the influence of the Royal Academy committee, this memorial was both personal and evoked values that by this time may have been anachronistic and heavily undermined by the terrors of the war. Nevertheless it must also have still chimed with some local sentiment, given the support for the memorial documented in private correspondence and the local newspapers.[42]

The arrangement and sizing of the figures on the memorial also demonstrates a personal quality linked to the estate, the locality and to the values of chivalry. Whilst officers were often shown in larger size, filling one blind arcade, this was not always the case (Table 4). The privately paid-for side three depicts three officers in a group, yet those who were active around Sledmere, even if of low rank, could be given individual treatment. Three local privates were portrayed in a small size to allow room for the long explanatory inscription on the right hand panel of side two, but that was also a face that many would have wished to read. Moreover, the other crowded panel was the left part of side five, where six captains were commemorated; professional men but interestingly from more distant parts of the area and so perhaps for this reason given less individual prominence. The variation in scale of figures and arrangements within the arcading further adds to the feeling of individuality, again a contrast to most community war memorials where just names, in identical lettering, are provided. The variability does have a deliberate inequality to it, but this was not based completely on class, as a chivalric model might suggest. Rather, it reflects a commitment to individuals, known to the commissioner and respected whatever their station in civilian life; it provided a personality to the commemoration that other war memorials lacked. This was something appreciated by the surviving family members, and no doubt by the wider public who saw this as the overwhelming message. The chivalric style would have been meaningful to a largely dead generation, but did not impede the quality and sincerity of the respect given through this physical statement of values and codes.

The individuals on the brasses had all been killed in the war, but the one blank face, side seven, was used to include Sir Mark, who died in Paris in 1919 from the influenza epidemic that decimated Europe at that time. The brass design is in the same genre as the others, and has a long inscription giving his qualities (Table 5), to match those of the war heroes on their brasses. Although a Roman Catholic, Sir Mark was buried in Sledmere churchyard with a service performed by the Abbot and monks of Ampleforth.[43] A detailed drawing of a medieval-style cross slab with symbolism and inscription informed by Catholic doctrine was designed by Walter Brierley of York,[44] and the original is still *in situ* (Fig. 3d). He also has a wall monument in the Catholic chapel (Fig. 4F) he had constructed when the house was rebuilt after a major fire in 1911.

The First World War led to the production of another notable monument (Fig. 4G), fully designed by Sir Mark Sykes and carved by Carlo Magnoni.[45] Rough sketches and a full outline of the three registers of carved scenes on the four faces of the central column drum survive,[46] demonstrating the evolving concept of the memorial. It was set up nearer to the village than the Eleanor cross, set a little back from the road. This memorial is to the Wolds Wagoners who were raised by Sir Mark to provide transport in the war zone. It is loosely based on Trajan's column, but is in a quaint rustic style (Fig. 6b). Most unusually for war memorials, it portrays fighting, German atrocities, and the steadfast and reliable qualities of the wagoners in all difficulties (Fig. 6d). This is in direct opposition to the chivalric repose of the individual dead commemorated on the Eleanor cross, though some of those figures do depict defeated enemies underfoot.[47] The two monuments may together reflect a more complex set of emotions within Sir Mark than those depicted on either one alone. This memorial also has a long inscription, in which the role of Sir Mark is given considerable prominence (Table 4); whilst it celebrated the Wagoners' contribution to the war, it also emphasised the dynamism of Sir Mark in raising this corps. The commemoration of the Wagoners was further expanded by an illuminated book that is now on display in the parish church (Fig. 4A). Created by Edmund Thomas Sandars over two years, it is an elaborate product in medieval style which listed all the names of local men who died in the war from the Green Howards and the Wolds Wagoners. The importance of this contribution was recognised following its author's death in 1942, as he was provided with a wall monument in the church nave.

The most recent Sykes monument erected in Sledmere followed the death of Sir Richard Sykes in 1978. He had succeeded Sir Mark whilst only a teenager and had been in charge of the estate for nearly 60 years on his death. The double-sided stone and wooden bench (Fig. 4H), decorated with incised greyhounds, was inscribed 'A good and generous Landlord Erected by Tenants and Staff of the Sledmere Estate' and was placed on the green near the

OPPOSITE Figure 6. (Clockwise from top left) Eleanor Cross converted by Sir Mark Sykes into a World War I memorial.
a) general view; b) side three with James Mortimer and Frank and Harry Woodcock; c) Wagoners' memorial designed by Sir Mark Sykes general view; d) detail showing loyal wagoners and British soldiers contrasted with menacing German soldiers.

MONUMENTS AND MEMORY 165

Eleanor Cross which commemorated his father. Though not as dramatic as the Gothic tower built a little more than a century earlier, this was still a considerable investment for the time, and one not often volunteered in the late 20th century. Sir Richard was a Roman Catholic like his father, and he is commemorated by three stained glass windows at the east end of the chapel at Sledmere House. In contrast his wife Virginia was an Anglican, and she has two monuments within the parish church (Table 3). A wall monument has been placed in the nave, and within the chancel is a marble urn on a pedestal, containing Virginia's ashes; she is also commemorated on the back of the bench to Sir Richard.

Iconic enough to be able to displace even Castle Howard from the cover of the Ordnance Survey Explorer 300 map (2000), the Eleanor Cross at Sledmere represents part of a monumentally rich landscape (Table 3). This was created over the 19th and 20th centuries to a landed family responsible for shaping that landscape, celebrating their power and success, and the community spirit which both led to the local efforts in the First World War, and its terrible consequent losses. That this spirit was not lost, and the links between family and estate were not broken, is symbolised by the lesser but still significant public memorial to Sir Richard Sykes who died in 1978, and to his wife Virginia, who had died 1970. This is a double-sided seat placed on the green near the Eleanor Cross, a form of publicly useful monument that has replaced the more monumental structures of earlier generations, but no less significant for that.

CONCLUSIONS

Memories on country house estates could be created, maintained and reinforced through a variety of commemorative strategies. These could be situated in and around the church, as seen at Bulmer, Welburn and Sledmere, or on the estate itself in more or less accessible locales. Some were designed to be visible even from a considerable distance, such as the Castle Howard mausoleum and the Sir Tatton Sykes monument. Others were appreciated in a more intimate manner such as the Sir Christopher Sykes rotunda and family pet memorial. The Sledmere war memorials also linked the family with the community. Whatever strategy was chosen, the scale and style of the memorials conveyed messages to those living and working in these landscapes for generations thereafter. Whilst the interpretations no doubt varied accordingly over time and social station, some forms of memory were nevertheless perpetuated, and family genealogies were given physical substance which could be socially active long after the death of those commemorated.

The landscape of historic commemoration has been little studied to date, yet it clearly has the potential to link many aspects of estate landscapes, church and churchyard memorials, and indeed other material culture which could perpetuate memories such as portraits, photographs, diaries and other heirlooms.[48] In a world where genealogy and inheritance was of such importance, the remembrance of family history was vital. How material culture influenced the creation, perpetuation and rewriting of these histories deserves further attention.

ACKNOWLEDGEMENTS

Undergraduate and graduate students from the University of York collected and processed graveyard memorial data from Bulmer and Welburn, under the supervision of Kate Chapman who also prepared Figures 1 and 4. Students also formed cleaning parties for the Castle Howard mausoleum that enabled access to its crypt. Fieldwork was possible through the co-operation of the clergy and parishioners of Bulmer and Welburn, and Christopher Ridgeway of the Castle Howard estate; all gave permission and made us welcome. The staff of the Bryn Jones Library Archive at the University of Hull were very helpful in locating primary material relating to monuments at Sledmere. I would also wish to thank Jon Finch for all his stimulating discussions regarding Castle Howard and memorials, and the conference delegates of the Society for Post-Medieval Archaeology who responded so positively to my original paper which has since been much expanded.

NOTES

1. Connerton 1989; Middleton and Edwards 1990.
2. Tarlow 1999.
3. Olick and Robbins 1998.
4. Burke 1989, 101.
5. Clabburn 1998; Morley 1971.
6. Mytum 2007b.
7. Litten 1999.
8. Mytum 2003; Mytum 2004
9. Downes 1969; 1977; Saumarez Smith 1990; Webb 1931.
10. Saumarez Smith 1990, 159.
11. Saumarez Smith 1990, 167-8.
12. Wilson 1995, 79.
13. Wilson 2000.
14. Wilson 1995, 81.
15. Webb 1931, 119.
16. Murray 1994.
17. Murray 1994, 220.
18. Both Bulmer and Welburn have been recorded using the methodology set out in Mytum 2000.
19. Pevsner 1966, 116.
20. Pevsner 1966, 116.
21. Clarke 1990; Dixon Hunt 1982.
22. National Trust 1997; Robinson 1990.
23. www.hull.ac.uk/oldlib/archives/landed/sykes.html.
24. Fairfax-Blakeborough 1929, 228-29; Pevsner 1972, 331.
25. Hutchinson 1984; Quiney 1984.
26. Wilkinson 2004.
27. Anon, The Builder 1865.
28. Bulmer's Directory 1892.
29. Banbury 2000.
30. Pevsner 1972, 346.
31. Banbury 2000; Meara 1996.
32. Banbury 2000.
33. Banbury 2000, 209.
34. Girouard 1981, 271.
35. Adelson 1975; Leslie 1923.
36. Banbury 2000; 209.
37. Hull University, Mark Sykes Papers 1918.
38. Hull University, Printed service booklet, Mark Sykes Papers 1918.
39. Banbury 2000, 210-12.
40. Hull University, Mark Sykes Papers 1918.
41. Meara 1983, 111, pl. 72.
42. Banbury 2000, 209.
43. Leslie 1923, 293-94.
44. Hull University, DDSY2/10/13.
45. Pevsner 1972, 346.
46. Hull University, DDSY2/6/32.
47. Meara 1996, 491, 493.
48. See Mytum 2007a for the use of dates and initials on a range of material culture in the creation of public and private memory.

BIBLIOGRAPHY

Adelson, R. 1975, *Mark Sykes: Portrait of an Amateur*, London: Cape.
Anon. 1865, 'Sir Tatton Sykes Memorial Tower', *The Builder* 1865.
Banbury, P. A. J. 2000, 'The Sledmere Cross', *Yorkshire Archaeological Journal* 72, 193-216.
Barker, D. & Cranstone, D. (eds) 2003, *The Archaeology of Industrialization*, Leeds: Society for Post-Medieval Archaeology Monograph 2.

Bulmer's Directory, 1892, *History and Directory of East Yorkshire,* Preston: T. Bulmer & Co.
Burke, P. 1989, 'History as Social memory', in Butler 1989, 97-113.
Butler, T. (ed.) 1989, *Memory, History, Culture and the Mind,* Oxford: Blackwell.
Clabburn, P. 1998, *Samplers,* Princes Risborough: Shire Publications.
Clarke, G. B. (ed.) 1990, *Descriptions of Lord Cobham's Gardens at Stowe 1700-1750,* Buckinghamshire Record Society 26, Aylesbury: Buckinghamshire Record Society.
Connerton, P. 1989, *How Societies Remember,* Cambridge: Cambridge University Press.
Dixon Hunt, J. (ed.) 1982, *The Gardens at Stowe,* The English Landscape Garden 16, New York: Garland Publishing Inc.
Downes, K. 1969, *Hawksmoor,* London: Thames & Hudson.
Downes, K. 1977, *Vanbrugh,* London: Zwemmer.
Fairfax-Blakeborough, J. 1929, *Sykes of Sledmere, the record of a sporting family and famous stud,* London: Philip Allan & Co.
Girouard, M. 1981, *Life in the English Country House: a social and architectural history,* New Haven: Yale University Press.
Hutchinson, J. 1984, 'Sledmere 1750-1800: the development of the house, the park, & the new farmstead', *York Georgian Society Annual Report for 1984,* 14-15.
Leslie, S. 1923, *Mark Sykes: His Life and Letters,* London: Cassell & Co.
Litten, J. 1999, 'Tombs fit for Kings: Some Burial Vaults of the English Aristocracy and Landed Gentry of the Period 1650-1850', *Church Monuments* 14, 104-28.
Meara, D. 1983, *Victorian Memorial Brasses,* London: Routledge & Kegan Paul.
Meara, D. 1996, 'Sir Mark Sykes and The Sledmere Brasses', *Transactions of the Monumental Brass Society* 15, 486-98.
Middleton, D. & Edwards, D. 1990a, 'Introduction', in Middleton & Edwards 1990, 1-22.
Middleton, M. & Edwards, D. (eds) 1990b, *Collective Remembering,* London: Sage.
Morley, J. 1971, *Death, Heaven and the Victorians,* London: Studio Vista.
Murray, V. 1994, *Castle Howard. The Life and Times of a Stately Home,* London: Viking.
Mytum, H. 2000, *Recording and Analysing Graveyards,* Council for British Archaeology Practical Handbook 15, York: Council for British Archaeology.
Mytum, H. 2003, 'Landscapes of Commemoration', in Barker & Cranstone 2003, 223-40.
Mytum, H. 2004, *Mortuary Monuments and Burial Grounds of the Historic Period.* New York: Kluwer Academic/Plenum.
Mytum, H. 2007a, 'Materiality and Memory: an archaeological perspective on an adoption of linear time in Britain', *Antiquity* 81, 381-396.
Mytum, H. 2007b, 'Domesticity and the Dresser: An Archaeological Perspective from Rural Nineteenth-century Pembrokeshire', in Symonds 2007.
National Trust 1997, *Stowe Landscape Gardens,* London: National Trust.
Olick, J. K. & Robbins, J. 1998, 'Social Memory Studies: From "Collective Memory" to the Historical Sociology of Mnemonic Practices', *Annual Review of Sociology* 24, 105-40.
Ordnance Survey 2000, *Howardian Hills and Malton.* Yorkshire Wolds North, Explorer 300, 1: 25000 scale, Southampton: Ordnance Survey.
Pevsner, N. 1966, *Yorkshire: The North Riding,* Harmondsworth, Penguin.
Pevsner, N. 1972, *Yorkshire: York and the East Riding,* Harmondsworth, Penguin.
Robinson, J. M. 1990, *Temples of Delight. Stowe Landscape Gardens,* London: George Philip/National Trust.
Quiney, A. 1984, 'Sledmere', *Archaeological Journal* 141, 51-54.
Saumarez Smith, C. 1990, *The Building of Castle Howard,* London: Faber & Faber.
Symonds, J. (ed.) 2007, *The Table. The Material Culture and Social Context of Dining in the Old and New Worlds AD 1700-1900,* Oxford: Oxbow.
Tarlow, S. 1999, *Bereavement and Commemoration. An Archaeology of Mortality,* Oxford: Blackwell.
Webb, G. 1931, 'The Letters and Drawings of Nicholas Hawksmoor relating to the Building of the Mausoleum at Castle Howard', *Walpole Society* 19, 111-64.

Wilkinson, G. 2004, 'Around the grounds', *Yorkshire Evening Press*, Saturday May 29, 19.
Wilson, E. (ed.) 1995, *Parish Register of Bulmer, 1571-1837*, Yorkshire Archaeological Society Parish Register Series 160.
Wilson, E. 2000, *St Martin's Church Bulmer near Castle Howard, N. Yorks. A brief guide,* Bulmer: Bulmer History Group.

Internet source consulted:
Sykes family, of Sledmere
www.hull.ac.uk/oldlib/archives/landed/sykes.html - consulted 5 February 2003

UNPUBLISHED SOURCES
Brynmor Jones Library, Hull University, Sykes Archive, Mark Sykes Papers, letters regarding memorial and printed service booklet, various dates in 1918
Brynmor Jones Library, Hull University, DDSY2/10/13 Design of memorial slab for Mark Sykes by Walter Brierley; 1919
Brynmor Jones Library, Hull University, DDSY2/6/32 Drawings and drafts of text for Wagoners' monument by Sir Mark Sykes; no date

Table 1

Monuments in Bulmer churchyard with explicit links to Castle Howard; details from partial inscriptions have been augmented where possible by information from the burial registers (Wilson 1995)

Name	Relationship to Castle Howard	Year of death	Age	Erected by	Memorial number
…r.i…	Earl	18thc (monument style)			274
William Sp…	Served Earl of Carlisle …	1728 (register)			175
James Nicholson	Groom to Earl for 20 years	1733	66		160
Thomas Row	Huntsman and Keeper	1744 (register)			46
Robart Row	Huntsman and Keeper for 25 years	1746 (register)			46
Christopher Thompson	Wrought in brass & iron for 3rd & 4th Earls	1748	78		275
Iveson Wise	Butler to 4th Earl	1748	65		163
Susanna Nicholson	Wife of Keeper	1763	41		158
John Turner	Servant	1788	59		179
Mary Hoyland	Widow of Gardener for 52 years	1779	99		177
Ann Massat	Daughter of housekeeper	1816	23		180
William Hussly	House Steward to 6th Earl for 16 years	18?? (register)			161
William Knight	Faithful servant to Frederick for 50 years	1841	81		238
David Smith	In service and confidence for 51 years	1848	73	Owners of Castle Howard	5
John Mander	Coachman to 2 Earls for 33 years	1849	59	Earl	211
William Drew	Stud groom for 40 years	1852	73	Heirs of 5th and 6th Earls	2
William Goodrum	Valet to 7th Earl	1854	34	7th Earl	86
Sarah Kimberley	Wife of Henry Kimberley of Castle Howard	1854	33		288
John Dursey	Served the Howard family for 51 years	1855	73	7th Earl	294
Ann Wild	In the service of the 6th earl for 46 years	1856	72		197
William Marshall	Served honestly & faithfully for 50 years	1858	70		25
Children of Thomas and Ezra Kirkby of Castle Howard		1848, 1860	2, 17		64
Mary Rowe	In service of Earl of Carlisle for 40 years	1850	88		165
Isaac Elliot	Of Castle Howard	1860	37		15
William Law	Lived with family as gardener & friend for 66 years	1861	92		73
Thomas Drew	True, faithful & devoted servant for 16 years	1864	48	George Earl of Carlisle	301
Isaac Elliot	Head game keeper to Earls of Carlisle for 44 years	1866	74		15
Thomas Franklin	In service of Earls for 52 years	1869	89		101
Thomas Cooper	Of Castle Howard Lodge	1879	61		28
Thomas Kirkby	Died at Castle Howard	1885	79		76
Anne Hill	Died at Castle Howard	1910	74		155

Table 2
Monuments in Welburn churchyard with explicit links to Castle Howard

Name	Relationship to Castle Howard	Year of death	Age	Erected by	Memorial number
David Beale	Upwards 17 years in service of 6th and 7th Earls	1865	32	Lady Taunton	18
John Hardwick	Of Henderskelf, Castle Howard	1869	75		144
William Chapman	Of Hinderskelf, Castle Howard	1871	53		190
James Sutherland	Died at Castle Howard	1878	26		114
Thomas Spofforth	Husband of Ann of Castle Howard	1893	77		52
Samuel Jackson	Drowned at Castle Howard lake	1893	14		102
John Broadie	Drowned at Castle Howard lake	1897	22		86
James Fisher	Castle Howard School	1897	17		183
..nni… Whitaker	Of Castle Howard	19thc (monument style)	??		187
Matthew Ward	Died at Castle Howard	19thc (monument style)	??		87
Jane Sheppard	Wife of late band master Castle Howard School	1915	??		94
Anne Bingham	19 years on staff of Castle Howard School	1917	58		13
John Pallister	Coachman and friend to 4 generations	1925	63		248

Table 3 List of the Sykes family members and their monuments

Baronet	Name	Death date	External Monument	Internal Monument	Comments
	Mary Kirkby	1714		Wall monument, Church chancel	Erected 1795 to Kirkby Family, especially Mary who married Richard Sykes, co-heiress, erected by Christopher Sykes
	Elizabeth Egerton	1763		Wall monument, Church chancel	Erected 1795 to aunt of Elizabeth, wife of Christopher Sykes, 2nd Bt, to whom she left her her fortune
1st	Mark Sykes	1783			
2nd	Christopher Sykes	1801	Rotunda		Erected 1840 by his son Sir Tatton Sykes
	Henrietta Masterman	1813		Wall monument, Church nave	Wife of Mark Masterman Sykes 3rd Bt; memorial later moved to the tower
3rd	Mark Masterman Sykes	1823		Wall monument, Church nave	Memorial later moved to the tower
4th	Tatton Sykes	1863	Sledmere spire monument Churchyard low coped slab	Wall monument, Church nave	Spire erected 1865 by public subscription; wall monument erected by grandson Henry Cholmondeley
	Jessica Sykes	1912	Churchyard graveslab		Wife of Tatton Sykes 4th Bt
5th	Tatton Sykes	1913	Eleanor Cross Churchyard graveslab	Wall monument, Church nave	
6th	Mark Sykes	1919	Eleanor Cross Wagoners' memorial Churchyard graveslab	Wall monument, RC chapel in house	
	Virginia Sykes	1970	Seat	Wall monument, Church nave Urn on pedestal, Church chancel	Wife of Richard Sykes 7th Bt
7th	Richard Sykes	1978	Seat	Stained glass windows, RC chapel in house	

Table 4

Inscriptions on external memorials in Sledmere village

Rotunda
This edifice was erected by Sir Tatton Sykes Bart in the memory of his father Sir Christopher Sykes Bart who by assiduity and perseverance in building and planting and enclosing of the Yorkshire Wolds in the short space of thirty years set such an example to other owners of the land as has caused what was once a bleak and barren tract of country to become now one of the most productive and best cultivated districts in the county of York AD 1840.

Sledmere monument
Erected to the memory of Sir Tatton Sykes Baronet by those who loved him as a friend and honoured him as a landlord.

Eleanor Cross brasses
This effigy was raised by the Tenants and Villagers on the Sledmere Estates as a mark of esteem and regard for a good Landlord and honoured friend.
[Each individual portrayed on the brasses and listed in Table 4 also had an inscription; for these see Bradley 2000, 210-12.]

Wagoners' memorial
Lieutenant Colonel Sir Mark Sykes Baronet MP designed this monument and set it up as a remembrance of the calling and services rendered in the great war 1914-1919 by the Wolds Wagoners Reserve A corps of 1000 drivers raised by him on the Yorkshire Wolds Farms in the year 1912.

Bench
In memory of Sir Richard Sykes Baronet 1905-1978 A good and generous Landlord. Erected by Tenants and Staff of the Sledmere Estate.

Pet memorial in the grounds of the house
East Face: Lambchop Bull Terrier 5 November 1986 Ae 13 Sic transit gloria mundi. Barley fidelis Greyhound 27 Februray 1987 Ae 13.
North Face: Venom died May 13 1920, Ae14. Minx 15 December 1921, Ae1 1/2. Puppy 6 August 1922 Ae 12.
West Face: Hic jacet Silva fidelis 5 May 1785 Ae10. Et suavis Julia 5 Nov 1788 Ae 7.

Table 5

Brasses at Sledmere (after Banbury 2000; Meara 1996).

Side (nos. from Banbury 2000)	No. Indivs	Rank on monument	Occupation (square brackets, data from Banbury 2000)	Name
1 L	1	Private	Footman	Walter Gorner Barker
1 R	1	Lce. Corp.	Agriculturalist	Harry Clifford Agar
2 L	1	Captain	[Soldier]	Edward Bagshawe
2 R	3	Private		William Holtby
		Private		David Cooper
		Private		George Potts
3	3	Lieut. Col.	[Soldier]	James Mortimer ***
		Captain		Frank Woodcock ***
		Lce. Corp.		Harry Woodcock ***
4 L	1	Major	[Businessman]	Harold Brown
4 R	1	Lieut. Col.	[Solicitor]	Frederick William Robson
5 L	6	Captain	[Bank manager]	T.E. Dufty
		Captain	[Architect]	D.H. Walker
		Captain	[Bank manager]	G.J. Scott
		Captain	[Solicitor's clerk]	G.C. Barber
		Captain	[Insurance]	E.R. Spofforth
		Captain	[Bank employee]	W. Vause
5 R	1	Lieut. Col.	[Miller]	James Albert Raymond Thomson **
6 L	2	Sergeant	Carpenter	Thomas Frankish
6 R		Lce. Corp	Carpenter	Harry Addison
7	1	Lieut. Col.	Bart MP	Sir Mark Sykes *
8 L	1	Private	Agriculturalist	David Scott
8 R	1	Lce. Corp.	Saddler	William Webster

Notes
* Placed by tenants and villagers
** Placed by his widow
*** Raised by Dora Mortimer (widow of James Mortimer) and Elizabeth Jane Woodcock, her mother and brother and sisters.

Part Three

Colonial Landscapes
―――――――――――

English Colonial Landscapes in the South-West of Ireland

By COLIN BREEN

The south-west of Ireland was extensively settled by English planters in the later decades of the 16th century and early years of the 17th century. Their arrival displaced the pre-existing Gaelic order and resulted in extensive landscape change and the intensification of industrial and agricultural activity. This in effect marks the advent of early capitalism across the region.

INTRODUCTION

Colonial plantations undertaken by adventurers from England, Scotland and Wales commenced in the south-west of Ireland in the later part of the 16th century. These ventures were to have a profound effect on the cultural character of the landscape and the political scenery of this part of the island. Prior to the arrival of these planters this area was dominated by the Gaelic-Irish sept of the O'Sulivan Beares. This family grouping had come to control this area from the beginning of the 14th century and owed political allegiance to the MacCarthy family, the dominant overlords in this part of southern Ireland. The plantations marked a movement away from the old Gaelic political order and the embracive collective power of the Gaelic lords and initiated the process of widespread Anglicisation of the Irish countryside. The plantations also marked the shift into an early capitalist society, exemplified by large investment in the development or regeneration of new settlements, increased formalisation and organisation of the landscape and the emergence of a new mercantile landowning elite. This paper will examine this process in the south-west of Ireland, specifically looking at the area around Bantry and Beara in west Cork (Fig. 1). It deliberately concerns itself with the plantations and does not examine in any great detail Gaelic responses to these developments. Varying responses of resistance, engagement and collaboration amongst the communities in the area to the new arrivals has been dealt elsewhere by the author.[1]

HISTORICAL BACKGROUND

Following the collapse of the 1583 Gaelic-Irish led Desmond revolt in the province of Munster, the English Crown quickly moved to plant these newly conquered lands, including some in the Bantry and Beara area. The plan was to people selected areas of the province with 'loving subjects of good behaviour and account none of the meer Irish to be

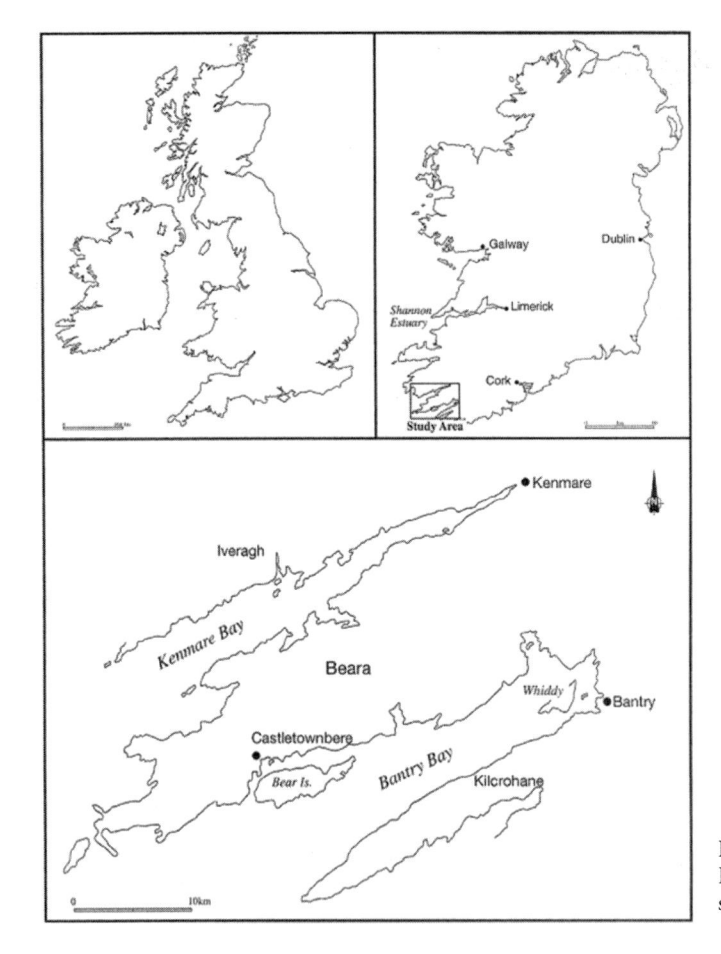

LEFT
Figure 1. Location map of the study area, south-west Ireland.

maintained in any family'.[2] Surveys began in an attempt to map out the forfeited lands and design a model plantation for this area. The first plantation survey proper was begun in 1584, under the direction of Sir Valentine Browne, which subsequently estimated the value of the attained lands at £10,000 and calculated that they included 577,645 acres.[3] Much of this Plantation had begun in 1586, with Bantry marking the most westerly extent of the grants centred around the lands of Clandonnell Roe and Clan Dermot. Clandonnel Roe are recorded as holding 8.5 quarters[4] at Bantry while Clan Dermod are recorded as originally holding four quarters in Beara in the locality around modern Castletownbere in the O'Sullivan family dispute Commission of 1593/4.[5] Three MacCarthys of ClanDonnell Roe and one of Clan Dermod are listed as having sided with MacCarthy Reagh during the course of the Desmond revolt and were therefore counted as traitors and as a consequence lost their lands. In 1584 these lands were found for the Crown and the area was originally to be settled but was subsequently restored to the Earl of Clancar (MacCarthy) in 1587.[6] This restoration did not happen and both of the lands were joined together to form the single seignory of Clandonnell Roe. The Attorney General, Sir John Popham wrote in December 1587 that this seignory had been granted to his son-in-law Edward Rogers, who could not take his claim up as the land 'was wholly environed by the Irish…and cannot be kept'.[7] However, a year later, in 1588 Rogers took possession.[8] The Earl of Clancar was much aggrieved at this grant and attempt at plantation and actively encouraged a campaign of harassment against the settlers over the next few years. Richard Beacon, from Suffolk, was subsequently granted 'the possessions of Clandonnell Roe in Bantry containing four ploughlands' in 1590.[9] He was to pay a rent of £33 6. 8d. on the grant per annum from 1594 and half of this for the preceding years and a further half d. for each acre of wasteland enclosed. Under the terms of the grant the Queen 'mindful of having her province of Munster repeopled and inhabited with civil, loyal and dutiful subjects' granted Beacon the lands of Clandonnell and Clandermot.[10] He was given rights to all waters, watercourses, creeks, ports, havens, fishings and custom of fishing, all to be held for ever in fee farm. The grant also licensed him to ship and transport all kinds of corn, grain and victuals into England and Wales, to undertake the enclosure of 300 acres for horses and deer and to have 'free warren and park'. Beacon was obliged to erect 'dwelling houses' suitable for 47 families – 'one for the principal dwelling of himself, his heirs and assigns; four for freeholders, unto each of whom must be assigned 200 acres, at the rate of 16 feet and a half to the perch, lug or pole, three for farmers, who shall each have 400 acres, and 21 others for copyholders' each allotted 100 acres.[11] Later in 1592 the lands were sold by Beacon onto Henry Goldfinch of London.[12]

There are currently several different opinions on what may have been the motivating factor behind the large scale English plantations of this period.[13] The first is the 'Renaissance' theory where historians contend that the planters were driven by a need for establishing a 'new way', rejecting the ways of old and borrowing heavily from classical Greek and Roman concepts of colonisation. The second theory is termed 'Little England' and is where planters were interested in establishing settlements and landscapes which replicated their homeland. This re-creation manifested itself in the elaborate designs for plantation schemes and the attempts to formalise and redesign the Irish landscape along English lines. There is also a suggestion that planters were only interested in the exploitation of new territories for short-term financial gain. The planters at Bantry were probably driven by a combination of all three factors. Beacon, one of the leading early settlers, was clearly motivated by the early classicists in his writings while the early settlements clearly had an obvious English character as epitomised through their buildings and material culture. A leading motivating factor however must have been financial and many of the planters were clearly entrepreneurial.

EARLY SETTLEMENT

Excavations at the site of Blackrock (Fig. 2), in the grounds of Bantry House, have uncovered extensive remains associated with the early Rogers/ Beacon plantation scheme.[14] Here a large linear settlement was established along the water's edge in the later part of the 1580s and early 1590s and was initially enclosed by a substantial palisade. While the presence of such a structure is reflective of the campaign of resistance mounted by some branches of the ruling Gaelic-Irish it is also indicative of the underlying philosophy of the early planters. Canny has argued convincingly that much of the process and form of the early plantations was led or heavily influenced by the writings of Edmund Spenser.[15] These writings argued for the subordination and subjugation by force of the pre-existing local populations if necessary in order to impose the authority and strong leadership of the English. This process was viewed as necessary and right given the perceived ethnic and cultural superiority of the English over other races like the Irish. Richard Beacon, an official on the Provincial Council of Munster with Spenser and a landowner in the study area, adopted a similar line in his own writings and advocated strong government enforced and supported by military rule. In one source he wrote that in quelling the Irish the English should follow the example of the Romans by placing 'strong garrisons in every of their fortresses, to disarm them, and to take sufficient pledges of the great and suspected men'.[16] It does not appear coincidental then that a palisaded enclosure was erected on Beacon's lands in the later part of the 16th century at Blackrock. Spenser advocated a similar strategy in his View of the State of Ireland, completed before 1598 and published in 1633 in an edition of Ancient Irish Chronicles. He argued that the only way of pacifying Ireland was through the establishment of a series of defended garrisons across the country.[17] This was partly because the Irish were engaging in guerrilla-type warfare and could not be fought or be confronted in a traditional manner and were also using the natural landscape to their advantage.[18] The fact that both of these writers were advocating such similar strategies is a clear indicator of the military thinking of the day. This was strongly influenced by classical models of subordination formed by Classical Roman period strategies.

Figure 2. Detail of the early 17th-century map of the Inner Bantry Bay Area (source: Yorkshire Archives DDCC(2)). The detail shows the settlement at Blackrock to the left and Balgobben (modern Bantry town) to the right. The site at Blackrock is now occupied by the Bantry House demesne.

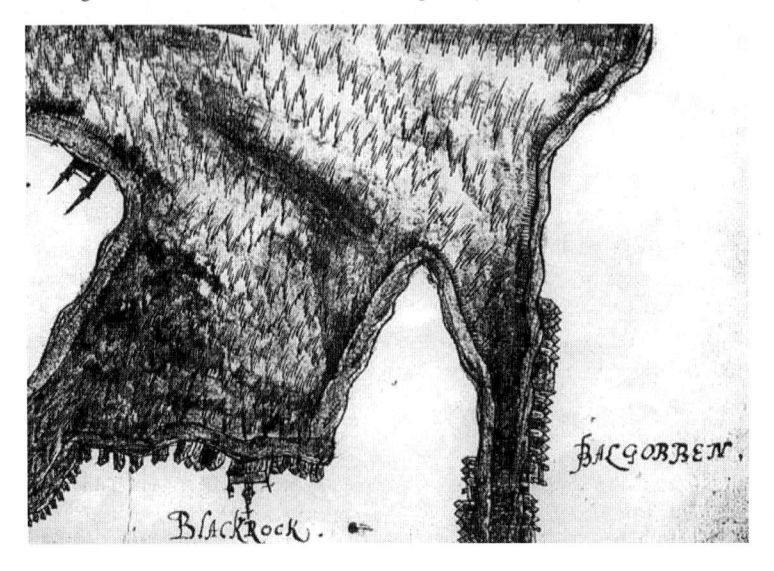

EARLY 17TH-CENTURY PLANTATION SETTLEMENT

While the earliest plantation schemes in the area took place in the late 1580s and early 1590s there was a more significant and successful phase of plantation after 1608/09. Owen O'Sullivan Beare, leader of the O'Sullivan Beare faction which stayed loyal to the English Crown following renewed conflict at the end of the 16th century began to lease out his lands to new arrivals. The landscape around modern Bantry town and Whiddy Island became the focus of the plantations with an emphasis on the exploitation of the extensive pilchard fishery in the seas off Bantry and Kenmare Bays. This can be seen as a continuation of earlier 15th and 16th-century O'Sullivan Beare financial control of the fishery resources in the region. Whiddy was an ideal base on which to establish speculative fishing ventures, a resource which was to serve as the focus for renewed plantations in the first and second decade of the 17th century. In leasing the island to the newcomers Owen O'Sullivan was maintaining indirect control and benefiting from the exploitation of the fisheries. In the early 1600s the seignory of Clandonell Roe was sold by Henry Goldfinch for £300 to Sir Nicholas Brown, a settler in neighbouring Kerry and married to a daughter of Owen O'Sullivan, while Goldfinch retained the original Clandermot lands around Castletownbere.[19] Valentine Brown, a ward, is recorded as being the King's tenant in possession of these lands in 1611, subject to one lease, in an *Abstract of the Inquisitions* into the state of lands undertaken in Munster.[20] Rent was reserved at £33 6s. and 8d. while rent was payable at the same. In the first quarter of the 17th century there was a major expansion of the fishing industry and activity in lands outside the realm of the original plantation and Owen O'Sullivan actively engaged in these developments through the mortgage and sale of lands. In many ways O'Sullivan was acting in his own interests. It is likely that the population around the study region had fallen dramatically in the wake of the Nine Years War (1593-1601/2) and was also effected by a number of famines which had preceded it. Sir Warham Sentleger had written to the Queen, for example, recording that 30,000 people had died from famine in Munster in 1582.[21] The situation had got so bad at the beginning of the 17th century that the Bishop of Cork writes in 1607 that the country west of Cork City to Bearehaven was so wasted from war that it was virtually uninhabited.[22] A new influx of settlers and investment would have been welcomed in these trying times, especially by 'loyal' subjects like Owen O'Sullivan. Details on these settlements are scant and are limited to a small number of documentary references and cartographic sources.

Edward Davenant had also established a base on Whiddy Island by 1609[23] and was to remain there for the next 30 years until his death, becoming one of the major economic influences within the region. Similarly Sir Thomas Roper, who had obtained the lease of the Castleisland seignory in 1605, had established fishery stations at Crookhaven, Skull and Bantry in the 1610s and 1620s.[24] His primary interest was in establishing stations to exploit the pilchard fishery. However, while these stations were based in the Inner Bantry Bay area, most of the actual fishing took place towards the mouth of the bay and on the fishing grounds which still lie off this coast.

The same degree of formality that was proposed for the earlier schemes does not appear to have applied to the early 17th-century undertakings. One reason for this is that much of the threat from Gaelic insurgents - a factor that hindered earlier settlement in the area - had now effectively gone. Much has been written about the process of plantation and subjugation by the proponents of the earlier settlements[25] but the later undertakings appear to be far more individualistic. Each grantee appears to have been able to operate without any political interference and was able to develop his own scheme. This movement away from formalisation is indicative of a broader conceptual movement away from recognised established centres of socio-economic power, a dominant paradigm during the high and late medieval periods, towards a much greater diversity of settlement in new centres and on the periphery. A much looser and less controlled market had almost sub-consciously been introduced and individual activity and initiative was actively encouraged. This is essentially *laissez faire* in operation, evidenced by the establishment of 107 new markets in Munster in the 1610s.[26] One of the direct consequences of this was that the actual morphology of the settlements in areas like Bantry is less rigid than that which was proposed for the earlier Munster settlements. There was, for example, no production of idealised plans of seignorys like those which had been produced in the 1585 plantation schemes.[27] It was also far less rigid than the ordered walled towns that were developed in Ulster at this time.[28] This conformity of style is expressed in the spatial layout of towns like Coleraine and Londonderry for example, both established in the first decade of the 17th century. The only example of such formalisation in West Munster is the development of Bandonbridge in Kinalmeaky with its surrounding wall and grid-iron street pattern.[29] However, the majority of the new settlements set up in association with the previously mentioned markets were far looser entities with no formal planning.

Detailed information on the nature and extent of the early 17th-century plantations comes from cartographic and archaeological sources. There is one informative map of the Inner Bay area which appears to date to the 1620s, and significant archaeological data from excavations undertaken at Blackrock, in the grounds of the demesne of Bantry House (Fig. 2). The map was located as a loose item in the East Yorkshire Archives[30] and was initially ascribed a late 17th-century date on the basis that it was a later copy of the Down Survey.[31] However, it is clearly early 17th-century in date. This earlier date is supported by the absence of the 1650s English settlement at Newtown, the illustration of the Franciscan friary at Abbey as a standing entity and the clear illustration of two separate settlements at Blackrock and Ballygobben. Blackrock was clearly the more prosperous, a factor which is amply demonstrated in the documentary sources. It is shown as a linear settlement located on the southern shores of the Inner Bay, running from the projecting bedrock at Blackrock Point to the inlet which lies immediately below the friary. In landscape terms the site was carefully chosen. It was positioned in an inter-drumlin hollow well protected from the prevailing south-westerly and westerly winds. A freshwater stream flowed through the site from the good grazing and agricultural land located immediately south of the site. It also overlooked the preferred anchorage in this section of the bay, an anchorage still used by the local sailing club and by visiting large ships. The bedrock point, Blackrock, not only gave the settlement its name but also served as the landing place. It was well suited topographically for this function, given the deep water that surrounded it and the ready access it provided to the immediate hinterland.

Ballygobben is shown as a less prosperous or less developed settlement; a linear settlement running along either side of a narrow inlet in the position where modern Bantry town is now positioned. It was referred to as a 'fisher town' in the documentary sources in the early part of the 17th century and the uniform illustration of its houses as small single-storey structures would seem to support this reference. It is known that the current inlet at Bantry was formerly far more expansive. Certainly analysis of the 1st (1840s) and later editions of Ordanance Survey six-inch Irish map series shows that there has been extensive reclamation of this area to expand the town and construct its present market place.

One of the most valuable aspects of the map is its depiction of Whiddy. Three areas of settlement are shown on the eastern shore of the Island overlooking the sheltered Inner Bay. These three sites must have constituted the pilchard fishing stations that were set up here in the early part of the 17th century. The largest of the sites is shown at the southern end of the Island in the townland of Trawnahaha. The location of the main house and compound shown are now occupied by a modern farmhouse, but traces of the foreshore activity illustrated still survive. The most obvious of these is the stone basal-foundations of a substantial pier. The remains consist of a rectangular feature measuring c. 6m by 4m built with uncut sandstone boulders, averaging 0.4m in length, as a foundation. It is probable that this foundation supported a timber superstructure.

This pier is clearly shown on the map and is associated with at least two further projections which must also have served as piers. Neither of these currently survives, probably due to the developed nature of the foreshore at this location. A number of modern slips and farm quays have been built over the last two centuries which appear to have destroyed the earlier features but may adopt their position and were built over them. The foreshore here is especially conducive to waterfront activities. It overlooks a natural sheltered location with good holding ground for vessels. There is also a significant exposure of clean inter-tidal area that would have allowed activities such as the graving of vessels,[32] an activity which is documented on the island at this time. A second concentration of settlement is shown centrally placed on the eastern shore, again in the townland of Trawnahaha. None of the foreshore features that are evident at the first site are shown here and all archaeological traces of the site were presumably destroyed during World War I when a US flying-boat airbase was constructed here. The final focus of activity is shown at the northern extremity of the site directly east of Reenavanny tower-house. This appears to be a far smaller settlement consisting of one to two possible house sites. Interestingly, aside from these sites, no other settlement is shown on the island.

ENCLOSURE

Enclosure of fields in Ireland in the later part of the 16th century and throughout the 17th century is well documented, although the main period of enclosure occurs in the 18th and 19th centuries.[33] This corresponds with a general upsurge in the enclosure of common fields, pasture and wasteland in England during the 16th century.[34] Enclosure was undertaken on a number of different premises in both Ireland and England. At this time agricultural thinking was of the opinion that enclosure would increase productivity and lend itself to the better management of the land and greater yields,[35] although it has been shown that enclosure did not result in improved productivity.[36] Johnson argues that enclosure in England begun a process of commodification of the landscape and paved the way for the generation of individual wealth through private ownership.[37] This was clearly taking place in the study area and can also be perceived on a number of different levels. Richard Beacon, in his grant of the area around Bantry in 1590 was to pay rent on each acre of 'waste' land enclosed.[38] He also undertook to enclose 300 acres for horse and deer, in a possible attempt to create a deerpark.[39] Sir William Hull's deposition of the 1640s made a claim for £180 in lieu of the 'Cost of breaking rocks at Lymcon [near Schull, West Cork] and stoninge the land five tymes all over to make it arable land and so divided it into many fields of 8-10-15-20 acres in a field which before a plowe could not worke in it also in draining the bogs and making gutters and for ditching and hedginge the saued land'.[40] This reference implies that enclosure was a new practice and that Hull appeared to be investing in and working land that had previously been neglected or ignored. At least this is the perception that the planters wished to give. The development of large-scale enclosures (certainly happening in the first two decades of the 17th century) marked a pronounced change in the character of the landscape of Bantry and Beara. The parcelling up of it by individuals and entrepreneurial enterprise marked a fundamental shift away from the open sept lands of the earlier period. Enclosure stamped new marks of ownership on the landscape and created new and evolving perceptions of identity and character. It also established overt expressions of private property. The vast majority of the new planters were English and not only did they bring their lifeways and cultural identity with them but they also brought their landscape identity with them as well. Of course this is not solely an English process; enclosure was happening in many different places and ways at this time, but in the study area appeared to mark a critical shift from the practices of the past. It also represented a breakdown in the traditional perception of landscape that preceded these developments. The effective closure of many units of landscape was a physical demonstration of a change in socio-economic and political structures of power. Whereas tower-houses and other high status residences were the previous manifestation of this expression, enclosure represented new investment and new arrivals in the area. Not only were the landowners erecting protective structures around their settlements, as shown through the construction of a palisade at Blackrock, but they were also physically ring-fencing their land investments.

This form of private enterprise was also an expression of the beginnings of capitalism, the origins of which can be traced in England from the middle of the 16th century onwards.[41] This can be seen in the direct association of enclosure with the individualism of enterprise and of the highly visible nature of the enclosed private property. The sheer size of the enclosure fences or banks, in excess of 2m in height, also literally changed the way people could view the landscape. Vistas were now broken and the same expansive examinations of the landscape were simply not possible anymore due to the height of the enclosing banks. This enclosure then, probably more than any other factor, represents the most obvious break with the past.

There is very strong cartographic evidence for this early enclosure. The early 17th-century map of the Inner Bay and Whiddy clearly shows the parcelling up of land on Whiddy. What is of particular interest is that many of these boundaries still survive and a number still function as townland boundaries. The surviving 17th-century boundaries from the map are illustrated in the accompanying survey map (Fig. 3). The existing townland boundaries, taken from the 1st edition OS six-inch map are shown as the dotted lines, while the 17th-century boundaries are shown as solid unbroken lines. It is argued here that the 17th-century planters adopted existing townland boundaries in whatever form they appeared and repartitioned them in a distinctive manner. Each townland is named and where an original property unit still survives it is labelled with its original alphabetic letter. The property boundaries highlighted in bold are those that also correspond to a route or roadway. From this particular evidence there appears to be strong a correlation between routeways, townland boundaries and the 17th-century divisions. Certainly the main boundary bordering Kilmore to the north is still the primary east-west running roadway on the Island. These 17th-century boundaries are very distinctive and clearly different to what came both before and after them in chronological terms. They are immediately identifiable from their size and are totally unlike the later 18th-and 19th-century divisions. The Whiddy boundaries average 2.2m in height and *c.* 1.2m in width with *c.* 12km of the banks surviving across the Island. They were constructed by first creating a substantial earthen bank and then facing it with large stones and boulders at their basal levels, presumably cleared from the surrounding fields. Many of the banks now incorporate large mature trees and are grass-covered. This type of structure differs greatly from the low-lying stone walls constructed as field fences in more recent centuries in the area.

INDUSTRY

The 17th century also witnesses the development of a number of new industries in the Bantry Bay region. In November 1608 Thomas Wilson, Dudley Norton and Thomas Crooke of Baltimore purchased lands and woods lying around Bantry Bay for development purposes.[42] Wood had become an extremely valuable commodity by this time for use in ship building and for charcoal production. In the late 17th century a number of iron furnaces were established taking advantage of the extensive supply of woodland.[43] A furnace had been established near Bantry Abbey before 1685,[44] while other works were known at Dunboy, Adrigole and a large works at Glengarriff exploiting oak and birch.[45] This activity resulted in large scale deforestation around the Bay especially in the Coomhola and Dunboy regions. Fishing continued to be an economic mainstay and a number of fish palaces were built to service this industry. Fish palaces were large stone-built structures in which barrels of pilchards were laid under press beams and weights in order to pack the barrels and extract oil. Independent walls and sections of exposed bedrock cliffs were also used for this purpose. Charles Smith in 1750 records that several fish palaces survived in creeks around the Bay which were built for the saving, preserving and salting of pilchards, while de Latocnaye in 1798 records that there were many pressing walls on Whiddy Island used for extracting oil from pilchards.[46] Other palace locations include one on the southern shores of Reenadisert, a curing house at Gerahies and possible sites in Bantry town and at Gurteenroe. The erection of these buildings reflected increased investment in the infrastructure of the fishing industry and the associated formalisation of this activity in the 17th century.

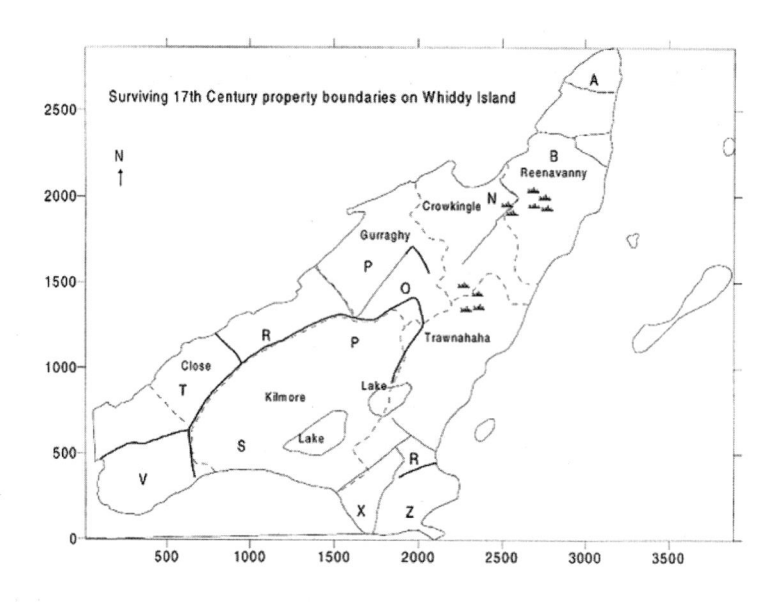

Figure 3. Survey detail of the enclosure and townland boundaries on Whiddy Island taken from the early 17th-century map of the Inner Bay area.

DEVELOPMENT OF CAPITALISM

It can be argued that the arrival of the plantations herald the advent of capitalism in the area. Capitalism is 'an economic system in which those who provide the capital control the production of goods'.[47] Capital is an inclusive term and covers modes of production and finance. These modes are owned or controlled by individual 'capitalists' who also control the productionists, i.e. the people who labour in the production process. This labour is rarely a choice but rather an economic reality of survival. Capitalists then create a subjugating system of control. A capitalist system produces commodities beyond the needs of the individual and is involved in a nationwide or international exchange market.[48] The emergence of capitalism is associated with individualism of enterprise, emergence of individual land-ownership, tenancy and private property.[49] There is a general consensus among researchers that the archaeology of capitalism is dominated by the central theme of individuality and the rise of the individual over community.[50] In the study area this is evidenced in a number of different ways. In the early stages of capitalism the small producer, e.g. local farmer or fisherman, is increasingly alienated from the control over his product leading to the eventual dependence of the individual to the sale of his labour to the market. That person has then moved into the status of wage-labourer. This transition is marked in general from a change from arable to pastoral agriculture as far less labour is required. This transition into a capitalist system is also marked by other occurrences. Organised manufacture occurs outside of the established urban guilds. Rural subsidiary operations such as fishing, spinning or iron working become organised. Individual producers become involved in exchange rather than just production.

This phase is evident in the emergence of a mercantile elite during the early 17th century at sites like Blackrock. It is also apparent in the establishment of modes of control over the monetary and productions systems. The development of a customs system at places like Blackrock is one manifestation of this. Protective measures were established to protect this economic activity, evidenced by the garrisoning of the country. This was done primarily to protect economic interests and was partially funded and controlled by the leading merchants and landowners in the area, i.e. the merchant class. The arrival of the military ensured forceful political structures of subjugation were put in place in order to protect production.

Capitalism is also intrinsically linked to exploitation, through the extraction and appropriation of surplus value and domination.[51] Here the advent of capitalism is seen through agricultural production for profit and the exploitation of the fisheries. Land in this context is seen as capital in the same way that resources are. Benjamin's statement describing the unchanging nature of capitalist relations and the process of commodity production is of relevance here – 'the always-new in the context of the ever-same'.[52] Further evidence for the extraction of surplus value in the absence of heavy industry can be seen in the appropriation of territory and through the initiation of an industrial base through iron-working. New power structures are then constructed in order to maintain capitalist production and this is reflected through the emergence of a new land-holding elite with tenant relationships. Arendt argues, that these types of transformations of class and State represent the first stage of the political rule of the bourgeoisie.[53] It is possible in the context of this study to see the bourgeoisie represented by the new economic elite emerging throughout the broader region of plantation Munster. What we are in effect seeing throughout the Atlantic world at this time is the globalisation of capitalist modes of production and the study area represents a tiny microcosm of this process. Colonialism represents the conquest and direct control of the peoples of the area and constitutes an intrinsic part of the development of imperialism. Gaelic society can be interpreted as being pre-capitalist and is effectively subjugated by new economic forces. Its pre-capitalist status is reflected in the dominant all embracing social role of the sept structure and the extent of political power and landownership that a tiny elite held at the head of the lordship.

The advent of capitalism must also be seen against the backdrop of the beginnings of modernity.[54] This is expressed in the physical change in the environment and the moulding of the landscape towards its contemporary form. Modernity is also expressed in the settlement forms which are heralded through the plantations. Larger complex settlements are established with multi-faceted roles and identities. Domestic space and architecture changes and increases in house sizes and personal space is reflective of broader moves within society towards individualism and societal privatisation right across the social spectrum. Changes in agricultural practice such as enclosure, private property, intensity of production and a movement away from community-based agricultural routine, are all indicative of this change. Redressing concepts of 'waste' landscape and the initiation of drainage schemes, planting and the disappearance of common space are also indicators.

CONCLUSION

A number of factors combined in the later part of the 16th-century that made the plantation of the study area an attractive option for settlement and investment by English settlers. The collapse of the Desmond revolt paved the way for initial settlement in the lands of Clan Donnell, allies of MacCarthy Reagh, in and around Bantry. A palisaded settlement was established here in the late 1580s and early 1590s in line with contemporary plantation theory. This also reflects the campaign of resistance mounted by some elements of Gaelic-Irish society to these new arrivals.

Regardless, large-scale plantation now takes place across the territory with the support Owen O'Sullivan. The plantations and ultimately unsuccessful resistance result in the continued exploitation of the fishery resource and the establishment of small nucleated town-like settlements in the Inner Bay area. In particular the settlement at Blackrock and Ballygobben are developed. Excavations at Blackrock uncovered two timber-framed houses and a range of early 17th-century material culture. Interestingly, the earlier of these two houses appears to represent a fusion of English and local building styles. There appears to have been some form of social differentiation between the two settlements, Blackrock constituting the mercantile and English area of settlement while Ballygobben represented a fisher settlement, inhabited primarily by Gaelic-Irish. These plantations are English but a continental involvement with the study area continued through trading and fishing. These developments radically altered the cultural character of the area, especially in the upper end of Bantry Bay. Power was largely removed from a handful of Gaelic-Irish lords and is essentially replaced by economic forces of exploitation. Merchants became the new brokers of power whose interests depend on the generation of capital through the exploitation of resources. Each individual was integrated in this new system of economic hierarchy and dependence and the old Gaelic-Irish systems were replaced by emerging capitalism and globalisation.

NOTES

1. Breen 2004.
2. MacCurtain 1972, 102.
3. Lennon 1994, 230.
4. A Quarter of land was equal to three ploughlands or carucates or the amount of arable land usually tilled in a season (i.e. 120 acres) but this varied because of the nature of the local terrain.
5. Cal S. P. Ire., 1592-96, 89.
6. Cal. S. P. Ire., 1587, 63, 27, 87, 145, 449.
7. Cal. S. P. Ire., 1587, 449.
8. MacCarthy-Morrogh 1986a, 86.
9. Eliz. Fiants 5536 (6558) 1590-91, 139.
10. Cal. Pat. Rolls. Elizabeth, 35, 1594, 266.
11. Cal. Patent & Close Rolls Elizabeth, 35, February 1594, 266.
12. MacCarthy-Morrogh 1986b, 119.
13. Klinglehofer 2000, 174.
14. Breen 2003, 13.
15. Canny 2001, 55-8.
16. Canny 2001, 123.
17. Hadfield and Maley (trans.) 1997, 96.
18. O'Conor 1998, 98-9.
19. MacCarthy-Morrogh 1986b, 142.
20. Cal. S. P. Ire., 1611, 220.
21. Cal. S. P. Ire., 1582, 361-2.
22. MacCarthy-Morrogh 1986b, 149.
23. MacCarthy-Morrogh 1986b, 158.
24. Cal. S. P. Ire., 1633-47, 156.
25. e.g. Canny 2001.
26. MacCarthy-Morrogh 1986a, 179.
27. NA, SP 63/121/55.
28. See Robinson 1984.
29. McCarthy-Morrogh 1986a, 180.
30. ERYA, DDCC(2); reproduced in Breen 2001, 32
31. Donovan and Edwards 1997, 272.
32. i.e. the cleaning of the hulls of vessels while they are beached above the high water mark.
33. Aalen, Whelan and Stout 1997, 136-44; O'Keeffe 2000, 64-66.
34. Rippon 1996, 101; Newman 2001, 106-11.
35. Buchanan 1973, 599.
36. Allen 1992, 17.
37. Johnson 1996, 10.
38. Eliz. Fiants 5536 (6558) 1590-91, 139.
39. Cal. Patent & Close Rolls, Elizabeth, 35, February 1594, 266.
40. Donovan 1993, 35.
41. Newman 2001, 5.
42. Cal. S. P. Ire., 1608, 101.
43. Hourihane 1985, 87.
44. Cox, 1902, 179
45. McVeigh 1995.
46. Quoted in Went 1946, 148.
47. Curtin 1990, 47.
48. Giddens 1971, 46.
49. Dalglish 2003, 1.
50. Dalglish 2003, 8.
51. Foucault 1972, 216.
52. Williams and Chrisman 1994, 12.
53. Arendt 1952.
54. Orser 1996.

BIBLIOGRAPHY

Aalen, F. H. A., Whelan, K. & Stout, M. 1997, *Atlas of the Irish Rural Landscape*, Cork: Cork University Press.
Allen, R. C. 1992, *Enclosure and the Yeoman*, Oxford: Clarendon Press.
Arendt, H. 1951, *The Origins of Totalitarianism*, London: Harcourt.
Baker, A. R. H. & Butlin, R. A. 1973, *Studies of Field Systems in the British Isles*, Cambridge: Cambridge University Press.
Bennett, I. (ed.) 2003, *Excavations 2001*, Bray: Wordwell.
Brady, C. & Gillespie, R. (eds) 1986, *Natives and Newcomers: the making of the Irish Colonial Society 1543-1641*, Dublin: Irish Academic Press.
Breen, C. 2001, 'The Gaelic Maritime Lordship of O'Sullivan Beare', *Journal of the Cork Historical and Archaeological Society* 106, 21-36.
Breen, C. 2003, 'Blackrock', in Bennett 2003, 31.
Calendar of Patent and Close Rolls of Chancery in Ireland, 1861, Henry VIII-Elizabeth, ed. J Morron, Dublin.
Calendar of Patent Rolls of Ireland, 1966, facsimile of the Irish record commissioners' calendar prepared prior to 1830, with foreword by M. C. Griffith, Dublin: IMC.
Calendar of State Papers of Ireland, 1860-1911, 24 vols, London.
Canny, N. 2001, *Making Ireland British, 1580-1650*, Oxford: Oxford University Press.

Cox, R. 1902, 'Regnum Corcagiense: or a description of the Kingdom of Cork', *Journal of the Cork Historical and Archaeological Society* 8, 65-75.
Curtin, P. D. 1990, *The Rise and Fall of the Plantation Complex: Essays in Atlantic History*, Cambridge: Cambridge University Press.
Dalglish, C. 2003, *Rural Society and the Age of Reason: an archaeology of the emergence of modern life in the southern Scottish Highlands*, New York: Kluwer.
Donovan, M. R. 1993, 'Notes on Sir William Hull and Leacom', *Mizen Journal* 1, 30-38.
Donovan, B. C. & Edwards, D. 1997, *British Sources for Irish History 1485-1641, a guide to manuscripts in local, regional and specialised repositories in England, Scotland and Wales*, Dublin: Irish Manuscripts Commission.
The Irish Fiants of the Tudor Sovereigns, 1994, 3 vols, Dublin.
Foucault, M. 1977, *Language, Counter-memory, Practice: selected essays and interviews*, Bouchard, D.F. & Simon, S. (trans.), New York: Cornell University Press.
Giddens, A. 1971, *Capitalism and Modern Social Theory; an analysis of the writings of Marx, Durkheim and Max Weber*, Cambridge: Cambridge University Press.
Hadfield, A. & Maley, W. (eds) 1997, *Edmund Spenser; A View of the State of Ireland*, Oxford: Blackwell.
Hourihan, J. K. 1985, 'Town Growth in West Cork: Bantry 1600-1960', *Journal of the Cork Historical and Archaeological Society* 96, 83-97.
Johnson, M. H. 1996, *An Archaeology of Capitalism*, Oxford: Blackwell.
Klingelhofer, E. 2000, 'Elizabethan Settlements at Mogeely Castle, Curraglass and Carrigeen', *Journal of the Cork Historical and Archaeological Society* 105,155-74.
Lennon, C. 1994, *Sixteenth Century Ireland, The Incomplete Conquest*, Dublin: Gill & Macmillan.
MacCarthy-Morrogh, M. 1986a, 'The English presence in early Seventeenth Century Munster', in Brady & Gillespie 1986, 191-213.
MacCarthy-Morrogh, M. 1986b, *The Munster Plantation: English migration to Southern Ireland 1583-1641*, Oxford: Clarendon Press.
MacCurtain, M. 1972, *Tudor and Stuart Ireland*, Dublin: Gill & Macmillan.
McVeigh, J. (ed.) 1995, *Richard Pococke's Irish Tour*, Dublin: Irish Academic Press.
Newman, R. 2001, *The Historical Archaeology of Britain c. 1540-1900*, Stroud: Sutton.
O'Conor, K. D. 1998, *The Archaeology of Medieval Rural Settlement in Ireland*, Discovery Programme Monographs 3, Dublin: Royal Irish Academy.
O'Keeffe, T. 2000, *Medieval Ireland, An Archaeology*, Stroud: Tempus.
Orser, C. J. 1996, *A Historical Archaeology of the Modern World*, New York: Plenum.
Rippon, S. 1996, *Gwent Levels: The Evaluation of a Wetland Landscape*, Council for British Archaeology Research Report 105.
Robinson, P. 1984, *The Plantation of Ulster*, Belfast: Ulster Historical Foundation.
Went, A. E. J. 1946, 'Pilchards in the South of Ireland', *Journal of the Cork Historical and Archaeological Society* 174, 137-57.
Williams, P. & Chrisman, C. 1994, *Colonial Discourse and Post-Colonial Theory: An Introduction*, New York: Columbia University Press.

UNPUBLISHED SOURCES
East Riding of Yorkshire Archives DDCC(2).
The National Archives SP 63/121/55.
Breen, C. 2004, The Archaeology and Landscape Cultural History of Bantry and Beara, 1200- c. 1650, Unpublished PhD thesis: National University of Ireland.

ABBREVIATIONS
ERYA East Riding of Yorkshire Archives.
NA The National Archives.

'In What Manner Did They Devide The Land'
The Early Colonial Estate Landscape of Nevis and St Kitts

By ROGER H. LEECH

A three-year research project funded by the British Academy has focussed on the colonial landscape of two islands in the eastern Caribbean. Methodologically the project has set out to utilise both archaeological and documented data, to reconstruct, deconstruct and interpret an enclosed European landscape of the 1630s onwards. It is this European landscape that provides the focus for this paper - how were the English islands of the Eastern Caribbean transformed into estate landscapes and what was the wider European context to this process?

INTRODUCTION

The English Leeward Islands were colonised from the late 1620s onwards. By the end of the century the islands were densely settled and their wealth, shipped principally to Bristol and London, far outstripped that of the North American colonies in total. This is a remarkable story, explored by historians but scarcely at all through its archaeology. Much of what might be known of the early settlement of the islands still awaits telling. The archaeological examination of the 17th-century colonial landscape, the plantations and fields has still largely to be undertaken, enabling the material record to be considered alongside the meagre documentary sources, decimated by fire, hurricanes, earthquakes, tidal waves and war.

Current understanding of the colonisation of the English Leeward Islands in the 17th century is based predominantly on documentary research. Historical studies point to the need for an archaeological perspective. Dunn's single chapter on 'life in the tropics' highlights the lack of archaeological data: 'nearly all the early houses on the islands have long since disappeared, victims of storms, fires and tropical rot'.[1] Watts's study in historical geography again highlights the need for an archaeological perspective.[2]

Archaeological research into the English settlement of the Caribbean has been undertaken on a number of islands including Jamaica, Barbados and various of the Leeward Islands.[3] For Jamaica there is now published Douglas Armstrong's monumental study of the Drax Hall plantation.[4] On Barbados research has been focussed on the archaeology of slavery.[5] In the Leeward Islands work has notably included Lydia Pulsipher's long-running research project on Montserrat, focussed on the Galway's Plantation, where fieldwork has now been halted because of the volcanic eruptions.[6] On St Eustatius an extensive research programme has been undertaken by William and Mary College at Williamsburg, accessible through a recent summary by Norman Barka and in a series of unpublished MA dissertations.[7] On Nevis research has been focussed on the 18th century onwards, as at Coconut Walk and Port St George.[8] On Barbados the widespread destruction of archaeology through modern ploughing[9] increasingly highlights the potential of Nevis and St Kitts for providing an archaeological perspective on the 17th century.

This paper will draw upon the research project on Nevis and St Kitts (for the latter see Hicks in this volume) commenced in 2001 by the Universities of Southampton and Bristol with the support of the British Academy, the Society of Antiquaries and in association with Bristol City Museum and the historical societies for the two islands. A preliminary assessment in 2000 had shown the potential for an archaeological perspective on the 17th- and early 18th-century colonisation of the two islands. On Nevis sugar production had fallen dramatically before the mid 1940s.[10] In the absence of post-war ploughing, archaeological deposits are often well preserved. On St Kitts sugar production continued until 2005, and there has been much more destruction of archaeological remains - but the early historic mapping and documentation for St Kitts is much better than that for Nevis.

The overall objective of the British Academy project was to formulate a strategy and plan for a wider study, reconstructing the colonial landscapes of the two islands from the sea to the mountains, using the field evidence in conjunction with documentary sources, to transform understanding of the 17th-century English colonisation of the Leeward Islands. The approach adopted was heavily contextual, using documentary and archaeological sources, using field survey alongside air photographic interpretation.

THE COLONIAL LANDSCAPE OF NEVIS AND ST KITTS

In 1624 the island of St Christopher, commonly known as St Kitts, was the first of the Caribbean islands to be colonised by English settlers under a patent granted to the Earl of Carlisle as Lord Proprietor for the settlement of the Caribees. The landings and settlement of St Kitts and then Nevis (from 1628) are described in the account of John Hilton c.1675, descendant of Anthony Hilton who led the first settlement of Nevis in 1628.[11]

It is from Hilton's account that my quotation is derived, 'In what manner did they devide the land'.[12] Hilton's answer focuses on the division of St Kitts between the English and the French - a path was cut around the island and found to be 32 miles in length. Leaving aside the dry savannah at the south end of the island the English took 8 miles to the leeward and windward of the centre line across the island. The French took 8 miles to the leeward and windward of the English lands, giving themselves each end of the island. Hilton's account goes on to describe the settlement of Nevis. Hilton's account does not then enlarge upon how this was carried out or how the lands within the divisions of St Kitts or of Nevis were then further subdivided to form estates. The accounts of Hilton and Sir Henry Colt make it clear that c.100 settlers, widely scattered, were involved in the initial settlement of Nevis.[13]

Historians and their documentary sources are silent on how the initial division of St Kitts, Nevis and the other English islands of Barbados, Montserrat and Antigua into separate estates was effected. Historical attention on the estates of these islands has instead focussed more on the gradual reduction in the number of estates, and on the later management of these increasingly large estates, notably those of the Pinney and Stapleton families.[14] The principal question that this paper seeks to answer is therefore 'how did they divide the land', how were the English islands of the Eastern Caribbean transformed into estate landscapes?

The present day map of Nevis[15] reveals an underlying structure of regularly laid out geometric linear estate boundaries. Many of these disappear into what is now forest. Iles's map of 1871[16], the first to show the settlement of the island in detail, shows many plantations in what is now forest. Iles's map did not though show land divisions and boundaries, and overall the cartography is grossly inaccurate; Burdon's map of 1920 is similarly inaccurate being derived from Iles's map.[17] The map of 1848 by Capt. Barnett is much more accurate, but does not show land divisions.[18] The earliest island-wide maps to show land divisions are of 1959 and of the 1970s, by the Directorate of Overseas Surveys.[19] By this date forest and scrub covered much of the former plantation landscape. To reconstruct the estates and enclosed fields now concealed by forest it is necessary to turn to documentary research, air photography and archaeological field survey.

Figure 1. Air photographic survey of 1956, the colonial landscape to the north of Hermitage Plantation, fields disappearing into regenerated forest (Government of St Kitts and Nevis, photograph for Directorate of Overseas Surveys).

In the absence of any detailed island-wide mapping earlier than the 1950s, estate maps of the 18th to early 20th centuries are of especial value. Maps of the 18th century exist for a small number of estates, such as that of 1755 for Jessops in the parish of St Thomas.[20] Some ostensibly of the 19th century are probably copied from earlier maps, for instance of Coconut Walk, the Potworks Estate and the Old Manor Estate.[21] Many more are new surveys of the 19th and earlier 20th centuries. The tenurial history of these estates can then be traced through documentary sources, notably the Common Records of 1707 onwards held in the Court House of Nevis.

The earliest air photographic coverage of Nevis is of 1946, taken by the US Air Force.[22] This is of especial value in showing estate and field boundaries, which are totally obscured on later photographs by forest and scrub. Later coverage is of particular value in providing greater clarity of landscape features still visible: by 1952, when the coastline of Nevis and other islands was photographed by the US Navy, and 1954, when the island was first photographed for overall mapping. By then superior cameras of German origin were possibly in use.[23] The 1968 larger scale coverage of the island shows a still more forested landscape, but with even greater clarity (Fig. 1).

The mapping of features concealed by forest and scrub even on the earliest air photographs can be achieved through archaeological field survey. North and south of Mountravers, GPS (Global Positioning by Satellite) survey over a four year period has reconstructed a landscape of fields and boundaries previously invisible (Fig. 2). Handheld GPS using the WAAS (Wide Area Augmentation Service) differential is sufficiently accurate for the mapping of features that will appear on maps of a scale of 1:1000 or smaller; using GPS here and then in Britain one is struck by the immediately greater number of satellites rapidly accessed in a Caribbean context.

Figure 2. Estate and field boundaries within and adjacent to the Mountravers Plantation, St Thomas's parish, Nevis, from documentary sources, air photographs and field survey (author).

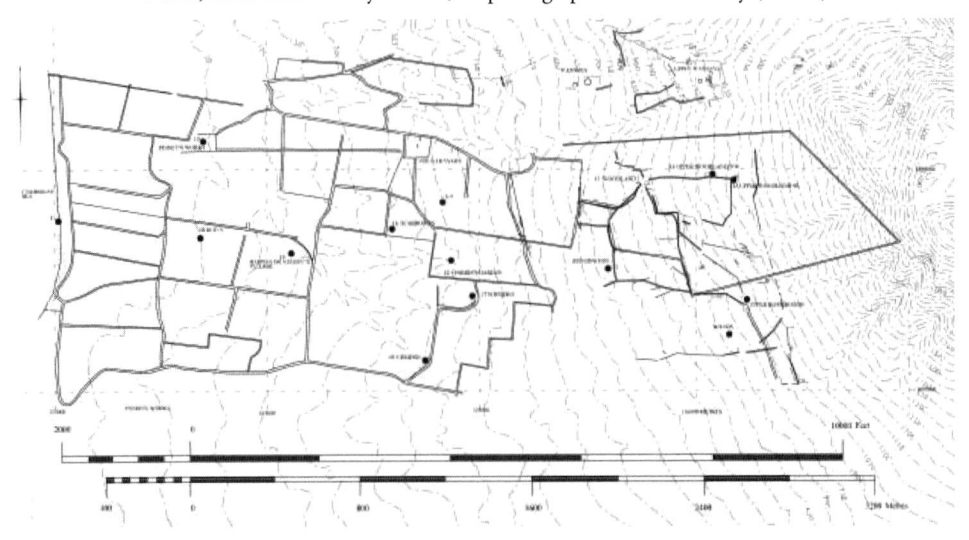

Here and in other parts of the island it is evident that the majority of longer boundaries are on a series of common alignments. In most instances these alignments run inland from the sea at approximately 90 degrees to the adjacent coast. In the central southern division, the alignments of the majority of the longer boundaries run approximately parallel to the coast. From the analysis of boundaries thus recorded from maps, documents, air photographs and field survey, it can be argued that, outside the towns of Charlestown and Jamestown, the land boundaries of Nevis have been laid out in some nine separate divisions characterised by consistent direction of land parcel and estate boundaries; the two towns may have constituted a further two divisions (Fig. 3).

Further archaeological study would probable enable the sequence in which the divisions were laid out to be established. The central southern division, with its property boundaries running parallel to the coast, was possibly the last division to be set out. On the west the inner round the island road forms part of the division boundary. The road must have been in use by the time that the division was laid out.

The use of the term 'division' can be contextually grounded in contemporary useage of the term. First, in the earliest land titles, estates on Nevis were located by reference to the division in which they were situated. In 1678 Sir William Stapleton's estate in the parish of St John was described as '... A certaine Plantation or Parcel of land Situate ... at or in the South West division ... Extending in length from the Sea near long Point to the figg tree Pond.'[24] In 1685 one Anne Kyrtland, widow, sold to John Haynes eight acres in the same 'South West Division' of the island.[25] In 1701 Stapleton's 'River Plantation' was said to be in the Old Windward Division of the island.[26] In 1738 the Potwork Plantation was said to be in the North West Division.[27]

A second contemporary use of the term 'division' was for the defence of the island. In 1678 the militia for the island consisted of thirteen divisions or companies. The lists enumerate for each division the white and negro men, women, and children.[28] The number of divisions here corresponds approximately to the number of divisions identified above by analysis of land boundaries. Possibly some of the largest land divisions were served by more than one division or company of people. The location of some of the divisions can be identified by correlation of personal names in the militia lists with those in land titles.

In early and later land titles and today, the island is divided into five parishes. Plotting of the parish boundaries in relationship to those of the eleven divisions reveals that the boundaries of the former are co-terminous with the boundaries of the land divisions. Each parish is therefore constituted of one (Charlestown) or more divisions (Fig. 4).

In the early 18th century visitors to Nevis described the island as cleared almost to the top of the mountain.[29] This clearance can be argued from the above to have been accomplished within the context of the island divided into eleven divisions, certainly in existence by the 1670s. These divisions are therefore likely to represent the way in which the island was initially divided and parcelled into separate estates. Archaeological and documentary records together provide some evidence as to how this was accomplished. Except in the central southern division the principal land boundaries run inland from the coast, approximately at right angles to the shore at that point. Within each division

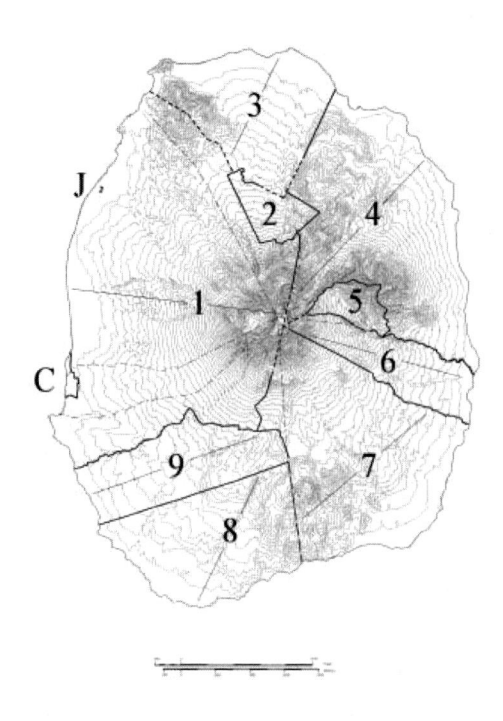

LEFT
Figure 3. The Divisions of Nevis, reconstructed from documentary sources, air photographs and field survey (author).

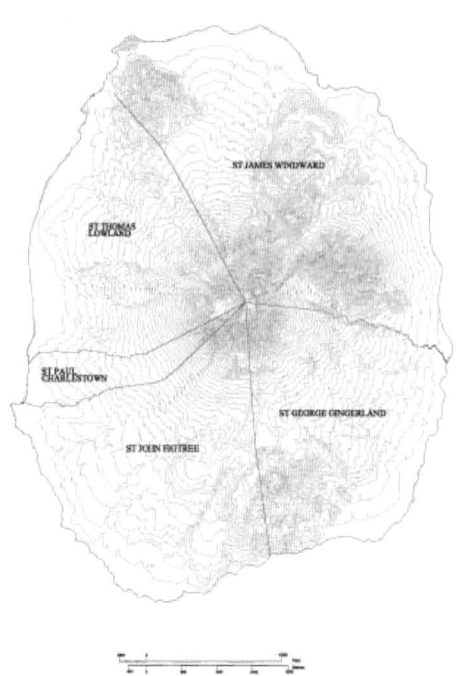

LEFT
Figure 4. The Parishes of Nevis (author).

the boundaries are remarkably consistent in following an identical compass bearing over distances of several miles (Fig. 3). How was such consistency achieved?

When first settled much of the island was densely forested. The consistency of the alignments over tracts of land up to four miles in extent along the shore was most probably achieved through the use of compass bearings. In some of the early land titles these compass bearings are actually given as a point of reference; the wording of the titles may in such cases be taken from the initial grants of land. For instance in 1728 the Windward Plantation in the Old Windward Division was said to be 'taking its beginning at the sea and running up south west half a point southerly to the farthest extent being the mountain'.[30]

Nevis was one of the Caribee islands settled in the 1620s and 30s through the patent granted to James Hay, Earl of Carlisle. Archives relating to his life are held in the Hay of Houston collection in the National Archives of Scotland. These contain no direct evidence as to how land on the islands settled under his direction was actually apportioned, but do reveal that surveyors were employed. On Barbados in 1638, less than ten years after settlement of that island had commenced, one settler wrote to Archibald Hay expressing his concern 'that the surveyors would not bound out' part of his lands. The surveyor had demanded of him 1000 pounds of tobacco for laying out 1000 acres of land, but notwithstanding his agreement to pay, he still could not get the surveyor to do the work.[31] On Nevis there was a similar consciousness of the need for estate boundaries to be confirmed by field survey. In 1676 the Assembly of Nevis ruled on the claim of one Captain William Digby touching the bounds of his Plantation. In 1643 the Assembly had adjudged that there must be 'an extent line' from Fig Tree Pond to Saddle Hill. In 1676, the present Governor had caused the Surveyor 'to draw a Platform', i.e. a plan, of all those Plantations that might cross one another. The Assembly now ordered that there be made 'an extent line' between certain Plantations from the Fig Tree Pond southerly down to Saddle Hill.[32] Extent lines that formed the boundaries between divisions were called 'division lines'. In 1726 a plantation of Richard Abbott esq., c.140 acres in extent, was bounded on the east with 'the Division Line'.[33] Running north to south down the middle of the island was the centre line, mentioned in many land titles. For instance, in 1714 the estate of John Symonds at Batchelors Hall in the parish of St George was said to be bounded on the south-west with 'the centre line; in 1725 John Ward esq. held c.148 acres of land late of Sarah Houblon, bounded on the east with 'the centre line.' [34]

The surveyors responsible for apportioning each estate were possibly working to a master plan. The earliest map to show Nevis in any detail has already been mentioned – Iles' map of 1871. However there was an earlier map, two centuries or more earlier, now lost but cited in at least two 17th-century records. Sir William Stapleton's 532 acre estate in St John's parish granted to him in 1678 had at an earlier date been on 'Mr Hiltons mapp ... Called by the name of Jennings and Balls Range'.[35] These same lands were held by one John Jennings by 1652. Hilton's map is also possibly mentioned in 1675 in a letter from Sir William Stapleton to his masters in London:[36]

198　ESTATE LANDSCAPES

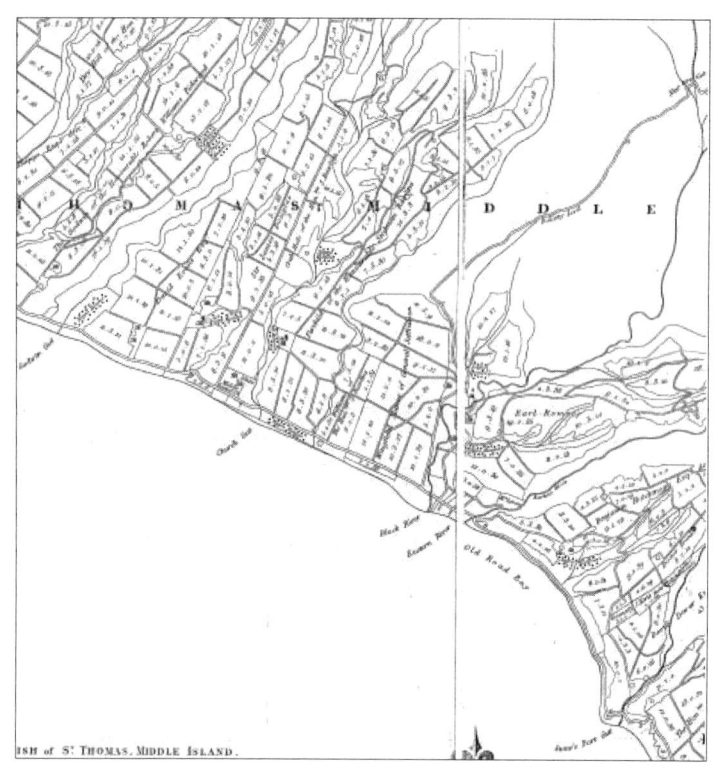

LEFT
Figure 5. St Kitts, the Wingfield and adjacent plantations, plan of 1828; note how the plantations of Wingfield Manor and Romney manor , two of the earliest on the island, are less regular than those to the north and south (McMahon 1828).

BELOW
Figure 6. Map of the island of Marie Galante, to the east of Guadeloupe, c. 1670 or earlier (du Tertre 1671, 360-1; reproduced by permission of the British Library).

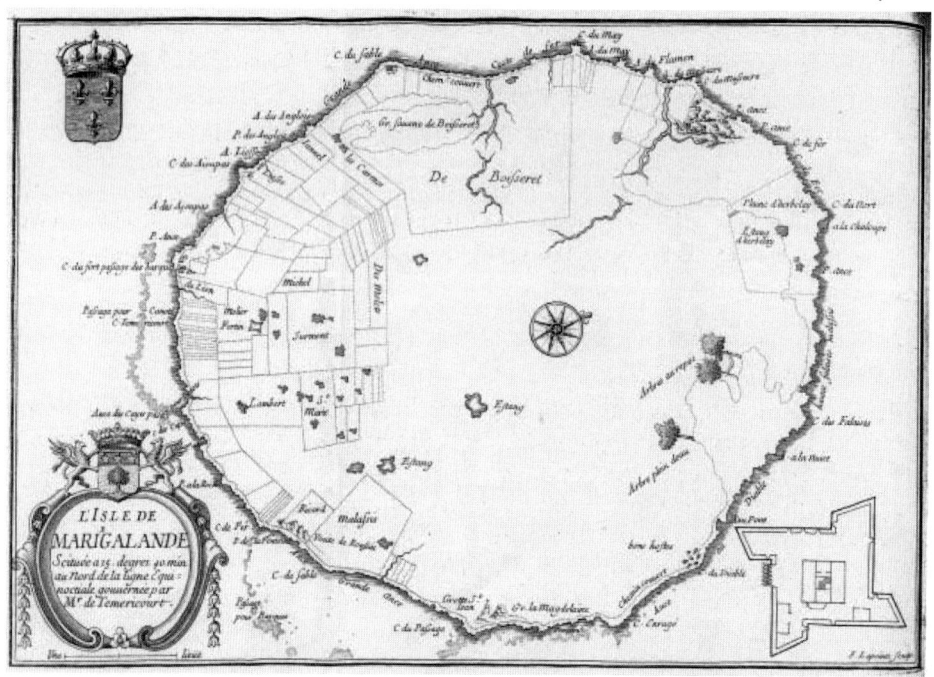

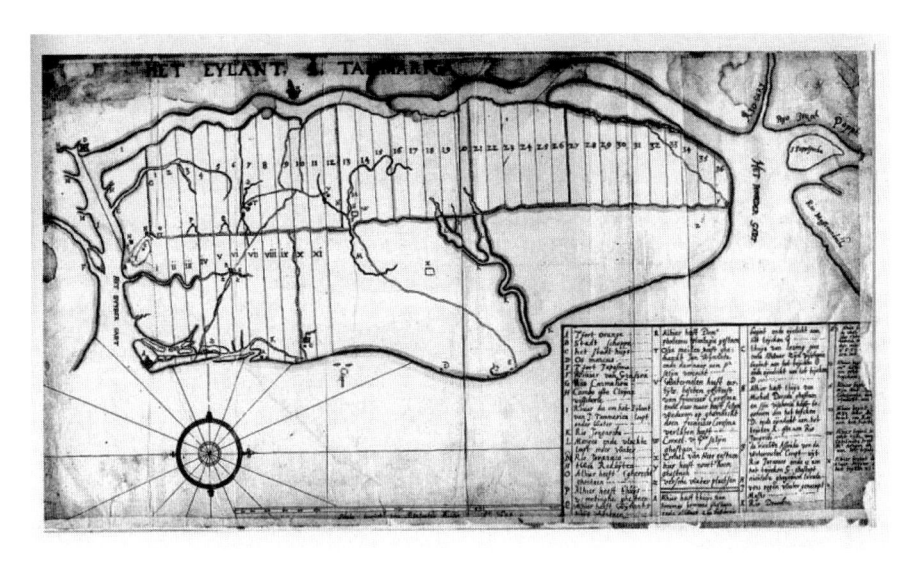

Figure 7. Plan for the division of land on the island of Itamaraca, off the coast of Brazil, 1648 (Algemeen Rijksarchief, Den Haag, VEL 707).

Nevis Jun.9.1675

My lords

By the annexed papers whereof here is a list I hope you have full satisfaction in what is required of me in your commands of 27.Oct.74, with an addition of acts and maps

Following sundry matters Stapleton annexed various papers – these included:

Narrative of St Xprs and Nevis by John Hilton old planter.

Narrative of St Xprs by ancient inhabitants to which is annexed the articles betwixt the English and the French at the takeing of it or rather surpriseing of itt contrarie to old articles.

Mapp of Nevis

[and]

Mapp of Montseratt

The 'Narrative of St Xprs and Nevis by John Hilton old planter' is probably the account published by Tarlow, from the manuscript in the Egerton MSS in the British Library. The map of Nevis cannot today be found in the Public Record Office / National Archives, but the map of Montserrat may survive, as the series of seven scenographic coastal profiles in the Blathwayt Atlas in the John Carter Brown Library, Providence, Rhode Island. These profiles were discussed at length by Lydia Pulsipher and dated to 1673, just two years before Stapleton's letter; Pulsipher identified Sir William Stapleton as the probable author of the coastal profiles, and of a scenographic map of the fortification at Pelican Point, Charlestown, Nevis.[37]

Since Stapleton had access to Hilton's narrative, it is likely that he had access also to Hilton's map of Nevis. The map sent to London in 1675 could have been that prepared originally by Hilton, or Stapleton's updated version. Possibly Stapleton's own inspiration for preparing the coastal profiles of Montserrat came from seeing Hilton's earlier map of Nevis. Such a map would have been drawn in large part from the sea.[38] Hilton's map would then have further demonstrated, as many might anticipate, that the settlement, division and apportionment of Nevis and other islands was accomplished from the sea. Maps similar to the Montserrat coastal profiles would have been necessary for the initial settlement of the island. On Montserrat too, estates were laid out in long narrow strips running from the sea to the mountain.

Looking briefly at other islands and lands newly cleared and settled in the first half of the 17th century we can discern a similar pattern. On St Kitts the subdivision of the island is clear on McMahon's map of 1828. The least organised area of landscape is that around the Wingfield plantation, probably the first of the island plantations to be established (Fig. 5). On St Kitts too the island was subdivided into units known as divisions, both as units of land and as components of the militia. In 1711 John Helden conveyed to Peter Millotte a parcel of land in 'the Old Road Division and in the parish of St Thomas Middle Island'.[39] On Barbados the organisation of divisions and estates follows closely that of the parishes, as on Nevis.[40] Looking further afield we find a similar mode of land parcel allotment being made by the Massachusetts Bay Company in New Hampshire in the mid 17th century. In

Figure 8. The settlement of the north shore of the St Lawrence, 1641 (Bibliothèque Nationale, Paris: Département des cartes et plans, portefeuille 200, pièce 5233).

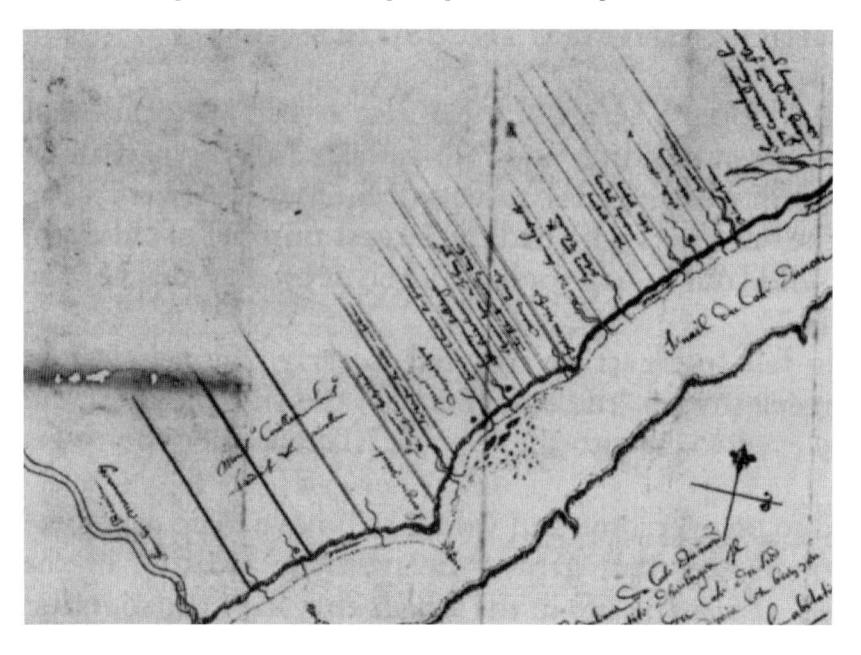

the subdivision of the Squamscott Patent of the 1650s long narrow estates were laid out at right angles to the Great Bay and to the coast.[41]

The colonial landscapes of other European countries were often formed to similar principles. Both St Eustatius, a Dutch possession, and Marie Galante, a French island, were laid out in a similar way to Nevis (Fig. 6).[42] Further afield Itamaraca, a Dutch island off the coast of Brazil, was similarly laid, as shown on a map of 1648 (Fig. 7).[43] On the north and south banks of the St Lawrence, the French subdivision of New France followed a similar pattern, recorded on a map of 1641 (Fig. 8).[44] Here the initial apportionment of land was probably achieved by survey undertaken initially from the wide estuary of the St Lawrence River.

CONCLUSIONS

The settlement of Nevis from 1628 onwards can be seen then in the wider context of contemporary European methodologies for land allotment. The processes of land division used by the surveyors of the Earl of Carlisle for islands such as Nevis, St Christopher, Montserrat and Barbados were similar to those being used for the settlement of French Canada, the French settlement of Marie Galante, the Portugese settlement of Itamaraca, and the English settlement of the coast of the Massachusetts Bay Company. Plans for the division of an island or coast made from coastal profiles would have enabled settlement to proceed in an orderly and profitable manner.

Regularly laid out divisions and land parcels were very much part of the mentality of 17th-century enclosure. The surveyors of the Earl of Carlisle would have been familiar with the application of such principles in the contemporary English landscape: in the draining of the Fens, the enclosure of waste and the reorganisation and enclosure of agricultural land formerly farmed in scattered open strips.

On Nevis and on other islands of the Caribbean, many of the land divisions laid out from the 1620s onwards remain today as prominent features in the post-colonial landscape, as the divisions between ecclesiastical parishes, as the boundaries of properties and as the limits of land parcels. They form an important element in the historic landscape of the islands. These same land divisions and boundaries must also be considered as archaeological data, illuminating the first years of European settlement, the survey of the coast and hinterland from the sea, and the division of the land into estates and plantations.

ACKNOWLEDGEMENTS

I am most grateful to Russell Fox for facilitating access to air photographs and maps in the now dispersed collections of the former Directorate of Overseas Surveys, Ordnance Survey, Southampton. I must also thank Vince Hubbard for many useful discussions, and Sheila Roberge for drawing my attention to the early maps of the settlement of New Hampshire. Finally I must thank my wife Pamela for reading through the manuscript and making many helpful suggestions. Any errors and omissions remain of course the responsibility of the author.

NOTES

1. Dunn 1973, 287.
2. Watts 1990, 335.
3. Watters 2001, 82-99.
4. Armstrong, 1990.
5. Handler & Lange 1978; Loftfield 2001.
6. Pulsipher & Goodwin 2001.
7. Barka 2001; unpublished MA dissertations in the library of William & Mary College.
8. Chiarelli 1999; Meniketti 1998.
9. Handler & Lange 1978.
10. Innis 1983 43-59.
11. Harlow (ed.) 1925; Hilton's account is BL, Egerton MSS 2395.
12. Ibid., 4.
13. Ibid., includes Sir Henry Colt's contemporary account of his voyage past Nevis to St Christopher in 1631.
14. Pares 1950; Johnston 1965; Mason 1993.
15. Ordnance Survey 1984.
16. Iles 1871.
17. Burdon 1920.
18. Barnett 1848.
19. Directorate of Overseas Surveys 1959, 1975 et al.
20. SRO, D/MW35/8a.
21. SuRO, HA178/1/56; Nevis Court House, Land Titles, Nevis Book 1, Old Manor 1893, Potworks 1904.
22. Formerly held by the Directorate of Overseas Surveys / Ordnance Survey, negatives now with the Government of St Kitts & Nevis.
23. Ibid.
24. JRL, Stapleton MSS, 2/1.
25. NCH, Common Records 1728-40, fol.21.
26. Bangor, Stapleton-Cotton MSS 1(1).
27. Caribbeana 3, 55 (Caribbeana: being miscellaneous papers relating to the history, genealogy, topography, and antiquities of the British West Indies ... Edited by Vere Langford Oliver, vols. 1-6. Jan. 1909 - Oct. 1919)
28. Caribbeana 3, 27-35, 70-80.
29. Smith 1740.
30. NCH, Common Records 1728-40, fols.87-91.
31. Hay of Houston MSS, letter of 24 May 1638, Mr Austen to Archibald Hay.
32. PRO Col. Entry Bk., No. 49, pp. 13, 14.
33. NCH, Common Records 1728-40, fols.92-7.
34. NCH, Common Records 1728-40, fols.39 and 98.
35. JRL, Stapleton MSS, 2/1.
36. PRO CO/1/34, item 85.
37. Pulsipher 1987.
38. Ibid., 414-6.
39. NCH, Common Records 1728-40, fol. 10.
40. Watts 1990, 205, Fig.5.5.
41. Merrill, Phinehas, 1793. Town of Stratham, New Hampshire (copy annotated by Bruce Parker to show land divisions, archives of the Great Bay National Estuarine Research Reserve, New Hampshire)
42. Eastman 1996, Fig. 9; du Tertre 1671, 360-1.
43. Zandvliet 1998, 203.
44. Bibliothèque Nationale, Département des cartes et plans, portefeille 200, pièce 5233 (map of the St Lawrence, 1641); Département des cartes et plans, Service hydrographique de la Marine, portfeuille 127.2. (map of the St Lawrence 1709).

BIBLIOGRAPHY

Armstrong, D. V. 1990, *The Old Village and the Great House: An Archaeological and Historical Examination of Drax Hall Plantation, St Ann's Bay Jamaica*, Urbana: University of Illinois Press.

Barka, N. 2001, 'Time Lines: Changing Settlement Patterns on St Eustatius', in Farnsworth 2001, 103-141.

Chiarelli, J. A. 1999, 'Archaeological Field Work Continues at Coconut Walk Estate / New River, *Nevis Historical and Conservation Society Newsletter*, August 1999, 6-7.

Dunn, Richard S. 1972, *Sugar and Slaves. The Rise of the Planter Class in the English West Indies, 1624-1713*, Chapel Hill: University of North Carolina Press

Eastman, J. A. 1996, *An archaeological assessment of St. Eustatius, Netherlands Antilles*, Williamsburg VA.

Farnsworth, P. (ed.) 2001, *Island Lives. Historical Archaeologies of the Caribbean*,Tuscaloosa & London: University of Alabama Press.

Handler, J. S. & Lange, F. W. 1978, *Plantation slavery in Barbados: An archaeologicaland and historical investigation*, Cambridge, Mass.: Harvard University Press.

Harlow, V. T. (ed.) 1925, 'Colonising Expeditions to the West Indies and Guiana,1623-1667', *Publications of the Hakluyt Society*, 2nd Series, LIV.

Innis, Sir Probyn 1983, *Whither Bound St Kitts –Nevis ?*, St John's, Antigua: Antigua Printing & Publishing Ltd.

Johnston, J. R. V. 1965, 'The Stapleton sugar plantations in the Leeward Islands', *Bulletin of the John Rylands Library* 48:1, 175-206.

Loftfield, T. C. 2001, 'Creolization in Seventeenth-Century Barbados: Two Case Studies', in Farnsworth 2001, 207-233.

Mason, K. 1993, 'The world an absentee planter and his slaves made: Sir William Stapleton and his Nevis Sugar estate, 1722-1740', *Bulletin of the John Rylands Library* 75:1, 103-130.

Morris, E. et al. (eds) 2001, *Nevis Heritage Project: Interim Report 2001*, Southampton: Nevis Heritage Project, University of Southampton.

Pares, R. 1950, *A West India Fortune*, London: Longmans.

Pulsipher, L. M. 1987, 'Assessing the Usefulness of a Cartographic Curiosity: The 1673 Map of a Sugar Island', *Annals of the Association of American Geographers* 77:3, 408-422.

Pulsipher, L. M. & Goodwin, C. M. 2001, '"Getting the Essence of It': Galways Plantation, Montserrat, West Indies", in Farnsworth 2001, 165-203.

Smith, Rev. William 1740, *A Natural History of Nevis, and the rest of the English Caribee Islands in America*, Cambridge: W. Thurlbourn.

Du Tertre, J. B. 1671, *Histoire générale des Antilles habitées par les Français*, vol. II, Paris.

Watters, D. R. 2001, 'Historical Archaeology in the British Caribbean', in Farnsworth 2001, 82-99.

Watts, D. 1990, *The West Indies: development, culture and environmental change since 1492*, Cambridge: Cambridge University Press.

Zandvliet, K. 1998, *Mapping for Money. Maps, plans and topographic paintings and their role in Dutch overseas expansion during the 16th and 17th centuries*, Amsterdam:Batavian Lion International.

UNPUBLISHED SOURCES

Bibliothèque Nationale, Paris: Département des cartes et plans, portefeuille 200, pièce 5233 (map of the St Lawrence, 1641); Département des cartes et plans, Service hydrographique de la Marine, portfeuille 127.2. (map of the St Lawrence 1709).

Archives of the Great Bay National Estuarine Research Reserve, New Hampshire, Merrill, Phinehas, 1793. Town of Stratham, New Hampshire (copy annotated by Bruce Parker to show land divisions) John Rylands Library, University of Manchester: Stapleton MSS, 2/1

Meniketti, M. G. 1998, *The Port St George Project: An archaeological assessment of a sugar plantation and harbour complex in Nevis, West Indies*, unpublished MSc thesis, Michigan Technological University.

National Archives (formerly the Public Record Office), Col. Entry Bk., No. 49, pp. 13, 14.

National Archives of Scotland: Hay of Houston MSS, GD34, letter of 24 May 1638, Mr Austen to Archibald Hay

Nevis Court House, Nevis: Common Records, 1728-1740; Land Titles, Nevis Book 1, Old Manor 1893, Potworks 1904.

Southampton Record Office, D/MW35/8a: *Plan of the plantation of Edward Jessup, esq., in the parish of St Thomas Lowland in the island of Nevis*. Surveyed A.D. 1755 by W. Cockburn, Delineated by S. Wilkinson, 1761.

Suffolk Record Office, HA178/1/56

University of Wales, Bangor. Stapleton-Cotton MSS: 1(1)

ABBREVIATIONS
JRL John Rylands Library
NCH Nevis Court House
SRO Southampton Record Office
SuRO Suffolk Record Office

MAPS
Barnett, Captain E. & assistants, HMS Thunder 1848, St Christopher and Nevis, 1:56,700, London: Admiralty (PRO WO78/603).
Burdon, Major J.A. 1920, Nevis, compiled and brought up to date from existing surveys by Major J.A. Burdon, London: Geographical Section, General Staff War Office.
Directorate of Overseas Surveys, 1959, Nevis, Lesser Antilles 1:25,000, Tolworth: Directorate of Overseas Surveys.
Directorate of Overseas Surveys, 1975 et al., revised 1980s by the Directorate of Overseas Surveys, Ordnance Survey. Nevis 3193[and other sheets for areas surveyed at1:2500], Tolworth: Directorate of Overseas Surveys.
Iles, John Alexander Burke 1871, An Account descriptive of the Island of Nevis, West Indies, Norwich: Privately Printed.
McMahon, William 1828, A New Topographical Map of the Island of St Christopher in the West Indies … by William McMahon Surveyor of the Island, (names of subscribers given, publisher and place of publication not stated).
Merrill, Phinehas 1793, Town of Stratham, New Hampshire (copy annotated by Bruce Parker to show land divisions, archives of the Great Bay National Estuarine Research Reserve, New Hampshire).
Ordnance Survey 1984, Nevis, Lesser Antilles 1:25,000, Southampton: Ordnance Survey.
Southampton Archives Office D/MW35/8a: Plan of the plantation of Edward Jessup, esq., in the parish of St Thomas Lowland in the island of Nevis. Surveyed A.D. 1755 by W. Cockburn, Delineated by S. Wilkinson, 1761.

'Material Improvements': the Archaeology of Estate Landscapes in the British Leeward Islands, 1713-1838

By DAN HICKS

This paper examines the archaeology of sugar estate landscapes in the Leeward Islands in the Caribbean, during the 18th and 19th centuries. It sets this study in the context not only of Caribbean studies, but also historical archaeology generally and post-medieval landscape studies in the UK in particular. It considers how the approaches of landscape archaeology can highlight the material (rather than purely ideational) dimensions of the changing estate landscapes of the colonial Caribbean, and the attendant conceptions of materiality that were bound up with colonial ideas of improvement. It points to some of the ways in which the archaeology of colonialism can inform that most British of fields of study - the history of the post-medieval English landscape – and to the potential of decentring our conceptions of 'Britishness' in British post-medieval landscape archaeology.

I

The global contexts of British imperialism are an increasingly common theme in historical archaeology. Focusing upon material remains to produce new accounts of the local complexities and contingencies of empire, such work is characterised especially by an acknowledgement of the central role of materiality – objects, landscapes, buildings - in the practice of colonial relations.[1] However, the study of the estate landscapes has been surprisingly uncommon in plantation archaeology in the New World, despite the central importance of agricultural estates and plantation slavery to the 17th-, 18th- and 19th- century histories of the much-excavated regions of the island Caribbean or the Chesapeake.

In the Caribbean, the development of historical archaeology has often been informed by perspectives from historical geography. Pioneering work carried out over the past three decades includes Lydia Pulsipher's studies of the historical landscape of Montserrat, Jerome Handler and Frederick Lange's studies of slave cemeteries in Barbados and Douglas Armstrong's study of a sugar plantation in Jamaica, and is increasingly built upon by new studies – as demonstrated by the recent collections of Jay Haviser, Paul Farnsworth and Kenneth Kelly and Mark Hauser.[2] However, such work has rarely aimed to contribute to thinking in historical archaeology elsewhere in the world: as Michel-Rolph Trouillot has observed for cultural anthropology, so also in historical archaeology the Caribbean region remains an 'open frontier…where boundaries are notoriously fuzzy'; a diverse and 'undisciplined' field that has rarely been able to contribute to metropolitan perspectives 'lessons learned on the frontier'.[3]

This chapter examines aspects of the archaeology of sugar estate landscapes in the Leeward Islands in the eastern Caribbean during the 18th and early 19th centuries in relation to British studies of post-medieval landscapes. It aims to use the idea of 'improvement' as a way of exploring two themes. Firstly, it considers how the approaches of landscape archaeology can highlight the material (rather than purely ideational) dimensions of the changing estate landscapes of the colonial Caribbean, and the attendant conceptions of materiality that were bound up with colonial ideas of improvement. Secondly, it points to some of the ways in which the archaeology of colonialism can inform that most British of fields of study - the history of the post-medieval English landscape – and to the potential of decentring our conceptions of the 'Britishness' in British post-medieval landscape archaeology.

***

The archaeology of plantations and designed landscapes forms a significant part of historical archaeology in North America and the Caribbean.[4] Much of this work has been focused upon excavation and artefact analysis rather than the above-ground archaeology of estate landscapes. Rich and sophisticated studies of the close relationships between people and things in colonial plantation contexts have been developed: for instance in Laurie Wilkie's study of Clifton plantation in the Bahamas, which has explored the importance of the consumption of European-made commodities to African-Bahamian identities.[5] Where such approaches have been extended to landscape and architecture, most notably in Anne Yentsch's account of the household of Charles Calvert (an early 18th-century Governor of Maryland), surviving material culture has been woven together with documentary sources, producing richly textured historical ethnographies of changing households over time.[6]

In the archaeology of landscapes, however, such nuanced work is less visible. Gardens and estates in the Chesapeake and Caribbean have been studied through processual approaches to spatial patterning,[7] through post-processual, and often Foucauldian, understandings of the effects of the built environment in relation to the structures of social power,[8] or through awkward combinations of the two.[9] Despite the broader regional traditions of North American 'landscape archaeology',[10] plantation estate design has often been presented as simply illustrative of, and embedded in, the ideologies of capitalism and slavery. So, James Delle's (1998) Lefebvrian study of Jamaican coffee plantations aims to 'read' capitalist power relations in local 'spaces', inspired by studies of designed landscapes as evidence of 'spatial inequality'.[11] Similarly, some 'critical archaeologists' in the Chesapeake associated with the Archaeology in Annapolis project have built upon its studies of gardens and towns by exploring how the designed landscapes and architecture of plantations were 'important arena[s] in ideological struggle' and the 'construction of difference' under 18th-century merchant capitalism.[12] The limitations of such approaches are clear in Charles Orser's discussion of 'plantations and space', which offers a general definition of plantations as 'a capitalist kind of agricultural organization in which a number of laborers produce a certain kind of crop under the direction of others':

> 'The size of [the planter's] house can be viewed as a physical manifestation of plantation power…A plantation's landscape is a bounded universe with clear limits…the spatial arrangement of plantation housing should reflect power relations to some degree. It can be expected, given the plantation's primary economic function, that plantation houses were located closest to the work places of their inhabitants. Thus the millwright…lived near the mill pond and the mill building…and the landlord's servant lived near the landlord. However, what may be more indicative of power relations are the relationships between individual buildings themselves. In other words, the relationships between the buildings should have carried a social meaning created to reflect, among other things, the power relations enacted within the dominant mode of production at the plantation' [13]

Such approaches tend simply to 'read off' power relations from unchanging, two-dimensional spatial organisation, modelling 'the plantation' as a category of comparative analysis: obscuring the complexities of local variation and historical process.

Meanwhile, in British post-medieval landscape archaeology, generalising studies of power and ideology as reflected in designed landscapes have been no less common. The 'improving' impulses of agricultural enclosure[14] and polite landscapes[15] have been examined as part of the ideology of capitalism, producing compelling and revealing analyses of the 'physical processes' of landscape change.[16] They have nonetheless been restricted by a normative conception of the general emergence of 'industrial capitalism'. While, as Mary Beaudry has put it, historical archaeology is at its best not when aiming simply to 'contribute…to our understanding of sweeping and amorphous cultural processes', but when also striving 'to inform us of the intimate and unheralded details of day-to-day life',[17] 'landscape archaeologies of capitalism' tend to smooth out the complexities and contingencies of particular circumstances, of particular regional or colonial situations for instance. The challenge for archaeologists is to find ways of weaving together fine-grained studies with broader scales of analysis:[18] a task for which landscape archaeology, which is characterised by an ability to work across different geographical dimensions, is particularly well placed.[19]

Two British archaeologists have recently used the idea of 'improvement' as an alternative way of examining elite landscape changes in Scotland during the 18th and 19th centuries. Chris Dalglish's study of improvement in the southern Scottish highlands traces a radical shift from nucleated townships (bailtean) and shielings to new patterns of dispersed settlement and isolated farmsteads. In his comparison of Kintyre and Kilfinan, Dalglish acknowledges that 'Improvement' was adopted in different ways in different places. Rather than 'reading power relations', Dalglish has emphasised the relationships between improvement, elite and national identity.[20] Similarly, in his examination of 'improvements' in South Uist in the Outer Hebrides, James Symonds has suggested that:

> 'Rather than trying to impose an "ideological confidence trick"…upon a mass of the population, the actions of the elite were in many ways geared to reaffirming their own social positioning, and to validating their own belief in the ideology of "improvement" through material expressions' [21]

Constructing broader archaeologies of improvement[22] might risk finding in improvement a kind of 'surrogate capitalism', replacing one grand, evolutionary process with another.[23] But the thoughtful work of Dalglish and Symonds provides insights upon the diversity of improvement: its contextual variation, itinerancy, the materiality of its performance, and the attendant changing conceptions of landscape. This is in keeping with the motivations for interest in improvement in historical geography as:

> 'usefully reposition[ing] enlightened culture, away from the prime focus on the metropolitan, libertarian world of London to the more regulated rural world of the landed estate'. [24]

Such 'repositioning', however, holds the potential to include still wider geographical contexts. In their studies of British agrarian landscapes, historical geographers have emphasised the significance of the notion of 'improvement' during the post-medieval period, whether between the 1780s and 1860s,[25] or between 1730 and 1914.[26] In their classic statement on 'landscape design and the idea of improvement' Stephen Daniels and Susanne Seymour described how from the 1730s 'improvement' was related to new elite landscape designs 'on a large scale and with great attention to detail', and hence to the management of parks and estates, and beyond:

> 'Landscape in Georgian England was not just a matter of conventions of taste; it was a highly complicated discourse in which a whole range of issues, which we might now discriminate as 'economic', 'political', 'social' and 'cultural' were encoded and negotiated.... The concept of improvement was integral to these negotiations. Initially used to denote profitable operations in connection with land, notably aristocratic enclosure, by the end of the 18th century 'improvement' referred not just to a variety of progressive farming practices but to a broad range of activities from music to manufacturing, with a series of overlapping resonances – financial, pragmatic, moral, educational, aesthetic. A central issue of 18th century polite culture, at least from a conservative point of view, was the relation between improvement in various spheres of life; the discourse of landscape provided a way of both diagnosing disharmony between these spheres and brining them into balance'. [27]

Daniels and Seymour, following Alistair Duckworth and Raymond Williams, suggest that the 'key word' of improvement was itinerant.[28] Williams sketched how between the 16th and 18th centuries 'improving' shifted from describing 'profitable operations in connection with land' to a 'wider meaning of "making something better"...often in direct overlap with economic operations', and then to 'the characteristic "improve oneself"', whereupon 'such phrases as "improving reading" followed':

> 'Jane Austen was aware of the sometimes contradictory senses of improvement, where economic operations for profit might lead to, or might hinder, social and moral refinement. In Persuasion [1818] (ch. v), a landowning family was described as 'in a state of alteration, perhaps of improvement'. The separation of the general meaning from the economic meaning is thereafter normal, but the complex underlying connection between 'making something better' and 'making a profit out of something' is significant when the social and economic history during which the word developed in these ways is remembered'. [29]

Williams suggested that the 'agricultural revolution' was in reality 'no revolution, but the consolidation, the improvement, the expansion of an existing social class'. Improvement shifted across 'soil, stock, yields, in a working agriculture' to 'the improvement of houses, parks, artificial landscapes', and into polite social life –

> 'Cultivation has the same ambiguity as improvement: there is increased growth, and this is converted into rents; and then the rents are converted into what is seen as a cultivated society. What the 'revolution is for, then, is this: the apparently attainable quality of life'. [30]

This itinerancy can be explored further. For example, Sarah Tarlow has extended the temporal dimensions of 'improvement', noting its appearance in literary sources from the early 17th century as well as clearly continuing in currency and importance into the 20th century.[31] The geographical mobilities of 'improvement', however, moving across the mercantile and estate landscapes of the British Atlantic world, are equally striking.[32] Richard Drayton has observed how the notion of improvement was central to English colonial activities from the early 17th century, representing a distinctive blend of agricultural, economic and political interests.[33] The colonial contexts of 'improvement' range from Kew gardens through the geographical networks of plant science,[34] across the Scottish highlands,[35] and Ireland, and more widely still. For the cultivation of sugar cane, Griggs has recently traced the improving activities of the Colonial Sugar Refining Company in New South Wales, Australia, between 1864 and 1915: including the introduction of ploughing, fertiliser use, land drainage and new paddock design.[36] In this vein, and building upon their previous work on improvement,[37] Susanne Seymour, Stephen Daniels and Charles Watkins have studied the close relationships between the development of Sir George Cornewall's Moccas estate in Herefordshire and his La Taste estate in Grenada (1771-1819). By 'examining landed estates and their owners in an imperial context', Seymour et al demonstrate a series of 'overlapping concerns…especially in terms of the management of land, labour and finance' at the two sites.[38]

The idea of studying colonial contexts to inform the study of British society 'at home' has been explored in other fields. In postcolonial literary studies, Edward Said's examination of the exclusion of references to Sir Thomas Bertram's Antiguan sugar plantations from his fictional rural elite landscape Mansfield Park[39] has inspired the acknowledgement of the influence of imperial worlds upon highly 'English' cultural situations.[40] Said famously observed how Austen described social life in the households and landscapes of the elite as 'implicated in the rationale for imperialist expansion':

> 'The "attainable quality of life", in money and property acquired, moral discriminations made, the right choices put in place, the correct "improvements" implemented, the finely nuanced language affirmed and classified' [41]

Here, Bertram's Antiguan estate landscapes are 'held in a precise place within Austen's moral geography' of improvement, as Austen 'connects the actualities of British power overseas to the domestic imbroglio within the Bertram estate'.[42]

Equally, historical studies of the colonial Atlantic have seen the emergence of what David Armitage has termed 'cis-Atlantic' accounts, aiming to provide a counterpoint to Victorian national historiographies by writing the history of particular locations in wider Atlantic perspective.[43] By seeking to define the uniqueness of a particular situation 'as the result of the interaction between local particularity and a wider web of connections', such historical studies bring 'methodological pluralism and expanded horizons'.[44]

Such impulses, across literary, geographical and historical studies, are united by an awareness of the entanglements of empire with metropole. In the study of Caribbean sugar plantations, such perspectives are indebted to another Williams: Trinidadian historian Eric Williams' 1944 study *Capitalism and Slavery*. The 'Williams Thesis' argued that the development of British industrial society was closely bound up with the cultural and economic capital produced by the sugar islands of the eastern Caribbean.[45] Similarly, in his classic examination of the relationships between urban and rural situations, The *Country and the City*, Raymond Williams acknowledged the 'larger context' of the British empire, and its profound effects upon British imagination and landscape from the late 19th century:[46] perspectives that can be applied before the 19th century as well.[47]

Seeking to bring together Eric and Raymond Williams' perspectives upon estate landscapes, in both Britain and the Caribbean in transatlantic perspective, the next section of this considers the changes in estate landscapes in St Kitts during the 18th and early 19th centuries.

II

This section considers the development of 'material improvements' described by Caribbean historian Jack Greene – which were 'practical' as well as purely 'aesthetic' – in the landscapes of the eastern Caribbean during the 17th, 18th and early 19th centuries, using St Kitts as a case study.[48] From the 1620s, British colonists established plantations on islands such as Antigua, Barbuda, St Kitts, Nevis, Montserrat and Barbados. Until the last decades of the 17th century, these landscapes were characterised by great agricultural diversity. The cultivation and processing of a range of tropical staples, including tobacco, coffee, sugar cane, cotton, ginger, indigo, pimento, and cocoa, was undertaken within walled or palisaded enclosures, not unlike the 'bawns' of 16th-century Ireland or 17th-century Virginia in which houses for planters, indentured servants and slaves were also built. Provisions such as cassava, manioc and sweet potatoes were also cultivated. Documentary sources describe close interaction and partnerships with native Carib populations in agricultural practices in the early decades of settlement.[49] The extent of pastoral and ranching activities and of clearance for a frontier timber trade at this time has been little studied, but may also have been significant.[50]

While the French *Companie des Isles* had begun 'a definite policy of encouraging the cultivation of the sugar cane' from its formation in 1635,[51] it was not until the last decades of the 1600s that the sugar cultivation began to dominate the landscapes of the French and English Caribbean Leewards. Under the Treaty of Utrecht (1713), British involvement in the slave trade was radicalised.[52] Under the same 1713 treaty, the French areas of St Kitts were ceded to Britain, and during the fifty years to the end of the Seven Years War, the island developed as one of the foremost British 'sugar islands'. Government plans to 'improve' the colony upon the ceding of the French lands by dividing up sugar estates into small, planned farms, thereby encouraging the development of a 'yeoman class' in an island that 'looked like a garden' failed,[53] and instead a new island landscape of fewer, larger estates emerged, filled with open, green fields of sugar cane, as:

> 'Economies of scale threw the balance in favour of the planter who possessed several hundred acres of arable land, and improved sugar works, and a labour force of [hundreds of] Negro slaves'. [54]

Planters bought up adjacent land, forming estates that ran, like the Pinney Estate on Nevis, 'from the sea to the mountain'.[55] Small cattle mills were replaced with new windmills, dedicated to the processing of each estate's own sugar. Larger fields and the new sugar monoculture brought changes in labour organisation: larger numbers of unskilled labourers, organised into gangs, were provided through a dramatic increase in the number of slaves. Where white indentured agricultural labour had formed, alongside African slavery, a major part of the mixed economy of the 17th century, gang labour now became synonymous with slavery. White servants were increasingly unwilling to labour in the large gangs of regimented workers that hoed the ground, planted the sugar, weeded the fields, and cut the cane,[56] as a transition from the 'paternalistic hierarchy' of servants and fewer slaves to 'industrial slavery' took place.[57]

Some of the changes in estate landscapes that accompanied the shift to sugar monoculture are visible the developments at the adjacent estates of Wingfield and Romney,

Figure 1. Photograph of Wingfield Estate from the early 20th century, showing 18th-century aqueduct and the chimney for a 19th-century steam engine (courtesy of St Christopher Heritage Society).

near Old Road, St Kitts, between 1713 and the effecting of slave emancipation in 1838 (Figs 2 & 3). This area was the subject of a programme of archaeological landscape survey, standing buildings recording and documentary research in 2001, which formed part of a broader study of the landscape archaeology of sugar landscapes in the eastern Caribbean between the early 17th century and the 20th century.[58] A water-powered sugar mill was established at the newly-styled 'Wingfield Manor' during the late 1670s by Christopher Jeaffreson (1650-1725), an East Anglian merchant, on the site of an earlier enclosure and works. Jeaffreson described establishing the works in a letter dated 12 May 1677 to his Father-in-Law:

> 'I goe on expending money upon my plantation, in hopes it will repaye mee with interest; but I must have patience, for it will require tyme, as well as a large expense, before the sugar-worke can be perfected. It is now esteemed here a great folly for a man to expose his tyme or goods to the hazard of indigo or tobacco, sugar being the only thriveing and valuable commodity.'[59]

From the 1690s Jeaffreson managed the estate from Dullingham House in Cambridgeshire through his Ensign in St Kitts, Mr Thorn, but from 1713 Wingfield was leased: between 1713-1728 to General L. Lambert, and then between 1728-1758 to Charles Pym. The relationship between Wingfield and the adjacent Romney estate became closer

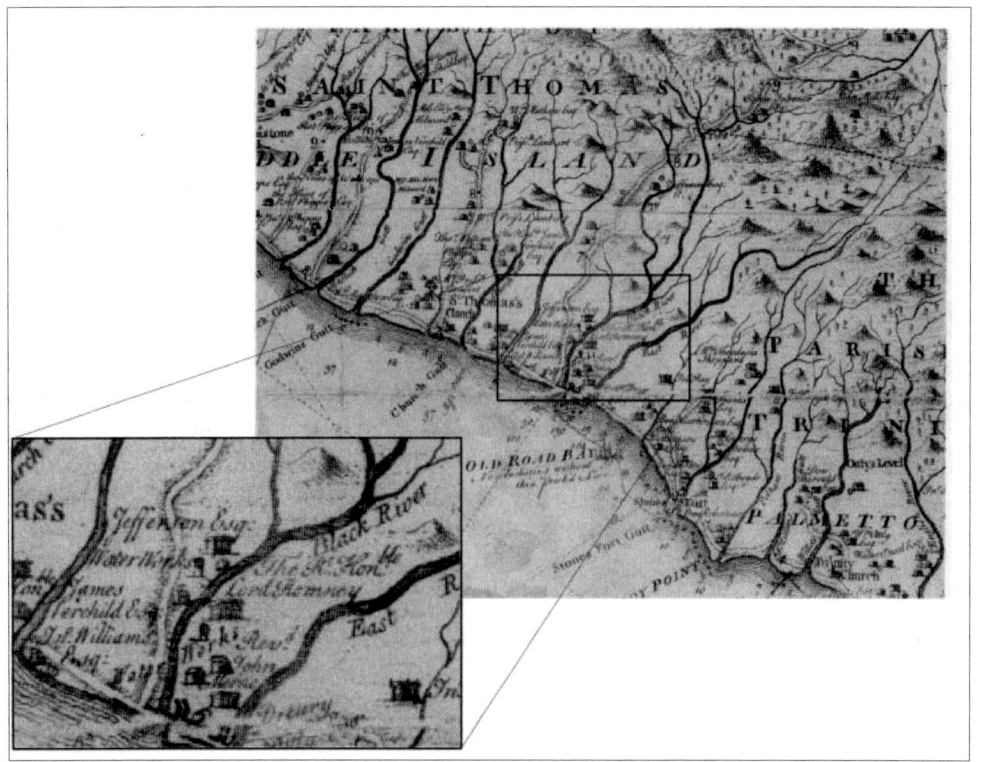

Figure 2. Detail of Baker map (1756), with inset showing Wingfield and Romney works

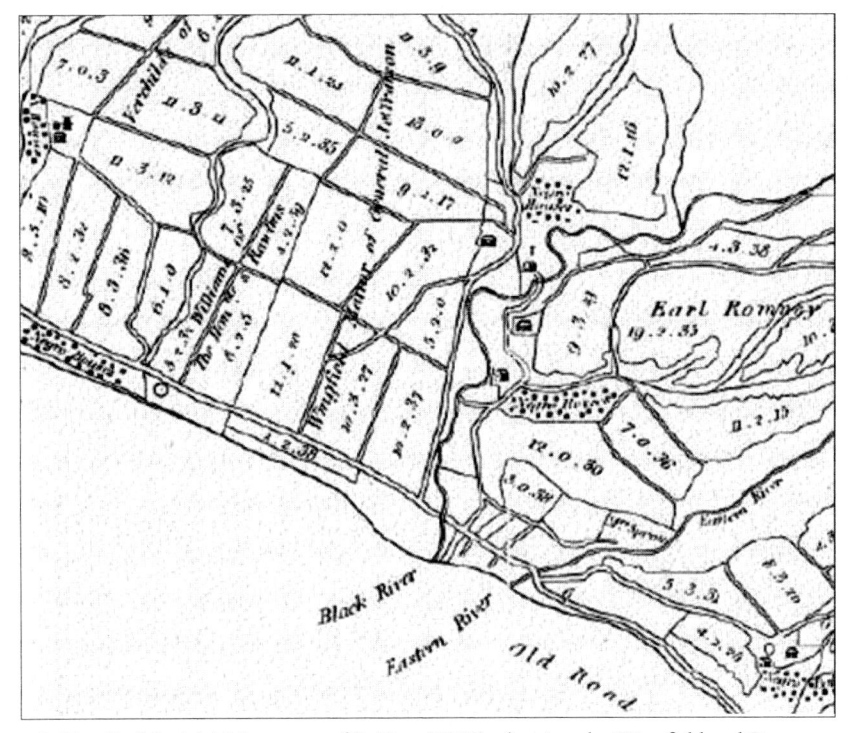

Figure 3. Detail of the McMahon map of St Kitts (1828), showing the Wingfield and Romney estates.

from 1742, when the Earl of Romney (Robert Marsham, 1712-93), owner of the Romney estate on St Kitts and the Mote in Maidstone, Kent, married Charles Pym's daughter and heiress Priscella.[60] Romney took over the lease of Wingfield in 1756, and for at least 30 years, from 1758 the Wingfield and Romney estates were managed as a single enterprise.

An inventory of Wingfield taken in 1713 listed only a few slaves, 'an old boiling house and walls', 'four mill posts and one bridge tree of the island wood' and 'one deal water spout rotten & of no value', along with 'a few negro houses'.[61] Over the next century, however, documentary and archaeological evidence demonstrates that a series of improvements were undertaken. The sugar works were continually remodelled in a highly complex construction sequence. The boiling house was entirely rebuilt on two occasions during the 18th century, each time rearranging the boiling and flue systems in order to increase capacity and efficiency. A massive, impressive brick and stone aqueduct (Fig. 1) replaced an earlier wooden launder, with impressive arches and fine brick dressings. A brick-built bell tower was added to the roof of the works.

A new Great House was constructed in the first half of the 18th century, replacing an earlier Jacobean house on the lower ground, high up above the works among the open, green cane fields. Commanding wide views, the house was approached by a new terraced road that wound uphill towards it, past the impressive works facade on their approach. An area of slave accommodation was located away from here, along the western banks of the Wingfield River, below the crest of the hill on which the plantation house was built.[62]

Wingfield was managed as a single enterprise with Romney from 1756, and a new sugar works at 'Romney Manor' was constructed. In this new arrangement, a new culvert was provided from the water wheel, through which the water passed, before being channelled along the side of the road to the new works. A new, substantial stone bridge over the Wingfield River between the Wingfield and Romney works was constructed. The road from Wingfield to Romney now passed below the aqueduct, around the Wingfield works, across the stone bridge, and along the side of the valley flanked by impressive stone terrace walls.

In 1819, an advertisement for the lease of Wingfield described the improved estate:

> 'To Let: The Plantation called Wingfield Manor situated in the Parish of St Thomas, Middle Island to the westward of Little River in the Town of Old-Road, the Property of Major John Jeaffreson, and now in the occupation of the Right Honourable Earl Romney, consisting of 960 Acres of Land, of which the Cane Land and Pasturage are inferior to none in the Island. The Cane Mill is turned by an abundant Stream of Water, and the Estate commands peculiar advantages. Immediate possession, with the standing Crop of Canes and Provisions, may be had. For the Terms and Particulars, apply to R.W. Pickwoad.'[63]

The changing estate landscapes of Wingfield and Romney provide a useful point of entry to studying the material dimensions of improvement in St Kitts during the 18th century. Sugar planters were 'combination farmer-manufacturers'.[64] The industrial nature of their plantations, involving the processing of sugar cane as well as its cultivation, made constant experimentation possible. These experiments, in the fields and the sugar works, were fuelled by fast-developing new concerns with the productivity and the application of scientific techniques to agriculture.[65] An Antiguan Committee described in 1788 how 'all…probable improvements in the Instruments of Husbandry have from time to time had a fair trial'.[66] New Asian varieties of sugar cane - such as 'Otaheite' and 'Bourbon' - were introduced during the 1780s, partly as a response to new concerns about the impact on harvests of pests such as caterpillars and sugar ants. Where appropriate, great attention was paid to water management, whether for water power or irrigation. Fertilisation with dung developed across the eastern Caribbean from the second half of the 18th century.[67] The use of ploughs in cane fields developed in Antigua from the 1750s in Antigua,[68] and was in 'almost universal use' there by 1820.[69]

A more efficient sugar cane crushing machine, with three horizontal rollers was invented in 1754 by John Smeaton: and widespread use of horizontal roller crushing machines in the eastern Caribbean had developed by the 1790s,[70] and the 'tied headstock' was introduced around 1830.[71] Further developments in sugar cane crushing included the use of solid iron rollers (rather than iron-clad wooden rollers) from 1721,[72] and the invention of a device known a 'doubleuse', which automatically fed the sugar cane back through the rollers. Concerns over efficiency in the use of waste crushed cane or 'trash' were alleviated through its use as a fuel for the boiling house furnaces from the early 18th century,[73] and considerable amounts of coal was imported to St Kitts during the late 18th century to increase the efficiency of the boilers further.[74] In the boiling houses, the use of clarifiers (or 'cold receivers'), and the mixture of juice with lime to promote crystallisation, became far more common from the mid 18th century. From around 1775 hydrometers were used at some estates to measure the specific gravity of cane syrup before transfer to the curing house,[75] and use was made of the vacuum pan, which increased the efficiency of evaporation by allowing it to take place under vacuum, after its patenting in 1813.[76] In 1808, microscopes were sent from London to one group of planters for the examination of the effects of different procedures on sugar crystallisation.[77] Centrifuges were introduced during the early 19th century, separating the molasses from the sugar granules in order to speed up the curing process.

At the same time, the improvement of estates also involved the negotiation of the complex systems of elite kin relations and land tenure that had been established during the 17th century in the creole gentry society of the eastern Caribbean. A small number of established families dominated land ownership and the Islands' Assemblies and Councils, and the careful development of pedigrees through exogamous marriage relations was central to the development of West Indian landed dynasties, especially in the face of a new emerging Atlantic merchant class. Many of these incoming merchant-planters were educated Scottish merchants who joined the planter societies of St Kitts and Antigua after the Act of Union.[78] During her visit to these two islands in 1774, Janet Schaw described how important Scottish identity could be in everyday polite social life:

> 'Just as we were preparing for Tea, my brother, Dr Dunbar, Mr Halliday, the Collector, and Mr Baird, the comptroller, and a very pretty young man called Martin came to us. Here was a whole company of Scotch people, our language, our manners, our circle of friends and connections, all the same.' [79]

Scottish doctor Walter Tullideph, who came to Antigua in 1726, described the manner in which such Scottish men joined planter society. In 1736 described how he had:

> 'married an agreeable young widow by whom I gott Possession of a very fine Estate to which I am making additions and improvements and am likely to have an heir of my own.' [80]

After arriving, Tullideph soon began to sell English commodities to planters as his brother's factor, worked as a doctor, and combined these trades by retailing medicines and drugs. He provided credit to planters by using his connections to borrow from London and lending at a higher rate of interest in Antigua. In a series of transactions over eighteen years, Tullideph proceeded to enlarge the estate from 127 acres and 63 slaves to 536 acres and 271 slaves. Similarly, in St Kitts the medically trained poet James Grainger (c.1721-1766) married a wealthy heiress, Daniel Matthew Burt, soon after arriving on the island in 1759. His wife's name was an amalgam of three of the planter families to whom she was related, reflecting her remarkable connections to an established plantocratic dynasty.[81] Her father was William Pym Burt, related to the Pyms who leased Wingfield Estate until 1758 (see above), and her paternal grandfather was William Burt of Nevis (d. 1707).

These incoming merchant-planters, from East Anglia and Scotland, brought distinctive attitudes to the 'improvement' of estate landscapes that engaged with the social and material relations of the gentry societies of St Kitts and Antigua. In the concluding section I shall examine how such 'improvements' were related to new conceptions of materiality - the entanglements of people, objects and landscapes – and to the broader geographies of the British colonial imaginary.

III

As well as simply understanding estate landscapes as illustrative of, or engaged in, the ideology of capitalism or slavery, the material focus of landscape archaeology can also explore the changing approaches to people and things that formed part of Georgian improvements in colonial estate landscapes. And rather than just underlining how designed landscapes were understood in different ways by different people, rather than 'duping' subaltern populations into compliance or false consciousness,[82] archaeology can be used to consider how the improvement of estate landscapes was part of a new set of attitudes and practices that related to the boundaries between people and things, by presenting material, both natural and artificial, as animate and active. It is difficult to think beyond understandings of improvement as concerned with meaning or ideology, especially because the influential account of the historical geography of improvement (e.g. Seymour and Daniels above) formed part of a more general approach to designed landscapes. This was set out by Stephen Daniels and Denis Cosgrove most clearly in the opening lines of their seminal statement on 'the iconography of landscape':

> 'A landscape is a cultural image, a pictorial way of representing., structuring or symbolising surroundings. This is not to say that landscapes are immaterial. They may be represented in a variety of materials and on many surfaces – in paint on canvas, in writing on paper, in earth, stone, water and vegetation on the ground. A landscape park is more palpable but no more real, not less imaginary, than a landscape painting or poem. Indeed the meanings of verbal, visual and built landscapes have a complex interwoven history. To understand a built landscape, say an eighteenth-century English park, it is usually necessary to understand written and verbal representations of it, not as 'illustrations', images standing outside it, but as constituent images of its meaning or meanings. And of course every study of a landscape further transforms it meaning, depositing yet another layer of cultural representation. In human geography, the interpretation of landscape and culture has a tendency to reify landscape as an object of empiricist investigation, but often its practitioners do gesture towards landscape as a cultural symbol or image, notably when likening landscape to a text and its interpretation to 'reading'.'[83]

Such a reduction of the material dimensions of landscape to 'the status of landscape as image and symbol' similarly characterises Daniels and Seymour's historical geography of 'improvement' (1990). As Tim Ingold has argued, approaches such as those of Daniels and Cosgrove tend falsely to divide mind from matter, meaning from substance.[84] In the context of ideas of improvement, landscape archaeology can reveal not only changing elite ideas but also how they were worked out in practice:

> 'the sites from which philosophes gathered their evidence, the settings in which their ideas took shape, the networks through which they were disseminated, the contexts in which they were interpreted'[85]

In the study of estate landscapes, at the heart of this issue is our conception of the relationship between design and material practice: whether the design of a landscape is envisaged as separate (following Daniels and Cosgrove) – an index of ideas, attitudes or ideologies – or as bound up with the more complex processes of the creation and enactment of estate landscapes on the ground. Where archaeologist James Delle's discussion of 'the imagined spaces of plantation theorists' discussion is limited to 'cognized plantation layout',[86] an alternative view would understand designed landscapes such as plantations as enmeshed with material enactment, or performance. As historian Robin Blackburn has argued:

> 'the planters of the English Caribbean and North America…saw themselves as sovereigns of all they surveyed….The Great Houses of the planters received African adornments, while echoing the Palladian mansions of the English or French aristocracy, the latter in turn being influenced by Versailles. Since plantation cultivation destroyed the forests, the planters has little difficulty finding sites with commanding views. They did not build fortresses or castles but theatres of gracious living.' [87]

During the 18th century, the design of Caribbean estates was increasingly informed by literature on 'plantership', which guided the practice of plantation management and improvement. Samuel Martin's Essay on Plantership (1750), described by James Grainger as 'an excellent performance',[88] argued that the properly managed plantation:

> 'ought to be considered as a well-constructed machine, compounded of various wheels, turning different ways, and yet all contributing to the great end proposed.' [89]

Martin's publication, in its fifth edition by 1773, outlined the 'art of managing' a plantation, and encouraged planters to gain 'proper qualifications'. He set up a 'school of 'plantership' at his 'Greencastle' Estate in Antigua from the late 1740s (Figure 4).[90] As seen at Wingfield above, the creation of carefully designed landscapes was a significant part of sugar planters' improving activities. Thus, William Beckford recommended the laying out of slave quarters:

> 'in strait lines, constructed with some degree of uniformity and strength, but totally divested of trees and shrubs.' [91]

Special slave quarters were set apart from the 'polite' landscape: in contrast with the early arrangements of smaller numbers of slaves and indentured servants living alongside planters. In 1745, William Smith wrote of Nevis that slaves:

> 'live in Huts, on the Western Side of our Dwelling Houses…because we breath the pure Eastern air, without being offended with the least nauseous smell; Our kitchens and Boyling-houses are on the same side, and for the same reason.' [92]

The focus in such arrangements in the emerging plantation management literature was upon the day-to-day business of running a plantation – the performance of management in the landscape. Some planters' manuals, such as William Belgrove's *Treatise upon Husbandry or Planting*, even provided a month-by-month schedule of activities.[93] More intervention in and regulation of slave lifestyles took place, and included the imposition of carefully regulated time-management, and dramatically increased surveillance.[94]

In the performance of estate management, the 'various wheels, turning in different directions' described by Martin constituted the larger 'machine'. The heterogeneous elements of the estate were juxtaposed, including not only the agricultural and technological elements described above, but also natural, animal and human slave components. Through

Figure 4. 'The Green Castle Plantation from the south'. A watercolour by Bristolian painter Nicholas Pocock from 1805, showing the estate house and outbuildings on the hill, slave housing on the slopes of the hill, and a sugar works with two windmills on lower ground, to the right. (From Andrews & Andrews 1921, between pages 104-5).

techniques of management, planters aimed to ensure and improve the productivity of all elements of this assemblage. Thus, the 'situation' of an estate, in relation to geology, wind and soil for instance, was emphasised.[95] Planters and overseers concerned themselves with the nutrition of slaves by encouraging 'provision grounds'.[96] In 1764, James Grainger drew on his medical training in publishing an Essay on the more common West-India Diseases: the 'first work from the anglophone Caribbean specifically devoted to the diseases and treatment of slaves'.[97] Scottish-trained plantation doctors and a thriving import trade in medicines contributed to the health of slaves.[98] Such 'improvement' of the health of slaves fitted well into the impulses towards the optimisation of production through science.

Janet Schaw, visiting Samuel Martin's Greencastle Estate in 1774, described how the planter effectively reared both slaves and animals through his careful management:

'Cultivated to the height by a large troop of healthy Negroes, who cheerfully perform the labour imposed on them by a kind and beneficent Master, not a harsh and unreasonable Tyrant. Well fed, well supported, they appear the subjects of a good prince, not the slaves of a planter. The effect of this kindness is a daily increase of riches by the slaves born to him on his own plantation. He told me that he had not bought in a slave for upwards of twenty years, and that he had the morning of our arrival got the return of the state of his plantations, on which there were then no less than fifty two wenches who were pregnant. These slaves, born on the spot and used to the Climate, are by far the most valuable, and seldom take these disorders, by which such numbers are lost that many hundreds are forced yearly to be brought into the Island…By turning many of the plantations into grass he…is able to rear cattle which he has done with great success. I never saw finer cows, nor more thriving calves, than I saw feeding in his lawns, and his waggons are already being drawn by oxen of his own rearing.' [99]

Through the enactments of estate management, the multiplicities of the estate 'machine' were made productive. Most important, however, was the provision of:

'a well-contrived plan of the buildings, their relative, convenient and appropriate situations, one to another, should be digested, and laid out on a piece of paper, of a size sufficient to have the whole delineated upon it' [100]

As geographer Barry Higman has argued, the sheer quantities of estate mapping in the British Caribbean requires explanation.[101] Over 20,000 maps and plans survive in Jamaica alone. The commissioning of estate maps and plans was part of the improvement, in the sense of being 'demonstrated' or 'shown to be true', of estate landscapes. Higman is accurate in his observation that the phenomenon of estate mapping , it is due to the existence of:

'a large group of wealthy individuals resident in Great Britain anxious to visualise their plantations and capable of paying the charges of professional surveyors and planmakers (and, sometimes, pictorial artists).' [102]

While plantation surveys were invaluable for the 'absentee' planter who desired documentary evidence of his West Indian possessions, in some cases 'the plantation map sometimes preceded the reality, enabling planter and surveyor to impose their ideal models of order on the landscape'.[103] The geographical limits of these ideal models were surprisingly loose, however. The phenomenon of 'absentee landlords', for instance, has conventionally been seen by economic historians as one that sowed the seeds of West Indian decline.[104] However, from a broader Atlantic context, these absences represented engagements in new, wide mercantile worlds described by historians such as David Hancock, who has explored the importance of cosmopolitanism in the emergence of a British Atlantic world. Merchants such as William Freeman of St Kitts and London had 'a world of business to do': 'the most critical asset a merchant could deploy in the first century of empire was acquaintance in the colonies'.[105]

The material construction and management of estate landscapes in both the Caribbean and Britain was increasingly important in planters' performance of such cosmopolitanism. Charles Tudway, for instance, after inheriting the Parham Hill Estate in Antigua in 1748 commissioned Thomas Paty in 1758 to build The Cedars in Wells, North Somerset, and combined absentee plantation ownership with a position as MP for Bristol from 1754.[106] The new survey technologies upon which the estate plans relied, in which direct measurement by paces between fixed points in the landscape was replaced by triangulation and chain and angle measurement, were closely associated with the military and maritime arenas to which the eastern Caribbean were especially exposed. The range of new surveying devices –box compasses, quadrants, pairs of compasses, plane tables astrolabes, geometrical squares and early angle measuring devices on tripods (theodolites or 'circumferentors') were inspired by sextants and navigation charts.[107] These bundles of paper and cloth, fair copies and embellished plans, were a central part of the new geographical imaginary of the improving planters. Just as in Britain, the improvement of estate landscapes was closely associated with improved transportation, especially by road,[108] so in the Caribbean mobility lay at the heart of the efforts of Scottish improvers in the Leeward Islands.

In the material practices of estate management, complex choreographies of maps and plans, soils, slaves, animals, kin relations, crushing machines, letters, rivers, bricks, verandas, teacups, the wind and rain, were enacted by the planter elite. Productivity appeared to emerge from climate, geology artefacts, people and animals. New attitudes to materiality lay at the heart of the improving impulse – bringing human and nonhuman actors together in the agrarian 'theatres' of plantation estates. Through such performances, planters sought to smooth out complexities and inequalities - the violence, horror and uneven materialities of racial slavery. People came to appear as objects or animals: bought, sold, reared, put to work as slaves. Incoherences were evened out, as the boundaries between people and things were blurred. These efforts can be illustrated by considering a poem. The new estate management literature was influenced by the increased interest in Virgil's Georgics during the mid 18th century.[109] In 1764, soon after his return St Kitts (where he would die two years later), the poet James Grainger, mentioned above, published his 'didactic poem' The Sugar Cane! It described, in highly laboured georgic diction, sugar cultivation in St Kitts, presenting 'some part of the science of husbandry put into a pleasing dress'.[110] Grainger described the Wingfield River, and Romney:

> 'The brawling Naiads for the planters toil.
> Howe'er unworthy; and, through solemn scenes,
> Romantic, cool, with rocks and woods between,
> Enchant the senses! but, among thy swains,
> Sweet Liamuiga! Who such bliss can boast?
> Yes, Romney, thou may'st boast' of British heart,
> Of courtly manners, join'd to antient worth.' [111]

In Grainger's vision, the Wingfield River 'enchanted the senses'. St Kitts was known by its native Carib name - Liamuiga, or 'Fertile Island'. Slaves were 'swains', and Romney's pedigree, 'join'd to antient worth'. Sitting in the shade of a tree by the river, Grainger described a picturesque landscape:

> Then should I scarce regret the banks of Thames
> All as we sat beneath that sand-box shade;
> Whence the delighted eye expatiates wide
> O'er the fair landscape; where in loveliest forms,
> Green cultivation hath array'd the land.
> See! there, what mills, like giants raise their arms,
> To quell the speeding gale! what smoke ascends

> From every boiling house! What structures rise,
> Neat tho' not lofty, pervious to the breeze;
> With galleries, porches or piazzas grac'd!
> Nor not delightful are those reed-built huts,
> On yonder hill, that front the rising sun;
> With plantanes, with banana's bosom'd deep,
> That flutter in the wind: where frolick goats,
> Butt the young Negroes, while their swarthy sires,
> With ardent gladness wield the bill; and hark,
> The crop is finish'd, how they rend the sky! [112]

It is not simply that these rural idylls sought to obscure slavery and inequality: the theatrical poetic diction was part of a broader effort – seen in the construction of new estate landscapes - to animate the assemblages of the plantation in new ways, and to reconfigure ideas of materiality. As Elizabeth Bohls has argued, this 'planter picturesque' was characterised by a certain 'staginess'.[113] These performative, georgic impulses in colonial improvement sought not only to 'obfuscate' tensions or inequalities, but to bring about the new permeabilities between people and things seen both in the ideology of racial slavery and in the new attitudes to landscape improvement. That is, the enactment in landscapes of ideas of improvement facilitated the rendering silent or absent of incoherences, just as at Mansfield Park. Improvement in this colonial context, then, involved the enactment of a new set of attitudes to materialities, which were concerned with breaking down firm divisions between places, people and material things. As Chandra Mukerji suggested in her examination of the relationships between designed gardens, national territoriality and material performance, so in the study of colonial improvement rather than 'see[ing] the creation of material culture as the manifestation of an idea – a realisation of a prior mental state' we must focus upon how 'human action and thought emerge from action on the material world'.[114]

It remains to consider how exploring the enactment of ideas of improvement in a colonial context can inform the study of more conventionally 'British' estate landscapes. Often, in the early nineteenth century, Caribbean estate landscapes reminded visitors of England. One visitor to the Leewards in the 1820s, for example, described how:

> 'the tall and moving windmills, the houses of the proprietors, the works and palm-thatched cottages of the negros embosomed in plantains, present the appearance, as indeed they are the substance, of so many country villages in England.' [115]

But as Elizabeth Bohls has suggested, this was not simply a case of metropolitan ideas being played out in new, colonial landscapes, the study of which might provide new perspectives on our understanding of these ideas 'at home', but a situation in which it is probable that colonial landscapes 'might actually have contributed' to 'supposedly metropolitan' developments.[116] After all, the vast open fields of sugar cane in St Kitts preceded the Capability Brown's turfed landscapes, in which from the 1760s mansions stood in a 'boundless sea of turf',[117] by more than a generation. Indeed, when we consider the financial connections between West Indian planters and British estate holders in the 18th and early nineteenth centuries, so clearly demonstrated by the Williams Thesis, the observation that the working out of ideas of improvement in the landscapes of the Caribbean might have played a central role in influencing the idea of improvement in Britain is still more compelling.

But this geographical connectedness, and perhaps historical causation, between metropole and colony cannot be studied in isolation from the enactment of new attitudes to places, people and things that, as argued above, characterized improvement in the British Caribbean. Historical archaeologists are well placed to take the lead of historical geographers such as Seymour, conducting further studies of the influence of the British colonies upon British landscape history. The challenge, however, is for archaeologists and landscape historians to consider how the creation of the wider 'landscapes' of the British Atlantic world – formed by treating humans as objects, and by producing 'drug foods' such as sugar, tobacco and coffee that were consumed into Western bodies - formed part of the new attitudes to people and things that colonial improvements involved.[118] Here, it is clear that our previous neglect of the material geographies of landscape change – the enactment of 'material improvements' in colonial as well as British situations - has served to masked our acknowledgement of a crucial dimension of British landscape history, just as the landscapes of Mansfield Park masked the horrors of plantation slavery.

ACKNOWLEDGEMENTS

An earlier version of parts of this paper was published as Chapter 4 of The Garden of the World: An Historical Archaeology of Sugar Landscapes in the Eastern Caribbean. Oxford: Archaeopress (Studies in Contemporary and Historical Archaeology 3).

NOTES

1. Lawrence 2003a; Gosden 2004; Lawrence & Shepherd 2006; Hauser & Hicks 2007.
2. Pulsipher 1977, 1994; Handler & Lange 1978; Armstrong 1990; Haviser 1999; Farnsworth 2001; Hauser forthcoming.
3. Trouillot 1992, 19-20, 35.
4. Singleton 1985, 1999.
5. Wilkie 2001.
6. Yentsch 1994.
7. Armstrong 1990; Clement 1997.
8. Epperson 1999; Leone 1984; cf Hicks 2004a.
9. Delle 1994.
10. eg Yamin & Metheny 1996.
11. Delle 1998, 9; cf Paynter 1982.
12. Epperson 1999.
13. Orser 1988, 321, 328, 329.
14. Johnson 1996, 61-69.
15. Williamson 1995.
16. Johnson 1996, 71.
17. Beaudry 1996, 496.
18. cf. Johnson 1996, 210.
19. see discussions in Hicks 2003 and Hicks & McAtackney 2007.
20. Dalglish 2003, 205.
21. Symonds 1999, 118.
22. eg Tarlow 2007.
23. see discussion in Hicks 2004b; cf Hicks 2005.
24. Daniels et al 1999, 346.
25. Briggs 1963.
26. Daniels & Seymour 1990.
27. Daniels & Seymour 1990, 488.
28. Duckworth 1971; Williams 1976, 132-3.
29. Williams 1976, 133.
30. R. Williams 1985 [1973], 115-6.
31. Tarlow 2007.
32. Hancock 1995, 281-5.

33. Drayton 2000: 55-9.
34. Drayton 2000.
35. Womack 1989.
36. Griggs 2004.
37. Daniels & Seymour 1990.
38. Seymour et al 1998: 341; cf. Seymour 2000.
39. Austen 1814.
40. Said 1993, 95-116.
41. Said 1993, 100.
42. Said 1993, 112, 114; cf Johnson 1996, 210.
43. Armitage 2002, 23-28.
44. Armitage 2002, 23, 29.
45. E. Williams 1944.
46. R. Williams 1985 [1973].
47. Said 1993, 98.
48. Greene 1974, 1513.
49. Labat 1724, 351-63.
50. See discussion in Hicks 2007, 10-28.
51. Higham 1921, 30; Mims 1912, 30-36.
52. Hicks 2007, 42.
53. Calendar of State Papers (Colonial Series, America and the West Indies) 1716-17, 118. Quoted by Niddrie 1966, 8-9).
54. Sheridan 1961, 343.
55. Pares 1960, 17-19; Pares 1950, 104.
56. Galenson 1981, 151.
57. Olwig 1993, 35.
58. Hicks 2007.
59. Jeaffreson to Colonel George Gamiell, London. 12 May 1677. Jeaffreson 1878, Vol. 1, 210-212
60. Gilmore 2000, 275.
61. Hicks 2007, Appendix 4
62. McMahon 1828.
63. The Godwin January 19 1819.
64. Dunn 1972, 189.
65. Ward 1988, 61-118; Watts 1987, 405-423.
66. Ragatz 1931, 23.
67. Ward 1988, 75.
68. Sheridan 1961, 353.
69. Ragatz 1931, 23.
70. Deerr 1943; 1950, figures 1-2
71. Deerr 1950, 539-41
72. Deerr 1950, 537
73. Sloane 1707; Labat 1724
74. Ward 1988, 75
75. Watts 1987, 424
76. Deerr and Brooks 1946, 4
77. Ward 1998, 102
78. Sheridan 1974, 368-370
79. Andrews and Andrews 1939, 81.
80. Sheridan 1961; 1974, 197-200.
81. cf Gilmore 2000, 13; Webb 1979, 486-7, 490.
82. See discussion in Hicks 2005.
83. Daniels and Cosgrove 1988, 1.
84. Ingold 1993: 152-4
85. Driver 2002, 229.
86. Delle 1998, 111.
87. Blackburn 1997, 21.
88. Gilmore 2000, 89.
89. Martin 1750, 37.
90. Sheridan 1957; 1960
91. Beckford 1790, Volume 2, 20; quoted by Higman 1988, 248.
92. Smith 1745, 226.
93. Belgrove 1755.
94. e.g. Ramsay 1784, 74-7; see Goveia 1965
95. Roughley 1823, 188.
96. Ward 1988, 109-11.
97. Gilmore 2000, 15.
98. Sheridan 1974, 372; 1985.
99. Andrews and Andrews 1939, 104-6.
100. Roughley 1823,188.
101. Higman 1988, 1-4.
102. Higman 1988: 1.
103. Higman 1988, 80.
104. Ragatz 1928, 1931.
105. Hancock 2000, 29.
106. Higham 1921, 217; Tudway Quilter 1985.
107. Taylor 1934, 158-176.
108. Daniels & Seymour 1990, 493-5.
109. Watts 1987, 384 ff.
110. Sandiford 2000, 69; Gilmore 2000, 27-8, 63.
111. Grainger 2000 [1764], 135 (Book III, 284-290).
112. Grainger 2000 [1764], 141 (Book III, 521-537).
113. Bohls 2002, 63; cf Bohls 1999.
114. Mukerji 1997, 326-7.
115. Coleridge 1826, 216.
116. Bohls 2002, 63.
117. Williamson 1995, 2.
118. Hicks forthcoming.

BIBLIOGRAPHY

Andrews, E. W. & Andrews, C. M. 1939, *Journal of a Lady of Quality: being the narrative of a journey from Scotland to the West Indies, North Carolina and Portugal in the years 1774 to 1776* [diary of Janet Schaw], New Haven: Yale University Press.

Armitage, D. 2002, 'Three Concepts of Atlantic History', in Armitage & Braddick 2002, 11-27.

Armitage, D. & Braddick, M. J. 2002, (eds) *The British Atlantic World, 1500-1800*, New York: Macmillan.
Armstrong, D. V. 1990, *The Old Village and the Great House: An archaeological and historical examination of the Drax Hall Plantation, St Ann's Bay, Jamaica*, Urbana: University of Illinois Press.
Austen, J. 1814, *Mansfield Park*, London: Nelson.
Beaudry, M. C. 1996, 'Reinventing Historical Archaeology', in De Cunzo & Herman 1996, 473-497.
Beckford, W. 1790, *A descriptive account of the Island of Jamaica: with remarks upon the cultivation of the sugar cane*, 2 vols, London: T. and J. Egerton.
Belgrove, W. 1755, *A Treatise upon Husbandry or Planting*, Boston: D. Fowle.
Blackburn, R. 1997, *The Making of New World Slavery: From the Baroque to the Modern, 1492-1800*, London: Verso.
Bohls, E. A. 1999, 'The Gentleman Planter and the Metropole: Long's History of Jamaica (1774)', in MacLean 1999, 180-96.
Bohls, E. A. 2002, 'The Planter Picturesque: Matthew Lewis. Journal of a West India Proprietor', *European Romantic Review* 13, 63-76.
Briggs, A. 1963, *The Age of Improvement, 1787-1867*, London: Longman.
Clement, C. O. 1997, 'Settlement patterning on the British Caribbean island of Tobago', *Historical Archaeology* 31(2), 93-106.
Coleridge, H. N. 1826, *Six Months in the West Indies in 1825*, London: John Murray.
Cosgrove, D. & Daniels, S. (eds) 1988, *The Iconography of Landscape*, Cambridge: Cambridge University Press.
Dalglish, C. 2003, *Rural society in the age of reason: an archaeology of the emergence of modern life in the southern Scottish Highlands*, New York: Kluwer/Plenum Academic Press.
Daniels, S. & Cosgrove, D. 1988, 'Introduction: iconography and landscape', in Cosgrove & Daniels 1988, 1-10.
Daniels, S. & Seymour, S. 1990, 'Landscape Design and the Idea of Improvement 1730-1914', in Dodgshon & Butlin 1990, 487-520.
Daniels, S., Seymour, S. & Watkins, C. 1999, 'Enlightenment, Improvement and the Geographies of Horticulture in Later Georgian England', in Livingstone & Withers 1999, 345-371.
De Cunzo, L. & Herman, B. L. (eds) 1996, *Historical Archaeology and the Study of American Culture*, Winterthur, DE: Henry Francis Du Pont Winterthur Museum.
Deerr, N. 1943, 'The evolution of the sugar cane mill', *Transactions of the Newcomen Society* 21, 1-10.
Deerr, N. 1950, *The History of Sugar*, Volume 2, London: Chapman and Hall.
Deerr, N. & Brooks, A. 1946, 'Development of the Practice of Evaporation with special reference to the sugar industry', *Transactions of the Newcomen Society* 22, 1-19.
Delle, J. A. 1994, 'A Spatial Analysis of Sugar Plantations on St Eustatius, Netherlands Antilles', in Linebaugh & Robinson 1994, 33-62.
Delle, J. A. 1998, *An Archaeology of Social Space: Analyzing Coffee Plantations in Jamaica's Blue Mountains*, New York: Plenum Press.
Dodgshon, R. A. & Butlin, R. A. (eds) 1990, *An Historical Geography of England and Wales*, London: Academic Press.
Drayton, R. 2000, *Nature's government: Science, imperial Britain and the 'improvement' of the world*, New Haven and London: Yale University Press.
Driver, F. 2002, 'Geography, Enlightenment and Improvement,' *The Historical Journal* 45(1), 229-33.
Duckworth, A. 1971, *The Improvement of the Estate: A Study of Jane Austen's Novels*, Baltimore: Johns Hopkins University Press.
Dunn, R. S. 1972, *Sugar and Slaves: The Rise of the Planter Class in the English West Indies, 1624-1713*, Chapel Hill: University of North Carolina Press.
Epperson, T. W. 1999, 'Constructing Difference: The Social and Spatial Order of the Chesapeake Plantation', in Singleton 1999, 159-72.
Farnsworth, P. (ed.) 2001, *Island Lives: Historical Archaeologies of the Caribbean*, Tuscaloosa: University of Alabama Press.

Galenson, D. 1981, *White Servitude in Colonial America*, Cambridge: Cambridge University Press.
Gilmore, J. (ed.) 2000, *The Poetics of Empire. A Study of James Grainger's The Sugar Cane* (1764), London and New Brunswick: Athlone Press.
Gosden, C. 2004. *Archaeology and Colonialism*, Cambridge: Cambridge University Press.
Goveia, E. V. 1965, *Slave Society in the British Leeward Islands at the End of the Eighteenth Century*, New Haven: Yale University Press.
Graham, B. & Nash, C. (eds) 2000, *Modern historical geographies*, Harlow: Longman.
Grainger, J. 2000 [1764] *The Sugar Cane: A Poem in Four Books*, in Gilmore 2000, 86-198.
Greene, J. P. 1974, 'Review: Society and Economy in the British Caribbean during the Seventeenth and Eighteenth Centuries', *American Historical Review* 79(5): 1499-1517.
Griggs, P. 2004, 'Improving Agricultural Practices: Science and the Australian Sugarcane Grower, 1864-1915', *Agricultural History* 78(1): 1-33.
Hancock, D. 1995, *Citizens of the World: London Merchants and the Integration of the British Atlantic Community, 1735-1785*, Cambridge: Cambridge University Press.
Hancock, D. 2000, '"A World of Business to Do": William Freeman and the Foundations of England's Commercial Empire, 1645-1707', *William and Mary Quarterly* 57(1): 3-34.
Handler, J. S. & Lange, F. W. 1978, *Plantation Slavery in Barbados: An Archaeological and Historical Investigation*, Cambridge, MA: Harvard University Press.
Hauser, M. W. (ed.) forthcoming, *Scales of Analysis in Caribbean Archaeology*, Special Issue of International Journal of Historical Archaeology.
Hauser, M. W. & Hicks, D. 2007, 'Colonialism and Landscape: Power, Materiality and Scales of Analysis in Caribbean Historical Archaeology', in Hicks 2007, 251-74.
Haviser, J. B. (ed.) 1999, *African Sites Archaeology in the Caribbean*, Kingston: Ian Randle Publishers.
Hicks, D. 2003, 'Archaeology Unfolding': Diversity and the Loss of Isolation', *Oxford Journal of Archaeology* 22(3), 315-329.
Hicks, D. 2004a, 'Historical Archaeology and the British', *Cambridge Archaeological Journal* 14(1): 101-6.
Hicks, D. 2004b, 'From the 'Questions that Count' to the Stories that Matter' in Historical Archaeology', *Antiquity* 78: 934-939.
Hicks, D. 2005, 'Places for Thinking' from Annapolis to Bristol: situations and symmetries in 'world historical archaeology', *World Archaeology* 37(3): 373-391.
Hicks, D. 2007, *The Garden of the World: an historical archaeology of sugar landscapes in the eastern Caribbean*, Oxford: Archaeopress (British Archaeological Reports International Series 1632; Studies in Contemporary and Historical Archaeology 3).
Hicks, D. forthcoming, *The Material Geographies of Sugar*, in Symonds forthcoming.
Hicks, D. & Beaudry, M. C. (eds) 2006, *The Cambridge Companion to Historical Archaeology*, Cambridge: Cambridge University Press.
Hicks, D. & McAtackney, L. 2007, 'Landscapes as Standpoints', in Hicks 2007, 13-29.
Hicks, D., McAtackney, L. & Fairclough, G. (eds) 2007, *Envisioning Landscape: Standpoints and Situations in Archaeology and Heritage*, Walnut Creek: Left Coast Press (One World Archaeology 52).
Higham, C. S. S. 1921, *The development of the Leeward Islands under the Restoration: a study of the foundation of the old colonial system*, Cambridge: Cambridge University Press.
Higman, B. W. 1998, *Montpelier, Jamaica: a plantation community of slavery and freedom*, Kingston: The Press Univ. of the West Indies.
Ingold, T. 1993, 'The Temporality of Landscape', *World Archaeology* 25: 152-74.
Jeaffreson, J. C. (ed), 1878, *A Young Squire of the 17th century. From the papers (AD 1676-1686) of Christopher Jeaffreson*, 2 vols London.
Johnson, M. H. 1996, *An Archaeology of Capitalism*, Oxford: Blackwell.
Labat, J. B. 1724, *Nouveau voyage aux isles de l'Amerique*, (Volume 2), Paris.
Lawrence, S. 2003a, 'Introduction', in Laurence 2003b, 1-13.
Lawrence, S. (ed.) 2003b, *Archaeologies of the British: Explorations of identity in Great Britain and its colonies, 1600-1945*, London: Routledge (One World Archaeology 46).

Lawrence, S. & Shepherd, N. 2006, 'Historical Archaeology and Colonialism' in Hicks & Beaudry 2006, 69-86.
Leone, M. P. 1984, 'Interpreting Ideology in Historical Archaeology: Using the Rules of Perspective in the William Paca Garden in Annapolis, Maryland', in Miller & Tilley 1984, 25-35.
Leone, M. P. & Potter, P. B. (eds) 1988, *The recovery of meaning: historical archaeology in the eastern United States*, Washington, DC: Smithsonian Institution Press.
Linebaugh, D. W. & Robinson, G. G. (eds) 1994, *Spatial Patterning in Historical Archaeology: Selected Studies of Settlement*, Williamsburg, VA: King and Queen Press.
Livingstone, D. N. & Withers, C. W. J. (eds) 1999, *Geography and Enlightenment*, Chicago: University of Chicago Press.
MacLean, G., Landry, D. & Ward, J. P. (eds) 1999, *The Country and the City Revisited: England and the Politics of Culture, 1550-1850*, Cambridge: Cambridge University Press.
Marshall, P. (ed.) 1998, *The Oxford History of the British Empire. Volume 2: The Eighteenth Century*, Oxford: Oxford University Press.
Martin, S. 1750, *An essay on plantership*, 2nd edn, Antigua: T Smith.
McMahon, W. 1828, *A new topographical map of the island of St. Christopher in the West Indies*, London: Edward Stanford.
Miller, D. & Tilley, C. (eds) 1984, *Ideology, Power and Prehistory*, Cambridge: Cambridge University Press.
Miller, N. & Gleason, K. (eds) 1994, *The Archaeology of Garden and Field*, Philadelphia: University of Pennsylvania Press.
Mims, S. L. 1912, *Colbert's West India Policy*, New Haven: Yale University Press.
Mukerji, C. 1997, *Territorial Ambitions and the Gardens of Versailles*, Cambridge: Cambridge University Press.
Niddrie, D. L. 1966, 'An Attempt at planned settlement in St Kitts in the early eighteenth century', *Caribbean Studies* 5(4) 3-11.
Olwig, K. F. 1993, *Global Culture: island identity - continuity and change in the Afro-Caribbean community of Nevis*, Amsterdam: Harwood.
Pares, R. 1950, *A West India Fortune*, London: Longmans, Green and Co.
Pares, R. 1960, *Merchants and Planters*, Cambridge: Cambridge University Press.
Orser, C. E. 1988, 'Toward a theory of power for historical archaeology: plantations and space', in Leone & Potter 1988, 313-343.
Paynter, R. 1982, *Models of Spatial Inequality: Settlement Patterns in Historical Archaeology*, New York: Academic Press.
Pulsipher, L. M. 1994, 'The Landscapes and Ideational Roles of Caribbean Slave Gardens', in Miller & Gleason 1994, 202-221.
Ragatz, L. J. 1928, *The Fall of the Planter Class in the British Caribbean, 1763-1833*, New York: Century.
Ragatz, L. J. 1931, 'Absentee Landlordism in the British Caribbean, 1750-1833', *Agricultural History* 5(1): 7-26.
Ramsay, J. 1784, *An Essay on the Treatment and Conversion of African Slaves in the British Sugar Colonies*, London.
Roughley, T. 1823, *The Jamaica Planter's Guide*, London: Longman, Hurst, Rees, Orme and Brown.
Said, E. 1993, *Culture and Imperialism*, London: Vintage Books.
Sandiford, K. A. 2000, *The Cultural Politics of Sugar. Caribbean Slavery and Narratives of Colonialism*, Cambridge: Cambridge University Press.
Seymour, S. 2000, 'Historical geographies of landscape', in Graham & Nash 2000, 193-217.
Seymour, S., Daniels, S. & Watkins, C. 1998, 'Estate and Empire: Sir George Cornewall's management of Moccas, Herefordshire and La Taste, Grenada, 1771-1819', *Journal of Historical Geography* 24(3), 313-51.
Sheridan, R. B. 1957, 'Letters from a Sugar Plantation in Antigua, 1739-1758', *Agricultural History* 31: 3-23.
Sheridan, R . B. 1960, 'Samuel Martin, Innovating Sugar Planter of Antigua 1750-1776', *Agricultural History* 34, 126-139.
Sheridan, R. B. 1961, 'The Rise of a Colonial Gentry: A Case Study from Antigua, 1730-1775', *Economic*

History Review 13, 342-357.
Sheridan, R. B. 1974, *Sugar and Slavery: An Economic History of the British West Indies 1623-1776*, Eagle Hall, Barbados: Caribbean Universities Press.
Sheridan, R. B. 1985, *Doctors and Slaves: A medical and demographic history of slavery in the British West Indies, 1680-1834*, Cambridge: Cambridge University Press.
Singleton, T. A. (ed.) 1985, *The Archaeology of Slavery and Plantation Life*, New York: Academic Press.
Singleton, T. A. (ed.) 1999, *"I Too am America": Archaeological Studies of African-American Life*, Charlottesville, VA: University Press of Virginia.
Sloane, H. 1707, *A Voyage to the Islands of Madeira, Barbados, Nieves, St Christopher and Jamaica, with the natural history of the herbs and trees, four-footed beasts, fishes, birds, insects, reptiles, etc*, London.
Smith, W. 1745, *A natural history of Nevis, and the rest of the English Leeward Charibbee Islands in America*, Cambridge.
Symonds, J. 1999, '"Toiling in the Vale of Tears": Everyday life and resistance in South Uist, Outer Hebrides, 1760-1860', *International Journal of Historical Archaeology* 3(2), 101-122.
Symonds, J. (ed.) forthcoming, *Table Settings: The Material Culture and Social Context of Dining in the Old and New Worlds, AD 1700-1900*, Oxford, Oxbow Books.
Tarlow, S. 2007, *The Archaeology of Improvement in Britain, 1750-1850*, Cambridge: Cambridge University Press.
Taylor, E. G. R. 1934, *Late Tudor and Early Stuart Geography*, 1583-1650, London: Methuen & Co.
Trouillot, M. R. 1992, 'The Caribbean Region: An open frontier in anthropological theory', *Annual Review of Anthropology* 21: 19-42.
Tudway Quilter, D. 1985, *A History of Wells Cathedral School. Volume 2: The Cedars and the Tudways*, Wells: Wells Cathedral School.
Ward, J. R. 1998, 'The British West Indies in the Age of Abolition, 1748-1815', in Marshall 1998, 415-439.
Watts, D. 1987, *The West Indies: Patterns of Development, Culture and Environmental Change since 1492*, Cambridge: Cambridge University Press.
Webb, S. S. 1979, *The Governors-General. The English Army and the Definition of the Empire, 1569-1681*, Chapel Hill: University of North Carolina Press.
Wilkie, L. A. 2001, 'Methodist Intentions and Sensibilities: The victory of African consumerism over planter paternalism at a Bahamian plantation', in Farnsworth 2001, 272-300.
Williams, E. 1944, *Capitalism and Slavery*, London: Deutsch.
Williams, R. 1985 [1973], *The City and the Country*, London: Chatto and Windus.
Williams, R. 1976, *Keywords: A vocabulary of culture and society*, London: Fontana.
Williamson, T. 1995, *Polite Landscapes: Gardens and Society in Eighteenth-Century England*, Baltimore; Johns Hopkins University Press.
Womack, P. 1989, *Improvement and Romance: Constructing the Myth of the Highlands*, London: Macmillan.
Yamin, R. & Metheny. K.B. (eds) 1996, *Landscape Archaeology: Reading and Interpreting the American Historical Landscape,* Knoxville: University of Tennessee Press.
Yentsch, A. E. 1994, *A Chesapeake family and their slaves: a study in historical archaeology*, Cambridge & New Haven: Cambridge University Press.

UNPULISHED SOURCES
Goodwin, C. M. 1987, 'Sugar, Time and Englishmen : A study of management strategies on Caribbean plantations', Unpublished Ph. D. dissertation, Dept of Anthropology, Boston University.
Pulsipher, L. M. 1977, 'The Cultural Landscape of Montserrat, West Indies, in the seventeenth Century: Early Environmental Consequences of British Colonial Development', Unpublished Ph. D. dissertation, Southern Illinois University, Carbondale.

Index

A

Acland Barton (Devon) 66, 67
Albaston (Cornwall) 67
America 2, 131, 133, 134, 137, 139, 143, 145, 203, 206, 217, 223, 225, 227
Antigua 192, 203, 210, 214, 215, 217, 219, 226
Atkyns, John Tracy 27, 35, 36, 37
Austen, Jane 202, 203, 208, 209, 223, 224
Avill, River 95, 97, 106
Axminster (Devon) 60, 64, 67, 70, 74

B

Ballinafad 80
Ballygobben 182, 183
Ballygubbin 188
Bantry (Co. Cork) 177-185, 188, 190
Barbados 191, 192, 197, 200-203, 205, 210, 225, 227
Barnwell, Paul 5, 13, 14, 125
Barrington, Sir Jonah 84
Barrow-in-Furness (Cumbria) 5
Beacon, Richard 179, 180, 184
Beale, David 157, 171
Beara (Co. Cork) 177, 178, 184, 190
Beaton, Donald 12
Beckford, William 217, 223, 224
Bedford County (Virginia) 129, 131, 133, 137, 146
Bedfordshire 7
Belgrove, William 217, 223, 224
Beresford Hall (Staffs) 118
Berriew (Powys) 39, 40, 42-49, 52-55
Bertram, Sir Thomas 209
Bindon, Francis 81, 87
Bishop's Clyst (Devon) 64
Blackrock (Bantry House, Co. Sligo) 179, 180, 182, 184, 187-189
Blagrave family 120
Blayney family 40, 50, 54, 55
Blenheim Palace 19
Bodmin Moor (Cornwall) 67, 73, 74
Bodrugan Barton (Cornwall) 67, 69
Bohetherick (Corwall) 67
Breckland (Norfolk) 3, 6
Brierley, Walter 164, 169
Bristol 97, 98, 101, 104-108, 110, 112, 191, 192, 219, 225
Bronsquilfa 51
Brown, Maj. Harold 163
Browne, Sir Valentine 178
Buckfastleigh Abbey (Devon) 63, 64, 71, 74
Bulmer (Yorkshire) 21, 28, 29, 31, 35, 37, 149, 150, 152-154, 156, 157, 166-170
Burrington (Devon) 65
Bury Barton (Devon) 67

C

Cadw 39, 53, 54
Caie, John 12
Calvert, Charles 146, 206
Capability Brown 9, 10, 221
Caribbean 191-194, 201-203, 205, 206, 210, 212, 214, 215, 217-222, 224-227
Carr, John 13, 14, 27
Cashiobury (Herts) 12
Castle Howard (Yorkshire) 5, 19-21, 23-28, 30-37, 149-154, 156-158, 166-171
Castle Howard School (Yorkshire) 157, 171

Castle Ward (Co. Down) 89
Charlestown (Nevis) 195, 199
Charlestown Barton (Devon) 67, 74
Chatsworth (Derbyshire) 4, 9, 12, 13, 19
Chesapeake 146, 205, 206, 224, 227
Chesterton (Warwickshire) 113, 120-128
Clan Dermot 178
Clandonnell Roe 178, 179
Clemenson, H. 2, 13, 14, 36
Clifton plantation (Bahamas) 206
Cobbs, Williams 132
Cobham, Lord 24, 168
Coconut Walk (Nevis) 192, 194, 202
Coke, Thomas William 4
Coleraine 182
Colleton Barton (Devon) 67
Colt, Sir Henry 192, 202
Coneysthorpe (Yorkshire) 28, 34, 150, 153
Conygar Hill (Somerset) 97
Coolidge, Ellen Randolph 132, 138, 143, 146
Cooper family 78, 79, 81, 82, 87-91, 93,
Coopershill (Co. Sligo) 78-84, 87-90, 93
Coopers of Markree 78, 90, 93
Corndon Down (Devon) 57
Cornwall 57-62, 64, 66-74
Cotehele (Cornwall) 67, 71
Cotton, Charles 116, 118, 127
Coxford Priory (Norfolk) 119
Crediton (Devon) 64, 71, 74
Cromwell, Oliver 116, 118, 123, 127
Crookhaven 181
Crosskill, Mr., of Beverley 33
Cumbria 19

D

Dart, River 57, 63
Dartmoor (Devon) 57, 58, 71, 72
Davenant, Edward 181
Denham, John 82, 83, 91
Dennis, Sir Thomas 63, 64, 73
Derbyshire 4, 9, 118, 128
Derwent, River 12, 116
Desmond revolt, The (1583) 177, 178, 188
Devon 57-67, 70-74, 101, 106, 107

Diderot Effect 88, 90
Dollas Farm (Berriew, Powys) 49, 51
Dorset 62, 71
Drax Hall plantation (Jamaica) 191
Driffield (Yorkshire) 160
Drumadderilohan 78
Dullingham House (Cambridgeshire) 212
Dunster 5, 95-97, 104-112
Dwyrhiw (Vaynor Estate) 45

E

Earls of Carlisle:
    3rd Earl 19, 21, 24, 27, 32, 151, 152
    4th Earl 154, 156
    5th Earl 33, 156
    6th Earl 33, 156, 157
    7th Earl 34, 151, 156, 157
    8th Earl 156
    9th Earl 156
Earth Barton (Cornwall) 67, 68
East Anglia 6, 15, 74, 215
East Lexham (Norfolk) 7
Edensor (Derbyshire) 12
Egerton, Elizabeth 158, 172,
Eleanor Cross (Sledmore, Yorks) 159, 162, 164, 166, 172, 173
Elliot, Isaac 156, 170
Eppes, Francis 131, 132, 134, 141, 144, 146
Essex 12, 42, 57, 119, 128
Evelyn, John 27
Ewenny (Glamorgan) 105, 108
Exmoor (Devon) 58, 73, 95, 96, 107, 108

F

Feely, Richard 79, 80, 83
Fitzherbert, *The Boke of Surveying and improvements* 58, 62-64, 70, 72
Fownes, Henry 95, 97, 98, 105, 106, 108, 109, 111, 112
Fownes Luttrell family 95, 98, 105, 106, 108, 109, 111, 112
Fox, Harold 60, 64
foxhunting 6
Freeman, William 219, 225

INDEX

Freer, Thomas 32
Fremington (Devon) 106

G

Gale, George 97, 98, 104, 105, 109, 111, 112
Galway's Plantation (Monserrat) 191
Ganthorpe (Yorkshire) 28, 32
Garthmyl (Powys) 40, 45, 50, 52, 54
Gawthorp, T. J., & Son 163
Girouard, M. 10, 14, 15, 162, 167, 168
Glansevern (Powys) 40, 43, 44, 53
Glin Castle (Co. Limerick) 89
Gloucestershire 108, 125, 127
Goldfinch, Henry 179, 181
Grainger, James 215, 217, 218, 220, 223, 225
Greencastle Estate (Antigua) 217, 218
Gregynog (Powys) 40, 46, 50, 54, 55
Grey, Thomas de 6

H

Haccombe (Devon) 62, 70, 74
Hackness (Yorkshire) 116, 117
Hampshire 15, 62, 113-115, 119, 128, 200-204
Hampton Court Palace 125, 128
Hardingstone (Northamptonshire) 162
Harrowbarrow (Cornwall) 67
Hawksmoor, Nicholas 21-23, 28, 36, 152, 168
Hay, James, Earl of Carlisle 192, 197, 201
Haye Barton (Cornwall) 67
Henderskelfe (Yorkshire) 21, 22, 24, 26-28, 31, 37
Henderson, John 30, 32-34, 37
Hertfordshire 12
Hilton, John 192, 197, 199, 200, 202
Hinchingbrooke House (Cambridgeshire) 123
Holkham Hall (Norfolk) 3, 12
Holne Moor (Devon) 57, 72
Honiton Barton (Devon) 67

Hooker, John 62, 63, 71
Houghton Hall (Norfolk) 3
Howard, Charles (3rd Earl) 21, 151
Howard, Geoffrey Algernon William 158
Howard, Georgiana 151, 154, 156, 157
Howard, William 20, 22, 150, 151
Hunstanton Hall (Norfolk) 118
Hutchinson, Col. John 117, 118, 128,
Hutter, Edward 132
Hutter, Christian 132

I

Iddesleigh (Devon) 65
Inigo Jones 123, 143
Ireland 5, 36, 77, 78, 80, 84, 87-93, 177, 178, 180, 183, 189, 190, 209, 210

J

Jamaica 191, 202, 205, 219, 224-227
Jamestown (Nevis) 195
Jeaffreson, Christopher 212, 214, 223, 225
Jefferson, Thomas 5, 129-147
Johnson, James 132
Johnson, Matthew 77, 90
Judith's Creek Plantation (Virginia) 133

K

Kenmare, Lord 87,
Kent 2, 97, 98, 107, 108, 143, 213
Kent, William 10
Killincarrig House 81
Kirkby, Mary 154, 158, 172
Kirkby, Thomas 170
Kirk Hill (Yorkshire) 151
Kirkstead Abbey (Lincolnshire) 119, 128

L

Lacock Abbey (Wiltshire) 116
La Taste estate (Grenada) 209
Lawrence, John 7
Lee, Sir Henry 114, 146
Leeward Islands VI, 191, 192, 203, 205, 206, 220, 225

Leez Priory (Essex) 119
Leighton Hall Estate 41, 46, 50, 127
Limerick, Co. 89
Little Comfort Farm (Rackenford) 69
Llanwyddelan (Powys) 43, 45, 54
Loch, James 30, 33, 36, 37
London 2, 12, 14-16, 21, 24, 36, 37, 54, 55, 71-74, 91, 92, 108, 121, 123, 127, 128, 133, 137, 143, 167, 168, 179, 189, 191, 197, 200, 202-204, 208, 215, 219, 223-227
Londonderry 182
Loutherbourg, Philippe Jacques de 98
Luttrell family 104, 107,
Lyveden (Northamptonshire) 113, 127

M

MacCarthy family 177-179, 188, 189, 190
Magnoni, Carlo 164
Maiden Bradley (Wiltshire) 120
Manafon (Powys) 45
Manchester 12, 14, 72, 127, 203
Mansfield Park 221, 222, 224
Markree Castle (Co. Sligo) 78
Marshall, William 32,
Martin, Samuel 144, 145, 169, 215, 217, 218, 223, 226
Marvell, Andrew 92, 115, 128
Metherell (Cornwall) 67
Mildmay, Lady Grace 116
Minehead (Somerset) 95-97, 104, 107, 109-111
Mogg, John and Ruth 104-106, 108-112
Montgomeryshire 39, 40, 43, 45, 52, 54, 55
Monticello (Virginia) 130, 131, 134, 137, 139, 140, 144, 145
Montserrat 191, 192, 199-201, 203, 205, 210, 227
Moorstone Barton (Devon) 63, 67
Morpeth, Lord 33
Mortimer, Lt. Col. James 163
Mountravers Plantation (Nevis) 194
Moxon, Robert John 42, 44, 46
Munster 177, 179-182, 187, 190

N

Naworth (Cumbria) 19, 34
Naylor, John 41, 50
Nesfield, William Andrews 12, 20, 34, 37
Nevis VI, 191-197, 199-204, 210, 211, 215, 217, 226, 227
Newenham Abbey (Devon) 65
Nicholson, James 153, 154
Norden, John 62, 64, 70, 73
Norfolk 3, 6, 7, 12, 16, 118, 119, 128
Norris, John 105, 111
Northamptonshire 113, 127, 128, 162
Nottinghamshire 78, 117, 127, 128

O

O'Sulivan Beares 177
Offwell (Devon) 67
Old Madeley Manor (Staffordshire) 115, 118
Old Manor Estate (Nevis) 194
Owen family 40, 43, 44, 53
Owthorpe (Nottinghamshire) 117, 119, 125, 126
Oxfordshire 115, 128

P

Palladio, Andrea 138, 142, 143
Pallister, John 157, 171
Pamber Forest (Hampshire) 114
Pandy Farm (Berriew, Powys) 49, 51
Parham Hill Estate (Antigua) 219
Paris 137, 164, 200, 203, 225
Paty, Thomas 219
Paxton, Joseph 12, 13
Peaks of Otter (Virginia) 133, 135
Penson, Thomas 47, 50
Pepys, Samual 123, 128
Peto family: 120, 121, 123, 124, 126
    Sir Edward 120
    William 121
    Edward 121, 123, 124
Phelps, Richard 97
Philadelphia 92, 140, 144, 226
Poling (Sussex) 106

Popham, Sir John 110, 179
Poplar Forest Estate (Virginia) 129-147
Port St George (Nevis) 192, 203
Potworks Estate (Nevis) 194
Powis Castle (Powys) 40, 43, 53-55
Powys 40, 46, 54
Probert, John 42, 44-46, 48, 53-55

Q

Quarrendon (Buckinghamshire) 114, 127

R

Rackenford (Devon) 65, 69
Rackham, Oliver 13, 15, 57, 70, 73
Rashleigh Barton (Devon) 67
Ray Wood (Yorkshire) 21-24, 26, 27
Repton, Humphrey 11, 14, 15, 52
Riverstown (Co. Sligo) 78, 90, 93
Rogers, Edward 179
Romney (St Kitts) 198, 211-214, 220
Roper, Sir Thomas 181
Roscommon, Co. 87, 89
Rushton (Northamptonshire) 113

S

Salisbury (Wiltshire) 62
Salvin, Anthony 97, 98
Sandars, Edmund Thomas 164
Saumarez Smith, Charles 35-37, 152, 167, 168
Saunders, James 104, 105, 110
Schaw, Janet 215, 218, 223
Scotland 2, 177, 190, 197, 203, 207, 215, 223
Sentleger, Sir Warham 181
Severn Valley 5, 39-43, 50, 54
Shadwell (Virginia) 138, 145
Shapcott Barton (Devon) 67
Shropshire 40, 43
Shrubland Park 12
Shurdington (Gloucestershire) 125, 128
Slapton (Devon) 64
Sledmere (Yorkshire) 5, 28, 149, 154, 158-160, 162-164, 166-169, 172-174
Sligo, Co. 77, 78, 83, 84, 93
Smeaton, John 214
Smith, Adam 30
Smith, William 6, 217
Snitterton Hall (Derbyshire) 118, 128
Somerset 5, 14, 57, 73, 95, 99, 102, 104, 105, 107, 108, 219
South Hams (Devon) 60, 64
Spenser, Edmund 180, 190
Staffordshire 104, 105, 108, 115, 118
Stapleton, Sir William 193, 195, 197, 199, 200, 202, 203
Staunton, Thomas 42, 113
Stith, William 131, 133
St Kitts 191-193, 198, 200, 202, 203, 210, 212-215, 219, 220, 221, 226
Stockland Hill (Devon) 58
Stoke Fleming (Devon) 64
Stowe (Shropshire) 24, 139, 168
Strokestown Park House (Co. Roscommon) 87, 89
Sussex 2, 106
Sutton, Anthony 31
Switzer, Stephen 21, 24, 35, 37
Sykes family:
    Christopher 158, 159, 166, 172, 173
    Richard 158, 159, 164, 166, 172, 173
    Sir Christopher 158, 159, 166, 173
    Sir Mark 154, 160, 162, 164, 168, 169, 173, 174
    Sir Tatton 154, 159, 160, 162, 166, 167, 173
Sykes of Sledmere 28, 168

T

Tackley (Oxfordshire) 115, 117, 128
Talman, William 21
Tanzyfort (Co. Sligo) 77-81, 83-90
Taunton, Lady 157, 171
Thirsk, Joan 3, 13, 14, 15
Tomahawk Creek (Virginia) 131
Tomkins, William 97, 104, 107
Trawnahaha (Whiddy Island) 183

Trebartha Barton (Cornwall) 67
Trefeglwys (Powys) 43, 45, 54
Trenowth Barton (Cornwall) 67
Tresham, Sir Thomas 113, 127
Tudway, Charles 219, 223, 227
Tullideph, Dr. Walter 215

U

Ulster 182, 190
Unshin, River 79, 81, 83, 85
Upcott Barton (Devon) 67
Utrecht, Treaty of (1773) 210

V

Vanbrugh, Sir John 19, 21, 22, 24, 28, 36, 37, 89, 152, 168
Vaynor (Powys) 5, 39-55

W

Wade Martins, Susanna 5, 13, 15, 36, 37, 70, 74
Wagoners Monument (Sledmere) 159, 164, 169, 172, 173
Wales 14, 15, 39, 40, 45, 50, 52-55, 73, 107, 108, 177, 179, 190, 203, 209, 224
Walpole, Horace 23, 35, 37, 98
Walton, Izaac *The Compleat Angler* 116, 118, 126, 128
Wardour Castle (Wiltshire) 120
Warwick Castle (Warwickshire) 120, 121
Warwickshire 113, 120, 121, 123, 127, 128
Wayles, John 131, 146
Welburn (Yorkshire) 20, 21, 28, 29, 149-151, 154, 156, 157, 166, 167, 171
Welshpool (Powys) 40, 41
Wessex 14, 62
Westcott Barton (Devon) 67
West Indies 2, 202-204, 223-227
Whateley, Thomas 7
Whiddy Island 181, 183-186
Whitby Abbey (Yorkshire) 116
Wicklow, Co. 81
Widworthy (Devon) 67
Williamsburg (Virginia) 136, 145, 192, 202, 226
Wiltshire 57, 62, 72, 74, 120
Winchcombe (Devon) 105, 108
Winder family 45, 47, 53
Windward Plantation (Nevis) 197
Wingfield Manor Estate (St Kitts) 198, 200, 211-215, 217, 220
Wise, Iveson 153, 154, 170
Woburn (Bedfordshire) 7, 12
Wyeford (Hampshire) 113-115, 119, 120, 128

Y

Yorkshire 6, 15, 19, 28, 32, 35, 36, 116, 151, 158, 163, 167-169, 173, 180, 182, 190
Young, Arthur 3, 29, 87